Battles at the Ballot

John Leston

Battles at the Ballot

The Politicians, Idealists and Cranks of Britain's
First World War By-Elections

John Leston

Haythorp Books

First published by Haythorp Books 2025

This edition published 2025

Haythorp Books is an imprint of Canbury Press Ltd (www.canburypress.com)

14 Beresford Rd, London, KT2 6LR, United Kingdom

EU Authorised Representative: Easy Access System Europe

- Mustamäe tee 50, 10621 Tallinn, Estonia, gpsr.requests@easproject.com

Printed and bound in Czechia

Typeset in Athelas (heading), Futura PT (body)

All rights reserved © John Leston

John Leston has asserted his right to be identified
as the author of this work in accordance with Section 77
of the Copyright, Designs and Patents Act 1988

This is a work of non-fiction

FSC® helps take care of forests for future generations.

ISBN:

Hardback: 9781914487514

Ebook: 9781914487521

Contents

Foreword   7

1. Introduction   9
2. Comrades at War   16
3. The Greatest Foe?   37
4. The Airman Cometh   60
5. A Second Sortie   89
6. A Prime Minister's Promise   114
7. Billing's First Dog Fights   142
8. Heads Above the Parapet   170
9. Trying to Wound   219
10. Nemesis Not Yet   234
11. Labour Pains   262
12. Billing's Final Missions   292
13. Windows on the Home Front   328

Appendix   *344*
Acknowledgements   *358*
About the Author   *361*

FOREWORD

Conventional party politics was put on ice during the 1914-18 war. An electoral pact ensured that in the event of a by-election the incumbent party's tenure was not challenged by its opponents. As a result, there was no contest for 89 of the 118 vacancies that arose in Great Britain during the war.

Yet in 29 instances one or more independent candidates intervened to ensure there was a contest. And as John Leston shows in his colourful and revealing analysis of these by-elections, they reflected the tensions of a country that was facing the biggest military challenge in its history. The contests raised questions about how effectively the war was being prosecuted, revealed doubts about whether military action should still be pursued, and provided a focus for debates about both conscription and liquor licensing. Although the independent challengers only won on three occasions, Leston indicates how these contests provided vital feedback to government about the public mood – much as by-elections do so today.

At the same time, these by-elections also provided vital clues that, despite the electoral truce, Britain's party politics were about to be transformed. A divided Liberal party was to be displaced by Labour as the Conservatives' principal rivals. Leston shows how the battle inside the Liberal party was evident in local disagreements about whether to nominate a follower of Asquith or of Lloyd George. Meanwhile, he indicates that the relative success achieved by some independent Labour candidates was a clear indication that the party was well-placed to win the support of working-class voters, many of them now newly enfranchised, in the post-war era.

Democracy is often put on hold during war time – and that perhaps helps explain why the by-elections of 1914-18 have largely been ignored. But this is a mistake. Leston shows how those contests gave voice to crucial debates between politicians and created an opportunity for voters to pass judgement. His book is a fascinating study of how in practice politics still managed to operate in what were undoubtedly difficult times.

Sir John Curtice
Professor of Politics at Strathclyde University

1.
INTRODUCTION

As 'the war to end all wars' began, the political guns across Britain fell silent. Or so the powers that be thought. In August 1914, the main British political parties agreed an electoral truce. Whichever party held a parliamentary seat, outside of Ireland, that became vacant had an unopposed right to nominate the replacement MP. The parties kept remarkably well to their agreement although cracks eventually appeared on the Labour side.

The truce was totally successful for the first 21 British wartime vacancies; then, in July 1915, an idiosyncratic Unionist reacted badly to not being selected as the official candidate and forced a blue-on-blue election. Whilst this unimportant fight did not open the floodgates, 28 further elections went to the polls before the Armistice. All these contested by-elections were held after the formation of the Coalition government in May 1915; however, they straddled Asquith's premiership and that of Lloyd George. Consequently, some of the later by-elections were complicated by the growing fissure within the Liberal party between supporters of the two leaders.

Because the truce held, these were not conventional elections between the big parties; instead, they featured challenges from an array of independents, fighting on specific concerns. The casus belli changed as the war progressed, or didn't, and as issues rose and fell in public significance. Consequently, the contests provide a fascinating insight into the priorities and concerns of the home front. They were fought by a miscellany of candidates, from the serious to the absurd, and provided a platform for mainstream politicians, failing politicians, party loyalists, idealists, single-issue fanatics, chancers, and no-hopers. One name among them stands out: Noel Pemberton-Billing. He fought two by-elections and mounted campaigns supporting candidates in others. His life story is remarkable, and his wartime political story, incredible. Early on he helped organise an air attack on a Zeppelin base in Germany. He then left the services to campaign for a more robust air policy to defend English cities and launch reprisals against German ones. As war-weariness grew, he became ever more extreme and peddled outrageous conspiracy theories. He claimed that the British establishment was being blackmailed by the Germans, largely for alleged homosexual behaviour, for which he was prosecuted for libel but won.

The poor quality of Britain's air defences was one of the debates played out in these elections. Other crucial, and not-so-crucial, topics made an appearance, including splits within the labour movement over attitudes to the war; opposition to restrictions on alcohol; controversy about the conscription of married men; dissatisfaction with the support for discharged servicemen; calls for ever harsher treatment of 'aliens' and general discontent at the perceived failure to pursue the war aggressively. Additionally, several by-elections featured men brave enough to challenge the consensus of unquestioning support for the war, arguing for 'peace by negotiation' rather than a 'fight to the finish'. They were generally not well received, suffering meetings being broken up and occasional barrages of rotten fruit and vegetables. One of the candidates, a conscientious objector, had to fight his campaign from prison, his arrest having been organised by his opponent's election agent, who was also the local recruiting officer.

The vacancies had multiple causes. Among the 29 contests, most (12) stemmed from the death of the sitting MP, four of whom were killed in action or died of wounds. Next most frequent, nine times, was the elevation of the sitting MP to the House of Lords. Five resulted from resignation due to ill-health, although in two cases that was probably a convenient fig leaf. One further resignation was due to an MP becoming a judge. Finally, two elections resulted from the rules of the time that someone appointed to government ('an office of profit under the crown') had to submit themselves for re-election. These involved big names, Herbert Samuel and Winston Churchill; in the case of Churchill, he was opposed by a socialist, pro-prohibition, and now overtly anti-war candidate. It was not to be their last fight.

The established party candidates had significant advantages over the insurgents but that did not prevent them from losing in three cases and suffering other close-run results. Fighting elections at the beginning of the twentieth century was a complex art so the parties were greatly aided by employing professional agents and deploying committed volunteers. Those complexities only grew through the exigencies of war. In a time before universal suffrage, knowing which men (for it was only men) should be on the voters' roll was far from straightforward; around 60 per cent had the vote, some more than one due to business qualifications. Essentially, property owners or lodgers paying more than £10 a year in rent were eligible. The party agents (mainly, but not exclusively, local solicitors) put in the hard graft to make sure their supporters got on the lists and, where they could, challenged the entitlements of known supporters of their opponents.

A related benefit was that the main parties knew where their voters were. This became more significant as the war progressed since the electoral register was not updated. Consequently, for all the wartime by-elections people qualified for the address where they were resident before it began. As time went on, voters moved away and, in some cases, even forgot that address. Local party machines were able to track down these so-called 'removals' and seek to get them to the polls. Insurgent independents had neither the information nor resources to do the same.

Another advantage for Liberal, Unionist and Labour parties was that they controlled the polling timetable and could use this to limit opponents' ability to mount an effective fight. While the allowable time between an election writ being received by the local returning officer and polling day was narrowly defined by legislation, the parliamentary party with the vacancy could decide when that writ was issued. Across all the contests, the minimum time from vacancy to poll was only nine days and the maximum, sixty. At least two, very short campaigns were deliberately organised to hamper effective opposition.

These by-elections were the 'last hurrah' of electioneering methods established in the late Victorian and Edwardian periods before the advent of universal male, and partial female, suffrage. The emphasis was on innumerable indoor and outdoor public meetings, leafleting, posters and systematic door-to-door canvassing if time allowed. High-profile speakers could be guaranteed enormous audiences. By-elections were a political event but also an entertainment and distraction. Expenditure limits applied but they permitted sizeable spends; in the most extreme case, Wimbledon, which was a very populous constituency, two candidates between them spent the equivalent of £400,000 in today's money. The wartime elections also witnessed novel campaigning techniques, such as one candidate's daily newspaper featuring conspiracy theories, jokes and cartoons. Other gimmicks included making speeches from an aircraft mounted on a lorry (see the photograph on the front cover) and positioning a 'dummy' (wooden) gun outside a committee room. Insults flew with abandon and there were more than isolated incidents of political violence.

The elections provided a platform for leading personalities to influence events or simply enjoy the limelight. One such was the former MP and charlatan, Horatio Bottomley, who almost certainly backed several candidates, at least in part, as a personal revenue-raising exercise. Bottomley was part of the third estate, through his ownership of the highly popular, and populist, John Bull magazine. Other press people involved included Howell (II A) Gwynne (editor of the Morning Post and hater-in-chief of Churchill) and, above all, Lord Northcliffe whose newspapers, and staff, aggressively backed several candidates.

Lastly, there is the question of how much these by-elections changed national politics. In truth, they were much like today's by-elections; many generated short-lived excitements but usually did not really change policy. But there were exceptions. The election of a 'patriotic' Labour candidate in Keir Hardie's former seat, at the peak of the conscription debate, did much to reassure a hesitant Asquith government to proceed with compulsion. Arguably, the threat of a by-election hurried along the response to complaints about the provision for discharged servicemen. And Pemberton-Billing's persistent highlighting of the Air War encouraged improvements in what was undoubtedly a chaotic and inadequate response by government and military alike.

On the other side of the coin, objections to restrictions on liquor had no effect. And complaints that the Prime Minster had broken his conscription promise to married men got nowhere; partly because the married men themselves were not united around a single alternative policy. But the greatest failure of all was by those putting themselves forward to argue for 'Peace by Negotiation'. Britain stumbled into the conflict, without codified war aims, and government resisted spelling out what those might be. The outcome was an unquestioning (and largely unquestioned) commitment to 'a fight to the finish' and the total surrender of the Germans. As war-weariness increased, attempts were made to question whether compromise might be found to bring the carnage to an end. Such heresy was promulgated by the American President, Woodrow Wilson, and even by Unionist grandees, such as the Lords Lansdowne and Loreburn. It had the backing of (minority) religious groups, some socialists, and the metropolitan-elite Union of Democratic Control. It was never to be enough. For most of the war, supporters of peace by negotiation were biding their time, waiting for more auspicious opportunities to raise their flag; often they felt the war was going too badly to talk peace and, sometimes, going too well. But they were a plaintive minority, and their only respectable performances came from well-established labour movement candidates able to draw on a portmanteau of grievances. However, their failure to win should not blind us to their bravery in standing up for their beliefs in a highly hostile environment.

Because of the political truce, these contests were restricted in their capacity to predict post-war party prospects. The antipathy generally revealed for those who questioned the conflict certainly continued into the 1918 General Election but, interestingly, it soon dissipated and the rising tide of Labour support in the 1920s lifted all socialist boats, including previous anti-war campaigners. Nonetheless, treated carefully, these elections do provide colour to the debate regarding the decline of the Liberal party and the rise of Labour. The stark wartime divisions between the 'patriotic' and 'internationalist' wings of the labour movement inevitably meant it was not as powerful a political force in the period up to and including the 1918 General Election as it was to become. But evidence emerges through these contests of a bleak future for the Liberals. Independent candidates with strong labour movement roots performed well against them. The highest polling percentages achieved for 'peace by negotiation' were where trade union-linked candidates were running against Liberals, such as in Rossendale and Keighley. Additionally, the Liberals did not help themselves. In North Salford and Wansbeck, their former MPs had strong links with, and fully backed, the labour movement locally. But the Liberals replaced both with non-working-class candidates who lacked those sympathies, one a high-flying 'carpet-bagging' lawyer and the other a successful shipping merchant brought into 'a miners' seat'. In response, independent labour candidates stood against them, winning one of the seats and coming perilously close in the other. These examples endorse the hypothesis that the Liberals harmed their prospects by unwillingness to adopt working-class candidates. More generally, as the end of the war came closer, Labour found it increasingly difficult to control its local organisations which were becoming more confident and assertive, keen to run their own men. By the time of one of the last by-elections of the war (Gravesend), where an independent labour man stood against the wishes of the national party, they had had enough and renounced the truce.

The structure of the book is thematic, grouping by-elections generally by the issue on which they were fought; this is largely but not entirely chronological. Chapter 2 covers the internal Labour fight in Merthyr Tydfil where the official candidate was opposed by 'patriotic' Labour. Chapter 3 explores two by-elections fought on opposition to alcohol restrictions and introduces the larger-than-life Horatio Bottomley. Chapter 4 introduces the even more colourful and eccentric Noel Pemberton-Billing. Chapter 5 moves on to Billing's second by-election and describes Britain's defence, or lack of it, against German airships, the Zeppelins, and bombers. Chapter 6 explores the muddle that the Asquith government got into over conscription and an apparent promise not to conscript married men before single men. Chapter 7 returns to Pemberton-Billing, his continuing campaigning on air defence and attempts to elect supporters, in Wimbledon and Tewkesbury. Chapter 8 is the most extensive and it brings together most of the by-elections featuring the core issues of peace and war. These ranged chronologically from North Ayrshire in October 1916 to Keighley in April 1918.[1] Chapter 9, by contrast, the shortest, covers a single by-election fought by a candidate of the National Federation of Discharged and Demobilised Sailors and Soldiers, highlighting the poor provision for the discharged wounded. It was fought between a private soldier and an Eton and Oxford-educated officer about to have a society wedding. Chapter 10 also features a single by-election, where

---

1 The other by-elections featuring 'peace' candidates of varying hues were in Dundee (covered in chapter 10) and Wansbeck and Gravesend (included in chapter 11).

the independent candidate, Ned Scrymgeour, is almost as fiction-like extreme as Pemberton-Billing. This by-election merits its own chapter because Scrymgeour was standing against Winston Churchill, and it is necessary to detail Churchill's reputation at that point. Chapter 11 has as its common theme by-elections in which Labour faced internal conflicts over whether to abide by the truce, including two where 'peace' candidates were adopted. Finally, Chapter 12 is a last hurrah for Pemberton-Billing and addresses three by-elections that advanced ever-more extreme policies against 'aliens', (despite Pemberton-Billing's own wife arguably falling into that category). There is, finally, an Appendix which contains brief descriptions of the remaining, less significant contests.[2]

Reviewing this aspect of Home Front life opens a window into the politics of the era, while highlighting the changing cares and beliefs of the population across four hard years of conflict and privation. They reveal what entertained and amused while also demonstrating how strong civilian morale proved to be and how much in favour of more war, rather than less.

---

[2] There is no coverage of elections in Ireland as they, generally, turned on the increasingly fundamental issues relating to the future of Ireland as exemplified by the rise of Sinn Fein.

2.
COMRADES AT WAR

Merthyr Boroughs, 25 November 1915

Contested by-elections began in earnest when a vacancy arose in Merthyr Tydfil, south Wales, with the death of Labour pioneer, Keir Hardie, on 2 September 1915.[1] Although the seat housed one of the country's largest Independent Labour Party (ILP)[2] organisations, it was not a socialist bastion and Hardie had been reliant for his success on the Liberals running a single official candidate in the two-member constituency.

The truce held and neither the Liberals nor Unionists[3] took part. But the outcome was a viciously fought election, between official and unofficial Labour. The result had a significant impact on the conscription debate and many decades later a surprising truth emerged about how the contest was won.

---

1 This was soon after the precedent of a contested wartime by-election had first been set (on 16 July 1915) in Glasgow Central. See Appendix for a brief description.
2 Until after the First World War, individuals could only join the Labour Party via an affiliated union or socialist society, of which the ILP was one. Unlike most of the left, the ILP (and many, although not all, of its members) broadly maintained an anti-war position throughout the conflict. Ramsay MacDonald articulated their position, by 1915, as being to not actively obstruct the war effort but to campaign for the earliest possible peace.
3 The terms Conservative and Unionist are used interchangeably throughout the book to designate candidates of the Conservative and Unionist party; this reflects common practice at the time. The Liberal Unionists had broken away from the Liberal Party in the 1880s, in protest against Gladstone's support for Irish Home Rule. They remained a separate entity until 1912 when they merged with the Conservatives.

Jingoism erupts in Hardie's backyard

The very first days of the war saw a rapid shift in sentiment in labour thinking. Owing to the movement's disparate organisation, pre-war British labour politicians held a complex mosaic of beliefs. Some were proudly internationalist in attitude, determined to resist 'capitalist' or 'imperialist' conflicts that would set working-classes against each other. Some, like Hardie, endorsed pacifism. Yet, others positioned themselves as strongly patriotic. One academic, D J Swift, argues: 'Most leading individuals on the British Left remained firmly against the war in the days preceding the start of the conflict'.[4] This was particularly true of the ILP who, on 2 August 1914, organised a major peace rally in Trafalgar Square, attended by around 10,000 people. Hardie planned to follow this with an anti-war rally in his constituency on 6 August. But by now, the mood on the left had been tilted in favour of the war, especially by the invasion of Belgium.[5] Opinion swung strongly against the ILP, even in Merthyr. Hardie tried to proceed with the meeting but faced massive disruption by protestors and after twenty minutes he had to give up and needed a police escort to leave safely.

The truce holds outside of Labour but not within

On Hardie's death, less than a month later, the party truce held, although not without debate. The local ILP unanimously nominated Robert Smillie, President of the Miners Federation of Great Britain, as their nominee for the Labour selection conference.[6] The Liberals reacted immediately with T Artemus Jones, their prospective candidate (who was expected to stand aside in line with the terms of the truce), saying the Labour candidate must

---

4 D J Swift, Patriotic Labour in the Era of the Great War (PhD Thesis: University of Central Lancashire, 2014)
5 In the Commons on 3 August, even Ramsay MacDonald had responded to Foreign Secretary Edward Grey saying: 'If the Rt. Hon Gentleman could come and tell us that a small European nationality like Belgium is in danger ... then we would support him'.
6 As the Labour Party comprised multiple, affiliated organisations its selection process was complex. Each organisation was permitted to nominate a candidate (often chosen by a ballot among their own members). Those candidates were then considered and voted on by an overall constituency selection conference at which all the organisations were given a voting strength that reflected the size of their individual membership. In Merthyr, easily the largest was the miners' union and so their nomination was the most important.

unreservedly support the government in waging war if the Liberals were to withdraw and he accused Smillie of being aggressively anti-war.

However, in the all-important miners' nomination ballot, Smillie came a distant fourth, trailing behind Charles Stanton, who was the Aberdare miners' agent, James Winstone, President of the South Wales Miners Federation, and a third candidate. In a final run-off between Stanton and Winstone, the order was reversed and Winstone was nominated. The ILP dropped its nomination of Smillie and switched to Winstone who was easily adopted at the constituency conference (on a card vote by 17,470 in favour to 745 against). Despite the clear outcome, Stanton announced he would oppose Winstone and stand as an independent candidate.

The colourful pre-war histories of James Winstone and Charles Stanton

Both protagonists had impressive records in the South Wales labour movement; one relatively staid, the other more mercurial.

James Winstone started work at the age of eight in a brickworks. Two years later he moved to Risca colliery from which he was eventually sacked for trade union activities. He was a prominent founder member of the South Wales Miners' Federation in 1898 and enjoyed considerable success in local government elections over the years. A Baptist lay preacher, his faith heavily informed his socialism and support for temperance. He was a committed, effective, and well-regarded working-class leader in South Wales.

Charlie Stanton was a labour movement firebrand from his early days. In an 1893 strike, he was accused of having fired a gun during clashes between miners and the police and was imprisoned for six months for possession of a firearm without a licence. He was again active in the 1898 miners' strike, after which he relocated, becoming a docker in London where he was once more prominent in strikes. He returned to South Wales and continued to be a leading union and socialist activist. He declared himself a 'revolutionary Marxian Socialist, believing in the class war' and in the pre-war period was described as 'one of the most notorious advocates of industrial unrest'. Much more exotic and unpredictable than Winstone, he was 'one of the wild men'[7]

---

7 K D Brown, The First Labour Party, 1906 – 1914 (1985).

of the labour movement. Aside from his industrial militancy, he was a fine amateur painter and a proficient violinist.

War brings immediate changes – especially to Stanton

As soon as war began, the firebrand Stanton switched from an anti-capitalist militant to an ultra-patriot. As one historian has it, he: 'at once abandoned his red flag for the red, white and blue of the Union Jack'.[8] He declaimed 'although I am a Socialist, I am a Britisher'. Kenneth Morgan wrote that Stanton was 'a Welsh Mussolini who turned as naturally to the advocacy of world war as of class war.'[9] He immediately left the ILP (which was one of few organisations still maintaining a broadly anti-war stance) and in April 1915, became a founder committee member of Victor Fisher's Socialist National Defence Committee, an ultra-patriotic, pro-war split from the British Socialist Party.

Winstone remained more consistent with his pre-war views. Although staying an active member of the ILP, he did not oppose the war; but he was firmly against conscription. Speaking in October 1915 he said: 'There were greater tragedies to come unless the workers rose in their power – compulsory military service. His (the speaker's) son went out of his own free will. Let every man who thought he should go join but, for the love of God, don't let us have this awful compulsory service'.[10]

The Labour Party, nationally and locally, was clear that Winstone was their validly selected champion. They recognised the electoral risk of an ILP candidate in a time of jingoism but were not going to oppose the miners. Likewise, despite Merthyr Liberals' sabre-rattling about the truce only holding if the selected Labour candidate endorsed the war, they did not object to Winstone on those grounds. Equally, the Unionists showed no inclination to step in. It seemed, despite his ILP associations, Winstone was sound enough on the war to be acceptable. Stanton, however, was having none of it and immediately resigned his position as the miners' agent for Aberdare in order to stand in the election. He wrote to the Aberdare Executive: 'I beg to state that I am fully determined not to work another day for your district ...There is a pro-German section in our district that has made my life a hell for many

---

8 Rev. Ivor T Rees, Stanton (Merthyr Historian 25, 2013).
9 K.O. Morgan, Keir Hardie: Radical & Socialist (1975).
10 Merthyr Express, 23 October 1915.

months.' He added 'I have always been loyal to my class without being a traitor to my country.'[11]

Campaigning off to a rapid start

The writ for the election was issued on 15 November 1915. However, supporters of the two battling Labour candidates had already been setting out their stalls. Victor Fisher, of the Socialist National Defence Committee (SNDC), organised a strong initial salvo via the *Clarion* newspaper.[12] On 12 November, the paper denounced Winstone as 'the nominee of the pro-German, pacifist, and friend-of-every-other-country-but-their-own, Independent Labour Party'.

By contrast, they said of Stanton: 'He comes before this great British electorate as THE BRITISH CANDIDATE in opposition to the candidate of the I.L.P., of the so-called Union of Democratic Control, and of the pacifists who, after all the sacrifices that Britain and her glorious Allies have made, are seeking to save our aggressors by a shameful and disastrous peace now that German defeat is happily looming in sight.'[13]

Meanwhile, the *Daily Herald* came out for Winstone as the official Labour representative, arguing:

> *'We hope every friend of Labour and the progressive movement for social salvation in Merthyr will rally to the support of Winstone. He stands as the representative of his class to carry on the traditional warfare on behalf of the workers' emancipation – that war which will not cease until monopoly and privilege is swept away. He is also an out-and-out opponent of Conscription, both military and industrial.'*[14]

---

11 Birmingham Mail, 1 November 1915.
12 Ironically, the SNDC had initially thought to back Winstone but withdrew their offer when he refused to support conscription. See: Charles Stanton and the limits to patriotic Labour: E May in Welsh History Review, 1997).
13 *Clarion*, 12 November 1915.
14 *Daily Herald*, 13 November 1915

Likewise, Arthur Henderson, Leader of the Labour Party and a member of the Asquith Coalition cabinet[15], stressed the legitimacy of Winstone's nomination, it being endorsed by the South Wales Miners' Federation, the Miners' Federation of Great Britain, the National Executive of the Labour Party and the Merthyr selection conference. He said of Winstone:

> 'His position is that he has one son engaged in the war, a second has just offered for enlistment, and he is in entire agreement with the allies' objects as defined by the Prime Minister. Under these circumstances, the Labour party will render Mr. Winstone full backing should a contest take place.'[16]

Meanwhile, Stanton remorselessly positioned Winstone as an unpatriotic hard-line supporter of the ILP and pacifism. Stanton also pleaded for help financing his campaign. He announced: 'In order that the returning officer's fees may be ready on time, I am today taking out a bill of sale[17] on my household furniture.' Interviewed in the press he said: 'Seeing that Mr. Winstone and his ILP friends have captured the money bags of the Miners' Federation, of which I am still a member, I can only go and appeal, cap in hand, to those who support me.'[18] A leading supporter also told the press that 'the source of all the necessary money was quite clear and that about 80 working men in Aberdare alone had already come forward with a pound note apiece to help the fund.'

Nominations[19] were set for Saturday 20 November with polling day to be Thursday 25 November. Winstone officially opened his campaign on the

---

15 Henderson had replaced MacDonald as Labour leader when the latter had resigned due to the party's decision to back the war. He had joined the cabinet in May 1915 when the Coalition was formed.
16 *Western Mail*, 18 November 1915.
17 Essentially, a means of obtaining credit. Ownership of the goods would pass to the creditor if the loan (and associated interest) were not paid.
18 *Western Mail*, 12 November 1915.
19 At least one, valid nomination paper had to be accepted by the returning officer for a candidate to be included in the election. Each paper had to be signed by ten electors (including a proposer and seconder) who were on the electoral register for the relevant constituency. Nomination papers were required to be submitted during set hours on the officially appointed day. Papers would be rejected if they contained any errors, so candidates sometimes submitted multiple papers as an insurance policy or as a demonstration of strength of support.

Friday with a meeting in Aberdare. He fought back hard against Stanton having painted him as pro-German. Rather, he claimed, he was a Welshman and had offered his services to his country which he maintained was more than Stanton had done. Both candidates released formal election addresses on nominations day. Winstone's made much of the fact that he was the 'official, democratically appointed Candidate' and attacked Stanton for causing a contest at a time of need for national unity. He described himself as 'a Democrat in Politics, and a Socialist in Economics on the Principles of the New Testament, from which I still draw my chief inspiration.' Yet again he countered Stanton's accusations, writing: 'I shall never shirk my duty to my Country and, as a Patriot, I would volunteer to fight myself.' But he did not shrink from including a strong statement of his anti-conscription views: 'I shall oppose Compulsion with all the strength at my command, believing, as I do, that the introduction of Conscription can but be productive of divisions, dissensions, and disruptions throughout this Coalfield and the Country at large.'

Stanton's address explained his justification for standing. Under normal circumstances he would, of course, abide by the selection decision taken by the Labour Party. However, he alleged: 'A comparatively small clique of unpatriotic intriguers have succeeded in possessing themselves of the machinery of party organisation' and that this clique 'composed almost entirely of members of the discredited and so-called 'Independent' Labour Party, have pursued a policy on the question of the War which I am convinced is as abhorrent to the overwhelming majority of their fellow citizens as their continued political influence is an actual danger to the safety of the country.'

He relentlessly made his campaign a referendum on attitudes to the ILP and conscription and portrayed Winstone as a mindless adherent to suspect, unpatriotic, views. The *Manchester Courier* was astute in its assessment that Winstone had 'apparently everything in his favour except his membership of the Independent Labour Party.'[20]

---

20 *Manchester Courier*, 23 November 1915.

Meetings the backbone of the rapid campaign

There was little time for widespread canvassing, so Winstone concentrated on a relentless barrage of public meetings, supported by notable speakers from across the country. These included: William Brace, MP, Under-Secretary at the Home Office, who had been Winstone's boyhood friend and next-door neighbour; David Gilmour, soon to be President of the Scottish TUC; Fred Jowett, MP (ILP); Ramsay MacDonald, MP (ILP); Tom Richards, MP; James Thomas, MP; Stephen Walsh, MP and Robert Williams, General Secretary of the National Transport Workers' Federation and a leading member of the Union of Democratic Control.

The presence of so many of Labour's 'aristocracy' confirmed Winstone's position as the official candidate and showed Labour firm in its resolve to ride out the allegations that their man was unpatriotic. But crucial for the campaign was the prominent support of the ILP big guns, Fred Jowett, MP for Bradford West and Ramsay MacDonald, MP for Leicester West and former Chairman of the Parliamentary Labour Party who had resigned that post in 1914 due to his firm opposition to the war. Both campaigns recognised their presence as a two-edged sword and MacDonald even attempted to use his speech to mitigate potential damage from his endorsement. He revealed he had been invited by the Winstone campaign but had had doubts about accepting because: 'for the past six months there had been a campaign of slander, malignity, and misrepresentation waged in the press against him'. He spelt out a nuanced position on the war, as reported:

> *'From the moment when war broke out, he had said nothing that in any way could divert the attention of the country from the task that was in front of it ... He and his colleagues had been talked about as being pro-German. "I doubt whether there is anyone in public life" he said "who is more anti-German than I am, if by that you mean antagonism to the spirit of Germany. My colleagues and myself are entitled to say not only are we opposed to a patched-up peace, but that we are working against a patched-up peace far more than those who thump the big drum and tell you to go thoughtlessly and heedlessly ahead."'* [21]

---

21 *Western Mail*, 24 November 1915.

MacDonald alleged there was a press technique of misquoting him, to make him sound favourable to the German position. That was then requoted with approval in the German press, following which the British press then condemned him for receiving supportive comments from the enemy. It was a tough mountain to climb but the *Birmingham Mail* felt his speech had achieved its objective: 'Last night Mr. Ramsay MacDonald delivered an ingenious speech to a big audience in support of Mr. Winstone, and so ingratiating were his arguments that there can be no doubt they had a steadying influence on a considerable section of the miners, who were disposed to vote for Stanton, and many of them have veered round.'[22]

But Winstone had not rid himself of the ILP albatross. The *Yorkshire Post* argued: 'To some extent Mr. Winstone has played into his opponent's hands, for it is generally recognised that the visit of Mr. Ramsay MacDonald ... has been a great tactical blunder.'[23] The *Manchester Courier* commented more widely: 'Because Winstone knows the ILP is unpopular he has been at pains to publish the fact that his personal conduct since the commencement of war has been that of a true patriot. Mr Stanton, his opponent, imputes to the official candidate, general adherence to, and sympathy with, the anti-war propagandists. It is on this issue alone that the contest will really be fought'.[24]

The other ILP titan, Jowett, concentrated on opposing conscription, which was the most important national issue at the time. The initial war enthusiasm of 1914 had seen large numbers volunteering but by mid-1915 those numbers had declined at the same time it had become obvious that the volumes required were going to be far greater than most (excluding the Secretary of State for War, Horatio Kitchener)[25] had ever imagined. For many, the idea of conscription was anathema, equivalent to the 'beastly Prussianism' they were fighting. The Labour movement was largely, although not entirely,

---

22 *Birmingham Mail*, 23 November 1915.
23 *Yorkshire Post*, 25 November 1915.
24 *Manchester Courier*, 25 November 1915.
25 On 7 July 1915, Kitchener publicly called for the formation of an army of 70 divisions, or over 1 million front-line troops, deployed on the western front alone. Realistically, such a size of army was beyond the resources that voluntary recruitment would provide.

opposed.[26] The Liberals were split; Churchill and Lloyd George in favour while Asquith remained hesitant. By June 1915, the Northcliffe papers *The Times* and *Daily Mail* were campaigning strongly for compulsion. Towards the end of August, Kitchener finally came out in support, severely weakening opposition. Despite this, the union movement remained hostile, with the TUC unanimously carrying a resolution opposing conscription. Asquith, too, was still unconvinced, although opinion within his government was hardening in favour.

The final throw of the dice for voluntarism was the Derby scheme. At the start of October, the Conservative politician Lord Derby was appointed as Director General of Recruiting. His plan was for all men of fighting age to be given the opportunity to 'attest' that, if called, they would volunteer for the armed forces. It was increasingly recognised that if too few, especially single, men came forward through this scheme, conscription would be inevitable. Those registering were given khaki armbands to show their commitment – to stop them being attacked as 'shirkers'. By 20 November, some 270,000 men had 'attested'. However, four days later (on the very eve of polling in Merthyr), Derby warned that: 'men must come in very much larger numbers in the next three weeks if they are going to make the position of voluntary service absolutely unassailable.' Thus, the Merthyr by-election was held at the height of controversy over compulsory military service. Winstone still firmly nailed his colours in opposition to conscription at a time when national opinion was moving inexorably against him. He was countering strident accusations of being anti-war because of his membership of the ILP while trying to stand on the increasingly slippery ground of opposition to compulsion. It was a subtle message in a campaign from which Stanton was removing all subtlety. Winstone agreed that the single objective of government was to bring the war to a speedy and successful end, and he fully endorsed that. He emphasised:

'Under no circumstances would he be a party to making peace while a German foot remained on Belgian or French soil. The Germans should pay to the

---

26 Organised labour, as well as being opposed to military conscription also feared that if the principle were accepted it could also lead to 'industrial conscription' with workers' hard-fought rights being removed.

> *uttermost farthing for the reconstruction of the towns and villages devastated by them. Great Britain should also be completely indemnified by Germany.'*

But he insisted that all this should be achieved under the principle of voluntarism.

Stanton also held numerous meetings, although with fewer outside supporters. His big draw was Victor Fisher who had worked his way through most socialist organisations in the country, ending up in the British Socialist Party and then leading the group (including such luminaries as Herbert (H G) Wells and Robert Blatchford) which established the pro-war Socialist National Defence Committee. He pulled no punches. At a mass meeting of over 3,000 at Aberdare, he positioned the election as being about the ILP. He said:

> *'It was not a contest between Mr. Stanton and Mr. Winstone, but a contest between everything they understood as British and the ILP. Robbed of all verbiage and pretence, Mr Winstone was the worthy standard-bearer of the particular principles of which Mr Ramsay MacDonald was the incarnation.'*

Stanton, meanwhile, concentrated on his feeling of injustice at having been denied the Labour nomination. He claimed, without evidence, 'had the ILP played the game at the ballot boxes he would now be in the happy position in which Mr Winstone found himself.' He responded to a challenge by Winstone that he should put himself at his country's service (as Winstone said he had done) by saying: 'So have I volunteered, but for the moment I propose to stay at home in order to fight the German Hun in our midst.'[27]

Stanton was happy to fight for conscription. He attacked Winstone by arguing that if he refused to help with voluntary recruitment and opposed conscription, then:

> *'it surely meant Mr Winstone was prepared to fold his arms while the Germans were allowed to beat us. He said deliberately that Mr Winstone was pro-German in his sympathies as the members of the ILP were also to a man. The ILP members in his own district of Aberdare had said that Nurse Cavell had only got*

---

27 *Western Mail*, 23 November 1915.

what she deserved. Men of that kind deserved to be treated in the same way that noble woman had been.' [28]

In his eve-of-poll speech, Stanton claimed a victory for Winstone: 'would be disheartening for the boys in the trenches and would bring joy to the Germans. It was a question of choosing between a pro-German and a Britisher.'[29]

While Winstone outgunned Stanton in numbers of meetings the latter made greater use of other campaigning tactics. Notably, he deployed letters, from himself and others, to hammer home key points. Particularly effective was the publication of a letter to Victor Fisher from the prospective Liberal candidate, who had stood aside, T Artemus Jones. Jones laid it on thick for the attention of Liberal supporters in the constituency, that the electoral truce did not mean that they must vote for the 'official' candidate. He argued that this election was outside the official truce as it was 'a domestic difference among members of one particular party.' He went on to claim that the only issue was the vigorous prosecution of the war and that 'I have nothing but admiration for Mr Stanton's sturdy championship of the national cause, right from the outset of the war and the manly and courageous fashion in which he has fought for his views.' His guidance was clear.

The letter was reproduced by Stanton as a leaflet and distributed on polling day. The Winstone campaign was heartily aggrieved by this interpretation. Instead, they maintained the truce meant that supporters (i.e. individual voters) of all parties should fall behind the duly selected candidate of the party that had previously held the seat. But that view was unenforceable and, truce or no truce, Jones' unsubtle nudge to his fellow Liberals was a powerful weapon in a constituency that was more Liberal than Labour.

Another letter was sent by Henry Hyndman, the founder of the British Socialist Party, (who had sharply changed his views since he spoke alongside Hardie at the peace demonstration in Trafalgar Square in August 1914). It was widely publicised in the press and again circulated as a leaflet by Stanton. The letter said:

---

28 Ibid
29 *Western Mail*, 25 November 1915.

> 'It was pointed out to me ... that if Mr Winstone, the ILP peace-at-any-price candidate, were to beat the Social Democrat pro-British miner, Mr C B Stanton, at Merthyr, such a political victory would have a very bad effect in France, Russia, Italy, Belgium, Serbia, and elsewhere. I attached little importance to this at the time, because I believe our allies know the position here very well, and are convinced that, in spite of the desperate blundering of our politicians, this nation is quite determined to win the war at all costs. Since then, however, I have learnt that the I.L.P. attach the greatest possible importance to the contest, and that they intend to represent Mr. Winstone's success, should he win, as clear evidence that the workers of Great Britain are ready to accept any terms of peace from Germany. Under these circumstances, the support given to Mr. Winstone by Mr. Arthur Henderson, as the Cabinet Minister representing Labour, cannot fail to be misunderstood and misinterpreted abroad. I hope sincerely no effort will be spared to return Mr. Stanton by a large majority.'

Finally, Stanton sent a letter of his own to Winstone, by registered post, asking him whether he would repudiate the war policy of the ILP leaders and condemn the Union of Democratic Control. He made much play of the fact that he had not received a response. Stanton also made widespread use of posters which highlighted a resolution passed by the ILP at its conference in Glasgow in January 1915 that its members: 'be requested not to assist the government in the recruiting campaign.'[30]

The Winstone team circulated only one further leaflet in addition to his election address. This was produced by the Aberdare Trades and Labour Council and stated:

> 'We cannot conceive of any Trades Unionist acting so disloyally to himself and his fellow workmen as to vote for any but the candidate of their own choice .... We further ask you not to be led astray by Mr. Stanton's persistent slander of the Labour candidate by calling him a pro-German.'

Winstone also tried to benefit from his strong commitment to non-conformity and issued testimonies from several religious leaders which, he said, showed

---

30 *Western Mail*, 23 November 1915.

his 'claim to the suffrage of the Nonconformist section of the Liberals in the constituency.' Examples he gave of specific supporters included Congregational, Baptist, and Methodist ministers. [31]

Prognostications and result

Both sides claimed to be confident of victory but, in a final campaign push, Winstone's team began to threaten that if he were defeated (as the official candidate) that might well mean the end of the parliamentary truce, at least on the part of the ILP. Among observers, *The Times* thought, generally, organisation wins elections and that the Winstone campaign was better organised and had greater resources. But local experts believed Stanton would prevail. They assessed that Winstone had failed to quarantine himself from the unpopularity of the ILP and, indeed, even on polling day, he toured the constituency in the company of the chairman of the local ILP branch.

In truth, the position of the ILP was confused and resulted in the worst of all worlds. On 13 August 1914, the ILP condemned the war, and five of the seven ILP members of Parliament upheld that stance.[32] However, it realised that total opposition would mean complete separation from the mass of the labour movement and the Labour Party. Consequently, during 1915 its positioning lacked clarity and MacDonald even appeared at a recruiting meeting in his Leicester constituency to blunt the accusation that he was anti-war. So, it was only at the National Conference of April 1916 that the ILP definitively adopted an anti-war position, and even then, they were always prepared to accommodate loyal members, such as Winstone, whose views did not go that far. But these were details in which 'patriotic' observers were not interested; so far as they were concerned, the ILP was against the war and, therefore, pro-German and, therefore, so was Winstone.

Locally placed commentators further recognised that a plea for Liberal and Unionist supporters to interpret the truce as meaning they **must** vote for the 'official' candidate was going to fall on deaf ears and that they would, generally, back the 'more patriotic' candidate. The one other electoral group

---

31 *Western Mail*, 24 November 1915.
32 Aled Eirug, Opposition to the First World War in Wales (Cardiff University PhD Thesis, 2016).

in the constituency was a sizeable Irish contingent and they came out mainly in favour of Stanton.

Overall, the expectation was Stanton would triumph, with a majority of around 2,000. In the event, he won a more considerable victory:

Dec. 1910 (2 members elected)			
Jones	Lib	12,258	42%
Hardie	Lab	11,507	40%
Watts	Lib Unionist	5,277	18%
Majority		6,981	
Electorate & Turnout		23,219	81%

25 Nov. 1915 (1 Member elected)			
Stanton	Ind Lab	10,286	63%
Winstone	Lab	6,080	37%
Majority		4,206	
Electorate & Turnout		24,192	68%

The aggressively pro-war campaign had won.

Assessment and implications

Counting took place on Friday, 26 November and the result was announced just before 1pm by which time a crowd of around 2,000 had gathered. Stanton's victory was well-received. He thanked the voters for their support and commented: 'the boys in the trenches will be glad that Merthyr Boroughs have stood loyally toward them.' Winstone was too hoarse to speak so his local agent, Mardy Jones, angrily commented on his behalf: 'In this election, Mr. Winstone was the victim of slander but after the war, he would come into his own.'³³ Later, Winstone continued the attack on Stanton saying: 'I have fought a clean fight and wish I could say the same about my opponent.'³⁴ He also took the opportunity to deny that he had run under the auspices of the ILP although, of course, he had received their nomination (as well as that of the miners) and welcomed their leading speakers to support him.

After the declaration, there was agreement about why the result had occurred. Stanton had been successful in making the contest a referendum on the ILP and its perceived anti-war policies. Much solace was found in their failure in what was assumed to be one of the country's strongest hotbeds of socialism. *The Times* described the outcome as 'one of the most significant events that have occurred at home since the beginning of the war' and stated 'this obscure by-election in South Wales is a decisive numerical test of the strength of patriotism in Great Britain at the very point where it is thought to be weakest.'³⁵ The result reassured the government about the reliability and patriotism of the South Wales miners, whose record of industrial disputes to that point had been a matter of considerable concern.³⁶ It also played heavily into the ongoing debate regarding conscription. The Times concluded: 'It shows that no candidate has the slightest chance of winning a contested election unless he is sound on the prosecution of the war with all the vigour at our command'.³⁷ Merthyr seemed to confirm that the great majority of the country was now ready to accept (and often, welcome) the move to the next stage of state control over the country and peoples' lives in order to win the war. On the day Stanton took his seat, *The Times* felt his victory was having a major impact, saying: 'it has acted as a wholesome tonic upon some whose firmness, until the other day, did not seem to be adamantine. It has braced their patriotism to the stalwart pitch.'³⁸ The paper assessed that, now, there was united backing for the policy of fighting the war to win.

---

33 *Nottingham Evening Post*, 26 November 1915.
34 *Western Mail*, 27 November 1915.
35 *The Times*, 27 November 1915.
36 There had been multiple strikes and disputes in the South Wales coalfield during the spring and summer of 1915 and Lloyd George had been forced to make major concessions to end them.
37 *The Times*, 27 November 1915.
38 *The Times*, 30 November 1915.

The results of the Derby scheme revealed many unmarried men of military age had failed either to volunteer or attest. Cabinet discussions were held on 27, 28 and 31 December by the end of which Asquith was willing to introduce the first Military Service Bill (published on 6 January 1916). The Merthyr result weighed in the scales on this decision and one analysis concluded: 'The results at the solidly working-class constituency were not lost on the conscriptionists of the Cabinet who argued that workers were ready to accept the policy. There was now little which could effectively stand in the way of compulsory service if the results of the Derby canvass were inadequate.'[39]

The truth behind Stanton's campaign

The belief at the time, and for decades afterwards, was that Stanton had fought a lonely campaign against the full force of the Labour and union machines. According to the *Scotsman*: 'Mr. Stanton fought practically single-handed, his only active friends being a few fellow Socialists who have put their country's cause higher than their economic views'.[40] Despite this, when the election expenses[41] were published, he was found to have spent only a little less than Winstone. The figures were:

Stanton	£801 5s 9d
Winstone	£1,099 8s 2d

Stanton's expenses were the equivalent of over £67,000 in today's money[42].

In truth, his campaign had been reliant on secret finance provided by Unionist sources. Evidence of this only emerged in the 1990s through research

---

39 R J Q Adams and Philip P Poirer, The Conscription Controversy in Great Britain, 1900 – 1918 (1987).
40 *The Scotsman*, 27 November 1915.
41 The expenses limits were £650 in County seats of up to 2,000 electors plus £60 for each additional 1,000 voters and £350 in Borough seats of up to 2,000 electors plus £30 for each additional 1,000. These amounts excluded the requirement to pay the Returning Officer's fees and personal expenses of the candidate.
42 Calculated at https://www.bankofengland.co.uk/monetary-policy/inflation/inflation-calculator.

by the historian, Barry M Doyle.[43] The proof was in the papers of Oliver Locker-Lampson MP, held in the Norfolk Records Office. Locker-Lampson was appointed in 1912 to manage the new Unionist Workingman Candidates' Fund, in conjunction with Howell Gwynne, the editor of the Morning Post. Its objective was to provide support to encourage more working-class Unionist candidates. Crucially, although an official Unionist organisation, it was not controlled by Central Office and so those in the party bound by the parliamentary truce did not need to know what it was doing. Certainly, there was anxiety at the highest level in the Unionist party about the possible outcome of Merthyr. The Chairman (Arthur Steel-Maitland) told Conservative leader Andrew Bonar Law of 'concern in the lobbies' that Winstone might be a pacifist. There was a wish to avoid any chance of an ILP victory and, also, a longer-term desire to build on the SNDC in the hope of creating a permanent split within Labour. In the event, a complex (albeit unofficial) network of Unionists secretly raised funds for Stanton. The organisation to do so was built on a combination of Locker-Lampson and Lord Alfred Milner's National Service League. The key letters in the archive were from the Secretary of the National Service League (Roderick MacLeod) to Locker-Lampson. In the first letter cited by Doyle, MacLeod refers to Locker-Lampson's 'very kind promise .... of £150 towards Mr Stanton's share of Returning Officer's Fees, in order to enable him to fight the Merthyr by-election, conditional on my raising another £150 for the same object.' He then goes on to confirm that he has managed to obtain the second £150, 'thanks to introductions from Mr. Gwynne of the Morning Post'.

MacLeod also confirmed he had informed Steel-Maitland what was happening and that the latter was very pleased 'in his unofficial capacity'. He further made clear the need for speed and secrecy saying:

> 'Will you be so good as to let me have the cheque ... as soon as you conveniently can? I shall have to pay the money into my private account and draw it out some time tomorrow as it must be sent down to Merthyr Tydfil by a reliable hand. May I venture to remind you that it is absolutely vital to Mr. Stanton

---

43 Barry M Doyle, *Who Paid the Price of Patriotism? The Funding of Charles Stanton during the Merthyr Boroughs* By-Election of 1915 (English Historical Review, Vol 109. No. 434, November 1994)

and the loyal labour men that it should never come out who has provided the preliminary sinews of war. It would not only ruin our chances at the by-election but would seriously damage those concerned in the eyes of the Labour world if it could be brought home to them that they were taking Tory money. I shall be grateful if you could see your way to destroying this letter as I do not quite like leaving this record on paper'.[44]

The letter was not destroyed, but the truth was hidden successfully for almost 90 years.

The road from Merthyr for Winstone and Stanton

Winstone and Stanton were to clash again, a year later, at the 'Battle of Cory Hall'. A meeting was organised by the National Council for Civil Liberties [45] in Cardiff on 11 November 1916. The Home Secretary had been asked to ban it but declined, arguing that to do so would encourage more troublesome underground opposition. He did, however, request that 'patriots' who were planning a counter-demonstration not go near the event. The meeting chairman was Winstone, and it was to be addressed by MacDonald, among others. The fact that a 'pacifist' meeting was to be held in Cardiff resulted in uproar. Opposition was led by the seamen's union who sent a telegram to the Home Secretary, saying: 'As you have not seen fit to prohibit the pacifist meeting ... the seamen of this port are taking the matter into their own hands, and you must take full responsibility for what will undoubtedly occur if the meeting is held.'[46]

An open-air protest against the meeting was followed by a procession which eventually split into two; part followed police instructions to avoid Cory Hall, but the other section headed towards it. *The Western Mail* reported the climax of the events: 'Upon the arrival of the patriotic demonstrators,

---

44 Quoted in Doyle: *Who paid the price of Patriotism?* 'Tory Gold', of course, already held a place in Labour history. Ironically, it was Hyndman (along with Henry Champion) who was the first socialist revealed to have accepted Conservative money. In 1885, the Tories gave £340 to fund the running of two Social Democrat Federation candidates in London seats in the hope of splitting the Liberal vote.
45 The National Council Against Conscription was renamed as the NCCL in mid-1916.
46 *Birmingham Daily Post*, 13 November 1916.

headed by Mr. C B Stanton and Captain Tupper, the scenes almost baffled description. The martial strains of the accompanying band had a tremendous effect upon the already excited crowd and their supporters stormed the doors successfully.[47]

A reporter described the scene inside the hall, immediately after the protestors, led by Stanton, had torn the doors off their hinges and marched up to the top table:

> 'Mr James Winstone JP, the chairman, held his ground for a time, and showed his teeth before he also quitted the chair... He then turned, with fire in his eyes, to his old opponent [Stanton] and almost everybody in the audience stood still for a few moments to take in the scene. They all knew the antagonism, embittered at the Merthyr election, existing between them and no one would have been surprised to have witnessed a regrettable personal trial of physical strength.'[48]

The Western Mail referred to 'Mr. Winstone's pluck'. It described how he (with a police escort) was followed from the Hall by many hundreds of protestors and that 'every conceivable epithet was hurled at him', especially by women. As he reached the station: 'a young man threw a squashy tomato, which hit Mr. Winstone on the back of the neck. This action was loudly cheered and, encouraged by its success, the crowd freely pelted tomatoes and other things at him.'

The abandoned meeting was eventually rearranged in Merthyr Tydfil and went ahead without incident. However, nationally from this time onwards, it became more difficult to arrange dissenting meetings, in part due to the fear by hall owners of damage, both physical and to their reputation, by allowing the open espousal of 'unpatriotic' views.

Winstone stood again in the 1918 General Election. The Merthyr seat had now been split into two (Merthyr and Aberdare) and he stood in Merthyr as the official Labour candidate. He lost narrowly to the sitting Liberal, Edgar

---

47 *Western Mail*, 13 November 1916.
48 Ibid

Rees Jones who had the Coalition 'coupon'.[49] On 23 July 1921, he was again re-elected as President of the South Wales Miners' Federation. Yet by 26 July that year he was reported to have fallen seriously ill. He was in London for the final stages of negotiation of a miners' dispute 'and was removed to a nursing home just before the settlement of the dispute was reached.'[50] He had originally been struck down by appendicitis and that was followed by a fatal heart attack. Over 25,000 attended his funeral.

In the 1918 election, Stanton stood in the new Aberdare constituency. He benefitted from the coupon and won easily against Labour's Thomas Nicholas, who had consistently opposed the war. He was elected as a National Democratic and Labour Party candidate.[51] The campaign continued his virulently anti-German positioning and added the prevalent violent distaste for 'Bolshevism'. In 1920, Stanton was awarded the CBE. He stood again for Aberdare in 1922 but was defeated by Labour. He later (1928) joined the Liberal Party but was never again returned to parliament. He relocated to Hampstead and subsequently worked as a violinist and a publican and acted in several films in which, due to his 'distinguished' appearance, he played parts such as clergymen (including the Archbishop of Canterbury) and an English butler. He died in 1946, aged 73.

---

49 The 'coupon' was a joint letter of endorsement by David Lloyd George and Andrew Bonar Law to selected candidates in the 1918 election. In total, 545 candidates received the coupon of whom 477 were elected.
50 *The Scotsman*, 28 July 1921.
51 The origin of the National Democratic and Labour Party was: In 1916, the Socialist National Defence Committee formed the British Workers League, which was funded by Milner. This, in turn, in 1918 became the National Democratic and Labour Party which, at the election, was led by George Barnes and returned nine MPs.

3.
THE GREATEST FOE?

Cleveland, 9 December 1915
West Newington, 10 January 1916

After Merthyr, the notion of using by-elections to raise contentious topics was taken up, beginning with protests about restrictions on alcohol. During 1915, a new Central Control Board for the Liquor Trade initiated the phased roll-out of limits on its production, sale and consumption. After the drinking public's initial acquiescence, controversy grew. On one side of the debate, David Lloyd George, the then Chancellor, claimed: 'We are fighting Germany, Austria and drink: and, as far as I can see, the greatest of these deadly foes is drink'.[1] Against this, a leading socialist activist and one of the by-election candidates, Joseph (Joe or JJ) Terrett, proclaimed that opposition would be massive: 'I promise you, unless you lock us all up, one of the most tremendous agitations that has ever convulsed this Metropolis.[2]

Consequently, by-elections were fought in the name of preserving an Englishman's right to drink. They also brought the flamboyant showman and charlatan, Horatio Bottomley, onto the wartime electoral scene, as a

---

[1] Replying to a deputation of shipbuilding employers, 29 March 1915. Quoted in J Grigg, *Lloyd George – From Peace to War 1912 – 1916 (1992).*
[2] Speaking as a member of a deputation to the Central Control Board by the London Trades Union Protest Committee. Quoted in the *Western Mail*, 27 November 1915.

committed advocate for the interests of 'the trade'. Despite this opposition, the government pushed ahead with restrictions, some of which remained in force for decades. Historical consensus is that the case for introducing regulation was not as strong as the government (and especially, Lloyd George) claimed; nevertheless, the changes were effective and brought productivity and social benefits.

Drink an early wartime concern and scapegoat

A perceived need for restrictions on alcohol surfaced in the earliest days of war. On 12 August 1914, naval and military authorities were granted powers to close licensed premises in or near a fortified place. The end of the month then saw the passing of the Intoxicating Liquor (Temporary Restriction) Act which allowed limitations on pub opening, typically to 9pm or 11pm instead of 12.30am as previously. By the end of the year, half the licensing authorities in England and Wales had curtailed opening hours. The budget in November 1914 tripled duty on a standard barrel of beer from 7s 9d to 23s., equivalent to an increase of around a halfpenny a pint, the average price of which was three pence. In a speech in Bangor in February 1915, Lloyd George said:

> *'But you must remember, a small minority of workmen can throw a whole works out of gear. What is the reason? Sometimes it is one thing, sometimes it is another, but let us be perfectly candid. It is mostly the lure of drink. They refuse to work full-time and when they return their strength and efficiency are impaired by the way in which they have spent their leisure. Drink is doing us more damage in the war than all the German submarines put together.'*

He was now on a mission such that Asquith complained he 'had completely lost his head' on the issue.[3] A contributor to the push for restrictions was the failure of an Allied attack at Neuve Chappelle in March 1915. Sir John French, the commander of the British Expeditionary Force, blamed the outcome on a shortage of munitions which, in turn, the government (and Douglas Haig, then commander of the First Army which was involved in the attack) attributed to working time lost through drink. In truth, Lloyd George was right to observe

---

3 Quoted in R Duncan, *Pubs and Patriots* (2013).

privately that: 'The idea that slackness and drink ... are the chief causes of delay ... is mostly a fudge.'[4]

But he was determined to reduce the production and consumption of alcohol. He successfully encouraged King George V to 'set an example' and, at the end of March 1915, it was announced that the monarch would abstain from alcohol until the end of the war and that no alcohol would be served in the Royal Households (a decision George rather regretted). The King's lead was followed by few. Lloyd George, the 'Welsh Wizard', also pushed for restrictive regulations. In April, he floated a plan for state ownership of public houses (which he felt more feasible than a total ban on alcohol) but could not get it through Cabinet. By the month end, he proposed instead further sharp increases in duties and the right in designated areas to close public houses and/or restrict the sale of drinks with high alcohol content. His plans initially were supported by the Conservative leader, Andrew Bonar Law, but strong opposition from the trade, numerous Conservative rebels and the Irish MPs meant that the taxation proposals had to be withdrawn. Bonar Law told Lloyd George that the Tory party 'is so much in the hands of the trade' that it must oppose the taxation proposals 'root and branch'.[5]

The introduction of the Central Control Board

The policy finally adopted, in the middle of May 1915, was the establishment of the Central Control Board. It was a free-standing entity, reporting neither to parliament nor government, and had a diverse make-up including individuals from the trade, the trades unions, the temperance movement and MPs. Its objectives were: 'controlling the sale and supply of intoxicating liquor in naval, military, munitions or transport areas, where such control should be found expedient for the successful prosecution of the war' as defined in an Order in Council issued under the Defence of the Realm Consolidation Act, 1914. On application by the Ministry of Munitions, the War Office or the Admiralty, specific areas deemed to need restrictions were reviewed by investigators – teams comprising naval, military and civil authorities plus representatives of employers and working men in the locality.

---

4 Reported comment by Lloyd George to Christopher Addison quoted in R Duncan, *Pubs and Patriots* (2013).
5 H H Asquith, Memories & Reflections, quoted in R Duncan, *Pubs and Patriots* (2013).

The first area to be subject to an order by the Board, in July 1915, was Newhaven where problems had arisen due to the drunkenness of soldiers bound for France. *The People* newspaper stated, 'Far-reaching and drastic are the regulations which are now put into force to secure the control by the State of the sale and supply of intoxicating liquor in areas where war work is to be executed'.[6] The powers of the Board included ordering public houses and clubs to be closed or compulsorily purchased; restricting opening hours; prohibiting the sale of particular types of drink in public houses or clubs; banning 'treating' and the purchase of alcohol on credit; regulating the strength of spirits; establishing refreshment rooms; and requiring any licensed premises to be subject to the supervision of the Board.

The Board worked at considerable pace. In August 1915 alone, restrictions were imposed in Barrow, Southampton, Dartford, Bristol, the North-east coast (Middlesbrough, Stockton, Darlington, Hartlepool, Newcastle), Liverpool and Merseyside, Newport/Cardiff/Barry, and East and West Central Scotland (Edinburgh and Glasgow). Generally, there was little opposition other than from local licensed victuallers' associations and the restrictions were successful in significantly reducing drunkenness. By late September 1915, news emerged that the Central Board was planning to designate the whole of London as a munitions area and to introduce restrictions, on the request of the officer commanding troops in the metropolis. The alleged cause was high levels of drunkenness amongst the armed forces, rather than concerns regarding 'broken time' in munitions works. On 11 October, limits came into effect on 'treating' (buying drinks for others, including the well-established habit of buying rounds) and on the strength of spirits. Maximum penalties were a draconian £100 fine and six months imprisonment with hard labour.

Then, early in November, rumours circulated of further restrictions in London to which greater opposition emerged. The *Manchester Courier* reported:

> *'Hitherto the drastic orders of the Central Control Board have on the whole been taken in excellent part by their various victims all over the country ... If, however, reliance is to be placed upon announcements in to-day's newspapers*

---

6 *The People*, 13 June 1915.

> that the Central Control Board is about to issue a new batch of even more stringent regulations ... the time has clearly come for the British public to adopt some more self-protective measures.'[7]

The newspaper was highly suspicious of what lay behind the plans, hinting that they were driven by pressure from 'teetotal propagandists' rather than real need. But confirmation came that stringent restrictions were to be imposed across London. Opening hours were to be from noon to 2.30pm and 6.30pm to 9.30pm (9pm in Woolwich) on weekdays and 1pm to 3pm and 6pm to 9pm on Sundays. Off-sales of spirits were not to be permitted in volumes smaller than one quart and credit and the 'long pull', where the publican provided a larger measure than had been paid for, were banned. Immediately, a trade union meeting condemned the move. Elsewhere the press reported:

> 'Over 300 delegates from the Postmen's Federation, the National Union of Paper and Printing Trade Workers, the National Union of Railwaymen, the National Vehicle Workers' Union, the London Labourers' Union, and Working-Men's Clubs attended a meeting at Hackney yesterday morning, and passed a resolution demanding the withdrawal within seven days of the "insulting restrictions imposed by the Central Control Board, and supposed to come into force on November 29".'[8]

The resolution stated that the meeting viewed the Order as a direct incitement to down tools. The resolution added—'Should the restrictions not be withdrawn within the specified time the meeting pledges itself to do its utmost to resist them by open revolt if necessary.'

The unions set up a London Committee to fight the new orders and the London licensed trade organised protests. A London trades union meeting on 27 November was presided over by Jack Jones, the leader of the Gasworkers Union. He declared that: 'the people who formed the Board of Control were as ignorant of the conditions of working-class life as the average Connemara pig was of astronomy.'[9]

---

[7] *Manchester Courier*, 8 November 1915.
[8] *Dundee Courier*, 22 November 1915.
[9] *The People*, 28 November 1916.

CLEVELAND – December 1915

Into this background came the announcement of a potential by-election in Cleveland in the north-east. On 25 November, the sitting MP, Herbert Samuel, the current Postmaster-General, was also appointed as Chancellor of the Duchy of Lancaster, replacing Winston Churchill. Churchill had been demoted from the Admiralty to this lowly cabinet position when the Coalition government was formed in May 1915, due to his unpopularity with the Conservatives, but he now decided to leave government entirely and take up active service on the Western Front. At that time, if an MP accepted 'an office of profit under the crown' he had to submit himself to a by-election. Samuel did not intend to take the additional salary, but the obligation still applied.

Challenging a Cabinet member about the new drinking restrictions in London seemed a good idea to some, even if it were via an election a few hundred miles away. Those first to consider the idea were associated with the London trades union protests. The potential candidate floated was the secretary of the London Protest Committee, Joe Terrett. According to newspaper reports, he said he would be unable to announce his decision until after a mass meeting to be held in Shoreditch that night:

> *'If Shoreditch tells me to fight", Mr. Terrett said, I will fight. I would be an Independent candidate in defence of the liberties of England, and for the assertion of Parliamentary Government.' On the war question, he went on, 'my views are exactly the same as those of Charlie Stanton. Stanton did for Ramsay Macdonald in Merthyr; I will do for Snowden*[10] *in Cleveland. If I win at Cleveland, there will be an end to pacifism in the Labour Party. If they withdraw the Liquor Order, I will stop my candidature at once.'* [11]

Terrett revealed that he had been offered financial help to fight the by-election by several influential citizens from Manchester. He told a newspaper that they wanted 'to burst the political truce, and they think that to attack a Cabinet Minister will be the most brilliant stroke of the agitation. They assured me

---

10 Philip Snowden was the MP for Blackburn and a leading light on the 'pacifist' wing of the Labour Party. He was also a strong temperance campaigner and a Board member of the Central Control Board.
11 *Birmingham Mail*, 2 December 1915.

on their personal guarantees that if I would consent to fight the Cleveland Division[12] of Yorkshire at this by-election they will immediately subscribe £2,000 for my election expenses.'[13] Terrett now announced he would stand.

Whilst some thought opposing a Cabinet minister was a good idea, others were less certain about fighting an election in the north-east about drinking restrictions in London and the labour movement was by no means united behind the notion. One senior Trades Union official said if Terrett went ahead 'it is calculated to make the Labour organisations the laughing stock of the country's enemies' and that he would find most of the unions in whose name he claimed to stand arrayed against him.'[14]

Time was now pressing. The government had decided on a rapid schedule for the election with only two weeks between Samuel's appointment and the nominated polling day. In the end, Terrett ducked the fight. At a meeting on 4 December, he gave as his reason that the constituency was a 'straggling' one and that he would be unable to reach the electors in the time available. He claimed the government had been frightened into rushing the election. There was, however, also recognition that it might be a mistake to fight a London issue in the far north-east. At the same meeting the Chairman, Jack Jones. said that they should confine their battle to London and that should any London constituency become vacant they should be prepared to fight it.

Horatio Bottomley steps in

Yet even before Terrett's retreat, a different candidate emerged. A major meeting in the Queen's Hall in London on 3 December, was presided over by the politician and publisher Horatio Bottomley and organised under the auspices of his 'League of the Man in the Street', although financed by 'the trade'. He said:

> *'He was appearing before the bar of public opinion as Counsel for the man in the street, for the munitions worker, for the wives of the soldiers that were fighting at the front, and that he was there to answer and to reject with indignation the*

---

12 The terms 'division' and 'constituency' effectively are interchangeable although, strictly speaking, 'divisions' referred to seats in county rather than borough areas.
13 *Burton Daily Mail*, 2 December 1915.
14 *Leeds Mercury*, 3 December 1915.

indictment made against them by the government of being slackers, drunkards and sots.' [15]

He then announced Reginald Knight, a resident of Leeds and a member of Bottomley's Business Government League, as his candidate. Another speaker at the meeting was the ever patriotic, Ben Tillett, who was to fight his own by-election in 1917 (see chapter 11).

Bottomley was a larger-than-life figure who was to play an always self-serving role in several wartime by-elections. He was one of Britain's leading crooks, charlatans, and eccentrics of the early twentieth century. Possibly the illegitimate son of Charles Bradlaugh,[16] he was raised in an orphanage. He started working life as a law reporter and then moved on to buying and starting small newspapers and printing companies. Elected as a Liberal MP in 1906 (South Hackney), in the same year he became the publisher of the populist magazine, *John Bull*. Early in his career, in 1891, he had filed for bankruptcy and eventually had to do so again in 1912, which meant his banishment from the House of Commons.

The war was to be the making of Bottomley. *John Bull* quickly adopted an ultra-patriotic stance[17] and achieved a claimed circulation of over 250,000. An impressive orator, desperate for involvement again in public life, Bottomley offered his services for recruitment meetings and 'patriotic rallies' across the country. (The latter were successful money-making events for himself). Through the course of the war, he spoke at over 300 meetings and became an influential figure.

---

15 *Manchester Courier*, 4 December 1915.
16 Bradlaugh was a charismatic figure who was an atheist and the founder of the National Secular Society. In 1880, he was elected as Liberal MP for Northampton but a parliamentary dispute over whether, as an atheist, he was allowed to affirm rather than swear an oath led to him being denied the right to take his seat. Four by-elections followed in which Bradlaugh was re-elected each time but still refused the right to sit. He was finally allowed to do so in 1886.
17 Bottomley was quick to see how the land lay. The first edition of *John Bull* to comment on the European crisis was vehemently anti the Serbs but he quickly changed his line to be militantly supportive of the war and savagely anti-German.

As early as 1887 (Hornsey), Bottomley had realised by-elections could be effective vehicles for publicity and self-promotion. As Henry (H J) Houston (his assistant and political agent) noted:

> *'He was quick to observe that a contest, which in a general election would pass unregarded by the nation at large, would attract considerable attention by the press when it happened to be the only political fight in progress. Thereafter HB had a special affection for by-elections. They were almost irresistible to him.'*[18]

Bottomley brought to elections the skills of a showman with a brilliant eye for attracting attention. Early examples are from his re-election in Hackney in January 1910. In one stunt, he gave money to each of fifty men to have their boots, in Houston's words, 'heavily soled and heeled, and liberally weighted with iron tips and nails.'[19] They were then despatched to his Conservative opponent's meeting. As the candidate began to speak the first of the men got up and very slowly and loudly, due to the boots, made his way to the exit, noisily protesting that he was leaving as quietly as possible. Immediately on his departure, the second man got up and repeated the performance. Well before all 50 had departed, the candidate had given up any attempt to speak.

Bottomley was also a firm supporter (and customer) of 'the trade'. Despite being a Liberal MP, in 1908 he played a major role opposing the Licensing Bill. Houston, his agent, remarked: 'Sometimes he would take charabanc loads of publicans out for a day's racing and give them a first-class champagne lunch.' When it came to the wartime patriotic rallies and recruiting meetings, Houston recorded that Bottomley always arranged for them to finish twenty minutes before closing time, saying: 'that was HB's consideration for the public, the publican and himself.'[20]

When news of Cleveland reached Bottomley, he was in Manchester. As Houston recalled: 'The Liquor Control Board had just come into being, and H.B. thought it an opportunity to exploit the natural annoyance of the working man when his drinking habits were interfered with. He immediately contacted Reggie Knight (in Leeds) and asked him to meet him the next day

---

18 H J Houston, *The real Horatio Bottomley* (1923)
19 Ibid.
20 Ibid.

in London.' In Houston's description: 'Mr Knight was a fine specimen of manhood who might have stood as the original of the figure on the cover of John Bull... When he journeyed to town that night, he had not the vaguest idea of H.B.'s purpose, which he only learned on arrival.'[21]

Knight, previously a Conservative, was now chairman of Bottomley's Business Government League in Leeds. In one incident at Christmas 1913, he was part of a group of businessmen who undertook street sweeping during a strike by municipal workers.[22] However, his most lasting claim to fame is probably as the person who published, in 1879, the first codified breed description of the Airedale Terrier, largely based on his own dog Thunder.[23]

A rapid election

Herbert Samuel, Cleveland's newly-resigned MP, travelled up to the constituency for the weekend before nomination day (6 December) and announced he would speak on the Monday evening were there to be a contest. Meanwhile, the Yorkshire Evening Post summarised an interview with the challenger Knight:

> *'As would be expected by all who have made acquaintance with Mr Knight's breezy, unconventional, outspoken manner, he will stand as an independent candidate with no other object, he says, than to fight the government on the drink restrictions, in the interests of the liberty of the subject.'* [24]

Knight's election address said: 'Electors are afforded an opportunity of entering a protest against the manner in which the authorities are abusing the patriotism of the people by gradually, under the guise of war emergency, filching from them all their rights and liberties.' He argued that it was in the national interest that a strong protest be made against the suggestion that the people could not be trusted with liquor. He claimed that: 'The Order was treachery to the working classes who were doing so much for the nation in this crisis and was the thin end of the wedge of prohibition.'

---

21 Ibid.
22 *Leeds Mercury*, 6 December 1915.
23 https://janedogs.com/airedale-terrier/
24 *Yorkshire Evening Post*, 4 December 1915.

Knight asked the returning officer for an extension of two days, to Saturday, so that polling would not disrupt munitions work. His request was rejected as arrangements were already in place and notices had been issued that polling would be on the Thursday. The *Yorkshire Post* reported Terrett as claiming that his, abortive, campaign had: 'frightened the government into the most cowardly, hurried election of the last 20 years.'

Bottomley's man introduced a note of tension to nominations by leaving it to the final half an hour before arriving. The establishment candidate, Samuel presented eight forms to demonstrate the breadth of his support. The local Unionists fully endorsed him and completed one of his papers. Others included the officials of the local miners' organisation and representatives from across the constituency, including a leading licensed victualler. The interloper Knight submitted only one paper, with the *Leeds Mercury* noting: 'Mr. Knight was nominated and seconded by two well-known local sportsmen, and, doubtless, a good sporting spirit will be shown by his backers during the few days that remain before the issue is to be decided.'[25]

Samuel did not hide his annoyance at being forced into an election when he was fully involved in the war effort. A supportive local press provided an extensive list of his roles. Examples of his efforts were proposing, and presided over, a government committee to address distress stemming from what proved to be a short-term rise in unemployment at the beginning of the war; dealing with arrangements for the large volume of Belgian refugees; working as Postmaster General to improve postal arrangements serving troops in the front line (which he visited); introducing free postage for books and magazines for the troops and initiating a scheme of cheap insurance for property damaged by aircraft or bombardment.[26]

His first speech was held, perhaps insensitively, at the Temperance Hall in Guisborough on the Monday evening. He commented on the reasons why the contest was occurring and described it as: 'a striking instance of the absurdity of our law with regard to the re-election of Ministers.' Because he had accepted an office additional to that of Postmaster-General, although he was paying the whole of the salary of that office into the Treasury, nevertheless,

---

25 *Leeds Mercury*, 7 December 1915.
26 *Daily Gazette for Middlesborough*, 6 December 1915.

the law required him to seek re-election, and 'the opportunity had been seized by a gentleman from Leeds, at the invitation of an organisation in London, to contest that seat, and, strangely enough, there had been found in the constituency ten unrighteous men to support his candidature.' Samuel continued:

> *'At an ordinary time this contest would be a nuisance; but in time of war it was an outrage. It is not fought on any great issue of national politics; instead, gentlemen come and plunge this constituency into the turmoil of an election because they think that five and a half hours a day is not enough to drink beer. An election fought against a member of the Government on such an issue at such time is, I venture to say, the most sordid incident that has yet occurred during the war.'*

He argued that the drink measures were necessary because of the behaviour of a minority and were not a comment on the working class (or any other class) as a whole and now revealed that he had followed the King's example, giving up alcohol for the duration of the war. He also told listeners that while restrictions had been in place for several months in Cleveland, he had received only one letter of protest, from the Stockton & District Licensed Victuallers Association.

Despite the brevity of the campaign, and the universal confidence of Coalition victory, Samuel put in considerable effort. *The Yorkshire Evening Post* reported:

> *'Some people are not inclined to treat the contest seriously, but this is not true of Mr. Samuel, for he is applying himself with vigour and enthusiasm such as one would have expected only if his opponent had been a much more formidable person. Nothing is being left to chance. The Postmaster-General intends visiting as many parts of the district as he can between now and tomorrow night, and Mrs. Samuel is coming down from London to represent him in the villages which he cannot visit in person. Half a dozen MPs are attending for meetings.'* [27]

---

27 *Yorkshire Evening Post*, 7 December 1915.

Samuel implored the electorate not to be complacent saying: 'Any man who voted for Knight, any man who did not vote, was failing in his duty to the country in the war.'

The Knight campaign was pepped up by the presence of Bottomley, always a popular and engaging speaker. Houston, who acted as Knight's agent, claimed that Bottomley addressed twenty meetings. The opening shots of the campaign were widely reported in the press:

> 'Mr Knight declared the Liberal Government had muddled the war, and the Coalition Government, had done little better. The time had arrived for a national protest against the constant interference with the liberties of the working classes. The Government had been made a tool of teetotal fanatics. The Liquor Control Order was the last straw. It was treachery to the working man and was the thin end of prohibition. The Control Board had stamped the whole nation in the eyes of the world as drunkards.'[28]

Bottomley arrived on 7 December and addressed four meetings. In an interview with the *Daily Gazette for Middlesborough*, he explained the reason for the campaign while setting low expectations:

> 'Mr. Bottomley ridiculed the idea that the question of liquor restrictions had no interest for Cleveland. He said it was not merely a question for London, because Cleveland was one of the officially declared drunken areas. "I have come down to resent this, and also because Herbert Samuel has always been a bigoted supporter of the so-called temperance legislation"... My main object is not so much to defeat Samuel as to give the indication that they are abusing the patriotism of the people by passing all these faddist regulations under the name of war emergency.'

Bottomley felt they were having an impact, noting that Samuel had originally announced he would only spend one day on the campaign but now he was there full time and 'is having MPs sent by express train from London to help him, no doubt as the result of an urgent appeal for reinforcements.' He went

---

28 *Dundee Evening Telegraph*, 6 December 1915

on to suggest: 'if the Government had been half as expeditious in sending reinforcements to the front to save the Empire as they had been to save Mr. Samuel's seat the war should have been over six months ago.'

One suggestion made by Knight was heavily criticised. This was that drinkers might be issued with a licence, similar to a driving licence, which could be endorsed or cancelled if the holder became drunk. Samuel 'wondered how the people of Cleveland would like to have to carry a drink licence that had to be shown every time they were thirsty, with a knowledge of the fact that a magistrate could condemn him to be a teetotaller for life by taking away his licence.'[29]

On the eve of poll, Bottomley claimed that 1,000 votes for his candidate would constitute a victory against the Coalition. Polling day was subdued; there were few posters and Samuel felt it necessary to issue a letter to electors asking them not to treat the election 'indifferently'. Turnout was hit by a blizzard late in the day.

Dec. 1910			
Samuel	Liberal	6,970	56%
Lewis	Unionist	5,343	44%
Majority		1,527	
Electorate & Turnout		14,811	84%

9 Dec. 1915			
Samuel	Coalition (Liberal)	7,312	83%
Knight	Indep.	1,453	17%
Majority		5,859	
Electorate & Turnout		16,424	53%

---

29 *Yorkshire Post and Leeds Intelligencer*, 8 December 1915.

The result was hailed as a smashing victory for the Coalition, demonstrating the country's unity behind the government's policies for the war in general and specifically to limit alcohol. Even Bottomley's faithful Houston admitted that the Showman had failed in this outing: 'It was one of those ill-conceived, impulsive schemes to which he frequently committed himself. It was a whirlwind fight with never a hope of success.'[30]

Yet others held that for almost 1,500 votes to be garnered by such a brief and exotic campaign hinted at levels of dissatisfaction that might become problematic. *The Times* commented:

> *'The result of the Cleveland by-election, sometimes hailed as a triumph for the government, should convey a moral and a warning to the more far-sighted among ministers. They will look at the surprising dimensions of the minority vote rather than at Mr Samuel's big majority. Nobody with a practical knowledge of electioneering could have imagined that the anti-government candidate would have polled as many as 1,453 votes. There must be a good deal of unorganised discontent in the country to account for these votes, the majority of which were certainly not cast on the merits of the drink orders.'*[31]

Even in a rapid campaign, both candidates spent more than £920 (2024: Over £75,000).

Samuel was to have a long snakes-and-ladders political career. He stuck by Asquith and so was denied the Coalition coupon and lost his seat in the 1918 General Election. Outside of parliament, he served as High Commissioner for the Palestine Mandate but later (1929) returned as a Liberal MP and was to become party leader before being defeated again in 1935. Knight embraced relative obscurity and did not run again.

Drink, however, would return to the election trail.

WEST NEWINGTON – January 1916

The *Liverpool Echo* now recommended to those opposing the drink orders that Cleveland should mark the end of their campaign: 'The signal rebuff which

---

30 H J Houston, *The Real Horatio Bottomley* (1923).
31 *The Times*, 13 December 1915.

they have suffered must convince them that until the end of the war, at any rate, their selfish personal interests must be subservient to the higher welfare of-the country.'³² However, the New Year provided immediate temptation for the London Trade Union Protest Committee when a vacancy arose in West Newington, just south of the river in the metropolis, due to the elevation to the peerage of the Liberal MP, Captain Cecil Norton. He had much earlier announced his intention to stand down at the next election and James Gilbert, a City merchant, was already in place as the intended Liberal candidate. The Unionists also had a prospective candidate, Warwick Brookes, who had fought the last two elections in the constituency and, surprisingly, the immediate response of the local Conservative Association was to call on him to stand. Meanwhile, on New Year's Day, the London Trade Union Protest Committee leapt to recommend its Secretary, Joe Terrett, to a delegate conference of the affiliated societies.

On 3 January 1916, Terrett announced his candidacy but offered that if Warwick Brookes agreed to oppose the drink orders, he would withdraw, saying:

> *'There is only one question upon which the average London Conservative has any quarrel with his leaders, and that is the drink orders of the Board of Control. If Mr. Brookes cares to put that question in the forefront of his programme and fight the election on that issue, I will withdraw and back him.'*

However, on 5 January, the West Newington Conservative Association confirmed they would, after all, back Gilbert, from the incumbent Liberals. Terrett remained in place and the election came down to a straight fight.

Joe Terrett: a Socialist warrior

Joe Terrett was a committed and feisty representative of British socialism. An early sighting is in 1891 as a twenty-year-old activist for the Social Democratic Federation. He worked for the SDF in London and lectured on socialism across the country and helped organise in Burnley. He next appeared in West Ham in 1895 and was part of the first Socialist/ Labour group to control a local

---

32 *Liverpool Echo*, 11 December 1915.

council (West Ham, 1898 – 1900). His early antics are well summarised by the *Daily Gazette for Middlesborough*:

> 'Mr Terrett is a meat trader in Smithfield Market ... He began to interest himself as a Socialist in public affairs at the age of 17 and he has been at it ever since. In 1892 he was elected to the Newington Vestry, London, and soon was talked about as a stormy petrel. Putting up a fight for the entry of the public to the meetings he was threatened with expulsion and the police were called in. He challenged the right of the police to act, and they withdrew, leaving the young vestryman master of the field. West Ham made him a town councillor in 1898. As the public were refused admittance, he brought a crowbar, forced open the Town Hall door, and let them in.'[33]

He moved in illustrious Socialist circles. In 1908, it was Terrett who wrote a letter of introduction seeking a Reader's ticket at the British Library for Lenin.[34] The war saw him continuing his socialist activism, but on the extreme patriotic wing of the movement. In April 1915, when Victor Fisher established the Socialist National Defence Committee, he stated its objective was 'to counteract the peace at any price policy of the anti-national elements in the Socialist and Labour movements in the country.'[35] Terrett was one of the founding supporters from the British Socialist Party. The SNDC had, of course, supported Stanton, another founder member, in the Merthyr Tydfil by-election (see chapter 2).

Another quick-fire campaign

Nominations for West Newington were set for Friday, 7 January with polling day on Monday, 10 January leaving less than two weeks for a campaign. Terrett started immediately, announcing his candidature on 3 January. He put up posters from the Protest Committee stating: 'Smash the Control Board

---

33 *Daily Gazette for Middlesborough*, 4 December 1915.
34 http://blogs.bl.uk/european/2015/10/i-beg-to-apply-for-a-ticket-lenin-at-the-british-library.html#
35 R. Douglas, The National Democratic Party and the British Workers' League (The Historical Journal, XV, 3, 1972), cited in M J Crick, 'To make twelve o'clock at eleven: The history of the Social Democratic Federation (University of Huddersfield PhD Thesis, 1988).

– No more Government by secretly appointed non-representative bodies, who tyrannize worse than any House of Lords'.

On 6 January, he issued his election address.[36] Its headlines were: 'No Prussianism at home or abroad' and 'No government by bureaucracy' and it described him as the 'Independent Trade Unionist Candidate'. On the front of the address, he commented: 'Owing to the manner in which the Government has hurried and rushed this contest a proper canvas is impossible.'

Although it was a detailed address, he did not go into the terms of the control orders he was opposing. Instead, his focus was on the undemocratic nature of the procedures adopted which he painted as part of a wider assault on British freedoms. He conceded: 'If this were a question of beer only, few of us would be concerned.' Instead, he claimed: 'It is more – it is one of a great conspiracy to subvert the rights and liberties of the British people and behind the plea of war necessity to effect the destruction of Parliamentary government.' He particularly attacked Lloyd George, saying: 'It is by this stateman's malevolent activity that England has been transformed from freedom to slavery. In ten short months Parliament is reduced to a cypher and our real administration transferred to nominated boards.'

Terrett also expounded his views on the war and conscription. He cited his membership of the National Socialist Defence Committee and said:

'I stand for the most complete and thorough prosecution to a successful finish. Only by the total and overwhelming defeat of Germany and Austria can militarism be abolished in Europe – not otherwise, and those Socialists who indulge in foolish peace talk, knowingly or unknowingly, defeat their own objects.'

On conscription, he declaimed:

'I have publicly stated at large meetings at West Ham that when Lord Kitchener declared Conscription necessary for the successful prosecution of the war, I would give him my whole-hearted support. That moment has arrived, and, though great opposition has developed in Labour circles – I would sooner lose

---

36 Copy available at the University of Bristol Library, Special Collections

> this and every other election than purchase one single vote by what in my conscience I believe would be a cowardly betrayal of my countrymen.'

He stressed his history as a fighter – 'Sixteen times I have stood in the dock in defence of public rights' – and called on all 'lovers of liberty' to back him:

> 'The battle which we fight is no brewers' struggle against reasonable restrictions, but once again we raise the old flag of Pym and Hampden and the champions of freedom – against the most coldly calculated and insidious attempt to destroy the liberties of the people which has arisen in our history for over a century.'

By contrast, Gilbert's election address[37] was highly conventional. He described himself as 'the official candidate of the Coalition Government' and stated: 'Owing to the truce existing between all political parties it is not my intention to refer to party questions.' He went on: 'The only question before the country at the present time is the winning of the war' and said he would give his support to the present Coalition government to enable them 'to bring the war to a triumphant conclusion and to make it impossible for such world-wide war to ever happen again at the dictation of military tyrants.' The only other content was a quick summary of his political record; he had represented the area for the past 17 years on the London County Council and been an LCC appointee on the Thames Conservancy and the Port of London Authority as well as being a long-standing magistrate.

Although the campaign was brief, Gilbert obtained an extension of polling hours to 7am to 9pm to secure the largest possible turnout. The earlier opening encouraged a higher turnout among the numerous electors who were employed in local markets. The major live political topic was conscription; however, the press noted: 'The question which is supposed to be tearing the nation asunder was barely referred to, as both candidates were in favour of the Compulsion Bill and equally keen on the more vigorous prosecution of the war.'[38]

---

37 Copy available at the University of Bristol Library, Special Collections
38 *Cheltenham Looker-On*, 15 January 1916.

Four nomination papers were presented for Gilbert, including one signed by Warwick Brookes and nine other Unionists, compared with one for Terrett. The latter's paper was signed by trades unionists, described as follows: 'The prominent trade unionists (by whom it was signed) prove in six cases out of ten to be interested in the licensed trade. Five are licensed victuallers and one is the son of a licensed victualler.'[39]

Limited campaigning was undertaken for Gilbert, his supporters considering it unnecessary. However, he held two meetings on the Friday evening where he acknowledged the full co-operation of the Conservative Party and pledged to support any measure the government thought necessary to win the war. The backing of two unions was announced, the Licensed Vehicle Workers Union and the Operative Plasterers. He then held a final, major meeting on the Saturday night at Newington Public Hall where the Lord Advocate, Robert Munro, also spoke.

Terrett's campaigning was more feisty. He arranged a parade of costermongers' barrows, adorned with his posters. He held open-air meetings on the Saturday and a final rally at Newington Public Hall on the Sunday. He drew attention to the recent suppression, under the Defence of the Realm Act, of the Glasgow radical journal, *Forward*, for publishing an unauthorised account of a meeting on Christmas Day 2015 at which Clydeside shop stewards had barracked Lloyd George, by now the Minister of Munitions. At the behest of Lloyd George himself, the authorities closed down the journal and sought to seize all copies of the issue concerned. The editor of *Forward* later wrote that Lloyd George 'had lost his head' over the issue and adopted extreme measures, even sending in the police to seize copies from the homes of known subscribers. Terrett's election address said:

> **'Tuesday's angry scene in the Commons over the suppression of the Glasgow 'Forward' is a sign that Parliament and the public are at last realising that that which Tudor Kings and Stuart princes failed to achieve Lloyd George has essayed to attempt – the subversion of British freedom and the destruction of the liberties won by the blood and struggles of our ancestors.'**

---

39 *Birmingham Daily Gazette*, 8 January 1916.

Terrett read extracts from the banned paper, stating that he might end up in the dock as a result but would be happy to pay that price to defend press freedom. He declaimed:

> *'It would be the proudest day of his life if he had to go into the dock to defend that journal. He did not care a brass farthing if he lost the election... If the Crown and all the forces of the Crown dared not arrest him, it would mean that he had vindicated the freedom of the Press.'*[40]

On polling day, The Times commented on a subdued campaign:

> *'A walk through the constituency on Saturday revealed curiously few of the usual outward signs of a contested election. Now and then one came across two bills posted side by side on the walls – 'Vote for Terrett, the Independent Trade Unionist '- in red and 'Vote for Gilbert, support the government and see the war through' in black. That was all. But one very unusual sight was the public-houses with window blinds drawn and doors closed during the early dinner-hour of the people; and in that spectacle one discovered the object of the contest'.*[41]

A short campaign put organisation at a premium. Terrett was unable to trace 'removals', an onerous task given the ageing nature of the register which contained only electors who had been in residence in the constituency in 1913. By contrast, Gilbert, backed by the two main party organisations, used fifteen motorcars to bring in voters who had relocated to other areas. Terrett also asserted that nearly all the 1,100 electors who were away with the forces would have supported him while Gilbert benefitted from the Conservative Chairman, Arthur Steel-Maitland, calling on all his party's supporters to vote for the Coalition candidate.

The expected victory

As was expected by all sides, Gilbert achieved a clear victory although nearly a quarter of the votes were cast for the protest candidate.

---

40 *The Scotsman*, 10 January 1916.
41 *The Times*, 10 January 1916.

Dec. 1910			
Norton	Liberal	4,038	54%
Brookes	Conservative	3,498	46%
Majority		540	
Electorate & Turnout		9,637	78%

10 Dec. 1916			
Gilbert	Coalition (Liberal)	2,646	77%
Terrett	Indep. Labour	787	23%
Majority		1,859	
Electorate & Turnout		9,809	35%

Terrett tried to claim a 'moral victory' saying: 'He did not expect to win. He estimated that 3,600 electors would vote, and that of these he would get 600. He considered that, in what was practically a one-day contest, the result from his point of view was satisfactory.'[42] He had, as promised, 'defied the ginger-beer crowd that rules Britain today.' The national press described the scene after the poll announcement: 'Mr Gilbert, who had a mixed reception, said that the result of the election was a vote for the government. Mr. Terrett, who was loudly cheered, said "We have done jolly well in the most hurried, scurried, and cowardly election that has ever been fought. We are now going to fight Mile End."[43] In the event, neither Terrett nor any other campaigner on the drink restrictions stood in Mile End (see chapter 4).

Gilbert went on to hold his, renamed, seat at the next three general elections before losing to Labour in 1924. He additionally sat on the London County Council until 1928. His brother was also an LCC Councillor, but a Conservative, and it was said that the two of them never spoke to each

---

42 *Aberdeen Press*, 11 January 1916.
43 *Daily Mirror*, 11 January 1916.

other. Terrett reappeared as a campaigner in later wartime by-elections; he supported the National Federation of Discharged Soldiers' and Sailors' candidate in Abercromby (see chapter 9) and patriotic labour stalwart, Ben Tillett in North Salford (see chapter 11). In the 1918 general election he stood in Rochdale as a National Democratic and Labour Party candidate, finishing fourth. He then tried again in the 1920 by-election in Stockport, this time finishing sixth (in a two-member election) standing as a Horatio Bottomley Anti-Waste Independent. Two years later, he was in disgrace. He was found guilty of fraudulently obtaining £671 from an ex-Servicemen's Fund and was sentenced to eighteen months in prison. The victim of this fraud was somewhat ironic, given Terrett's earlier support for the NFDSS.

4.
THE AIRMAN COMETH

Mile End, 25 January 1916

January 1916 saw the arrival on the election scene of the Daily Mail, which began backing independents who aimed to 'ginger up' the government. It also saw the debut of the most exotic of all the wartime candidates: Noel Pemberton-Billing (often known as PB or Billing). An early pioneer of aviation, he had served in the Royal Naval Volunteer Reserve and the Royal Naval Air Service[1] before resigning his commission in frustration at inadequate prosecution of the air war. His biographer's summary certainly does not exaggerate his story:

> 'During his 67 turbulent years he was a prolific inventor, an aircraft designer, a pioneer aviator and motorist, yacht-broker, gunrunner, spy, soldier, sailor, author, playwright, newspaper proprietor – and much more besides. His appearance was as striking as his lifestyle for he was well over six foot tall, wore a monocle and clothes of his own design ... It was once said that his main fascinations in life were 'fast aircraft, fast boats, fast cars and fast women'.[2]

---

1 Until 1918, Britain's air forces were divided between the Royal Flying Corps and the Royal Naval Air Service. These were amalgamated in 1918 to form the Royal Air Force.
2 Barbara Stoney, *Twentieth-century maverick* (2004)

This chapter reprises his action-packed life prior to 1916 and the events and outcome of his participation in the Mile End by-election of late January 1916. It explores the issues raised by Zeppelin and aircraft attacks up to that time and the reaction to those by the public and politicians. The 'blitz' may be indelibly linked to the Second World War but the realisation that Britain, in military terms, was vulnerable from the air and no longer an island was born in the First World War.

PB's early life – a remarkable story

So dramatic are the events of PB's early life that any self-respecting fiction author would shy away from them. He was sent to school in France aged eight but ran away three times, on the final occasion managing to cross the Channel to freedom. At 13, he again absconded. Now, even a large ocean proved no barrier as he joined a ship to Mozambique as a deckhand (having lied about his age). Once in Africa, he reached Durban and there followed a bewildering series of occupations. He initially became a self-taught carpenter and then bricklayer. His next jobs were as a tram conductor, followed by locomotive cleaner (then shunter, then stoker). At the age of 17, he joined the Natal Mounted Police with whom he became a useful boxer, a consequence of which was an injury that meant he wore a distinctive eyeglass/monocle for the rest of his life. In 1899, the outbreak of the Boer War saw PB involved in active service, including as a bodyguard and later a 'galloper' for General Redvers Buller. Having become ill with dysentery, he returned to England, working his passage as a crew member on a hospital ship.

In 1903, he married Lilian Schweitzer; his persistence having overcome her original refusal. He proposed by sending a telegram: 'Will you marry me? Wire reply Adelphi'. This elicited the prompt response 'No' but he eventually persuaded her otherwise. Lilian (Dot)'s parentage was to feature as an issue in Billing's later career; she was to claim during the war that her father was originally Swiss but many (rightly) believed that he was actually German. By 1905, PB became obsessed with flight and his personal involvement started with an (unsuccessful) attempt to design a glider. When Wilbur and Orville Wright came to Europe in 1908, Billing formed the view that England could potentially be threatened from the air, nullifying its naval strength. A year later, his practical involvement in the embryonic aircraft industry began. He tried to develop an 'aerodrome' in Essex and founded a monthly magazine, Aerocraft. These initial forays, which also included attempts to design and build aircraft, all failed.

Forced to find new sources of income, Pemberton-Billing decided he should become a barrister. As he did not have a degree, it was necessary for him first to pass the Bar Preliminary Examination. However, this route into the profession was being closed and so PB's only opportunity to use it meant taking an exam very quickly. Unhelpfully, one of the papers was Latin, of which he was wholly ignorant. Undaunted, he hired two tutors each of whom taught him for six hours a day while he worked on his own for four more. He also gambled on which set text (of two) would come up and then, realising he could not cover it all, decided to learn only the odd-numbered sections. Remarkably, this strategy worked, and, of sixty candidates, he was one of fourteen who gained entry as a student to the Middle Temple.

But the law was not to detain him for long and his next 'career' move (and one of his most successful) was the world of yacht-dealing or 'ship-running' as he called it. A friend was to refer to this as 'the time PB bought luxury yachts with money he hadn't got, in order to sell them for cash to people who didn't really want them'.[3] Three years of buying and selling yachts were to generate many incidents and scrapes but also a lot of money. With his finances now in a good state, in 1913 he turned his attention once more to aviation. With typical impetuosity, he challenged Frederick Handley Page, an industrialist and aviation pioneer, to a £500 wager (broadly the equivalent of £47,000 today) that he could learn to fly within 24 hours and would do so before Handley Page. At the time, pilots typically took weeks to qualify for their Royal Aero Club certificate. On the day set for the wager, PB began his instruction in a two-seater plane at 5.45am; three and a half hours later, the Royal Aero Club's observer concluded that Billing's then solo performance in the air was sufficiently competent that he had earned RAeC certificate No.632. He had not only achieved his aim within 24 hours, but he had done so before a leisurely breakfast. At this point, Handley-Page had not yet taken off.

Inspired by his reintroduction to aeroplanes, Billing decided his next initiative would be to design and build *supermarine* aircraft – 'boats that

---

3 Quoted in Barbara Stoney, *Twentieth-century maverick* (2004)

would fly, rather than aeroplanes that would float'.[4] This enterprise was founded in Southampton and, within weeks, the first design (the PB.1) was on display in London at an exhibition (March 1914) where it was viewed by both Churchill and George V. It never flew successfully.

PB and active service

The start of the war found PB still designing prototype aircraft and trying to win orders from government for them, achieving only limited success. However, in October 1914, he was recruited by the Royal Naval Volunteer Reserve (RNVR) to organise an attack on the Zeppelin factory at Freidrichshafen on Lake Constance, within flying distance of a French airfield at Belfort. Leading an initial reconnaissance in mid-October 1914, he and a colleague crossed the Swiss border from France in the guise of commercial travellers. They then persuaded local fishermen to take them across the lake at night and leave them on the German side, close to the factory, and to collect them 24 hours later. The reconnaissance was successful, but it ended in drama with PB being shot at by German officers as he drove away in their motorcar (he had knocked out the driver using an ornamental lion he had taken from a house in which he had been hiding). In mid-November, a group of five pilots and eleven mechanics were transported from Southampton dock in a cargo boat that also carried their biplanes packed in wooden crates. After arrival in Le Havre, the men and aircraft were loaded onto a special train that PB had negotiated with the French authorities. Billing briefed the pilots with the information gleaned from his reconnaissance but did not, himself, take part in the attack. The raid was reported to be highly successful and was later described by Churchill as 'a remarkable feat of aerial initiative'. German records show that while no Zeppelins were destroyed a complete hydrogen-producing plant was demolished and one Zeppelin was damaged.

After this excitement, in January 1915 Pemberton-Billing transferred from the RNVR to the Royal Naval Air Service as an acting flight lieutenant. He was attached to the Air Department of the Admiralty.

---

4 Ibid.

The road to Mile End

Billing's work at the Admiralty lasted less than a year. He continued his involvement with aircraft design and manufacture, culminating with being granted indefinite leave of absence to work on an aircraft which he believed could be an effective counter to the Zeppelins. The first German airship attack on Britain had been on 20 January 1915, when Great Yarmouth and King's Lynn had been bombed while the first hit on London was 31 May 1915, an attack in which children had been killed. Billing's offering to the Admiralty was the PB.29E which he was designing as an airship-interceptor at his own expense. It was a twin-engined, quadruplane destined to fail early in its winter 1915-16 testing. According to Billing, his experience of working with government on this project directly led to his decision to leave the Admiralty and try to enter parliament. On Christmas Eve 1915, after multiple telephone calls, he had been promised that a vital instrument, needed to finish his prototype, would be despatched to him that evening. It never arrived, despite his having kept the factory open and staff on site. When he called again to complain he was told to wait until after the Christmas holiday. That was too much for this man of action and, on 28 December, he applied to resign. This was accepted but, at the same time, he was informed that: 'Mr Churchill and Lord Fisher were very pleased with the way you organised the Lake Constance raid'.[5]

Trying to be elected was not a spur-of-the-moment thought. He had previously shown an interest in public policy and was confident he would make an admirable MP. As early as 1904-5, he had been thinking about a public insurance scheme, similar to the one later adopted by Lloyd George at the 1909 'People's Budget', which began a putative welfare state. PB was also, already, concerned about the potential risks to the country's defence from air attack and felt that parliament needed someone who was an aviation expert.

He reported that he had a meeting with the Conservative Whip, Lord Edmund Talbot, to argue for a more effective and coherent air policy, with the Leader of the Conservative Party (and currently Secretary of State for the Colonies in the Coalition government) Andrew Bonar Law in attendance, but that it had no effect. So PB resigned without a clear route in place to find his way into parliament. Nevertheless, he started planning immediately and

---

5 Barbara Stoney, *Twentieth-century maverick* (2004)

quickly moved into larger accommodation and employed a secretary and a typist in preparation for a suitable by-election. On 9 January 1916, he was notified of a vacancy at Mile End in east London. The seat was held by the Unionist MP, Harry Levy-Lawson, who was elevated to the peerage on the death of his father, Baron Burnham, owner of the *Daily Telegraph*. Quickly, Billing appointed as his agent someone 'who had the reputation of being an expert in political affairs'. This may have been Bottomley's aide, Houston, who certainly acted as PB's agent once the by-election was underway. However, before the by-election commenced this 'agent', according to PB, introduced him to a 'very well-known and experienced' politician who promised to get him into the Commons within the month in return for £3,000.[6] Billing turned down the proposition and next, against the advice of the agent, went directly to Conservative Central Office to make his case to be selected so he could enter parliament as an expert on the air war. He held discussions with the Conservative Chairman, Arthur Steel-Maitland, and claimed he was told the Party would accept him as an official candidate but only if he gave 'certain undertakings' should he be elected. He declined the offer.

Nevertheless, PB still wanted to win the Conservative nomination and so participated in the constituency selection process. At this, he argued that he wished to enter parliament solely to address Air Policy and that, since Conservatives and Liberals were now working together in Coalition, they should be prepared to choose him as an Independent. He also said that he had wished to 'avoid undesirable publicity to our aerial unreadiness.'[7] In a hyper-marginal seat (the majority over the Liberals had only been six votes in the December 1910 election) local Conservatives rejected him. In his autobiography, PB expressed shock at what this process taught him about party politics. He wrote:

> *'Thereupon began my education in "Party" methods .... I had long considered the Party system rotten, but hitherto had no idea of its inner workings and, as*

---

6 There is no evidence, but this may have been Bottomley. The sum is equivalent to more than £200,000 today.
7 *Daily Mail*, 13 January 1916.

a hereditary trait, I suppose, I had cherished an almost pathetic belief that the Conservative Party was more straightforward.'[8]

He stated that he had discovered that the nomination of candidates is 'wangled' between HQ and the Local Committee, so that HQ gets its way. Billing had told the local committee that, if they did not select him, he would stand anyway, which he proceeded to do.[9]

The Air Policy issue

By January 1916, the war in the air was causing concern, especially the threat it posed to civilians. A nation that expected to be protected by the overwhelming strength of its navy had been shocked enough by German cruisers bombarding Hartlepool, Whitby and Scarborough[10] but potential attack from the air was even more frightening. PB had voiced concern about air attack, specifically from Germany, prior to the outbreak of war. In 1908, when commenting about the Wright brothers, he said he 'feared this achievement would make the country no longer an island, protected by its seas, and that its security in the future might well depend on its supremacy in the air'. Popular fiction posed the scenario of hostilities by Germany, sometimes including air attack. Particularly influential was H G Wells: The War in the Air (1909). This commenced with a German airship attack on New York, but Britain was brought into the scenario later when Wells envisioned that 'the little island in the silver seas was at the end of its immunity'. In response, a 'wave of Zeppelin mania' swept through the country in the winter of 1913-14.[11]

In the immediate run-up to war, there was official consideration of the aerial threat. However, sizeable complacency or lethargy was reflected in Churchill's hostage to fortune when he told the Commons in March 1914: 'Any hostile aircraft, airships or aeroplanes which reached our coast during the coming year would be promptly attacked in superior force by a swarm of formidable hornets.' He made these public comments despite raising concerns in private about the lack of coordination for home air defence between army

---

8 N Pemberton Billing, *The story of his life* (1917).
9 Ibid.
10 The attack took place on 16 December 1914 and resulted in 137 deaths.
11 C. Cole, *Air Defence of Britain 1914- 18* (1984).

and navy and regarding what he saw as an urgent need for the development of a specific home-service fighter aeroplane, believing (rightly, as it transpired) that searchlights and guns alone would be ineffective.

Early on, the reality was that the Zeppelins faced no effective opposition. At the start of the war, London's defences comprised one, unarmed, aircraft and three anti-aircraft guns. It was soon agreed (September 1914) that home defence would be the responsibility of the Admiralty (and the two months' old Royal Naval Air Service) rather than the War Office and the Royal Flying Corps. Also, in early October somewhat half-hearted regulations came in to reduce lighting at night – 'no more than a dim out'. The consequence was an increase in deaths from road accidents. By the start of 1915, around 40 RNAS aircraft, located on the coast and inland, were available supposedly to intercept hostile aircraft and airships and London's number of anti-aircraft guns had increased marginally. But when the attacks began it was quickly apparent that neither the aircraft nor the guns were a threat to the Zeppelins. The aircraft could not climb rapidly enough to engage the airships while nearly all the guns lacked the range to hit them.

Despite these weaknesses, the impact of Zeppelin attacks was restricted by their limited numbers (at the start of the conflict, Germany could muster just 11 airships and added to that net total only slowly) and their vulnerability to adverse weather; several intended attacks ended up hitting other areas than their target or being aborted as the airships were forced off course or became lost. Another restriction was the Kaiser's initial refusal to accede to his military's requests to bomb London. Partially, his ambivalence was claimed to be due to a wish to avoid harming his relations in the British Royal family but, gradually, this self-imposed restriction was removed. In January 1915, he gave permission for bombing (but not in London). In February, he authorised the London docks as a legitimate target, and this was extended in May to London east of the Tower and finally, in June 1915, to all of London.

By the start of the Mile End by-election campaign in January 1916, across the country there had been 19 raids by Zeppelins and six by aircraft, resulting in 207 civilian fatalities. The population at large was unaware of the limitations of the Zeppelins and concern was widespread. The first London raid on 31 May 1915 had produced limited public unease, but complaints grew after attacks were conducted on consecutive nights in September. An early historical review noted: 'The fact that Germans came back the next night showed they had no fear of challenge... The next day, therefore, citizens of all classes, from the Lord Mayor downwards, took steps to ensure their participation in the general demonstration of dissatisfaction.'[12] A more recent commentator recorded that: 'Thousands observed [the Zeppelin] sailing relatively unmolested over the heart of London. No aeroplanes appeared in opposition.'[13]

In fact, the September raids did prompt action. Lord Kitchener, the War Secretary, now instructed the Royal Flying Corp to join in defending London, even though it was not their responsibility. The Admiralty appointed the country's foremost naval gunnery expert, Admiral Sir Percy Scott, to organise the artillery defence. He quickly improved the situation, not least by importing a far superior French gun (a 75mm auto-cannon) which had the range to reach the Zeppelins. As of mid-September, London was defended by 12 guns but by mid-November, this had increased to 24, nine of which were mobile. All had searchlight units attached to them. The beginning of October also saw the introduction of more comprehensive lighting restrictions. The German crews noticed that the defences over London were strengthening.

However, the public and political unrest which surfaced after the September raids was reinforced by a Zeppelin raid in October 1915 over East Anglia, Hertford and London, resulting in 71 deaths, the greatest loss of life to date from a single raid. Several issues emerged. A contentious debate began as to whether the 'German murders by Zeppelin' should be opposed via reprisal raids, of which Arthur Conan-Doyle, writer of the Sherlock Holmes mysteries, was one of the highest-profile advocates. There was also concern about the fragmentation of responsibility for the air defence of London. Both issues were raised at a public protest meeting organised by *The Globe* newspaper immediately after the raid. That meeting, reportedly comprised of mainly businessmen who were hostile to the government, called for reprisals, the speedy formation of a Ministry of the Air and a unified command for air raids covering aeroplanes and guns.[14]

Members of Parliament were disturbed that only three defending aircraft had been airborne over London to counter the deadliest raid in October. There

---

12 A Rawlinson, *The defence of London 1915-18* (1924).
13 Ian Castle, *The first blitz* (2015).
14 *The Times*, 15 October 1915.

were discussions about whether the public should be given advance warning of attacks, although the government's firm view was that to do so would increase the risk of civilian casualties since nothing would stop Londoners rushing out to watch 'the entertainment' rather than head for cover. Doubt was also expressed as to whether the harsher lighting restrictions were of any benefit. Finally, adverse comparisons were drawn between London and Paris where the French authorities seemed to have had more success in preventing attacks.

Undoubtedly, the government was struggling with the Zeppelins. Much publicity was given to the appointment of Sir Percy Scott and to the increase in the number of guns available. Additionally, it was revealed that the gunnery teams were undergoing additional training, a roundabout acknowledgement that performance had been poor. In late October, Arthur Balfour, the former Conservative leader and now First Lord of the Admiralty, admitted to the House: 'it was still a matter of anxious study whether the defence of London could be secured best by guns or aeroplanes and he hoped that the defence was undergoing constant improvement' while worries about co-ordination issues were probably not allayed by his answer that: 'The military are responsible for sending up military aeroplanes and the navy are responsible for sending up naval aeroplanes'.[15] Without doubt, the stage was set for Pemberton-Billing to launch his political career.

A Mile End contest

As the Mile End seat in East London was held by the Tories, they nominated the 'Coalition' candidate, selecting Warwick Brookes, who had very recently stood down in favour of the Liberals in West Newington (see chapter 3). Initially, there was talk of a leading local figure, Frederick Charrington (who had been turned down by the Tories), standing as an Independent Patriotic candidate. He was the founder and superintendent of the Tower Hamlets Mission, an anti-poverty charity. According to the *Western Mail*: 'he will be recognised as a member of the well-known family of London brewers and, according to popular belief, has renounced all participation in the family fortunes owing

---

15 *The Times*, 29 October 1915.

to his pronounced teetotal opinions'.[16] The issues exercising Charrington, on which he said he would stand, were conscription and the post-war treatment of Germany. He was a strong supporter of the Military Service Bill which had just been introduced in Parliament and wanted the highest possible tariffs imposed on German goods after the war. Episodes from his life suggest that he would have made a colourful adversary for Brookes. When war broke out, he embarked on a personal crusade against the playing of professional football and attempted to visit the bar of the House of Commons to protest about alcohol being provided for members. In the event, Charrington's 'campaign' was short-lived, and it was reported on 13 January that he had decided to retire 'from patriotic motives and in order not to clash with the political truce'. Another potential 'one issue' candidate, Harry Biner, who opposed the drink restrictions, had also sought the Conservative nomination but now claimed he would stand on a platform of 'Lloyd George or Liberty'. In the event, he too did not go forward as a candidate.[17] So, it was anticipated that Brookes would be elected unopposed as the Mile End Liberals made clear they would support him.[18] However, Billing now confirmed he would stand, solely on the issue of Air policy, warning that far greater air raids were coming and that bomber aircraft would be much more of a threat than Zeppelins; so much so, he said they would make the Zeppelins look like a 'Christmas toy'. The Northcliffe-owned *Daily Mail* immediately swung into action on his behalf. On 12 January, it gave him space to outline his fears about the air war and, the following day, approvingly reported his candidacy. On 14 January, the *Daily Mirror* (now owned by Northcliffe's brother, Lord Rothermere) joined in, starting with an eye-catching photograph of Billing flying.

Ranged against Billing in Warwick Brookes was an old childhood friend of his who today might be characterised as an 'identikit establishment candidate'. Brookes was a successful businessman with considerable political experience. He had already twice fought West Newington, reducing the Liberal majority

---

16 *Western Mail*, 10 January 1916.
17 Biner was later to appear as a member of the Union of Attested Married Men and the founder of the People's Fairplay League which complained about poor air defences, soft treatment of aliens and food profiteering.
18 One other potential candidate was mentioned, a local licenced victualler, George Lardner, intending to continue the fight against the drink restrictions, but this came to nothing. Indeed, he ended up signing one of Billing's nomination papers.

significantly through innovative campaigning methods; one was to record the occupation of everyone he canvassed and then write to them whenever something impacting their profession was discussed in Parliament. His business activities were diverse. He owned an iron foundry in Essex which he expanded to manufacture military requirements. Immediately after the start of the war, he became Managing Director of the Junior Army and Navy Stores and was also Director of the Civil Service Co-operative Society. In his spare time, he was a keen yachtsman. Somewhat outside the typical establishment mould, Brookes had been involved as co-respondent in a divorce due to his adultery with Beatrice de Minciaky; he had fathered a child with her and, following the divorce, they lived together and married. The question to be settled was how well could the newcomer Pemberton-Billing campaign and how would the establishment cope with him?

A high-octane election

Somewhat bizarrely, the two candidates, Brookes and Billing, met regularly to compare notes on the campaign; they 'used to lunch together daily at the Savoy Hotel in the sincerest good fellowship, returning afterwards to the division to fight each other to the last ounce of energy.'[19] And there was no stinting in energy by either side.

Amateur or not, from the very beginning PB launched an effective campaign. He was significantly assisted by Horatio Bottomley and his organiser, Henry Houston, who described it as 'A real 'stunt' election from beginning to end.'[20]

No doubt benefitting from Houston's PR skills, Billing managed to set the terms of the campaign immediately it commenced, the day after Baron Burnham's funeral, before which he had been advised no electioneering should take place. Examples of initial press coverage summarise his campaign. Firstly, in the *Portsmouth Evening News*: 'He has resigned his commission in order to bring before the public his opinion that stronger measures should be taken to protect London from a great air raid which he expects the enemy to

---

19 H J Houston, *The Real Horatio Bottomley* (1923).
20 Ibid.

attempt. He also stands for organised air attacks on Germany as a regular part of our war policy.'[21]

Secondly, on the same day from the *Manchester Courier*: 'Pemberton-Billing believes he will be greater use to the service which he has at heart when he is no longer subject to its regulations and discipline and his object in entering parliament is to ensure for the country the same supremacy in the air that she now holds on the sea.' The same paper also added that PB's programme was: 'Up with the lights of London. Don't hide but send up our own airmen to fight' in reference to growing frustration at the negative side-effects of the blackout regulations.

Billing's campaign had an unfortunate start. The plan was for a cavalcade of motorcars, mainly Rolls-Royces, to travel to the constituency in advance of an open-air meeting. As well as Billing, Houston and others associated with Bottomley and his John Bull magazine, the cars also contained several officers from the Royal Naval Volunteer Reserve. Each vehicle was decorated with posters calling on people to 'Vote for Billing'. PB's own car had on its bonnet a bronze model of a lion swallowing a Zeppelin, a reference to his Friedrichshafen reconnaissance. However, the problems with this effort were, firstly, that the destination (for the speeches) was outside the constituency and, secondly, as it was a Saturday, it was the Jewish Sabbath. As Houston recollected, 'although the Mile End Road was thronged with Jews in top hats and Jewesses in elegant short frocks and fancy hose, they had very little interest in politics on that day'. As a result, he described their entire initial audience as comprising 'two small boys ... who stood sucking oranges and gaping at cars'.[22]

Houston conceded it was a farcical opening but there were plenty of thrills to come. In his recollections, he was very positive about Billing: 'PB, a fine fellow of over six feet, young, fresh and alert, was one of the most attractive candidates it has ever been my lot to handle as agent. He could never be given enough to do. He wanted to speak all day and all night, although he had never before spoken in public.'[23] Billing stressed that he intended to enter Parliament as a true independent, concerned only with air policy and argued that while

---

21 *Portsmouth Evening News*, 13 January 1916.
22 H J Houston, *The Real Horatio Bottomley* (1923).
23 Ibid.

the Commons contained many members with army or navy experience, there was no-one who was an air expert. In terms of practical policy, he predicted that once the Germans 'know we have an aeroplane capable of going up at night and dealing with raiders, they will treat London with the same respect as Paris. And it is possible to produce such an aeroplane in a few weeks.' He further maintained that the 'darkening' of London was ineffective as German pilots could still see the streets silhouetted as if on a map.

Brookes hit back immediately. He sought to establish support for the strongest possible blockade of Germany, using the fleet, and also to take up PB's ideas. The *Chelmsford Chronicle* laid out his riposte. It claimed that Brookes was 'interested in flying from the start and was one of the first aerial passengers'.[24] It also reported 'Mr Brookes said: I make this offer to Mr Pemberton-Billing: I am as strong on the air defence of London as he is; I will adopt the whole of his programme to avoid a contest. I will ask his questions in the House'.

PB was never going to stand down, especially as Bottomley and Houston were so heavily invested in his 'jape'. So, it is unsurprising that the *Daily Mirror* reported him saying: 'I will fight this election to a finish. If I do not win, I will fight every vacant seat independently on a war ticket until I get in to the House of Commons.'[25] In his autobiography, PB explained that when he left the services he had £5,000 (equivalent today to £350,000) ready to support his planned entry into politics:

> *'I knew that after 17 months of bloody war, we had no definite Air Policy, I knew the hideous danger in which we stood on that account, and I knew, moreover, that the one thing that stood between the Air Service and efficiency was the absolute apathy of the Political Heads; that the one way to force the Government to abandon that apathy was by rousing the Public; and the one way to get the Public to rouse and act was to enlighten it. I decided that the speediest and most effective way to rouse Public opinion would be to fight one election after another, even if I didn't have the ghost of a chance of winning anyone of them. With my £5,000 I could fight ten elections in sequence, if necessary. Mile End should be the first!'*[26]

---

24 *Chelmsford Chronicle*, 14 January 1916.
25 *Daily Mirror*, 14 January 1916.
26 N Pemberton-*Billing The story of his life* (1917).

Initial assessments were that Billing would struggle. The *Western Daily Press* argued that he was 'being 'boomed' by that section of the London press which is always 'booming' somebody or something.'[27] More importantly, it was expected that an independent would stand little chance against an 'official' campaign drawing on the combined resources of two (Unionist and Liberal) strong, local political organisations that had grown up fighting in a highly marginal seat. As early as 14 January, the *Daily Mirror* reported that Brookes' campaign had opened its central committee room the day before and would have four further committee rooms within a few days.

An early argument used against PB was of aiding the enemy. It was said that much care had been taken, largely through self-censorship, not to discuss information which might help inform the Germans about the nature and state of British military arrangements. The *Westminster Gazette* commented: 'The question does suggest itself to us whether a man who has just resigned from one of the defensive forces of London should be allowed to discuss on the platform what he calls 'the present inadequate use of the men and material already at the disposal of the Government for the defence of London''.[28]

The rival campaigns used different tactics to argue for almost identical policies. PB, who lacked on-the-ground resources, relied on eye-catching stunts while Brookes methodically mobilised his own more conventional organisational skills and the impressive Unionist and Liberal machines. Yet each candidate set about adopting, or echoing, the policies of the other. The *Daily Mirror*, backing PB, confirmed that his focus on defence against the Zeppelins had seized local imagination but acknowledged the Brookes campaign was also singing from the same song sheet. The anti-Billing, *East London Observer*, felt, at the beginning of the campaign, that PB stood 'no chance whatever'. It raised the very real question (again, later to be stressed by the Brookes campaign) of how PB thought he could influence air policy as a single, Independent MP and argued that Brookes was an equally firm advocate of strong air defence.[29]

The early days of electioneering highlighted the contrasting campaigns. Brookes felt unable to begin before official endorsement by the Unionist

---

27 *Western Daily Press*, 14 January 1916.
28 *Westminster Gazette*, 13 January 1916.
29 *East London Observer*, 15 January 1916.

organisation and so his first public meeting was not scheduled until Monday (17 January). However, in the background, he was busy setting up his campaign organisation and bringing in agents from neighbouring constituencies, with one, for example, dedicated exclusively to establishing and running a team to undertake the process of tracing an estimated 1,000 'removals'.

By contrast, Billing had only a single committee room but was highly active with much more visible work. Following on from the Saturday afternoon open-air speech, Billing held two meetings at the Mile End Palladium on the Sunday (16 January) accompanied by outside patriotic 'celebrities', Horatio Bottomley and leading trades unionist, Ben Tillett.[30] The supportive *Daily Mirror* first published photographs of his outdoor meeting and then, the next day, reported that the Palladium meetings were 'very enthusiastic and so crowded that people were standing at the back and in the gangways.'[31] In his speeches, Billing stressed:

> *'I know for a fact that the enemy are building thousands of aeroplanes with which to attack London; that the use of these machines is not dependent on the weather; and that unless we prepare by some definite fighting policy to meet the danger, half of London will be burnt down'.*

He also downplayed improvements made to date and claimed that he had better answers. He argued: 'The proper place to fight the raiders is in the air and if the men of the Air Service were given the chance to go up there would be no more raids on London'. He protested that a British airship which had flown over London a few days previously would be no use against a Zeppelin[32]; but that 'we had a machine – it had flown for the first time that morning – which carried an armament before which a Zeppelin would turn back and never come again'. Horatio Bottomley, who was chairing the meeting, claimed

---

30 Tillett was a hyper-patriot. He was to stand at the Salford North by-election in 1917 (see chapter 11).
31 *Daily Mirror*, 17 January 1916.
32 Unlike the Germans, the British generally had not been impressed by the potential of lighter-than-air airships and had invested very little in their development. It was also certainly true that an airship would offer little effective defence against another airship. In his speech at the Palladium, Billing said the British airship 'was as much good as a snowball in hell against Zeppelins'.

that 'Mr Billing was not only the inventor, but the builder of the machine in question, and the day he was returned to Parliament he would fly in it over Mile End and drop his vote of thanks to the electors from the skies'.[33]

Billing made other populist points. He would name the new aeroplane 'The Mile End Hawk'. He told the audience: 'I do not come here to talk to you boys about politics. To hell with politics – it's time we got on with the war'. When asked if he would take a salary as an MP, he claimed he only expected the war to last a further six months; that would be £200 in salary, and he would use that to buy one of the aircraft he had designed and would fly it himself. As well as arguing his policies would make people safer, he said adopting an approach of defence in the air would allow London to abandon the generally unpopular lighting restrictions. Given a plentiful supply of aeroplanes, the streets would not need to be darkened at night, 'with the consequent toll of mortality and all the discomforts the present conditions involve.'[34]

Newspapers opposed to Billing castigated him for being parochial, fastening on what, in objective terms, was a minor part of the war – the air attacks on London. They also reiterated that the official candidate had given similar commitments. The *Sheffield Daily Telegraph* observed: 'The Mile End election is developing into a contest, not on the conduct of the war, but on how far the lights of London need to be turned down.'[35] More aggressively, the *Newcastle Journal* declaimed:

> 'It seems almost incredible that, while the Empire is struggling with the supreme crisis of the greatest war mankind has ever known, an important constituency in the very heart of it, should be asked to regard such an issue as one of overwhelming importance. Pemberton-Billing's sole policy is that we should send out aeroplanes to fight Zeppelins, that we should turn up all the lights of London, and that the Londoner should go to bed o' nights and never worry about Zeppelinitis anymore'.

---

33 This aircraft was the PB.29E, which had been designed and built within seven weeks. It underwent further tests in February 1916 when it crashed and was wrecked. A variant, the PB.31E was designed but only one was ever flown and that was scrapped in July 1917.
34 *Derby Daily Telegraph*, 17 January 1916.
35 *Sheffield Daily Telegraph*, 17 January 1916.

In addition to his large-scale meetings with the draw of Horatio Bottomley as guest speaker, Billing also revitalised the old tradition of postering. In the period immediately before war an unspoken understanding between the main parties had resulted in a significant reduction in the use of posters; in particular, it was often agreed at a local level that full-sized posters would not be deployed to reduce election costs. However, from the beginning of the campaign, Billing made extensive use of them. Early on, *The Globe* reported that he had 'liberally covered the hoardings with large and effective posters.'[36] As the campaign continued, the poster battle became more prominent. An early Billing example, drawing considerable attention, was one representing a Zeppelin in flames from the effects of a bomb dropped by an aeroplane with the legend 'Send Up your own airman'. Others read 'Vote for Pemberton Billing and the defence of London', 'Vote for Pemberton Billing – The member for Air', 'Billing and Business versus Brookes and Bungling', 'Save your wives and children – vote for P.B.' and 'Pemberton Billing is the End-the-war candidate'. The *Daily Telegraph* commented that Billing's posters were 'as plentiful as blackberries in autumn'. Early in the campaign, Brookes had fewer but used one proclaiming: 'Poll for Warwick Brookes and Business – not Bunkum.'

The two candidates issued their election addresses before the writ for the election was issued on Monday 17 January 1916. Brookes' was the more professional. It emphasised that he was the unanimous choice of the Conservative Association to stand as the official candidate of the Coalition Government. Unsurprisingly, in so marginal a constituency, he stressed that 'owing to the crisis at the present time, the old party issues are dormant' and emphasised that he did not propose to enter into controversial party questions. The policy issues he chose to stress were:

- His long-term support for the 'two power' standard for the navy (whereby British policy was to be that its navy was more powerful than that of the next two largest navies combined).
- Fullest possible backing for the conscription bill introducing compulsion of single men which was making its way through the Commons during the by-election campaign.

---

36 *The Globe*, 17 January 1916.

- Seeking to steal Billing's thunder, he said he would support anything 'which has for its object the better organisation and further development of the air service (army and navy)' to place it 'in the same predominant position that our Navy occupies today', arguing 'in my opinion, no effort or expense should be spared to make London impregnable from Aircraft attack'.
- That Britain's supremacy at sea should urgently be used to implement a fully effective blockade of Germany.

Billing's 'address' was printed and published by Houston (The Houston Advertising Company) but was typed, rather than typeset, and single-sided and looked amateurish compared with Brookes' more traditional offering. Initially, Billing paid Bottomley £100 to draft it for him, money he borrowed from Hannen Swaffer, the editor of the Weekly Despatch. Swaffer and Billing visited Bottomley who dictated a version of the address to them. However, Swaffer was of the view that 'it was rubbish' and proposed 'let's go back and write it ourselves', which Swaffer and Billing did.[37] Inevitably, the main pitch was about air defence and Billing's personal expertise: 'I ask you to send me to the House of Commons to obtain for this country a Strong Fighting Policy in the Air' on which he said he could give the government the benefit of his expert knowledge. He referred to 'the gravest danger that besets you' being 'an early renewal on a much larger scale than we have ever experienced of bomb raids on London'.

He claimed that a strong air policy would mean no more air raids so that:

- The lights of London shall be raised.
- London will return to normal life and conditions.
- Further interference with civil liberties will be unjustified.

In summary, he said that he stood for three things:

- The winning of the war.
- The defence of London.
- The freedom of the people.

---

[37] Tom Driberg, *Swaff* (1974).

The address also contained a counter to Brookes and stated: 'This is my programme. My opponent cannot take over this programme. He has not been on Active Service. He is not a practical Airman. He is not a Fighting Man. My opponent can TALK to you about these things, but he cannot DO them'. One other policy area justified a long paragraph in an otherwise sparse address: this was Billing's (or Bottomley's) continuing opposition to the liquor restrictions (see chapter 3). Billing wrote: 'I am entirely opposed to the ridiculous and grandmotherly restrictions imposed by the Central Control Board (Liquor Traffic), and when returned to Parliament will do my utmost to secure their withdrawal.'

The issue of the drink restrictions made only a minor appearance in the election. The East London Licensed Victuallers' Association decided not to run a candidate but talked to Billing and Brookes to choose whom they should back. Brookes, even though he was the Coalition candidate, came out against the Control Board and its constitution, methods of working and its 'crushing' restrictions. Billing was even more strongly opposed and, following a vote of its members, secured the support of the Association. Bottomley, via his League of the Man in the Street, also used the by-election to continue his attacks on Lloyd George and the Control Board. He advocated: 'If you want your liberties restored and a speedy end to the war vote for Billing, freedom and fairplay'.

As the campaign moved into its only full week, Billing added to his eye-catching stunts. On Monday, 17 January 1916 he brought in an aeroplane on the back of a lorry and began to make speeches from it, attracting much attention; indeed, shortly afterwards film of this was to appear in cinema newsreels. The *Daily Mirror* reported that 'everyone' in Mile End was discussing the war in the air and that enthusiasm for Billing's campaign was growing.[38] The *Daily Mail* also highlighted Billing's ability to attract attention, saying: 'He is tall and powerful, drives a high-power car with an exhaust that to say the least is audible, and addresses the electors in a great megaphone voice that could be heard above the roar of his engine if he set his aeroplane going'.[39] On the same day, Warwick Brookes held his first public meeting. At this he was supported by leading Liberal, Herbert Samuel, and letters of support were read out from

---

38 *Daily Mirror*, 18 January 1916.
39 *Daily Mail*, 18 January 1916.

the former member, the now Lord Burnham and from Bertram Straus, the previous Liberal candidate. Further, the seconder of the motion in support of Brookes was Frederick Charrington. Several arguments were deployed at the meeting. Samuel continued the line that 'If a man is a good flyer, as Mr. Billing claims to be, surely his place is with our air fleet' and that 'It is a dozen pities we have to waste our time on a contest when we should be presenting a united front to the Prussians.' He had, of course, argued this strongly in his own recent by-election (see chapter 3).

Brookes was gracious about his old friend, Pemberton-Billing, remarking 'All good luck to Mr. Billing but I say that in Mile End you want a businessman and I come before you as a businessman'. He stressed his record of being supportive of strong national defence. Now, he further emphasised the need for conscription and the economic strangulation of Germany. On the key topic of air defence, he still argued that he was equally as strong as Billing. However, two interesting themes began to emerge. Firstly, Brookes maintained there was no need to become obsessed with the issue. He said:

> *'While I fully appreciate the seriousness of the air raids on London, I do not think we should give way to hysterics or adopt in haste panicky measures which are likely to do more harm than good. I have every reason to believe that since Sir Percy Scott took in hand the defence of London our position has been immensely strengthened'.*

Secondly, he expanded that argument to set up a straw-man assault on Billing by saying: 'We are dealing with a serious matter and I am strongly against taking the defences of London out of the hands of Sir Percy Scott and putting them in the hands of a man simply on the qualification that he can fly'; Billing had claimed by going to parliament he could encourage, or force, the government to do more to defend London but had not implied that would involve him, personally, taking charge. Still, Brookes realised that Scott's standing was so strong that it would be damaging to Billing to imply he was intending to remove him, possibly in favour of himself.

Something of a carnival air set in as the two vigorous campaigns continued. On the Thursday, *The Globe* newspaper noted that by now Mile End street vendors were 'hawking miniature models of aeroplanes as a topical novelty' and predicted that, by polling day, 'there should be all the fun of the fair'. The Billing campaign made use of model aeroplanes as well as their real one and decorated the windows of supportive tradesmen with them, and models of Zeppelins, to interest children and remind people of their message. At another large meeting, Billing had put flesh on the bones of his proposals for Air Defence. He explained that, once in the Commons, he would demand that a committee be set up with fifteen members, of which he would be one, to review: the position of the air service, the manufacturers, sources for engines and 'what tactics they should employ to beat the Hun in the air and to defend London.' At the end of ten days, Billing was confident that 'they would be able to decide upon a policy so bold and so great and so ingenious that we would have the German airmen at our mercy.' In a more incendiary comment, he claimed that Britain had thrown away initial supremacy in the air and that Germany's aircraft were now so superior that 'every man we were sending in the air now was murdered by the mechanical ingenuity of our enemy. And we are taking no steps to prevent it.'

Formal nominations took place at Stepney Public Library. Brookes submitted eight papers, and his nominators included Charrington, Straus and the Chairman, Secretary and Treasurer of the Mile End Liberal Association. Pemberton-Billing had more papers with eleven. His signatories included the Chairman and Deputy Chairman of the East London Licensed Victuallers' Association and, it was claimed, representatives of all the trades unions in the division. Inevitably, Billing ensured his aeroplane was parked prominently outside the library whilst the nomination process was underway. He also, successfully, requested that the Returning Officer agree to longer-than-usual polling hours of 7am to 9pm. Press observers now suspected the battle would not be the walk-over many had presumed. Whilst the advantage of strong organisation was recognised, Billing's verve, and the saliency of his campaign topic, were having an impact. Moreover, the Northcliffe press was supportive with, for example, the *Weekly Dispatch* including a sizeable piece written by Billing, headlined: 'Why the Germans are beating us in airfights.'

Two themes now emerging were speculation about the allegiance of the Jewish vote and an apparent attempt to smear Pemberton-Billing. The Jewish vote was estimated at around one-third of the total, sufficiently significant that some campaign speeches were made in Yiddish and polling day had been set to avoid the Sabbath. Billing said he was confident of winning their support and there was speculation his campaign against the blackout would find favour in that community as many were shopkeepers. Against this, the former Liberal MP, and candidate, Straus, had strong Jewish backing and was supporting Brookes. Further, key local Jewish leaders, Leopold de Rothschild and Colonel Lionel de Rothschild, had written to Jewish electors calling on them to do the same. In the event, it seems likely that the rival campaigns fought themselves to a standstill within the Jewish community and that it did not vote as a bloc.

Regarding the personal attacks (or innuendoes) on Billing, one paper, *The Globe* commented: 'The amazing Mile End election has now got down to personalities, a surest sign of a hotly-contested fight.'[40] There were rumours the Brookes campaign was suggesting that Billing had left the RNAS under a cloud. Obviously, Billing was not able to reveal anything about his service and, specifically, the Freidrichshafen raid. On the other hand, he was probably happy enough to see multiple comments that he had led air raids. The Brookes campaign was now pursuing a 'damned if you did, damned if you didn't strategy' arguing that, either, Billing left the service as a result of some personal failure, in which case he wasn't the hero and expert it was claimed, or he didn't, in which case he should be back there fighting on the front line rather than seeking an easy billet in the Commons. Billing immediately responded to the attacks by showing *The Times* a copy of the letter he had received accepting his resignation. The paper reported it was a letter in which 'their Lordships accepted, with regret, his resignation, and in recognition of his services promoted him to the rank of squadron commander, with seniority of January 1st 1916.'[41] The Admiralty letter was sufficient to take the wind out of the attempts to question Pemberton-Billing's war service but was used instead to support the argument that he should, rather, be fighting than seeking a place in Parliament.

Numerous meetings and intensive canvassing filled the final weekend of the campaign. Both campaigns made appeals for people with motorcars to come and assist them. Brookes' canvassing was also aided by Unionist and

---

40 *The Globe*, 20 January 1916.
41 *The Times*, 22 January 1916.

Liberal supporters from nearby constituencies. The *East London Observer* carried an advertisement for Brookes: 'Vote and work for Warwick Brookes – The Coalition candidate – Recommended by Men you trust'.[42] It also advertised his planned meetings for the eve of poll on Monday night. At one, the chair was to be taken by Frederick Charrington and the supporting speakers were to be Arthur Steel-Maitland (Conservative party chairman and Under-secretary for the Colonies), Bertram Straus and William Glynn-Jones MP, the Liberal member for the neighbouring constituency of Stepney. Another meeting was advertised as taking place at the same time (8pm) with a different chairman. Pemberton-Billing's meeting schedule was more extensive. Described as 'the Airman candidate', meetings were planned at the Mile End Palladium on Saturday afternoon, Sunday afternoon (2 meetings) and Monday evening (2 meetings). His supporting speakers were, as before, Bottomley and Tillett, and now also Arnold White. White was an interesting choice. At the time, he was giving almost daily lectures in London on 'The Triumph of British Seapower' in which he stridently called on the government to 'unshackle the navy' and to enforce the blockade against Germany by closing all Mediterranean and North Sea ports 'to all neutral powers.' His involvement no doubt boosted Pemberton-Billing in his efforts to match Brookes' strong commitment to a more effective blockade. However, White also represented another, disturbing, strand in British politics. He had stood, unsuccessfully, in Mile End for the Liberals in 1886 but soon split with the party. Dating from that period he displayed significant, and growing, anti-Semitism and, in 1899, wrote a book, *The Modern Jew*, which attacked Jewish immigrants for a failure to assimilate and blamed them for many of the problems of the East End.

The potential controversy of involving White does not appear to have concerned Houston who, in later years, considered his novel format for Billing's final meetings to be one of his greater campaigning innovations. In Houston's own words:

'The great feature of the election was a non-stop meeting I organised on the last Sunday at the local picture-palace. It started at two o'clock and an hour later the

---

42 *East London Observer*, 22 January 1916.

first audience was ejected by the back door and the second audience admitted by the front. That process was continued until six o'clock'. [43]

The Times was impressed and reported that: 'On Saturday, Sunday and Monday he is to have two meetings daily in the Mile End Palladium with an orchestra in attendance and a display of films showing him in his aeroplane'.

As chairman, Bottomley used the meetings to reinforce Billing's patriotic standing saying that Mile End electors had the chance to 'administer a much-needed tonic to the present government by sending to the House of Commons a man who knew the business of war and wanted to help Lord Kitchener to win it.' Houston's initial assessment was that the Sunday meetings had been a great success and must have won hundreds of votes. However, the next day, the police reported a lengthy queue of complainants who discovered that their pockets had been picked at the meetings. Houston later noted: '"The boys" had evidently patronized us and had a very successful time.'[44] Compared with this hive of activity, in another indication of the contrast between Billing's unconventional campaign and that of Brookes, the latter had no events on the Sunday, instead observing the customary day of rest.

The next controversy revolved around comments Pemberton-Billing was claimed to have made about the Zeppelin attacks on different parts of London. It surfaced in a letter (23 January) from the First Lord of the Admiralty (Balfour) to Brookes, in reaction, he said, to a request from Brookes for his views on statements on the subject made by Billing. Balfour's letter alleged that Billing, in one of his speeches, had implied the government was not interested in defending working-class areas such as the East End and only stirred into action when the affluent West End was hit. PB was alleged to have said:

> 'You know the history of the Zeppelin raids. There was one raid over the East End, but the papers, under Government orders, said nothing... But when a Zeppelin went over the West End of London, the Government woke up, and then England went mad. Why should you discriminate between men and women being blown up in the East End and the West End?"

---

43 H J Houston, *The Real Horatio Bottomley* (1923).
44 Ibid.

Balfour's strong letter said that the claims were totally untrue. Further, he accused Billing of being 'unpatriotic' by trying to make political capital out of false claims that government policy was based on 'class selfishness'. The Brookes campaign made good use of the Balfour letter and sought to distribute it to all electors. Billing hit back. His reply said: 'As a fighting man, I can only interpret the occasion and singular violence of Mr. Arthur Balfour's letter to Mr. Warwick Brookes as a sign that the Government realises it has lost Mile End.'

The final twist in the election coincided with Balfour's letter. Having argued that the next, and greater, risk was aeroplane attacks, it played into Billing's hands that the Germans started the 1916 air attack season over the weekend with aircraft, rather than Zeppelin, raids on East Kent; especially since, for his predictions, Billing had been denounced by the Coalition campaign as 'a bogey-monger and a mountebank'. The *Western Daily Press* commented:

> *'In the course of the weekend, Mr Billing's campaign has received an excellent fillip from the enemy. The East Coast of Kent, where an aeroplane raid took place last night, and a further raid today, is just sufficiently near and sufficiently far away to provide an additional stimulus which may turn a lot of doubtfuls to his way of thinking'.*[45]

Similarly, the *Daily Mirror* said: 'If any one event could increase interest in the election it is yesterday's double air raid .... Mr Pemberton-Billing has all along contended that daylight raids by aeroplane are to be expected in the future. He speaks as an expert. Yesterday his forebodings were proven correct'. But the final word went to Brookes. He flooded the constituency with hundreds of posters, harshly declaring in large type: 'Pity Billing was not in Kent and not Mile End yesterday'.

The campaign was the first to attract widespread coverage in the national press. *The Times* and *Telegraph* gave daily reports. *The Daily Mirror* and the *Daily Mail*, while covering a by-election essentially for the first time, increasingly offered exclusively positive coverage of Pemberton Billing, attracted both by his policy focus on the air war and the 'box office' nature of his campaigning.

---

45 *Western Daily Press*, 24 January 1916.

A near run thing

Expectations of the result now changed. Newspapers had anticipated a similar outcome to those at Cleveland and West Newington, where independent, single-issue candidates were easily dismissed. In contrast, by the culmination of the Mile End battle, most papers thought the result would be close and that a Billing victory could not be ruled out. The day before polling, the *Western Daily Press* summarised:

> 'The Mile End air election looks as if it were not to be the fiasco which was anticipated.... Mr Pemberton-Billing ... is certainly making an impression and though to prophesy his success .... would be a bold proceeding, it is pretty certain that he will make an excellent show.'

The Daily Mail summarised the fight as 'Man versus Machine' as Billing's personality and popular cry took on the quiet efficiency of the established political organisations. Warwick Brookes agreed and said directly to one of Billing's main organisers: 'You have the popular cry and the popular meetings. But our organisation will beat you'. He would need that organisation for the general news about the progress of the war was not in his favour and the country was still digesting the final withdrawal from the Dardanelles which had been accomplished, actually with fewer casualties than feared, on 8 January 1916. Polling Day (25 January 1916) saw the hard campaigning by both camps continuing to the end. The polls opening at 7am meant, as one reporter noted: 'The agents of the candidates had the unusual experience of opening their committee rooms in moonlight.'[46] Both campaigns brought in as many helpers and motorcars as they could muster and among those providing vehicles for Brookes were Lord Curzon, Arthur Balfour and several other MPs. The *Lancashire Evening Post* said there would be a 'great incursion of the West End into the East today' as 'both the Liberal and Unionist Parties are bringing all the forces they can to secure the Coalition candidate as large a majority as possible'.[47] Mile End was one of the smallest constituencies in the country both geographically and numerically. Consequently, the paper also thought

---

46 *Hull Daily Mail*, 25 January 1916 and *Daily Mail*, 24 January 1916.
47 *Lancashire Evening Post*, 25 January 1916.

there would be so many motorcars that 'very few of its free and independent electors should require to walk to the polling booths'. The comprehensive nature of the party machines meant nearly everyone on the register who now lived in neighbouring constituencies was traced and could be offered transport to return to Mile End to vote. That, and the extremely high-profile nature of Billing's campaign, meant there was a heavy poll, despite so many electors being away on active service.

The result was a narrow win for Brookes by fewer than 400 votes:

Dec. 1910			
Levy-Lawson	Liberal Unionist	2,176	50%
Straus	Liberal	2,170	50%
Majority		6	
Electorate & Turnout		5,467	79%

Jan. 1916			
Brookes	Coalition (Unionist)	1,991	55%
Pemberton-Billing	Indep.	1,615	45%
Majority		376	
Electorate & Turnout		5,800	62%

Brookes was gracious in victory and complimented Billing on the way he had fought and said he hoped to have the pleasure of fighting him again when he had a local organisation behind him. Billing felt he had fought hard but that it was difficult to succeed as an independent. Nevertheless, he reiterated his pledge to keep contesting elections in the name of an efficient air service.

The consequences of Mile End, for Brookes and Billing

Warwick Brookes was as good as his word and immediately became involved in the air defence issue. As early as 27 January 1916, he joined a delegation of Unionist and Liberal London MPs who met with Kitchener and Balfour at the

War Office to seek assurances about the defences of London against aeroplane attacks. He also made his first speech in the Commons about the air defence of London. This was on 16 February 1916 which, in normal circumstances, would have been considered unseemly haste. He duly apologised for speaking so soon after his entry into the Commons but getting to the substantive issue said he was entirely in support of the policy of appointing a Minister of Aviation to take over the control of both wings of the Imperial Air Service of the country. He felt that this new minister should be of equal status with the First Lord of the Admiralty and the Secretary of State for War and so be a full member of the War Committee of the cabinet.[48]

For the rest of his time as a wartime MP, Brookes continued to show an interest in air defence, participating in debates and asking questions and he was appointed a member of the Joint Air Committee of the two Houses of Parliament. However, as the war ended, so did his parliamentary career. At the 1918 'coupon' election, the Mile End constituency was abolished, and Brookes needed an alternative seat to fight. He was selected for the two-member seat of Preston and immediately set about campaigning. He was renowned as an assiduous constituency MP at Mile End at a time when such behaviour was uncommon and, on 5 November 1918, advertised in the *Lancashire Evening Post* his availability to help Preston residents in his guise as 'one of the Unionist and Lloyd George candidates' for the borough.

Brookes' move to Preston, a highly marginal seat, was brave and he was unsuccessful. In 1910, both seats had been held narrowly by the Unionists. This time, however, the single sitting Unionist who was standing again, George Stanley, held his seat but Brookes lost out to Labour. He was never to stand for parliament again. The rest of his career, centred around business and yachting, was a roller-coaster and he was declared bankrupt during the Great Depression. As will be seen in the next chapter, Billing was also as good as his word about fighting the next convenient by-election, once more as an 'Air Candidate'.

---

48 Hansard: HC Deb 16 February, 1916 vol. 80 cols 126 – 127.

5.
A SECOND SORTIE

East Hertfordshire, 9 March 1916

Opinion was sharply divided over Billing's near win at Mile End. The pro-Coalition press interpreted it as good sense by electors, who were not to be diverted by showmanship and scaremongering. Bottomley, however, trumpeted the outcome as a stunning result. He quickly gave his views in an article, 'The moral of Mile End', in the Sunday Pictorial. He argued that Billing had only been denied victory by the large number of 'removals'; voters that the party machines had managed to bring back into the constituency who had not been exposed to Houston's highly effective campaigning. He joked: 'there is consternation in the Party dovecots. There is no cooing at the moment it is all "Billing"!'

The candidate himself coped with defeat better than his long-suffering wife, Dot, had anticipated. Initially, he was buoyed by the acclamation from delighted supporters and, although his mood turned darker after a few days, Dot persuaded him to carry on campaigning and he reiterated his intention to 'fight the next by-election in any constituency within reasonable distance of London on the policy of Great Britain's supremacy in the air'. That opportunity arrived rapidly when the East Hertfordshire seat became vacant.

The Zeppelins return

In the days after Mile End (25 January 1916) the Zeppelin threat was talked about, even before the new 'season'. The tone was not always serious:

newspaper letters speculated whether some animals, notably cats and rats, had a sixth-sense premonition of their impending arrival. A newspaper in Hull felt it would be no loss if a Zeppelin bombed the Town Hall since they would then get a more pleasant building to replace it. (There were problems with the lavatories, apparently). But real concerns remained, and rumours circulated that the Germans had up to 200 factories equipped to build Zeppelins. And while not many Londoners were so scared of them that they invested in Zeppelin-damage insurance, a drunk in Bayswater was fined £2 for shouting (falsely) 'Put all your lights out, the Zeppelins are about' because of the anxiety that caused. At the end of January, fears increased with news of Zeppelin attacks beginning again on Paris, resulting in substantial civilian casualties, including children.

Then, on the last day of the month, all nine of Germany's serviceable naval Zeppelins attacked the Midlands.[1] Seventy-one people were killed and 114 injured. Twenty-two British aircraft took off, trying to oppose the raiders, but none made contact, and several were damaged in crash-landings in which two pilots died. It was clear that the Zeppelins remained a problem and, the day after the attack, *The Times* was underwhelmed by the state of London's defences saying: 'London's principal efforts consist of guns, largely manned by the cheery but inexperienced and ill-equipped amateurs in naval uniform whom we owe to Mr. Churchill.'[2] The 31 January raids revived debate regarding defence tactics and reprisals. *The Times* (3 February) noted that towns without a black-out tended to suffer greater damage.[3] It argued that the best defence was to attack enemy Zeppelins and aircraft on the ground, 'in their lair'. A few days later (7 February) a long article by its Aeronautical Correspondent illuminated the state of public opinion, and policy. It opened:

> *'There are probably few editors of important English newspapers whose letter bags, since the Zeppelin raid of a week ago, have not been full either with*

---

[1] As in Britain, there were separate Army and Navy air arms in Germany and strong competition between them.
[2] *The Times*, 1 February 1916.
[3] Just over a week later, the Home Office extended the areas of the country subject to black-out to include the Midlands and the North-West.

> *indignant inquiries as to why these raids are not prevented or with equally urgent demands that the Government shall take immediate steps to prevent them.'*

It echoed Billing's complaints about lack of expertise on the subject in Parliament and his proposal for a committee to be appointed that could receive secret information and develop realistic responses. The correspondent warned: 'The government should be aware that, on this occasion, the country is in no mood to be trifled with and will not be content with the customary soothing and confusing assurances.'

On 11 February, *The Times* again warned about air defence: 'The Government must by this time be fully aware of the rising tide of feeling on this subject.' The article was stimulated by another aircraft raid, this time over Ramsgate. Little damage was caused and there were no fatalities, but it was a reminder that the country was likely to be attacked frequently as flying conditions improved. The paper painted a bleak picture of Britain's preparedness and put forward suggestions that again closely mirrored those by Billing. It demanded aircraft construction be put under a single decision-maker and condemned: 'The present ruinous and wasteful system of competition between the Army and Navy' and proposed that 'the whole system of our air defences, from lighting to fighting, from warnings at sea to the warnings to local communities, should be under one authority and not under several'. At the same time, the *Daily Mail* was providing invaluable publicity, keeping Billing's name in the public eye, by allowing him to write detailed articles on aspects of air defence.

Discussions in Parliament

On 16 February, the main parliamentary advocate of Air Defence, William Joynson-Hicks, the MP for Brentford, moved an amendment: 'That this House humbly regrets that no mention is made in the Gracious Speech from the Throne of any proposals for placing the Air Services of the country on a firmer and stronger basis.' The debate revealed widespread concern about neglect of the 'air' issue. No backbench speeches were made in defence of the government while concerns were raised by Conservatives and Liberals alike. MPs commented on public opinion. While they all agreed that air raids, and perceived lack of defence against them, were not resulting in panic, there was growing dissatisfaction. Joynson-Hicks warned: 'There is no subject, I imagine, upon which public feeling is stronger at the present moment than the subject of our Air Services. It has been brought to a head very largely by the effects of the undisputed raid which the German Zeppelins made over us on the 31st of last month.' A similar contribution was made by Sir John Rolleston:

> 'I have been asked to express the wishes of my Constituents, some of whom have been victims of air raids. They wish representations to be made to the Government that there is much need for development of our aerial defences and other safeguards against invasion of this kind, and they are justified in expressing that wish, because they have themselves been the victims on various occasions of visitations by airships, with terrible and fatal results.'

Rolleston was the MP who was about to leave the House and so trigger Billing's next by-election opportunity and his constituents had suffered heavily; over 40 bombs had been dropped on Hertford during the 13 October 1915 attack, killing nine, injuring 15 and damaging 151 buildings. MPs complained that the government lacked urgency and about confusion over who was responsible for what. Several speakers called for the formation of an Air Ministry which would take over control of both air wings and be led by a powerful, Cabinet rank Minister.

The official reply was divided between Harold Tennant (War Office), Herbert Samuel (Home Office) and Arthur Balfour (Admiralty), rather reinforcing the persistent complaints about split decision-making. Some initiatives and actions were announced. The Navy would now deal with aircraft trying to reach the country and the Army with those that did so. Much tighter black-out restrictions had been imposed across much of the country, and a new 'early warning' process had been established to alert local police authorities if a raid seemed imminent. Finally, previous strict censorship had been lessened so that the press was permitted to provide more details on raids. Subsequent speakers were underwhelmed, still feeling that the government lacked the urgency demanded by the 'air question'. The reforms were not enough to mollify the House and the failure to move towards a single Air Minister was particularly poorly received by MPs.

Air War: How to wage it

Pemberton-Billing's first activity following Mile End was to pull together his recent articles into book format. He achieved this at breakneck speed and, within a month, the book (*Air War: How to wage it*) was on sale at one shilling a copy, just as the Hertfordshire East campaign began. It laid out his comprehensive manifesto, attacking failures to date but confidently arguing these could be reversed:

> 'After the pitiable confessions of His Majesty's Ministers in the House of Commons of their hopeless unpreparedness against the menace from the air, and their attempts to shield themselves behind the plea of the impossible, it becomes more than ever necessary to prove to the nation that Great Britain's supremacy in the air is simply a question of hard cash, hard work, brains, and bravery.'[4]

The opening chapters laid out Billing's case for leaving the Royal Naval Air Service in order to campaign; he stressed warnings he had been giving since 1908 of the need to achieve strength in the air and what he saw as the unforgiveable failure of the 'powers that be' to act accordingly. The next sections detailed his recommendations and demonstrated that, setting aside his hyperbole, he had practical knowledge and foresight. He advocated attacking Zeppelins in their bases rather than fighting an unequal and perhaps impossible battle in the air at night. The approach described was a thinly veiled account of his attack on Freidrichshafen.[5] As he claimed: 'This is no romance; I know of what I write'. He outlined a plan for 'The defence of Great Cities – By night and by day'. This set out how many aircraft (of what, detailed, specification) were needed and how many pilots. The following chapter was remarkably prescient; it described, in full, a plan for an early warning system which bears remarkable similarity to the approach adopted in 1940. The country would be split into areas, each of which had local sub-areas and all the areas were in communication with a central controller. In later chapters, Billing laid out comprehensive plans to produce a 'great fleet' of five thousand aircraft, how to train the necessary pilots and how to specify and obtain the engines for them. He finished by describing what kind

---

4 *Air War: How to wage it* (N. Pemberton-Billing), 1916.
5 See chapter 4.

of person would be required to fulfil the, much-needed, role of Air Minster and, similarly, Commander-in-Chief of a new, unified air service. *Air War: How to wage it* was somewhat cobbled together, at pace, and was undoubtedly produced to assist Billing's mission to get into the Commons. It included some point-scoring post-Mile End against Balfour and Asquith and praised Northcliffe and his newspapers that had been friendly to him. It was also promoted for sale in the local newspaper in Hertford during the by-election campaign. Nevertheless, it contained sufficient information and good sense to make clear he could not be treated dismissively. Having survived one scare at his hands, the government was now going to face another.

Hertfordshire East & Billing's rapid start

A mystery of the Hertfordshire East by-election, in the northern Home Counties, is why the government business managers initiated it so soon after Billing's impressive performance at Mile End and his commitment to fight all future vacancies, 'convenient to London'. The sitting Conservative MP, Sir John Rolleston, was in ill health and had long made it clear he intended to resign. His putative successor, Brodie Henderson, had been chosen before the outbreak of war. However, in a personal statement to the electors (only published after the by-election) Rolleston revealed that he had offered to stay on as MP until September 1916, but that proposal had been rejected. After the election, Pemberton-Billing said that the statement had been sent to the local paper before the campaign, but the editor decided to hold it back as it might damage Henderson's campaign. Billing further recounted he had been encouraged to publish the statement himself but had not done so as he wanted to fight fair: 'I did not want to be returned as a protest against dirty political tricks, but on my own merits as an Independent Imperialist – with a strong Air Policy as the basis and safeguard of that Imperialism.'[6]

For whatever reason, the Unionists went ahead and found themselves in a tough fight. News of Rolleston's impending departure emerged on Friday 18 February. Billing responded straightaway. He told the press he would stand, so that nearly all the news stories the next day announcing the impending vacancy also reported that he would be a candidate, and, further, that he

---

6 *Pemberton-Billing: The story of his life (1917).*

intended to speak in Hertford that very afternoon, Saturday 19 February. Billing's autobiography claims that when he heard about the coming vacancy, he called the telephone exchange in Hertford, got the number for the Superintendent of Police, told him his MP had resigned and that he, Billing, was arriving to give a speech the next afternoon and asked him where the best place was to do so. According to Billing's account: 'He was extremely gracious and interested and advised 'Bull Plain'. I then rang up two or three of the dailies and told them I was holding that meeting.'

But Billing had a diary clash since that Saturday he was to be at the wedding of an old friend. By his own account, he didn't leave the reception in central London until 2.20pm and then raced the thirty miles to Hertford at high speed and in very wet weather. His autobiography said that he was speaking 'from the altitude of an orange box in Bull Plain, Hertford' having arrived at 3.10pm – after all, he did claim at that time to own the fastest motorcar in England.[7] *The Hertford Mercury and Reformer* was impressed by Billing's speed and commitment, commenting that: 'moving with characteristic rapidity... Mr. Pemberton-Billing motored down to Hertford on Saturday afternoon and addressed a large meeting of townspeople and farmers from the outlying districts.'

A crowd had waited patiently in quite heavy rain and on his arrival, heralded by 'the throbbing sound of a high-powered motorcar', moved in tightly to hear him. He began by saying, more in sorrow than anger, that the country's air forces were unacceptably poor but that things could be turned round quickly, with the right policies and people. Then, Coriolanus-like – although he took to the role with considerably more enthusiasm than Shakespeare's character – he claimed:

> 'It was the greatest sacrifice of my life, in the middle of a great war like this, and with a physique like mine, to get out of uniform, put on civilian clothes and come and stand on boxes like this to ask for the votes of the people. But I was willing to make the sacrifice, or any other sacrifice, if only I could have a hand in helping this country to gain supremacy in the air.'

---

7 Ibid.

He made a strong emotional appeal to patriotism and British exceptionalism, declaiming: 'If this country does dictate to the rest of the world it will do so for good but there are other countries who, if we are not very careful, will dictate to us and the rest of the world and whose dictation will not be good for the world.' Billing said: 'What I want you to send me to the House of Commons to do is to prove to the government by my experience and knowledge that what they say cannot be done can be done.'

The time and place were right for this message. The right time, because, as a new air attack season loomed, air policy had now climbed the political and public agenda. The right place because of the still recent memories in Hertford of the Zeppelin attack the previous autumn. That was reflected in a letter from 'A Resident Elector' in the local newspaper arguing that the town should welcome Billing and saying: 'East Hertfordshire will seriously remember what happened somewhere in the constituency last October, and if anything can be done to prevent its repetition then surely it is fair and honest ... to give the expert an opportunity of showing what can be done to prevent it.' It also, helpfully, advised readers 'to remember, the ballot is absolutely secret, no one can tell how you vote, notwithstanding how you may be conveyed to the polling station.'

The arrival of the Airman was going to bring excitement. The question remained how feasible it would be for an Independent, even with such a powerful 'cry', to compete with the strength of the party machines. Opinions were divided. The same issues applied as in Mile End of sizeable numbers of voters being either on active service or having moved elsewhere. However, some felt the geography of this constituency gave the party machines less of an advantage. The East Hertfordshire division of 1916 was large, straggling and predominantly rural and so would be hard to canvass. The *Hertford Mercury* concluded about the Unionist 'machine' that:

> *'There are important parts of it which, owing to the removal from the district on military service of many active and influential workers, are missing and which in the short space of time available before the day of the election, cannot be adequately replaced ... Given a good supply of motorcars, which we understand is assured, Mr. Pemberton-Billing will be almost as well able to see the electors and make his influence felt among them, in a general sense, as his opponent.'*

The Northcliffe press rapidly moved to back Billing. *The Times* published a leader indirectly endorsing his campaign. It called for practical experts on the subject to be heard in parliament. The Thunderer also endorsed a series of 'air policies', all advocated by Billing. These included the need for the air to no longer be a 'Cinderella' service, starved of investment; an end to the separation of air procurement between army and navy; the establishment of a unified administration, headed by an Air Minster and, overall, an aggressive air policy and campaign, not restricted to passive defence but, by implication, including reprisals. In summary, the paper felt: 'The one hope of reform is public pressure, preferably in Parliament.' In similar vein, the *Daily Mail*, announcing Billing's intention to stand, included a puff piece by a correspondent named 'An Air Pilot' who praised Billing to the skies.

The East Hertfordshire contest: The establishment versus the new

Brodie Henderson was a popular, local, and entirely expected choice by the Coalition, having been selected as Rolleston's prospective successor more than two years earlier. Aged 47, he was a partner in a civil engineering firm and the Chairman of the local Conservative Association. He was a Justice of the Peace, a staunch member of the Church of England, and a hunt supporter. Among his hobbies were shooting and art (He was the original owner of Waterhouse's Gather Ye Rosebuds While Ye May) and he owned more than 400 acres of park and agricultural land. He was a railway bridge designer and builder.

He and his wife were well-known figures in Hertford society, featuring regularly in the lists of attendees at society balls such as the annual County Ball and the Marchioness of Salisbury's Ball. Indeed, Brodie's wife was considered a major asset to his campaign. *The Hertford Mercury and Reformer* waxed lyrical about her believing: 'In his charming wife, Cpt. Brodie Henderson possesses an asset which in a closely contested election might easily tip the scales in his favour.'[8]

Henderson's adoption on 22 February was agreed unanimously by the Conservative Association; he also received full support from the local Liberals and a joint Unionist-Liberal campaign committee was established.

---

8 *Hertford Mercury and Reformer*, 26 February 1916.

In his acceptance speech, Henderson announced support for Billing's position regarding the Air War. Feeling potentially vulnerable in comparison to Billing's tales of derring-do, he detailed his own wartime activities. He told his gathered supporters he had realised very early that the Germans were having great success due to their excellent supply of machine guns and so, as an engineer, had offered to help in that area. He became the machine-gun Officer for the Hertfordshire Yeomanry but was soon appointed into that role for the entire Eastern Command. He had by now trained many machine gunners and was 'absolutely convinced it was good practical work.'

Using the same tactic employed in Mile End, he then questioned why Billing, as a practical airman, was not similarly devoting himself to active service –' he could not help feeling that if this gentleman, Mr. Billing, who was giving them all this trouble of a contested election, were such an expert in aircraft as he said he was he ought to be doing his bit also.' Of course, he was at risk of a similar challenge and so announced that even as an MP he would not abandon his military duties. Attacking Billing, Henderson laid out his own aviation credentials, saying that he and three friends owned an engineering works in the Midlands and around 55 per cent of their business was aircraft work which, he argued, meant even in that field he was doing more than his opponent.

The campaigns came to life on Thursday (24 February). In the afternoon, as it was market day, Billing addressed a meeting in the market square which was well attended. He was followed by Henderson. However, this was not the end of the procession of potential candidates. When Henderson finished, a well-known local figure, William Rolfe, came forward and expressed surprise that the other two were planning to stand when he 'was already in the field'. In fact, Rolfe had announced in 1914 that, when the next election came, he would stand against both the Unionists and the Liberals as an independent Agriculturalist candidate, and he held a few meetings at that time. Now he claimed that he would indeed stand in the by-election. One issue he addressed was that of an MP's salary. Henderson said he would not take a salary and Billing announced (as he had in Mile End) that he would use his to fund the building of aircraft. Rolfe took the opposite view and announced that he most assuredly would take the salary since 'he knew the value of money and would take it and he certainly knew how to spend it.'

A Second Sortie

The same evening, Billing addressed a meeting in Hertford. Here, he announced a 'deal' he had proposed to Henderson. He said:

> *'I understand that Captain Henderson, if elected, does not intend to give up his Army work to follow his Parliamentary duties until the end of the war. In these circumstances, I am prepared to make him the following offer to avoid the expense and excitement to the constituency of an election at this time: If he is prepared to stand down so that I may be elected without a contest I will apply for the Chiltern Hundreds at the end of the war and surrender the seat to him.'*

He also revealed that he had had made a Master's Voice record of his speeches so that he could 'address' multiple gatherings at the same time – the first time this had been done.

Henderson's initial big meeting was at the Conservative Club in Waltham Cross the following night. He had multiple speakers including Sir George Reid MP, the ex-Australian High Commissioner, and a former Liberal candidate for the constituency, Edmund Barnard.[9] Attendance was reduced due to snowy weather but, even so, there was a crowd of around 300. The speeches were robustly aggressive towards Pemberton-Billing, arguing that were he to succeed that would bring great encouragement to Berlin and no aid to Hertford. Herbert Gibbs, a local businessman and leading Unionist, said that Billing's programme could be summed up as 'Supremacy in the Air', but, to him, that seemed 'an extraordinarily modest programme' when what was needed was supremacy in the air, on the sea, on the land and under the sea. He raised the spectre that, were Billing to be elected (with the support of Northcliffe and his newspapers) that might be the beginning of a separate party with the aim of harassing the government. Henderson continued the attack, saying:

> *'Let there be no panic speeches. If they had read their papers, they would find that the candidate that was against him had been making speeches which, if there was such a thing as a Potsdam Daily Mail or a Berlin Times, if they could*

---

9 Barnard was to essay a political migration and reappeared as the first ever candidate for the National Party at the East Islington by-election in 1917 (see chapter 12).

> be published in those papers, no greater encouragement could be given to the Germans. Pemberton-Billing said the country was open for them to come. Was that right? It was a most disgraceful thing for a man who posed as an expert to say the country was open to Zeppelin raids.'

He then repeated that Billing should be using his skills more directly saying:

> 'Mr Billing said that he had a wonderful cure by which the Zeppelins would be kept away from England. He would not tell them what the cure was, and if he was a patriotic Englishman he ought not to be in East Herts, he ought to be with Lord Derby – chairman of the Air Services Committee – laying his scheme before him and offering it to the country.'

Sir George Reid forced home the attack, insinuating that perhaps Billing had only chosen to come to Hertford because the town had suffered air raids. He argued:

> 'The one thing that would encourage the Germans would be that some respectable English electorate would show that some damage done amongst them had made them feel frightened... horrible as those air-raids were, they were a fleabite in the face of that gigantic struggle in which millions of the king's subjects had risked their lives every day and night. What they needed was machine guns --- Capt. Henderson, when he brought his scientific knowledge as an engineer to bear upon the problem of the machine-gun supply of the country did not carry out his patriotism by resigning. ... If they put Mr Billing in it would be a most popular election in Germany, for the Germans would say 'By Jove, we have frightened them'.'

Frenetic and increasingly vicious campaigning

The campaign rapidly picked up pace with both candidates holding multiple meetings daily. By the end, Pemberton-Billing had impressively held over 160 meetings in twelve days in a constituency of 260 square miles, across which he estimated he had motored more than 1,460 miles. Furthermore, he achieved this with less support than in Mile End as Houston was not available to be his agent, and he was the sole speaker at most meetings. Henderson also undertook a punishing schedule, but enjoyed the assistance of many speakers, including MPs such as James Campbell (Irish Unionist), Col. Sir Hamar Greenwood (Liberal) and Reginald Neville (Unionist). The peak effort came on the Saturday before polling day (4 March) when Billing gave ten speeches, but Henderson topped that with twenty.

The two campaigns issued diametrically different election addresses whilst largely agreeing on policy. Henderson's was in traditional format and as well as being distributed door-to-door, it was reproduced in the local newspaper. He started by regretting the need for a contest and reminding voters that due to the electoral truce, he was receiving substantial support from the Liberals. He stated: 'I stand, firstly, to secure the efficient conduct of the War' and declaimed his backing for 'a strong Navy' and an Army that was 'maintaining its glorious traditions'. On the air issue, he combined adopting Pemberton-Billing's ideas whilst turning attention away from any earlier failings:

> 'Our Air Service has been greatly neglected and starved but it is useless at this time to rake up past errors although I feel very strongly on this subject. Our endeavours must be directed towards making up for lost time and our command of the air must be as supreme as our command of the seas ... From personal experience I know that our airmen will not hesitate to face any dangers and that what we need are more aircraft, more and better guns and efficient organisation and every effort in this direction must be made and will be made by me.'

In total contrast, Billing issued what was claimed to be the shortest election address in history. It comprised illustrations of air raid damage and two sentences, saying:

> 'The accompanying illustrations express with far greater eloquence than any words of mine the urgent and crying need of having an airman in the House of Commons who understands the job. Never let it be forgotten that the ballot is secret and you can vote according to your judgement and conscience without fear of any man.'

The illustrations were by the Dutch cartoonist, Raemaekers and showed damage from Zeppelin attacks.

Billing's and Henderson's campaign arguments remained as in their initial salvoes. Billing felt vulnerable having no outside speakers supporting him so tried to turn that to advantage, saying he had received offers of influential support from MPs and various political and social organisations, but had declined them all as he preferred to fight single-handedly. He also modified his position in response to the, entirely logical, questioning as to how he, alone, was going to stop Zeppelin attacks if elected. He said his presence at Mile End had already had a good effect, for it had forced upon the House of Commons the fact that the nation was clamouring for a more vigorous prosecution of the war on land, at sea and in the air; he further claimed his candidacy in East Hertfordshire had resulted in the appointment of Lord Derby to chair the Joint Naval and Military Committee on Air Service. He then upped the ante on his personal expertise claiming that in the past six months he had built two aircraft that had broken all records, and they were now in service. His key emotional argument was: 'It hurts my pride as an Englishman to think that the centre of the greatest Empire the world has ever known should have to admit that its only defence against enemy air attacks was darkness and silence.'

The Coalition campaign launched sharp personal attacks against Billing. Henderson repeatedly tried to counter the argument that this was an 'air' election; instead, he argued it should be referred to as the 'unnecessary' or the 'scare' election. He savaged the idea that Billing should be standing as a candidate because he had a secret plan, saying:

> 'If his opponent was the patriot he wanted them to believe why did he not state what his scheme was to deal with raids instead of waiting until he got in the House of Commons? ... If he [Henderson] had a scheme for stopping Zeppelins he would jump off that platform get in his motorcar and go and lay his scheme before Lord Derby ... Why did this wonderful man not do the same? It was absolute nonsense.'

Additional assaults were made, directly and through innuendo, on Billing's claimed achievements. Rumours were circulated that he was being financed by Northcliffe and, also, that he had failed while in the Royal Naval Air Service and that was why he left. Billing fiercely rejected the accusations. Regarding the support he was receiving from the Northcliffe papers, he denied that his campaign was being financed by anyone other than himself. He was adamant that he was paying the entire cost of East Hertfordshire, as with Mile End. He also released the letter from the Admiralty to counter claims that he had been asked to resign.

The squabble deepened and Henderson's people hit back. As one newspaper reported:

> *'The Air Candidate and his supporters have keenly resented attempts which have been made to discredit a number of his statements by the publication of particulars respecting his past career, and more particularly with reference to the nature of the services rendered by him as an airman and inventor during the period he was in the Naval Air Service. The constituency has been flooded with handbills and posters on the subject and the Air Candidate appears to have been persuaded into an indiscretion in publishing, by way of reply to the attacks, a personal and confidential letter he received in December from Commodore Murray F Sueter, Director of Aircraft Construction, against the latter's expressed wish.'*[10]

One of Henderson's guest speakers, Frederick Lanchester, was a member of the Government Advisory Committee for Aeronautics. He joined Henderson at a meeting aimed at 'working-class' supporters. Lanchester had checked with the Admiralty on PB's claim that he had 'built a wonderful machine for attacking Zeppelins at night and that it was now flying at Chingford.' He read out the reply he received from the Admiralty: 'This machine was badly smashed at Chingford in its trial flights a month ago and was removed in an absolutely wrecked condition and nothing has been heard of it since.' But such attacks were not necessarily hitting home, and Lanchester was poorly received at the meeting. When the audience were told that he had come down specially to talk about the air service, 'He can't beat Billing' was the retort. Lanchester complained about what he described as 'Mr Billing's misstatements', and said they made his blood boil, to which one heckler responded: 'You have been

---

10 *Hertford Mercury and Reformer,* 11 March 1916.

talking about yourself for the last half-hour, get on with your job'. When Lanchester said that Billing's claims to be an expert designer and builder of flying machines, who had built record-breaking machines, were 'pure moonshine' it caused an angry uproar in the audience, and he was howled down. Even though this was a meeting in support of Henderson, the chairman did not risk calling for a vote of support for him and it finished with three cheers for Billing and the singing of the national anthem.[11]

The disruption of the Lanchester meeting by the Billingites was not an isolated incident and the Henderson campaign grew angry at their tactics. Speakers were heckled at other meetings, to greater or lesser effect, and Henderson's eve of poll meeting was disrupted. The exuberance of the Billing supporters reached a peak on the eve of poll with the local newspaper reporting that 'supporters of Mr. Billing defaced with red paint and mud the posters on Cpt Henderson's committee room and on private houses and polling stations and posted his bills on the residences of several electors. This proceeding undoubtedly lost him a lot of votes.' Despite this, Billing personally was generally recognised to have fought a 'clean' campaign and to have 'studiously avoided personalities'.[12]

Smears and attempted smears?

The Henderson team may not have defaced posters, but they were fighting an 'aggressive' campaign, recognising that Billing was in with a chance. At the end of February, Billing repeated the claim that he had been told that if he didn't fight Mile End he would soon be rewarded with a safe seat. The Unionist Chairman, Steel-Maitland, had a letter published in *The Times* (3 March) categorically denying the claim. He also wrote the same letter to the *Hertford Mercury and Reformer*; offered by that paper the chance to respond, Pemberton-Billing limited himself, rather enigmatically, to the repost *'Qui s'excuse, s'accuse'* (Roughly: he who excuses himself accuses himself or making excuses reveals a guilty conscience). In his later autobiography,

---

11 Frederick Lanchester was one of the founders of aeronautics and made a great contribution to the development of aviation. However, somewhat ironically, an experimental aircraft he co-designed crashed in 1911 and from then onwards he abandoned the practical side of aviation.
12 *Hertford Mercury and Reformer*, 11 March 1916

Pemberton-Billing made numerous claims against the Unionists. He said: 'as polling day grew nearer the Party Machine was getting hot and bothered' and he maintained that they had arranged for numerous women 'coming down from London' and spreading 'all sorts of vile rumours concerning myself and my wife'. He claimed the Henderson campaign was also alleging that he was an undischarged bankrupt, that he had been flung out of the Navy for many grave misdemeanours, and that he was a spy for Germany. In response to claims like this appearing in handbills in the constituency, Billing had them reprinted but with the addition of a comment from himself that: 'Mr Pemberton Billing thinks too much prominence cannot be given to this type of electioneering.'

Another alleged letter formed the centre of a more substantial potential smear. Billing claimed that the Unionist Chief Agent, Sir John Boraston, had written to Balfour saying 'I am sorry to trouble you so much about Billing, but he has undoubtedly captured the imagination of the public. The seat is in danger and unless we can discredit him, I fear he will be returned for East Herts' and that Balfour had then passed on the letter to the Air Department of the Admiralty to see if anything negative about PB could be found. Billing said he was told of the letter by someone in the department (possibly Maurice Sueter). If it existed, Billing did not use it, but he wrote afterwards that he had a photograph of it, to use should he be defeated. [13] He also, in the last days of the campaign, issued numerous leaflets that simply said: 'VOTE FOR A CLEAN FIGHTER'.

Billing also rumbled a plan by Henderson's people to keep watch on him. Allegedly, they arranged to have an observer at all his meetings, to note everything the Airman said, in the hope of capturing some major faux pas. Tipped off by Billing, Northcliffe's *Weekly Dispatch* provided full coverage of how that played out:

> 'Ever since he began his first speech on the Bull Plain in Hertford, Mr PB has been kept company by a mysterious reporter... Every word that the airman said was taken down verbatim. ... And now it has transpired that this reporter is the

---

13 In a later libel case, Billing was asked in court to produce the photograph of the letter and confessed that he could not do so, weakly claiming that he had destroyed it.

Coalition reporter, and that the Coalition is taking a very deep interest in all that the candidate says. But the airman's car is one of the fastest in the country and the Coalition reporter found it impossible always to arrive at the same time as the Candidate ... Mr PB felt so flattered at this keen curiosity of the Coalition that, out of consideration for the government note-taker and also for the public purse, he offered him a seat in his own car. He has thus saved important expenditure at a time when there was never greater need for economy in our government departments and, in addition, the Coalition is now certain of not missing a single utterance of the airman.' [14]

Building up to Polling Day

Polling day ended a 19-day campaign; Billing had started campaigning on 19 February and polling was set for Thursday 9 March. The close of nominations had produced one partial surprise in that Rolfe, the putative agriculturalist candidate, did not put himself forward even though he had issued an election address. Although never a serious contender, he would have been a colourful addition, as evidenced by his description in *The Times* that he smoked a clay pipe and 'wore a grey felt bowler hat, knee breeches, green and blue plaid stockings, and brogue shoes'.[15] Even more colourful had been his past; in 1914 he had purchased a motorcar which he proceeded to paint red, white and blue and have inscribed with the words 'Lord Clavering of Essex'. These facts emerged in his court appearance for being ejected from a local hotel for being drunk and disorderly.

Significant outside events now intervened. On Sunday 5 March, the Zeppelins returned. Thirty-six people were killed and 104 injured, mainly in Kent and Hull. As before, defensive measures were largely ineffective; it is likely one airship was damaged by anti-aircraft fire but only a single aircraft went up and it did not make contact. Inevitably, the raids received newspaper coverage in the final days before voting. On 7 March, *The Times* expressed strong dissatisfaction with the government and concluded the events could only strengthen Billing's prospects, saying of the raids: 'They have already,

---

14 *Weekly Dispatch*, 5 March 1916.
15 *The Times*, 28 February 1916.

we imagine, improved the prospects of the independent enthusiast who is standing for Parliament in East Hertfordshire against the united forces of officialdom. They will certainly exercise a considerable influence on opinion'. The same leader also referred to 'the apparent incompetence of the government against this form of attack' and echoed Billing's call for 'a single Department presided over by a strong minister of cabinet rank.' The *Daily Mirror* helpfully reminded their readers that this was: 'the fifth raid this year and the thirty-second since the start of the war'.

Then, there was a major debate in the Commons on the navy, led by Balfour. Churchill had returned briefly from his posting in France to participate and made some controversial comments, one of which could be viewed as backing PB's position. Churchill said:

> *'A great remedy against Zeppelin raids is to destroy the Zeppelins in their sheds. I cannot understand myself why all these many months, with resources far greater than those which Lord Fisher and I ever possessed, it has not been found possible to carry on the policy of raiding which, in the early days even, carried a handful of naval pilots to Cologne, Dusseldorf, and Friedrichshafen, and even to Cuxhaven itself.'*

This, too, gave publicity in the papers to Billing's arguments.

Finally, on the eve of polling, there was an air debate in the House of Lords when Lord Montagu of Beaulieu, the leading air enthusiast in the House, who had first lectured on 'Aeriel Machines and War' as early as 1910, asked whether the government would establish an Air Ministry. He informed their Lordships:

> *'It cannot be denied that the present position of our Air Service is thoroughly unsatisfactory ... We have had over this country something like twenty-five raids by Zeppelins since the commencement of the war. On none of those occasions have we been able to bring down a Zeppelin, and with the exception of part of a propeller which was said to have been found in Kent last week I think I am right in saying that there is no evidence that any German Zeppelin has been seriously damaged'.*

The government maintained that a separate ministry was unnecessary; indeed, government supporters questioned the constant clamour for 'push and go' policies, saying that they encouraged 'violent action before thinking, instead of violent thinking before action'. The message provided by the debate was not going to deflate Billing's campaign cry.

Although Henderson had sought to echo Billing's positions on air defence, he had not committed himself as strongly as Brookes had done at Mile End. Henderson argued that while steps should be taken to strengthen home defence, the issue should not be seen out of proportion, compared with the massive conflict on the western front. Lord Salisbury, the son of the former Prime Minister, as one of his supporting speakers, argued that what people wanted was a man who would look after the country as a whole and look at things in perspective – given the scale of losses abroad they 'must not think too acutely of the comparatively little things that were happening at home.'

Thus, Billing went into polling day with a simple and attractive position on a major issue while Henderson's was more complex and called for loyalty to a Coalition government that had not shaken off the aura of Asquith's 'wait and see' image. Moreover, he could not condemn Billing as holding unrealistic policies; rather, the lines of attack had to be ad hominem and with Billing, that was not easy either. The essence of the Coalition campaign was neatly summarised by the *Staffordshire Sentinel*, published on polling day itself:

> *'The fight has turned solely on the air service of the country ... Captain Brodie Henderson, the official candidate, ... insists that Britain shall be mistress of the air, and he wants many more aeroplanes and airships, more and better anti-aircraft guns, and one supreme authority in charge of air defence and offence. Even this comprehensive scheme, which is but one item in his programme, has not been sufficient to stave off opposition. Mr. Pemberton-Billing... undertakes to provide a preventive for Zeppelin raids, and to beat Germany by wonderful machines which are to be superior to anything ever seen. Details may be lacking, but the electors are asked, none the less, to return Mr. Pemberton-Billing, and all will be well.'*

Henderson had the advantages of greater resources and electioneering experience. He was also a well-established and popular local figure; in contrast, Billing had fewer campaigners and was clearly a 'carpetbagger'. However, both he and his motorcar were exotic figures that brought welcome excitement. He also had the benefit of constant 'booming' by Northcliffe's *Daily Mail*, far more extensive than the support it had provided in Mile End. Day after day, articles appeared praising him to the roof-tops while, simultaneously, damning Henderson with faint praise. As early as 25 February, the *Mail* said Billing's personality and enthusiasm were creating an extraordinary impression while they reminded readers of his opponent's divided attention saying he had appeared in khaki. The next day, the paper contrasted Billing's plucky individual campaign with the Unionists throwing everything into the constituency, including drafting in their champion election agent, Mr Gale. Henderson they maintained was taking very little part in the contest as 'the machine is doing everything for him and he does not even control the machine'. By the end of the month, the *Mail* reported there were only eight days left for Billing 'to put his commanding policy and his engaging personality' before the electorate and that, at the beginning of March, he was 'stirring up the electors of East Herts'. By contrast, it concluded that Henderson's election address must have been 'difficult to draft' given that he was forced to defend the record of the Coalition. The bias was unrelenting.

Polling Day and the result

Polling Day closed what the *Hertford Mercury and Reformer* described as: 'A short, desperately hurried and tiring campaign'. The day saw the usual election rituals and both candidates were 'early astir' in the press cliché and toured the constituency. The hours of polling had been extended to 7am to 9pm; this had been requested by Billing and was expected to result in a higher turnout among working-class voters. It was an election in which motorcars played a particularly important role, given the size of the division; as the *Mercury* said: 'It may be doubted whether in any other election the utility of the motorcar has been more fully demonstrated ... otherwise it would not have been possible to visit or call on the villages and even most of the hamlets in so short a time'.

The newspaper felt the contrast between Henderson's and Billing's vehicles neatly symbolised the difference between the two campaigns:

> 'The chief cars on either side formed about as striking a contrast as the candidates themselves. Cpt. Henderson has progressed from place to place in a handsome limousine, the very embodiment of dignity and stability; whilst Mr Pemberton-Billing has pinned his faith to a rakish-looking craft, torpedo-shaped, and extremely fast – said to be the fastest travelling car in England – and with originality apparent in every line of it.'

Henderson had more motorcars, but Billing was, nevertheless, also well provided with them (*The Daily Mail* had published almost daily appeals for vehicles to support his campaign). Billing may have made more effective use of his resources. There was a high turnout of those in Territorial Army uniforms who were brought in from Tring and Newmarket in Pemberton-Billing's cars. Obviously, the ballot was secret but many of the soldiers made it clear that they intended to return Billing's hospitality by voting for him.

Polling Day was a delightful spring day. Both Billing and Henderson toured with their respective wives; Henderson visited all of the polling stations, and his car carried a horseshoe decorated in Coalition colours. Billing, meanwhile, travelled twice round the entire area. A report from Hoddesdon noted that voters had come in from places as far apart as Salisbury Plain and London. Locally, it was commented that while window portraits of the two candidates were broadly evenly distributed, more adults, especially women (who, of course, could not vote) were wearing Henderson's colours while Billing was strongly winning the children's non-vote.

Both camps claimed to be confident of victory. Henderson announced that the voting in Ware was estimated to be two to one in his favour, but the Billing camp said they would offer very long odds in favour of the Airman. The press expected a close result. Henderson's backers were quoted as saying they expected that his local influence and the 'exceptional platform support he had received' would ensure victory. However, against that, *The Times* assessed that Billing 'had made wonderful progress, chiefly among the working classes' and particularly in the large towns.

It was recognised that Billing had the clearer, more popular, cry on the air war and, beyond that, it was suggested that he was gaining support by backing the also topical issue of the plight of conscripted married men.[16] Billing pledged to look after the 'civil interests' of married men who were called up saying 'when a man is fighting for his country he should not be troubled with thoughts of a home broken up through a lack of means to meet charges for rent, rates and other obligations.'

A stunning, shocking victory

Billing not only won, but did so with a four-figure majority:

Dec. 1910			
Rollaston	Conservative	5,594	57%
Pawle	Liberal	4,226	43%
Majority		1,368	
Electorate & Turnout		12,684	77%

9 Mar. 1916			
Pemberton-Billing	Indep.	4,590	56%
Henderson	Unionist	3,559	44%
Majority		1,031	
Electorate & Turnout		12,684	64%

The result, announced just after noon the day after the poll, was greeted with strong cheering and singing in favour of Billing. PB said: 'I have only one thing to tell you. My labours here have finished, and my labours now commence.' From the balcony of his HQ (a local hotel), he appealed to supporters: 'I want to ask you to spare what voice I have left to tell them in the House of

---

16 See chapter 6 for the by-elections which were primarily fought on this issue. Essentially, the argument was over whether the government was keeping to a pledge that, under conscription, married men would only be called up after those who were single.

Commons what has to be done'. Nevertheless, with his wife and friends, he proceeded, in a cavalcade of eight or nine motorcars, to make a victory tour of the constituency before then retiring to his bed for four days to regain his strength.

Henderson was gracious in defeat, saying: 'I hope our new member will have strength and good health to carry on his work'. He also thanked his supporters and announced that he would live to fight another day. But he never again stood for Parliament. He was knighted, in recognition of his war service, in 1919, and went on to be Vice-President and later President, of the Institute of Civil Engineers but did not pursue a political career.

The post-mortems began immediately, especially as most observers had been surprised that Billing won so easily; the result was widely described as 'sensational' and 'startling'. It was noted that East Hertfordshire had an unbroken Unionist history and, further, *The Times* summarised:

> *'It has been an electioneering axiom for generations that no independent candidate, no matter what his personality or programme might be, could win a contest without the backing of a party organisation. Mr. Stanton gave a severe shock to this comfortable theory at Merthyr last autumn. He, however, had the advantage of local associations, friendships and sympathies. It has been left to Mr. Pemberton Billing, a stranger to East Herts, a candidate without a party and all that means in the way of canvassers, speakers and conveyances, to put his foot through the whole scheme of modern political selection'.*[17]

There were some suggestions that Billing's victory was not solely due to the air question; the recruitment situation of married men (see chapter 6) and the liquor issue (see chapter 3) were both mentioned. Certainly, Billing had aligned himself in support of conscripted married men, but he did not think that had swayed the result; he also strongly rejected any notion that his position had been bolstered by the liquor interest saying that 'the liquor restrictions were never mentioned on his platform' and that 'the biggest brewers in the division were among his chief opponents'. Nor had Billing outspent his opponent;

---

17 *The Times*, 11 March 1916.

indeed, it was quite the opposite with Billing having committed £786 (£56,500 today) compared with £1,159 (£83,000 today) by Henderson.

Billing took his seat in the Commons on the Tuesday after his election and then, in a major break with convention, proceeded to make his maiden speech on the same day. He attacked the Coalition from the start, both within parliament and outside, including by participating in other by-elections (see chapters 7 and 12). He featured in numerous, dramatic, controversies throughout the war.

6.
A PRIME MINISTER'S PROMISE

Harborough, 23 March 1916
Hyde, 29 March 1916

In January 1916, conscription began. Ironically, while this brought in compulsion to join the forces for single men between 19 and 41, the primary political fall-out revolved around a furious reaction among some married men who believed that Asquith had reneged on a promise to them. Their complaints had begun to be heard towards the end of the East Hertfordshire by-election but became the dominant issue at Harborough and one of the focuses at Hyde.

The tortuous road to conscription

Compared with the great continental powers, Britain entered the war with a tiny army. Long-established mistrust of a large, standing force, based on conscription, combined with a preference to rely on the navy for the nation's defence. In August 1914, Britain's army stood at around 120,000, all volunteers. By comparison, Germany and France could, respectively, deploy 1.9 million and 1.3 million troops.

Despite this huge disparity, Britain decided both to send an expeditionary force to the continent and to continue relying on volunteers. Whilst the idea that the war was expected 'to be over by Christmas' is largely a myth, there was little conception of how all-encompassing the struggle would become;

consequently, few initially recognised the ultimate necessity for conscription, which was anathema to a Liberal government.[1]

Initial voluntary recruitment was more than adequate. Indeed, the army struggled to train and equip the surge of volunteers, whose ranks included a large number of essential workers, such as miners and skilled engineers, hitting the war economy. So high was the response in September 1914 that height and chest measurement requirements were changed to make them more restrictive. But by 1915, the rate of voluntary enlistment had declined markedly, and Unionists began demanding conscription, backed by *The Times* which opined: 'the voluntary system has limits and we are rapidly approaching them'.[2] As the true nature and likely length of the conflict became apparent it was increasingly felt that voluntary recruitment would not meet the needs, especially of Lord Kitchener at the War Office, who wanted an army of 70 divisions (although, ironically, he was a strong supporter of voluntarism as he believed conscripts made poor soldiers). The peak figure for volunteers was September 1914 with 462,901 for the month. From then on, the total never exceeded 170,000 a month and the average across 1915 fell to around 100,000 a month.

Through the summer of 1915, debate over conscription intensified. Newspapers, led by Northcliffe, demanded it while, on the opposite flank, the Independent Labour Party was opposed. A fissure within the Liberals became clearer, with Asquith unconvinced while Lloyd George and Churchill were supportive. In a critical development, on 24 August 1915, Kitchener finally came out publicly in favour and, in September, the debate intensified. Asquith remained uncertain but the Unionists, with the Lord Privy Seal, Lord Curzon, in the lead, were increasingly vocal in their demands. Against this, the TUC unanimously passed a resolution in opposition, and, at the end of the month, the Labour party also maintained that compulsion was unnecessary.

Kitchener now launched the last throw of the dice for the voluntary system. In a move supported by the Liberal government, the labour movement

---

[1] Although not to Churchill who, on 25 August, called (in Cabinet) for conscription of single men. At the same meeting, Kitchener conceded it might be necessary, but he did not publicly endorse compulsion until much later. Simon Heffer, *Staring at God* (2019).
[2] *The Times*, 6 May 1915.

and the Northcliffe newspapers, in early October Lord Derby was appointed Director General of Recruitment. He was a supporter of conscription but introduced one more big push for volunteers with what became dubbed 'the Derby scheme'. Every male of military age was to be asked either to volunteer immediately or to *attest* that he would do so if called upon later. The scheme involved a large-scale house-to-house canvass and major recruitment meetings. Derby proposed that men who attested be put into groups, based on age and marital status, with the intention that the single men would be called before the married and younger age groups before older ones. In total, there were 46 groups, 23 for each of the unmarried and married men. There was strong support for the principle that unmarried men should be called first, in recognition that they did not have dependents to support.

On 2 November, Asquith made a Commons speech which was to come back to haunt him and to play heavily in these by-elections. He said: 'The obligation of the married man to serve ought not to be enforced or held binding upon him unless and until – I hope by voluntary effort, but if it be needed in the last resort by other means – the unmarried men are dealt with.' A few days later Bonar Law asked for clarification since this appeared to suggest that no married man who had attested under the scheme would be called up until all available single men had been taken, which he felt impractical. Derby, in response, said that if insufficient unmarried came forward, the government would either release the married men from their pledge or introduce compulsion.

The entire country now recognised that if too few came forward under the Derby scheme, compulsion would follow, at least for single men. Asquith's 'pledge' to those who were married was widely used to promote the scheme and reprinted on official leaflets. Towards the end of November 1915, Derby said: 'men must come in very much larger numbers in the next three weeks if they are going to make the position of voluntary service absolutely unassailable', while the Merthyr by-election result (see chapter 2) suggested that working-class opposition to compulsion was not as great as Asquith had feared. The Derby scheme was due to close at the end of November but, in a last attempt to attract greater numbers, it was extended until 11 December.

The day after the scheme closed, *The Times* argued that many of those choosing to attest had done so in the belief that, in practice, they would not be called upon. The paper said there would be a lot of married, starred[3] and unfit who attested as they believed they would not be called but could be seen to be patriotic by putting themselves forward. (The incentives to attest included being given an armband so that people knew the wearer had done so). Regarding married men, Derby re-iterated the pledges that had been made to them. On 15 December, he said in the Lords that faith must be kept with the married men and three days later that Asquith would keep his word to them in the spirit as well as the letter.

On 20 December, the outcome of the Derby scheme was announced. Out of 5.0 million men of military age, 2.8 million had enlisted, attested or been rejected, leaving 2.2 million who had failed to do anything; in particular, over one-third of single men had not come forward. These numbers were universally considered disappointing, and Derby commented: 'the men in the married groups can only be assumed to be available if the Prime Minister's pledge to them has been redeemed by the single men attesting in such numbers as to leave only a negligible quantity unaccounted for'.[4] Immediately, the first three Derby groups (the youngest, single men) were informed they were to be called up. The next day, Asquith repeated his pledge to the married men but also called for a further one million volunteers. He had now positioned things such that conscription of single men was unavoidable.

The cabinet held multiple discussions between Christmas and New Year, but the outcome was inevitable and the Military Service Bill, or the 'Bachelors Bill' was announced on 5 January 1916. This made conscription compulsory for all single men of military age, other than those in 'starred' occupations, such as farmers, teachers and those employed in manufacturing industries which were vital to the war economy. Asquith denied that it represented general compulsion and positioned it as the redemption of his pledge to married men. The political fall-out was less dramatic than he had feared. The Home Secretary, Sir John Simon, resigned, as did the three Labour members of the Coalition government; however, by the end of the month, the Labour

---

3 Starred men were those in roles considered vital to the war effort who should not be enlisted.
4 Quoted in R J Q Adams & P P Poirier, *The Conscription Controversy in Great Britain 1900 – 1918* (1987).

representatives had returned. When the Bill was voted on, only 11 Labour and 34 Liberal MPs opposed it, and it passed on 27 January 1916.

The case of the married men

By the end of February 1916, problems emerged over the married men who had attested. The battle of Verdun began, meaning that a greater burden on the Western Front would fall on Britain, requiring yet more recruitment. *The Times* reported that attested married men were worried about the number of exemptions among unmarried men and, additionally, that while conscripts could claim to be Conscientious Objectors, those who had attested could not.

On 7 March, the youngest attested married men were called up, generating immediate controversy. The complaints were numerous. Firstly, that far too many single men were being allowed to slip through the net by being deemed 'essential workers'. It was argued that too little had been done to replace single men by married men in such roles and so free them up to serve. Also, married men disliked the tendency for employers to persuade tribunals to exempt an unmarried employee by promising that they would not come back later for further exemptions (which, of course, potentially put married men at a disadvantage). But the greatest anger was generated by Asquith now saying that he was not prepared to extend compulsion; in other words, while unmarried men were to be compelled, the same would not be true of married men. Consequently, attested married men would be called up while married men who had not come forward would be left alone. The attested married men were unpersuaded by the argument that they had expressed their willingness to serve and all that was happening was that their voluntary pledge was being redeemed. Instead, they felt duped, saying they had been led to believe that, in the event of married men being required, those who had attested would have been put in a better position than the married men who had not come forward.

A major protest movement rapidly formed. On 8 March, meetings were held in Portsmouth, Leicester and Cardiff, later followed in other cities. The attendees wanted all single men from reserved occupations, single clerks in government offices and so on, to be taken, before married men were called up; there was a strong feeling that many single men were 'hiding', having deliberately entered government/ munitions work to protect themselves. They also called either for compulsion for unattested married men before attested ones were called up or, at the least, for compulsion for all. Additionally, there was real concern about what arrangements the government intended to make to protect the financial position of married men's households. The controversy emerged at the end of Billing's successful campaign but the first substantive electoral challenge on the issue was the next by-election, at Market Harborough in Leicestershire.

HARBOROUGH – March 1916

Another rapid election

The Market Harborough MP was a Liberal, John Logan. His resignation, due to ill health (stemming from a past hunting accident), had long been expected and his proposed Liberal successor, Percy Harris, had been selected in February 1914. On 4 March, Logan announced he could no longer continue, and the writ was issued almost immediately on 7 March with nominations set for 15 March and polling, if required, on Thursday 23 March.[5]

There was immediate speculation about a contest, with both the liquor trade and the attested married men viewed as likely instigators. A mass demonstration of over 4,000 attested married men in Leicestershire on 12 March resolved to raise funds to run a candidate. The name of Charles Pearse, a local Conservative councillor, was mentioned and, despite the truce, he indicated a willingness to stand before he was pre-empted by a much bigger name: Tommy Gibson Bowles. Gibson Bowles, a veteran political figure, rushed up from London and met with the local attested married men's organisation on the morning of 14 March (the day before nominations), offering to stand in their support.[6]

Born in 1842, the illegitimate son of a former President of the Board of Trade, Gibson Bowles became a highly successful businessman, founding The Lady and Vanity Fair magazines. In a long and chequered political career, he stood for parliament 11 times, winning on four occasions. He was

---

5 There was no doubt that Parker was in poor health, but he survived until 1925.
6 Gibson Bowles was clearly keen to return to the House of Commons (having lost his seat in December 1910) since, earlier in the year, he had briefly announced he would stand in a by-election in the St.George's, Hanover Square constituency as a 'Sea candidate' although, in the end, did not do so.

never a committed party man and across his contests stood as a Conservative, Independent Conservative, Unionist Free Fooder, Free Trader (with Liberal support) and a Liberal. He was MP for King's Lynn from 1892 to 1906 as a Conservative and then, between the two 1910 elections, as a Liberal. His political migration from Unionist to Liberal was considerable. Initially, a militant opponent of Gladstonian Liberalism in the 1880 election, he was 'an anti-Liberal first and a Conservative afterwards.'[7] Yet, by 1904, he was voting in Parliament with the Liberals in support of free trade and against 'tariff reform'. This led to a dramatic election in King's Lynn in 1906 where Gibson Bowles lost his seat. The local Conservative association decided to repudiate 'Tommy' and de-selected him, choosing a pro-tariff reform candidate instead. Not being one to go quietly, Gibson Bowles also stood (as a Unionist Free Fooder). The inevitable consequence, in a highly marginal constituency, was that the Liberals won on a split vote. Yet his revenge was not complete for in the next election (January 2010) he re-appeared as the Liberal candidate and won. In his political career, he was known for two things. Firstly, he became an expert on the procedure of the House of Commons. But more important was his specialism in the sea (he was a keen yachtsman) and, particularly, international law as it affected naval warfare and blockade. This issue was to make a significant appearance in the by-election.

His opponent, Percy Harris, was an established Liberal campaigner, having previously fought in Ashford in Kent and Harrow (he had been educated at the school), significantly increasing the Liberal vote on both occasions. He was Chief Whip of the Progressive Group on London County Council. If Gibson Bowles' specialism was the sea, then Harris's was the Volunteer Training Corps, an organisation aimed at those beyond military age or others whose personal or family circumstances made it difficult to volunteer for the regular forces. Harris could claim to be the originator of the idea, having written a letter to *The Times* on 6 August 1914 first floating the concept. The authorities were ambivalent, concerned it might conflict with recruitment into the regular forces and compete for available guns; nevertheless, as the war progressed, the VTC was accepted and allocated duties such as guarding

---

7 Leonard E Naylor, *The Irrepressible Victorian* (1965).

sensitive installations, and Harris played a major role serving as its Honorary Secretary.

Gibson Bowles was another independent candidate who benefitted from the support of Northcliffe's *Daily Mail*. The journal of the professional Liberal agents noted: 'It was quite clearly understood by the man in the street that the contest was hatched in London by the same clique that tried to get Kitchener out of the War Office'.[8] Reminiscing in his autobiography, *Forty Years In and Out of Parliament*, Harris observed: 'Northcliffe was going to leave nothing to chance, and threw into the fray the whole force of the Press he controlled. The hoardings were covered with *Daily Mail* posters, 'Buy Daily Mail and vote for Bowles', and a special edition of the *Daily Mirror*[9] was published and distributed free to the electors.'[10]

In the run-up to nominations, the issue of the attested married men dominated politics. Several hundred founded a protest organisation in Manchester while a major demonstration was held at Tower Hill in London on Monday 13 March. Leaflets were distributed, advising that a resolution would be put to the meeting, proposing: 'That this meeting calls on the government to fulfil its pledge that single men who did not attest should be compulsorily attested before attested married men under Lord Derby's group scheme are called up'. Tensions were running high as it was rumoured that older married men were about to be called up at a time when speakers estimated almost one million single men had not yet joined up. The *Belfast Newsletter* reported: 'The calling of married men aged 35 has caused the indignation against the single shirkers to pass all bounds.'[11] Over two thousand attended the Tower Hill meeting and the resolution was passed unanimously.

The meeting tried to send a deputation to meet Asquith and Derby; Asquith declined to see them but an emergency pause was placed on the call-up of the outstanding married men's groups and options were investigated to reduce the number of occupations treated as 'starred'; changes which Gibson Bowles claimed were the first fruits of his decision to stand. A further Tower Hill

---

8 *Liberal Agent*, July 1916.
9 Northcliffe had sold the Mirror in 1914 to his brother, Lord Rothermere (Harold Harmsworth).
10 P Harris, *Forty Years In and Out of Parliament* (1948).
11 *Belfast Newsletter*, 13 March 1916.

meeting expressed anger at Asquith's refusal to meet with them and called on electors at Harborough to back Gibson Bowles' campaign. When Gibson Bowles arrived on the eve of nominations, he was met at the railway station by officials of the Leicestershire Attested Married Men's Protest Society. Two hours later, he was their candidate and according to the *Newcastle Journal*: 'before tea-time he had given an interview to the Press, sketched a plan of campaign, and issued his election address, while his supporters secured the Corn Exchange for his first public meeting in the evening'.[12]

His whirlwind campaign led the *Daily Mail* to claim that Gibson Bowles 'having been nominated, suddenly as if by a touch of magic, discarded about thirty of his years and became of the same age and energy as Mr Pemberton Billing.' [13] He articulated multiple attacks against the government. He maintained it was the Coalition he was standing against rather than Harris as an individual, claiming that, had Harris agreed to stand as an Independent, he would not have opposed him. Inevitably, the policy difference to which he gave most prominence was that of the attested married men. He argued they would accept 'compulsion all round' but felt the present situation did not represent the government keeping Asquith's pledge. There were too many single men 'hiding' in reserved occupations and too little had been done to think through how the households of married men were to be supported financially. He also launched a wider attack saying: 'He was beginning to be seriously alarmed by the way the Government were carrying on the war, and he could not see that the present Cabinet had done any better than its predecessor which had confessed its incompetency.' Therefore, criticism was 'more and more necessary'. He saw problems with the army and navy and in the air on the last of which he claimed to have received support for his candidacy from Lord Montagu of Beaulieu, even though the latter had just accepted appointment to the Inter-Departmental Committee on the Air Service. Montagu denied having given his support and Gibson Bowles issued an apology for having claimed it. As well as the married men's issue, Gibson Bowles argued for a more effective blockade of Germany, his specialist subject, with the press frequently referring to him as the 'Navy and Married Men's candidate'.

---

12 *Newcastle Journal*, 15 March 1916.
13 *Daily Mail*, 16 March 1916.

Blocks on the blockade

The blockade issue was complex, although viewed as straightforward by a public that recognised no valid impediment to starving Germany into submission. The government, however, did not want to alienate neutral nations. In truth, Britain had been 'hoist by its own petard'. British foreign policy had long anticipated being more likely to be neutral than a belligerent. Consequently, it had supported policies that stressed the rights of neutrals and reduced the economic warfare options of belligerents. A key example was the Declaration of London (1909) which strengthened protection for neutral shipping. The Liberal government had supported this although its attempt to bring it into law had failed when it was defeated in the House of Lords; significantly, an important contributor to the defeat was a book by Gibson Bowles, *Sea Law and Sea Power*.

Despite failing to ratify the Declaration, Britain initially behaved as if it had. Action against Germany's own merchant fleet was rapid and highly effective and during 1915, it became evident that the economic blockade was impacting the German economy and population. However, the blockade was porous due to limited action being taken against trade via neutral ships and neutral ports. Admiral Sir John Jellicoe, now Commander of the Grand Fleet, was furious with constraints placed on his blockade forces, the Dover Patrol and the Tenth Cruiser Squadron. But government felt it had to keep neutral nations like the Americans and Dutch onside since Britain's war effort was itself reliant on imports from them.

Towards the end of 1915, Parliamentary criticism surfaced of the nuanced blockade. Dissatisfied MPs complained that: 'the government's desire to avoid angering neutrals was being put above the needs of the country at war'. The government responded and on 23 February 1916 a new Ministry of Blockade was founded. This marked the beginning of a more assertive policy, but opposition continued especially when negative, confidential reports and complaints about the Foreign Office by Jellicoe were leaked. Consequently, by the time of the Harborough campaign, blockade was a prominent issue and turned into another focal point for dissatisfaction with the government's perceived lack of assertiveness. Additionally, Gibson Bowles was recognised as an expert in the area, who had led opposition to government policy. The *Daily Mirror* pushed the issue strongly, remarking that: 'Mr. Bowles is making part of his policy a call for the unhindered use of our naval power. As the man who smashed the infamous Declaration of London, Captain Bowles is sure of a sympathetic hearing.'[14] The *Sunday Mirror* continued the theme stating:

> 'The electors of Market Harborough must elect Mr Gibson Bowles by a great majority. They owe more than they know, as does the Empire, to the destroyer of the Declaration of London. Under the provisions of this extraordinary document, the great German mercantile marine would have had free and unmolested passage over the oceans of the world.'[15]

Gibson Bowles himself told electors that he had 'wearied heaven and earth' protesting against the curbing of the liberty of the Fleet while 'A Real blockade' and 'Give the Navy a Chance' were two of his campaign slogans. He put out circulars detailing the level of importation of iron ore into Germany via the North Sea and by land and, according to the press: 'holds the Government responsible for the prolongation of the war through the failure to stop the supply of iron ore for the Huns'.[16]

The married men's issue in the campaign

Support for the attested married men was claimed by both candidates, continuing the trend of a Coalition candidate arguing he was as firmly opposed to the policy of the government he was supporting as his rival. Harris protested he had been a keen proponent of the attested married men's rights well before Gibson Bowles arrived on the scene and that such men had 'just grounds of complaint'. He maintained no married men should be called up until the single men had been 'dealt with'; inevitably, he was not as aggressive in his criticism of the government as Gibson Bowles but nevertheless promised to fight the married men's corner in the House of Commons. He put forward a plan to tackle the issue and, in a specific leaflet on 'Married men and recruiting', he proposed:[17]

---

14 *Daily Mirror*, 18 March 1916.
15 *Sunday Mirror*, 19 March 1916.
16 *Aberdeen Evening Express*, 21 March 1916.
17 *Western Morning News*, 20 March 1916.

- The government should make clear which married men are now recruited and when they are wanted
- That the calling up of the groups should be spread over considerable time, each group being called separately
- That single men should only be exempted if they were engaged in skilled work that could not be undertaken by untrained married men or women
- The state should make more ample provision for married men called to the colours to enable them to meet their liabilities and keep their homes together
- Married men to be trained in the Volunteer Training Corps in their home districts and readiness to undergo such training to be taken into account on application for postponement of service

The proposal to use the Volunteer Training Corps was novel; of course, it played to Harris' strength as the acknowledged 'father' of the Corps but it was also a creative reaction to comments by Kitchener that the reason for the rush to call up the attested married men was the considerable time needed for training before they could strengthen the numbers at the Front. By suggesting that training was undertaken locally, under the auspices of the VTC, Harris raised hopes of long delays before the married men were forced to leave their homes. However elegant this solution might have been, the *Daily Mail* was having none of it and described the proposal as 'queer', claiming that his position meant that neither the 'single shirkers' nor the married men would become available to the front line.

In response, Gibson Bowles, while protesting support for the 'unfairly treated' attested married men advocated a policy of universal conscription. He argued for 'a consistent, coherent, scientific, well-considered scheme which will allow every man to know exactly where he is, what he has to do, and when he has to do it' and explained what that would entail, saying: 'I believe it will be necessary to adopt conscription of a scientific character, in which every man of military age and physical capacity, whether married or unmarried, attested or unattested, would be called to the colours.'

The policies proposed by the candidates served to blunt the protest campaign by the attested married men as a decisive electoral factor since both offered some, but not all, of what that group wanted. Harris did not address their anger at the non-attested married men being left alone, but at least by drawing more unattested single men into conscription, he was trying to find means to improve the treatment of the attested married men. By effectively promising conscription for all, Gibson Bowles was offering less relief to all potential combatants. Although his scheme would widen the pool of possible conscripts and thus make the call up of attested married men less likely in the short term, they still faced the surer medium-term prospect of being called up, as did the married who had not attested. So far as the single men were concerned, the *Daily Mail* pointed out that neither candidate was offering them solace, saying: 'The single man voter who fights shy of active military service is in a quandary to know which candidate to vote for.'

Some observers believed Harris had done enough to nullify Gibson Bowles' main point of attack while the latter, with his 'compulsion all round' cry, was not offering an attractive alternative. The *Birmingham Daily Gazette* commented about Gibson Bowles: 'Apparently, he would not oppose the conscription of all the unattested married men, a fact that those men will do well to note.' Meanwhile, the paper said of Harris' proposal of training via the VTC: 'This proposal was given a very cordial reception at a meeting of attested married men last night, and the Attested Married Men's Protest Society, which invited Mr. Bowles to try to rush the constituency, is finding it hard to vamp any arguments against it.'[18]

Further government action also took force out of the issue. News emerged of plans to reduce the list of reserved occupations and to remove protection from single men in munitions factories while the expected call-up of the second tranche of married men was put on hold, pending a review. A little later, rumours began that the government was planning policies to ameliorate the financial position of households headed by married men who had attested. Interventions from Derby and Kitchener sought to buttress the government's position. Derby protested that Asquith had never meant no married men would be called up until all single men had been taken, while Kitchener made it clear that, even if all single men were called up, the numbers needed would require married men also to be taken. Actions and arguments like these made the issue less clear-cut and powerful than the air defence cry so effectively

---

18 *Birmingham Daily Gazette*, 17 March 1916.

exploited by Billing. By 22 March, the day before polling day, the *Western Daily Press* was reporting: 'Although the agitation, against the calling up of married men until all bachelors have enlisted, continues, undoubtedly its fury has considerably abated.'

Gibson Bowles and Northcliffe face the full force of the coalition

Although the venom of the attested married men's question was waning, Coalition business managers, chastened by Billing's victory, were concerned that the outcome in Harborough could be the same. According to the *Evening Despatch* there was 'some perturbation in Ministerial circles as to the recruiting position' and that 'Mr. Gibson Bowles's candidature in the Market Harborough division is looked at askance'.[19] There was wide press speculation that another defeat was coming; according to the *Leeds Mercury*: 'In political circles the return of Mr Gibson Bowles, who is fighting the Coalition nominee on the married men's issue in the Harborough Division, will occasion no surprise, for it is recognised that he is on a very popular platform.'[20]

Consequently, significant efforts were made, and the battle was fought between Gibson Bowles' access to Northcliffe's advertising resources and the Coalition's ability to bring in external forces and to encourage local Unionists to support the truce. Harris was supported by exceptional numbers of outside speakers. So prominent was this effort that a pro-Bowles MP, Sir Arthur Markham, claimed in the Commons that the reason the administration had opposed a sitting of the House (to discuss the recruitment issue) on the Monday before polling day was that the Whips had arranged for so many MPs to travel to Harborough to campaign.

The Unionists played their part. Their Chairman, Sir Arthur Steel-Maitland, accompanied by a Liberal Whip, Geoffrey Howard, travelled up to Leicester to meet with the Conservative Association and pressurise them fully to support Harris. Following their meeting, the Association resolved: 'That this meeting decides, in the interest of the nation, to support the candidature of Mr. Percy Harris'.[21] Further Unionist support came from an even more

---

19 *Evening Despatch*, 15 March 1916.
20 *Leeds Mercury*, 18 March 1916.
21 Before the meeting, Steel-Maitland had also visited the Liberal Club for lunch with Percy Harris.

unexpected quarter. Charles Pearse, who had indicated a willingness to stand as the Attested Married Men's candidate, in a sharp volte-face, emerged to chair a Harris meeting. He said he had been informed by the Conservatives national Chief Agent that:

> 'The defeat of Mr. Percy Harris would be as much a defeat of the Conservative party as anything in this world could possibly be. It is your duty to go back to the constituency and tell the Conservatives in Harborough Division to vote and work for Mr Harris.'

How genuine his conversion was is open to debate since the Gibson Bowles supporters hit back by saying that had they been able to raise sufficient funds locally, Pearse had agreed to stand against the Coalition and that it was only due to lack of local money that they had been forced to approach a standard-bearer from London.

It was not only MPs drafted in to speak for Harris. For the first time, paid speakers, initially recruited for the Parliamentary Recruitment Committee and the War Savings Campaign, were used to support the 'official' candidate in election meetings. Letters from one of those speakers, Will Toynbee, a trade union official and Labour supporter, provide insights into the process. He told his family:

> 'Stupidly enough, but hitherto the Party whose candidate was attacked has been left to defend the seat: but, evidently, the East Herts. catastrophe has put the fear of death in the hearts of those who realise that a few losses will shake them to their fall. So, when the renowned tergiversationalist, 'Tommy' Gibson Bowles, made his mind up, supported by the Northcliffe faction, to contest this corner, the Coalition woke up. Consequently, all Parties are requisitioned to support the Coalition nominee. Hence, behold me supporting the Government! What cheers? Really, I don't see what else could be done. All the same, the irony of me being on a Government platform is really funny.'[22]

---

22 J Travers, *A Toynbee to Remember* (2013).

Toynbee was paid at a lower rate than for his recruiting and war savings efforts but was glad of the income. He also revealed: 'I hope my ministrations will help to defeat Tommy Bowles and the *Daily Mail*. Before the vote is complete, I, with a few 'selected' speakers (mark the adjective) will have left Leicester en route for Hyde Division of Lancashire, where another 'Independent' candidate is having a fling.'

Other Labour representatives put their weight behind the campaign against Gibson Bowles due to his perceived antipathy to unions. A leaflet was widely distributed, signed by officials of the hosiery, typographical and boot and shoe operative unions. It reminded readers that the previous year, the TUC had pledged itself to assist the Coalition Government in the successful prosecution of the war and that the National Labour Party Conference in January 1916 had argued that the best interests of the nation would be served by the Labour Party's representatives remaining in Government. Turning specifically to Gibson Bowles, it attacked a piece he had written in The Candid, a quarterly magazine which he founded in early 1914, demanding the repeal of the Trades Disputes Act, which had reinstated trade union immunity from claims for damages resulting from strike action. Consequently, the leaflet argued: 'We, therefore, claim that any vote given for Bowles is a vote against trades unionism'.

In addition to meetings and leafleting, the Harris campaign postered, although not on the same scale as the Independent; a late example was one stating: 'This is no time to be playing at Bowles'. In a flurry of arguments, Harris moved the debate away from the attested married men. Gibson Bowles was an obvious candidate for attacks on inconsistencies during his career. Steel-Maitland said of him:

> *'I am bound to say the Independent candidate is a politician pure and simple. In fact, he has the peculiar record in this that he ratted from the Unionist Party and he ratted from the Liberal Party and now he has the opportunity of ratting from both at once.'*

Gibson Bowles was happy to hit back, arguing: 'in defence of the rat' that 'It earns its own living, sponges off nobody, and when he is attacked he fights like a gentleman'. He went on to say that: 'To rat' is a political term for honesty, and I take it as a great compliment to be called a rat by a parasite.' In addition, when challenged by a heckler for having left both the Conservatives and the Liberals, he responded: 'I've had to leave them both because they sacrificed their principles, and I wouldn't.' The government campaign, however, also drew attention to a relatively recent statement by Bowles that everyone should back the Coalition.

Gibson Bowles had fewer supporting speakers than his opponent. Arnold White, the antisemitic advocate of British sea power, made yet another by-election appearance, arguing in support of strengthening the blockade. From Parliament, Sir Arthur Markham came to speak. He was a long-standing Liberal MP and a forceful advocate for the strongest possible prosecution of the war, hence his willingness to oppose the government. Newly-elected Pemberton-Billing had been rumoured to be coming to speak for Gibson Bowles but in the event restricted himself to sending a telegram offering: 'Sincerest wishes for your success and consequent air support.' However, a more potent and subtle telegram was received from Sir Edward Carson who, at this point, was a virtual Leader of the Opposition in the Commons. Cleverly worded, it first thanked Gibson Bowles for his contribution to halting the Declaration of London but then went on to say:

> *'I am a supporter of the present Coalition Government, and every opportunity ought in my opinion to be taken to strengthen its hands by the election to the House of Commons of men who could help by criticism to solve great international problems. No such criticism can rightly be resented when the whole country is in absolute unity as to our determination to win the war. It is, of course, for the electors to judge who is best qualified to bring about that result in the speediest manner. —Yours sincerely EDWARD CARSON'.[23]*

Gibson Bowles was also supported by the *Sunday Times* who backed opposition to the government to restore the supremacy of parliament over the Cabinet. Meanwhile, in an unsavoury attack, his campaign raised questions about Harris' ancestry. Sir Arthur Markham challenged Harris to say whether he had any relatives serving with the Austrian or German forces. Such an

---

23 *Dublin Daily Express*, 22 March 1916.

accusation was potentially fatal to his campaign. However, Harris saw off the attempt; his father had been born in Poland, but he had repudiated Austrian rule and migrated to New Zealand where he built a successful career before moving to England. It was widely felt that the Gibson Bowles team had blundered by questioning Harris' loyalty, especially as he had never disguised his connection with Poland.

Given the backing of the Northcliffe machine, much of Gibson Bowles' campaigning effort went into distributing thousands of handbills, typically calling on the electors to support 'a real blockade, an efficient air service and a square deal for married men'. There was insufficient time for canvassing, but he did his best to take his message to the electors. He took long drives across the constituency, sixty miles on one day, preceded by an outrider vigorously ringing a bell to announce his arrival to hold small, informal meetings before moving on to the next village. His campaign summary was that: 'This is an election for the freedom of the elector and the assertion of his right to speak his mind in a grave national crisis and the intimation to the government of the fact that he is 'fed up' with waiting and seeing'. In conclusion, he said the government 'must either mend its ways or end its days'. Immediately before the election, the *Daily Mirror* announced that Gibson Bowles was already promised 100 motorcars for polling day, but that he needed more and especially as many donations of petrol as possible since it was in such short supply locally.

The Coalition strikes back

By eve of poll, expectations of the result were mixed and a final twist on the attested married men's issue raised Gibson Bowles' hopes. Lord Derby in London received a protest delegation, led by the organiser of the Tower Hill mass meetings. However, his responses were considered highly disappointing as he claimed that the spirit of Asquith's pledge had been met and that he expected all men, married or not, to be prepared to serve their country. Gibson Bowles seized on the resulting disappointment, saying that the married men 'were in a more desperate position now than ever'. Rumours further circulated that the delayed call for the next Derby Groups of married men would soon be issued. Despite this, while Billing's victory in East Hertfordshire had been a major shock, in Harborough the surprise came in a widely unanticipated, substantial defeat for Gibson Bowles.[24]

Dec. 1910			
Logan	Liberal	8,192	54%
Marshall	Conservative	7,115	46%
Majority		1,077	
Electorate & Turnout		17,921	85%

23 Mar. 1916			
Harris	Liberal (Coalition).	7,826	68%
Gibson Bowles	Leicestershire Attested Married Men's Protest Society	3,711	32%
Majority		4,115	
Electorate & Turnout		19,203	60%

The Times reported that the outcome was 'received with undisguised relief in the party camps yesterday' and the *Liverpool Echo* noted that the result 'has caused great surprise in certain quarters and is a blow to the absurd section of the whimperers.'[25] Observers identified multiple reasons for the reversal of fortunes compared with East Hertfordshire, in favour of the government. Firstly, the considerably greater effort by both Coalition parties was noted. The *Western Morning News* remarked: 'It is evident that the Coalition government are anxious that their position should not be prejudiced by any further opposition and this view is supported by the efforts made at the Harborough

---

24 Although possibly not unanticipated by Gibson Bowles himself, who failed to attend either the count or the declaration of the result.
25 *Liverpool Echo*, 24 March 1916.

election to secure the return of the Coalition candidate'.[26] On a similar theme, The Times praised the Unionist contribution: 'Unionists, as other events have shown, are more punctilious about the 'party truce' than are Liberals, and Mr. Harris (a Liberal) received a good deal more support from the local Unionists than the Liberals of East Hertfordshire gave to Captain Brodie Henderson.'[27] The visit by Steel-Maitland showed willing on their part, although the Liberal Agents were equivocal in their assessment, commenting of the Conservatives that: 'Many of them came on our platforms; a few helped in other ways; some voted with us; many against; most refrained'.[28]

A second contribution was the government candidate's co-opting of his opponent's policies working better than it had against Billing. The *Western Morning News* was depressed by this, saying: 'It is noteworthy that Mr. Harris, the Coalition candidate at Harborough, has had to follow Mr. Bowles closely in his criticisms of the Government he stands to support in order to propitiate the controlling element in the constituency—the married voter.'[29] *The Times* remarked: 'The recruiting question might have proved embarrassing to a government candidate of the traditional type, but Mr. Harris tacked the married men's grievance against the government on to the official programme, and both on that question and on the question of a stronger air service, expressed himself as much in favour of 'gingering up' the Ministry as Mr. Bowles.'[30]

Although the recruiting issue was causing political heat, it lacked the clear-cut nature that could motivate electors as the Zeppelin raids had in East Herts. The evidence of the preceding elections was that insurgent candidates polled well when arguing for more aggressive prosecution of the war. Gibson Bowles announced that he was a candidate for Harborough as a protest against 'wait and see' and was looking for increased aggression. But the attested married men's issue was more complex. If Gibson Bowles wanted to maintain a 'strong' position on the war it was difficult, at the same time, to argue for delays in the recruitment of the attested married men while more was done to comb out

---

26 *Western Morning News*, 22 March 1916.
27 *The Times*, 25 March 1916.
28 *Liberal Agent*, July 1916.
29 *Western Morning News*, 25 March 1916.
30 *The Times*, 25 March 1916.

the single 'shirkers'. Consequently, he was left with supporting 'compulsion all round' such that the unattested married men would be called up alongside their attested colleagues; some attested men felt that they should be called upon after the unattested, as a reward for their patriotism, but that was not a logical position. The policy of all-round compulsion undoubtedly had its adherents, but it did not form a winning base since such a development had unattractive elements for single men, unattested married men and attested married men alike. Combined with the subtle way Harris responded, the recruitment issue was not a firm base from which to attack the Coalition. The 'air war' cry was also weaker in Harborough than in Hertford. Neither Leicester nor Harborough had suffered a raid. The nearest locations that had been hit were Loughborough, Burton, Ashby and Melton Mowbray.

Gibson Bowles was something of a 'curate's egg' as a candidate. He was a well-known figure and his main claim to fame, opposition to the Declaration of London, was popular. He was also an effective debater. However, his unbending and unrelentingly hostile attitude was not to the taste of many. The *Liverpool Daily Post* summarised this view: 'Mr. Gibson Bowles is a man whose ability commands respect, but he has not raised himself in esteem by identifying himself with all the petty criticism to which the Government is being subjected.'[31]

Finally, the support of the Northcliffe newspapers was a mixed blessing. After the result, Harris remarked: 'Bowles fought a good fight but throughout the division there was a very strong feeling of resentment against the attempt of a certain newspaper to dictate a candidate to the electorate. That fact very much helped me in the large majority I have secured.'

Harris' election was a timely boost for the government; there was relief at avoiding another defeat so soon after East Herts. and it was anticipated the Coalition would now become more confident. Whether it would provide a long-term boost for Asquith would be tested, rapidly, at the Hyde by-election (see below). For Gibson Bowles, it marked the end of a long political career. He did not stand for parliament again. In contrast, Harborough was just a parliamentary beginning for Harris. In 1918, he sided with Asquith and being denied the Coalition coupon, he lost the seat. Nevertheless, he re-appeared in

---

31 *Liverpool Daily Post*, 24 March 1916.

the House in 1922 as the MP for Bethnal Green Southwest, a seat he then held until defeated in 1945.

HYDE – March 1916

The 'hi-jacked' election

Polling day for the Cheshire seat of Hyde (29 March) was only six days after Harborough. This election was fought on two issues – the conscription controversy and the Liquor Control Board. Once again, Bottomley and Houston were involved and Houston hoped to run the campaign very much in support of the Attested Married Men. However, despite his best efforts, the campaign rapidly became as much about the restrictions on alcohol, which he considered a guaranteed losing ticket.

The election began in controversy regarding the Liberal MP who resigned. Francis Neilson had been in the United States for many months, allegedly for health reasons. Fortunately, these were not too serious, and he eventually died in 1961 at the age of 94. However, he was essentially anti-war, and rumours circulated that 'when Neilson went to the US, he said it was for health reasons but once there he embarked on a platform crusade denouncing Britain for taking part in the war.'[32] However, according to a sympathetic *Derby Daily Telegraph*: 'His views in regard to the war are not altogether in accord with the sentiment of our people as a whole. They are nearer those of a very small group in the Commons who indicate their opinions vaguely. Needless to say, he has never expressed himself against our fighting though. The message from States which suggested that he did, was altogether in error.'[33]

What is true is that, soon after the by-election, Neilson published a controversial book – *How Diplomats Make War* – that vigorously challenged the orthodoxy of sole German guilt. His arguments echoed those of the Union of Democratic Control that the country was now paying the price for 'secret diplomacy'. Overall, the Liberal hierarchy welcomed his resignation, despite it providing an uncomfortable starting position for a by-election in a marginal

---

32 For example, the *Dumfries & Galloway Standard*, 4 March 1916.
33 *Derby Daily Telegraph*, 4 March 1916.

seat; in December 1910, the Liberal majority had been 294, an increase from the majority of just 15 achieved in January 1910.

The Liberals adopted Thomas Jacobsen, the senior partner of a stationery manufacturing business located in Hyde and London. Although based in London, he was described as 'a leading figure' and 'well-known' in the constituency where he was a vice-president of the Liberal Association. His opponent was to be David Davies from Manchester, where he was the local agent of the National Trade Defence Association. Despite Davies' connection to 'the trade', the contest was initially described in the press as 'another husbands' election' and early developments revolved around the married men's issue. It was first suggested that Helsby Moss, an active leader of the Attested Married Men's Union in the north-west, would accept the Union's request to be their candidate. However, the next day, Davies met a delegation from the Union and committed to adopt its programme, thereby gaining its backing. Simultaneously, Jacobsen announced his strong support for the attested married men. He telegraphed:

> *'My sympathies are entirely with the attested married men. I emphatically support their view that all possible single men should be taken first, and married men's interests protected by the Government. Am willing to champion the cause of married men. I canvassed under the Derby scheme and expect what we canvassers were promised be carried out.'* [34]

The fact that both candidates backed the married men meant that the real area of conflict became the actions of the Control Board as well as, again, more general dissatisfaction with the conduct of the war. Houston was bitterly disappointed about this, commenting: 'unfortunately for his [Davies] prospects, however, he was the secretary of an organisation that had as its object the protection of the interests of the brewing industry.' According to Houston, the official campaign saw him as a 'trade' candidate and so began to make the running on that issue and: 'As a result, I was forced to abandon my

---

34 *Manchester Evening News*, 15 March 1916.

plan of fighting the election on the broken pledge to the married men who had attested under the Derby scheme.'[35]

Nevertheless, that did not prevent him running a lively and innovative campaign, nor did the bad weather, including snowstorms, although these did limit the degree to which Bottomley played an active part. Houston's main innovation was a daily campaign newspaper for Davies (The Daily Paper), for which he received congratulations from Northcliffe himself. It was to appear for nine successive days, excluding Sunday.

Whilst Houston felt the link to 'the trade' cost his candidate, the Liberal campaign was impressed by the resources that the brewers deployed. According to *Liberal Agent* (July 1916): 'from the first day of the contest it was evident that all the tricks known to the trade would be used to defeat our man,' The journal highlighted the 'lavish display' of posters and the daily newspaper. Its final summary commented: 'The liquor trade made special efforts, and on polling day sent in large drafts of publicans from a huge area around Hyde. It can readily be imagined what effect the presence of a thousand of these gentlemen had in one division.'

Neilson's resignation was announced in early March 1916 and the writ was issued on 13 March with polling day set for 29 March. The first edition of Houston's campaign newspaper appeared on Monday 20 March. The lead story stressed support for the Attested Married Men. However, sizeable space was given to exploiting the controversy regarding the previous MP. Houston asked whether the reasons for his resignation related to his 'anti-war attitude and the belittling and bespattering of his country's actions' and whether the Liberal Association approved of 'his anti-war sentiments and his pro-German tirades against this country?'

The paper also attacked the Control Board, fully supported Pemberton-Billing's Air Policy and demanded a more active pursuit of the war generally, including air reprisals and calls for Empire preference in post-war trade policy. An array of speakers coming to support Davies were announced. These included Pemberton-Billing (although, in fact, he sent a message saying that his absence abroad meant he could not visit in person) and Ben Tillett (see chapter 11). The next edition made the patriotic case for opposition, called

---

35 Quotations from H J Houston, *The Real Horatio Bottomley* (1923).

on voters to send Davies to Parliament to support Pemberton-Billing and attacked the Control Board. It asked: 'What is better for the country – healthy opposition when called for or dog-like submission? In support of Pemberton-Billing it demanded action to 'put an end to the murderous attacks of the German Zepps on our defenceless women and children' and policies to carry the war into the enemy's territory.

The salvoes against the Control Board echoed those from earlier by-elections. They described the drink restrictions as a scapegoat for the government's failure to prepare for war and claimed that what had been originally presented as limited powers in a few areas had been transformed into 'teetotal fanaticism'. The paper complained: 'If you ILLTREAT your wife you are fined five shillings or seven days. If you TREAT her you are fined £100 and six months in prison!'

The *Daily Paper* employed popular press techniques and aimed to entertain. By Thursday, 23 March, it was pulling no punches. It quoted Davies: 'Unless lawyers, Jews and Quakers were cleared out of the Cabinet and the conduct of the war left in the hands of soldiers and sailors it would never be brought to a conclusion.' Trying to paint the Liberal candidate as insufficiently anti-German, it attacked what it viewed as his soft policy on commercial links with Germany by stressing: 'think of the Hun-dogs who murder women and children, even Red Cross nurses and infants at their mothers' breasts'.

By the final edition of the newspaper, Davies was majoring on the combined themes of attacking the government for its poor conduct of the war and opposing the drink policy. He blamed the Liberals for the country not being ready for war, saying they had opposed conscription and always opposed funds for the army and navy. He also continued attacks on the local Liberal association, arguing they were not committed to the war, and on his opponent with the suspiciously non-English surname [Jacobsen], asking: 'We are at war. Are there no full-bloodied Englishmen left in England?'

In his campaign, Jacobsen struggled against this populist attack. An initial concern was whether local Conservatives would abide by the truce. There was some call, motivated by dissatisfaction with the attitudes and behaviour of the previous Liberal MP, that the Unionists' prospective candidate, Major James Knott, should be recalled from the Western Front where he was serving in order to stand. Davies made it clear that, were Knott to do so, he would immediately withdraw. This died away with the Chairman of the Conservative Association stating: 'I do not for an instant think that Major Knott would care to leave the trenches at the present time to contest an election.'[36] However, there was no clear Unionist endorsement of the Liberal candidate, with their Chairman telling the *Manchester Evening News:* 'We have not considered the question of adopting Mr. Jacobsen as a Coalition candidate. No invitation to support him has been considered or even received from the Liberals.'[37] However, by 20 March, Knott had made it clear he would not leave his military duties and the Conservative Association, strongly encouraged by the party nationally, announced their full support for Jacobsen. Labour, despite having a firm base in the constituency, abided by the truce from the beginning.

When Jacobsen's election address was published it confirmed there was very little difference between his policy on the Attested Married Men and that of Davies. However, he took a fundamentally different position on the drink question. Not mincing his words, Jacobsen stated: 'I think the action of the Liquor Control Board and the steps they have taken are entirely in the interests of the people of this country and have been necessitated by the terrible crisis we are passing through.'

Davies advertised an array of 'exotic' speakers. One of these was an officer who had served on HMS Baralong which was a Royal Navy Q ship (Disguised but armed merchant ships used to tackle German submarines) which in August 2015 sank a German U-boat (U.27). Several of the German crew managed to board the merchant vessel they had intended to attack whose own crew had abandoned ship. However, the crew of Royal Marines on board the Baralong were ordered to shoot all the German survivors, fearing they might seize armaments or even scuttle the ship. All survivors in the water, including the U-boat captain, were also killed. This ruthless approach possibly stemmed from outrage at the earlier sinking by a German U Boat of the liner, the Lusitania, on 7 May 1915. That sinking occurred just off the coast of Ireland, caused 1,197 deaths and resulted in huge international controversy (and riots and attacks on individuals in Liverpool, the Lusitania's home port). In any event, it is claimed that the Baralong's commanding officer had

---

36 *Manchester Evening News*, 17 March 1916.
37 Ibid.

been told by the Admiralty that: 'it was most undesirable to take any enemy submarine prisoners.' Certainly, he was not disciplined for what happened but, rather, awarded the DSO for the sinking of U27. The following month, September 1915, the Baralong sank another submarine, U.41, in a further controversial incident; allegedly, it sank the U-boat with gunfire then returned and deliberately ran down a lifeboat containing two German survivors. The Germans were to condemn the Baralong incidents as 'war crimes' but the Davies' campaign clearly saw association with them as a positive.

Meanwhile, Jacobsen was distancing himself from the retiring member. Challenged about the Liberal Association having passed a vote of thanks to Neilsen, Jacobsen stated: 'I have nothing whatever to do with that resolution. I was not a party to it, and while I do not question the discretion of the Liberal Association, I must say I do not agree with it.'[38] By nomination day, it was clear that the party truce would hold as Jacobsen was unopposed by Conservative and Labour. The Independent Labour Party, which was strong in the Division, eventually argued for abstention, a move which assisted Jacobsen as ILP supporters might well have voted for Davies. Additionally, Redmond called on Irish voters to support Jacobsen.

The short campaign attracted limited local interest. The Attested Married Men issue rapidly disappeared; few felt that the election was really justified and attendance at meetings was poor. Houston did his best to overcome his candidate's organisational weaknesses. The Manchester Evening News reported: 'Up to the present ... in the Market Place at Hyde ... it has been no uncommon thing to see a strident-voiced champion of the 'trade' haranguing in the bleakest of weather to three or four women and a small boy on the evils of the Liquor Control Order, but a fair has now commandeered the Market Place, and a more attractive entertainment is thus provided.'[39]

Jacobsen was returned but the result was closer than anticipated with over 3,000 supporting Davies. This was interpreted as reflecting general dissatisfaction with the government's handling of the war rather than protest about the Control Board or the treatment of the Attested Married Men. Certainly, the military news remained bleak; the Germans had renewed their

---

38 *Manchester Evening News*, 21 March 1916.
39 *Manchester Evening News*, 23 March 1916.

attacks on the French at Verdun while the British had suffered a significant reverse at Dujaila in their ill-fated attempts to relieve the force trapped at Kut (see chapter 7 for more details on this Mesopotamian military disaster).

Dec. 1910			
Neilsen	Liberal	5,562	51%
Smith	Conservative	5,268	49%
Majority		294	
Electorate & Turnout		12,169	89%

29 Mar. 1916			
Jacobsen	Liberal	4,089	56%
Davies	Indep.	3,215	44%
Majority		874	
Electorate & Turnout		13,349	55%

Davies did not fight another parliamentary election. Jacobsen gained minor office in 1917 as Parliamentary Secretary to the Minister of Shipping. However, he was never successful again in parliamentary elections. He was defeated for Stalybridge & Hyde in 1918 and in each of the 1923 and 1929 general elections. James Knott, who had declined to come back from the front to stand for the Unionists was to be killed on active service, later in the year.

7.
BILLING'S FIRST DOG FIGHTS

Wimbledon, 19 April 1916
Tewkesbury, 16 May 1916

Noel Pemberton Billing took his Commons seat on 14 March 1916, the Tuesday after his election and, against convention, made his maiden speech the same day. He attacked government conduct of the war from the start:

> *'Eighteen months ago, when the material at the disposal of the Royal Naval Air Service was something like one-twentieth of what it is to-day, we succeeded in raiding Zeppelin bases and carrying the air war into the enemy's country ... For the first six months of this war our Air Service was rich in leadership and poor in material. During the last six months we have been somewhat richer in material, but infinitely poorer in leadership ... I do ask the right hon. Gentleman the First Lord of the Admiralty to insist, not in six months' time, not in six weeks' time, but, if necessary, in six minutes' time, that the material which is now waiting shall be used, and that the bombs which are now being stored and which are due for delivery in many places in Germany shall be delivered forthwith'.*[1]

The Times approved: 'The House laughed and cheered, well pleased with Mr. Billing's first appearance in debate.'[2] For the government, this was the first of

---

1 Hansard: https://api.parliament.uk/historic-hansard/commons/1916/mar/14/mr-tennants-statement.
2 *The Times*, 15 March 1916.

innumerable irritations caused by the Air Man. This chapter reviews Billing's antics during the rest of 1916. He was to ruffle feathers in the Commons, begin to create a national organisation, and intervene in other by-elections.

An accusation of murder

Just over one week later, Pemberton-Billing made a less well-received intervention. On 22 March 1916, he denounced the quality of aeroplanes ordered by the Royal Flying Corp saying they were known at the front as 'Fokker fodder'. He claimed that because of the poor quality of British machines, numerous RFC officers had been 'murdered rather than killed'. *The Times* noted: 'The speech created a great sensation, and it was heard with expressions of impatience. Later two or three members were seen to be in angry expostulation with Billing.'[3] Fortunately, this did not extend as far as fisticuffs – it did later. Billing refused to withdraw the accusation and pledged he would bring substantiating evidence before the House. He then appealed to contacts to help him compile a list of flying casualties proving his point and, taking the campaign outside Westminster, repeated his claims at a large meeting at the Cannon Street Hotel in London. Then, in the Commons on 28 March, he read out a letter from the father of a recently killed airman, detailing all the problems he had experienced with 'dud' aeroplanes, and described other incidents. He particularly condemned the aeroplanes being used from the Royal Aircraft Factory which he said were grossly inferior to the Fokkers. Surprisingly, the government undertook to conduct an enquiry into his allegations. This took time to establish during which Billing continued his pressure. Every week, he asked parliamentary questions related to the air campaign while, outside Parliament, he called the first meeting of his new 'Imperial Air Convention', held at the Royal Albert Hall and attended by almost 5,000 people; he was tapping a rich seam of public disquiet.

The Committee of Enquiry eventually met on 16 May, but its terms of reference only covered the Royal Flying Corps, part of the Army, and excluded the Royal Naval Air Service, belonging to the Royal Navy. Pemberton Billing found this unacceptable and so boycotted the opening sessions but, inevitably, he was attacked for doing so and eventually had to appear. He was

---

3 *The Times*, 23 March 1916.

to be, according to Charles Grey, the founding editor of the weekly magazine, *The Aeroplane*, who also testified, 'the star turn', providing a list of airmen who had died, Billing claimed, due to inadequate equipment.[4] An interim report in September 1916, in Grey's and Billing's opinion, whitewashed the service against Billing's claims of 'murder'. The final report emerged between Christmas and New Year and this, at least, recommended the formation of a more powerful Air Board, representing some progress in Billing's direction. He continued asking innumerable questions but made little parliamentary headway. However, he also carried on being active across the country, as did the German Zeppelins and aircraft.

The Zeppelins keep coming

Billing remained a prominent critic as German air attacks continued. In 1916, after his election, there were 28 raids, 8 by aircraft and 20 by Zeppelins. Thirteen of the raids resulted in fatalities, totalling 209 deaths. Several themes emerged. Firstly, although the concentration was on the east coast, now Scotland and the west were vulnerable too; this was becoming a national issue. Secondly, the number of casualties was relatively low and attacks were limited during the summer, due to there being insufficient hours of darkness for safe long-distance Zeppelin raids. Thirdly, London was not hit very hard during 1916, although the fear of attack remained. Finally, at this stage, sorties by German aeroplanes were less common and less damaging than those by Zeppelin although (as frequently predicted by Pemberton-Billing) that was to change.

In addition to his persistent questions in the House, Billing also took part in by-elections, this time as an elected MP supporting independent anti-Coalition candidates. Harborough (23 March) and Hyde (29 March) came too quickly (see chapter 6) but he participated in the next two contested by-elections, at Wimbledon (19 April) and Tewkesbury (16 May).

---

4 C G Grey, *A history of the Air Ministry* (1940).

WIMBLEDON – April 1916

Once bitten, twice shy

The government had learned from East Hertfordshire and tried to sneak through a vacancy in Wimbledon with insufficient time for opposition to gather. As late as 3 April, the sitting member, Henry Chaplin, having failed to attend his constituency party's AGM nevertheless sent apologies saying he was prevented from joining the meeting on doctor's orders but 'would be back among them shortly'. He was now in his mid-seventies and a replacement candidate, Sir Stuart Coats[5], had been selected in August 1914. But out of the blue a peerage was announced for Chaplin on 10 April with nominations for the resulting by-election timetabled for just two days later and polling day set for 19 April, thereby giving just over one week for a 'campaign'.[6] The local Liberals supported the political truce and so were unconcerned and the Unionists were entirely ready and formally adopted Sir Stuart Coats on the day the vacancy was declared. The *Aberdeen Press* smelt a rat, saying: 'Mr Chaplin's Peerage was kept a great secret up to the last minute, so that all the Coalition election arrangements could be completed before an opponent could get time to prepare.'[7]

Yet within 48 hours, there was a small queue of non-government candidates expressing interest. The first names were William Boosey, referred to as 'a member of the well-known firm of music publishers, and a man who has recently taken a strong line in public affairs, who has been approached by a number of electors with a view to his standing as independent candidate' and Robert Walker Dixon, who agreed to fight on behalf of the London branch of the National Union of Attested Married Men. Then, a higher calibre non-government candidate emerged. The *Dundee Courier* reported:

---

5 Coats had three unsuccessful parliamentary campaigns behind him in Morpeth (1906) and then Deptford (1910, twice).
6 Towards the end of the campaign, there were press rumours that the peerage was offered directly on the initiative of the King and that government business managers would have preferred not to have to deal with parliamentary vacancies at this time, fearing possible defeat.
7 *Aberdeen Press*, 12 April 1916.

> 'The discreditable endeavour of the Government organisers to evade public opinion in the Wimbledon Division of Surrey by rushing the election is not (says the Daily Mail), after all, to succeed. Last night, Mr Kennedy Jones, who has achieved high distinction as a journalist and man of business and has done a great deal of useful work at the headquarters of the British Red Cross ... announced his intention of submitting himself to the electors as an independent candidate for the vigorous and efficient organisation of the war'.[8]

Kennedy Jones had a massively successful business career in newspapers behind him, and his decision meant that the by-election was to be contested by two Scottish millionaires. In his early fifties, Jones was a journalist by training. He had purchased a share in the *Evening News* and quickly arranged the sale of the paper to Northcliffe, whose Business Manager he became. Jones was the driving force behind the establishment and unprecedented success of the *Daily Mail*. Additionally, he became Chairman of the very profitable Waring & Gillow company, the furniture manufacturers, until retiring in 1914. His putative campaign received immediate boosts when the London branch of the Union of Attested Married Men decided to support him rather than nominate Dixon and then Boosey abandoned his potential candidacy and supported Jones, even becoming a platform speaker for him. An organiser to his core, the announcement of Jones's campaign included an appeal for 300 clerks and typewriters.

A fevered week of campaigning

Jones' first meeting took place immediately and while the Northcliffe press was fully behind him, he received harsh notices from newspapers backing the government. The *Birmingham Daily Gazette* reported:

> 'Heartened by a breezy invitation to enter and listen to Mr. Kennedy Jones, the new candidate for Wimbledon, the 'Gazette' representative walked up into a small hall, which could have accommodated comfortably three times as many people as were already inside. K. J. proved a very modest sort of hustler, with none of the dash and breeziness of his friend 'P-B.' He did a singularly unexpected

---

8 *Dundee Courier*, 12 April 1916.

thing for a candidate out on a livening campaign— he read his speech laboriously from a printed proof-slip.'[9]

The *Daily Mail* had a different view. It referred to Jones' 'fine start', describing the same speech as 'so eloquent and earnest' that 'all who heard it recognised that a new power had appeared in public affairs.'[10]

The *Gazette* predicted that even with Billing's help, Jones 'has the task of his life if he expects seriously to impress his personality upon the huge and straggling constituency of Wimbledon which includes places as far apart as Mitcham, Caterham, Merton and Whyte-Leaf.' Undeterred, Jones issued his election address which stated:

> 'Under the guise of the party truce the Government have attempted to play on you a political trick. By rushing this election, they are trying to rob you of your right of electing your Member of Parliament. It is because I believe you resent this attempt on the part of the Government to obtain a dummy vote of confidence that I have come forward as an independent candidate. If you return me to the House of Commons, I shall regard it as my duty to you and the nation to insist upon a more vigorous prosecution of the War in all its phases. To that end, I am a keen supporter of the demand for an efficient Air Service, and the appointment of an Air Minister, and I would do what I could to aid Mr. Pemberton Billing, M.P., in his splendid campaign for such an offensive force as will put an end to the long series of hostile air raids over this country.'

He also bitterly noted that the government: 'apparently believed in quick elections and long wars.' The *Daily Mail* was, of course, on side, calling his effort 'plucky', and condemned the fastest-ever election campaign in a county seat. Jones expressed disgust at the attempt to 'rush' the election, noting that Coats' election address had been at the printers' three days before the public announcement of Chaplin's resignation.

As in Hertford, the Coalition candidate issued an entirely conventional election address. In it, Coats addressed the twin current issues, air defence

---

9 *Birmingham Daily Gazette*, 14 April 1916.
10 *Daily Mail*, 14 April 1916.

and the conscription of attested married men. However, he only moved partly towards the positions of his opponent. On air defence, Coats agreed action was required but that, nevertheless, it was of a lower priority than seeking absolute victory through the strength of the British navy and army. He told electors:

> *'The needs of our Navy and Army, of course, come first. Then the food supplies and the commerce of the nation must be adequately protected. Afterwards, when these are as far as possible secured, those who are of the civilian population have every claim that all protection which can be extended to them in the way of defence against hostile raids, whether by air or by sea, shall be provided... The problems connected with aerial defence have advanced distinctly toward solution, but a great deal still remains to be done, and I urgently appeal for a strong and intelligent policy to be adopted and persistently followed.'*[11]

The Globe commented: 'The contest will probably be one of the shortest and sharpest on record. Mr. Jones has a big task. For one thing the constituency is one of the most extensive in the country;[12] for another it is essentially Conservative.'[13] The Coats' campaign tried, disingenuously, to claim complaints about a rushed election were 'sheer bunkum'. Its campaign chairman wrote to *The Times* saying that 'diligent enquiries' had failed to find evidence of any opposition candidate wanting to come forward but that, had he known of Jones' intentions he would: 'for the sake of old friendship, have done my best to secure for him a fair run for his money, and for the exposition of his views, which, I am sure, would be both refreshing and original.' As a sop, he said that Coats would ask the returning officer for an extension of polling hours to 7am to 9pm but then closed by commenting:

---

11 Coats' election address available at University of Bristol library, Special Collections.
12 Although named Wimbledon, the constituency was large in terms of numbers of electors (34,719, the second greatest in the country) and covered a sizeable area in addition to Wimbledon itself.
13 *The Globe*, 14 April 1916.

> 'I hope Mr Kennedy Jones will accept this in the contrite spirit in which it is offered, and as the best atonement we can make for daring to support greatly a National Government whom he prefers to discredit in the eyes of our Allies, and other nations, in the middle of a life-and-death struggle.'

Despite the brickbats, the move to extend polling hours was important in a large commuter constituency.

As in East Hertfordshire, the campaign matched an effective and well-prepared Coalition machine against a hyper-active, talented, independent. The Unionists and Liberals were cooperating well together, reprising their effective collaboration under the Derby recruitment scheme and the Unionists, especially, poured resources into the seat. The *Conservative Agents Journal* subsequently reported that 35 agents from London and the Home Counties had joined the team.[14] Indeed, the Coalition campaign was leaving nothing undone; despite the shortness of the campaign and the sheer scale of the constituency, they mounted an extensive canvass. *The Times* reported that they had 800 workers in the field, aiming to achieve a complete canvass in under a week. The *Daily Mail* stated that every hotel in the division was full of party officials brought in from outside. It was also noted that a 'platoon' of MPs and other speakers were drafted in, including MPs as diverse as Sir George Cave, the Solicitor-General and MP for nearby Kingston, and Will Crooks, the MP for Woolwich and a leading member of the 'patriotic wing' of the labour movement. A vast number of meetings were arranged including twenty open-air meetings on a single day and then twenty-five the next, in addition to major indoor ones.

Kennedy Jones also organised numerous meetings including novelties, such as addressing groups of working men as they gathered for early morning trains. But he relied more on his printer and election stunts than did Coats. As well as his election address, he circulated copies of his first campaign speech widely. Another of his numerous handbills stated: 'K is for Kitchener. J is for Joffre. KJ is for Wimbledon'. Additionally, he made great use of posters, attracting significant attention. They were so ubiquitous that the *Birmingham Daily News* remarked:

---

14 *Conservative Agents' Journal* (July 1916).

> 'It is not merely the battle of the billposter; it is assault by advertisement; and, though Mr. Jones bitterly complains in print that the contest is being rushed, most privately replied that the cost of advertising alone would exceed his election expenses, as allowed by law, if it were prolonged even a very few days beyond the present mid-week.'

One Jones poster warned voters to be wary of the party truce which, it claimed, had resulted in: 'the shortage of munitions, the blunders of Gallipoli, the Mesopotamian 'crime', the 'blockade' which is not a blockade and the recruiting failure.' A second said: 'The Coalition needs critics not supporters' while a third exhorted: 'Don't put a dummy gun into Parliament'. Coats responded with posters of his own, but without the volume achieved by Jones. Among the Coats versions were: 'Vote for Coats, the Businessman'; 'Munitions for Men at the Front—a 10,000 majority for Coats' and 'Wimbledon does not want a whimperer'.

Jones ran a whole theme, built around the word 'dummy'. It had its genesis in late March, when an MP alleged that a dummy gun, guarded by soldiers, had been sent to an east coast location subjected to Zeppelin attack. Then, Pemberton Billing picked up the story and asked in the Commons whether it was true that a wooden gun had been erected on the roof of a foundry to reassure residents. The government did not deny it but said it was a *ruse de guerre*, aimed at misleading the enemy, not the public. The story took off, even in Germany, where their commentators referred to it as a 'tranquilising cannon'. Kennedy Jones claimed that some influential people on the east coast had demanded protection and that, in response, the War Office had ordered a wooden gun and sent it with a guard of 40 soldiers. The next night, in repeating the tale, Jones asked his audience whether they knew the full story of the dummy gun. A heckler called out 'Made in Germany' but Jones responded: 'They never make dummy guns in Germany. They only make them in the Coalition government'. He continued the 'dummy' theme to highlight more failures, saying: 'When Mr. Pemberton-Billing was returned for East Herts they appointed a dummy Air Committee. Who has called it a dummy Committee? Lord Montagu, who was put on it and who resigned because he found it out.'[15] Finally, Jones had a dummy gun placed outside his main committee room on the last day of campaigning, attracting further press coverage, including a large photograph in the polling day edition of the *Daily Mirror*. Montagu's resignation was also likely to bolster Jones' prospects. He stated that he resigned because the Joint Air Committee was 'lulling the public into a sense of false security' and he was supported by the Bishop of Birmingham who wrote: 'for a long time there was culpable negligence and quite unnecessary ignorance in this country on the question of air defence.'

The Northcliffe media fully supported Jones, and the Conservative Agents' Journal noted that he was: 'backed every morning by the *Daily Mail* and in the evening by the *Evening News*, two of the most widely circulated and popular newspapers in London.' Against this, Coats was endorsing a predominantly Liberal government when many natural, Unionist, supporters were minded to show their dissatisfaction at 'wait and see'[16] by voting for a 'push and go' candidate.

According to the *Western Morning News*: 'Wimbledon shares in a very large measure the vague feeling that the government would be all the better for 'gingering' and Mr Kennedy Jones' audacious raid, backed up by Mr Pemberton Billing in his torpedo-shaped motorcar, is calculated to appeal to the spirit of the electors.'[17] Jones was gathering to his favour all the discontents against the government. Air defence, bolstered by Billing's extensive participation, was the main part, although its impact was reduced as there were no Zeppelin attacks during the campaign. But concern about the attested married men, residual liquor protests and discontent regarding 'wait and see' generally – when it came to fighting the war overall and deciding on conscription in particular – all played their part. In his speeches and literature, Jones promoted a litany of policies. He called for the establishment of an air ministry, a tightening of the blockade on Germany and, in response to the worries of the attested married

---

15 *Surrey Mirror*, 18 April 1916.
16 The phrase, 'wait and see' had been indelibly linked to Asquith after he had used it multiple times when answering questions in the Commons in 1910. Now, it was viewed as appropriate shorthand for the perceived failures of his government to pursue the war vigorously.
17 *Western Morning News*, 17 April 1916.

men, a call for equal military service for all of military age and 'consideration for married men's homes.'

But the theme tying together Jones' appeal was the contrast between the indecent speed of the election and the continuing 'wait and see' fudge. In a harsh attack on Coats, he argued 'we have dummy guns and dummy committees; we don't want another dummy member of parliament.' He was especially aggrieved by the sharp tactics over timing (the *Daily Mail* consistently referred to Wimbledon as the 'trick election') and he noted: 'If the government were as eager to get on with the war as it is to get on with the Wimbledon election, much of the criticism I shall offer would have been unnecessary.'

Jones claimed that the government only acted when it faced criticism and that, therefore, supporting him was the patriotic thing to do. To back this up, he took extreme positions stating: 'there is only one thing I want to do and that is to starve and kill Germans ... to exterminate the brood.' Building on this, he sought to bring to his side all malcontents, saying: 'If you are satisfied that the Coalition government has done everything for the safety of the nation you will vote for Sir Stuart Coats. If you are not satisfied, you will vote for me.'

Billing arrived on the Saturday and stayed actively involved throughout the brief campaign. Coats hit out at him, using the same attack as previously: 'If Mr Billing was such a wonderful airman, he could be much better employed than spouting round the theatres in Wimbledon on a Sunday afternoon.' In a speech on the Saturday, Billing focused on Coats' party-political weak point by arguing that Asquith's position was as strong in the Coalition government as it had ever been when the Liberals were ruling alone. However, it was his speech (and that of Jones) on the Sunday evening that was given the most effusive write-up by the Northcliffe press which claimed that the mass meeting at the Wimbledon Theatre had been a dramatic one that would secure victory for Jones. According to the *Daily Mirror*: 'Neither Mr Kennedy Jones nor Mr. Pemberton Billing had ever spoken with such force, fervour or simple direct eloquence.' In his speech, Billing again argued for a powerful Air Board and claimed that producing 100,000 aeroplanes was nothing, saying he could give the government a price for them tomorrow and a date to deliver them. He further said that a hundred thousand pilots were also nothing and he could teach a man to fly quicker than to drive a taxicab. Speaking about the Commons, he claimed:

> 'I told them what they didn't know and didn't want to know. I'm sick, I'm tired and I'm bored with the men who sit at Westminster .... I was told I could do nothing. It is because I found what one man could do, even if alone, that I am asking you to send Mr. Kennedy Jones to help me.'

Billing was speaking again on the Monday evening, now calling for Lloyd George's resignation as Minister of Munitions unless war policy and effort were immediately strengthened. Finally, on the eve of poll, he called on voters to return Jones 'to help him in his rather lonesome job'.

There was one final twist, two days before polling. A leading Conservative, who had signed one of Coats' nomination papers, stated he would now be supporting Jones. Frank Rosher was a ward Chairman and a member of the Wimbledon Conservative Executive. In a resignation letter, he said due to the nature of Mr. Kennedy Jones's candidature he had decided to support him, because he was convinced that the present policy of the Coalition endangered 'that absolute and crushing victory anything short of which will be equivalent to defeat.' In another twist, Jones claimed that Coats had told him, privately, that he was also dissatisfied with the government's performance, a suggestion which Coats strongly repudiated.

One campaign aspect was less intense than hoped, certainly by the Coalition forces. They noted a considerable shortage of motorcars, vitally important when it was estimated up to 40 per cent of the register had 'removed' out of the constituency. The *Conservative Agents' Journal* post-mortem gave reasons for the shortage: many people had either disposed of their motorcars or laid them up owing to the increase in duties and price of petrol; across London there were placards everywhere calling on people not to use a motorcar for pleasure. Further, an extra tax of sixpence had been imposed on every gallon of petrol so that to run a car on polling day would mean about three guineas for oil and petrol. Yet the need for motorcars was 'increased a hundred-fold' owing to the large number of removals. Partially in response, the *Daily Mail* made the plea that it didn't have to be large cars that were provided; motorcycles with side cars would be fine.

A close-run thing

By polling day, both campaigns were confident. Jones had achieved substantial impact in the limited time available, aided by Northcliffe's press coverage. His backing was thought particularly strong among working-class voters but, also, from Conservatives dissatisfied with the Liberal Asquith. Against that, Wimbledon was a staunchly Unionist area, enhanced now by support from the Liberals. When the result was announced, local political professionals were shocked by how close Jones came to defeating the Coalition candidate and almost universally, the result was interpreted as reflecting widespread dissatisfaction with government lethargy.

Dec. 1910			
Chaplin	Conservative	Unopposed	
Electorate		27,810	

19 Apr. 1916			
Coats	Conservative	8,970	56%
Jones	Indep.	7,159	44%
Majority		1,811	
Electorate & Turnout		35,063	46%

The general assessment of the outcome was well summed up by the *Dundee Courier*:

> 'The Coalition Government is being weighed in the balance. East Herts, by returning Mr Pemberton Billing, showed that it has been found wanting. And now Wimbledon has given a distinct warning. It cannot be claimed that the return of Sir Stuart Coats is a victory for the Government. Does not the fact that out of 16,129 electors, 7,159 voted against the Government afford convincing proof of public dissatisfaction with the 'wait and see' policy? The result of the election is

all the more significant when it is remembered that seven days before the polling Mr Kennedy Jones was unknown in the constituency.[18]

Jones blamed the speed of the contest for his failure to win, saying: 'It was really Mr Asquith with the adroitness of the sharp attorney who prevented me from winning Wimbledon.' Coats' own election committee chairman acknowledged 'it was a marvel we won' as he recognised that 'old-time Unionists were dissatisfied with Asquith's 'wait and see'. He predicted that no seat would now be safe unless the government changed its ways. Jones was furious that the Unionists had been arguing that everyone should be backing the government only now to acknowledge that the very changes he had been calling for were necessary, saying: 'Having won the dirty little game of political shove ha'penny ... he admits what he denied last week about the need for real action.' Jones also claimed that Coats had only won because of strong allegiance from the 5,000-strong Catholic electorate 'by virtue of his high position in the household of the Pope.' He was a 'Private Chamberlain of Sword and Cape' in the papal household, one of the top positions open to laymen in the church.

The expenditure in Wimbledon was enormous (reflecting the size of the electorate), with Coats reporting £2,657 (equivalent to £190,000 today) and Jones, £2,939 (equivalent to £210,000). Coats remained the Wimbledon MP until the 1918 election when he switched to East Surrey which he then represented until standing down in 1922. He remained a backbencher. Jones was not far behind him in entering the Commons, remarkably being chosen as the Unionist Coalition candidate in Hornsey, north London, in December 1916; he was elected unopposed. He worked for the Ministry of Food in 1917 and held the seat, again unopposed, in the 1918 general election. He died of pneumonia in October 1921, aged 56.

---

18 *Dundee Courier*, 21 April 1916.

TEWKESBURY – May 1916

On to the west country

Billing's next involvement was the Tewkesbury by-election, held on 16 May. This was a very different scenario; it was born of tragic events for the dominant political family of Gloucestershire and proved much less welcoming terrain. The need for an election became public on 27 April when the death was announced of the sitting MP, Michael Hicks-Beach. He had been on active service in Egypt and died of wounds, a little less than two months after the death by typhoid, also in Egypt, of his wife. Hicks-Beach was the son of the veteran Conservative former Chancellor of the Exchequer, Earl St. Aldwyn.

News of the election can hardly have come at a worse time for the government. The Easter Rising in Dublin had begun on 24 April and then, on 29 April, information emerged of the surrender of British forces in Kut after a near six months siege and the abject failure of a relief expedition. This is recognised as one of the greatest defeats ever suffered by the British Army and the post-mortem discussions made uncomfortable reading, largely ascribing the disaster to political dithering rather than military errors. Part of the Indian Army had arrived in Mesopotamia in late 1914 with the objective of defending the oil fields, now vital given the conversion of the British fleet to oil. Initially, they enjoyed remarkable successes in the region. But over-reach and over-confidence resulted in a failed attempt on Baghdad, following which the 8,000 strong Imperial force had to retreat to Kut where it was besieged for almost five months before surrendering to the Turks. For *The Times*, Kut was close to the final straw and in a leader on 1 May they argued 'the case for reconstruction' and called for major changes to what they considered an unsatisfactory government.

Immediately on the news of Hicks-Beach's death, William Boosey (who had considered fighting in Wimbledon – see above) said that he would run against whomever the Coalition selected. The *Daily Mail* expected him to fight on air policy and the situation in Ireland. Then, almost straight after Boosey's decision, Earl St Aldwyn died (on 30 April). Despite the intense family tragedy, the local Conservative Association felt it essential to make an early decision about a candidate, given that Boosey was already in the field. They offered the seat to Michael Hicks-Beach's 74-year-old uncle, William Hicks-Beach.

Although, unlike his brother and nephew, he had not attained national political prominence, he was a major figure in Gloucestershire public life. One press profile said of him: 'He has for many years taken a prominent part in local government, both as an alderman of the County Council and chairman of the Cheltenham Board of Guardians. He is chairman of the Health Committee of the county and has been on the Commission of the Peace for Gloucestershire for many years.'[19] More colourfully, the *Gloucestershire Echo* wrote: 'A specimen of the cultured rather than the bucolic type of country squire, Mr. Hicks-Beach, however, long was a notable figure in the hunting field'. The *Daily Mail* predicted that he would be considered too old for a wartime MP.

At his selection meeting, Hicks-Beach agreed to stand but with conditions. He stressed he would fight as a Conservative and stated: 'Any Government in wartime needs frank and responsible criticism. Our present Ministry is no exception, and I can only accept your support on the understanding that I have a practically free hand.' Nevertheless, he had not entertained too many doubts about accepting since he also read extracts from a draft election address. The policy issues he emphasised were:

> 'There must be no delay in the settlement of the recruiting problem; prompt measures must be taken to ensure that our aircraft service shall be second to none in the world and that can best be attained by a special department and a Minister of Aerial Defence; and the responsibility for recent events in Ireland demands the most searching investigation.'[20]

Were he to be successful, Hicks-Beach would break the record for the oldest man to be elected to the Commons for the first time.

Although the local Unionists had a candidate, they resolved not to begin campaigning until after Earl St Aldwyn's funeral. Boosey, however, arrived in Tewkesbury on Sunday, 30 April, planning a rapid start. He had previously helped Thomas Gibson Bowles at the Market Harborough by-election (see Chapter 6), when he came to the attention of Lord Northcliffe who had

---

19 *Birmingham Daily Post*, 1 May 1916.
20 The Easter Rising, which had shocked British public opinion had taken place in Dublin between 24 and 29 April and so was very much the key political issue of the time.

personally asked him to stand as a 'National' candidate in Tewkesbury because he was 'anxious to speed up the war'.[21] An early press summary of his priorities suggested that: 'He is interested in the National Service movement, and stands for compulsion all round, and the constitution of a strong War Council'.[22] Boosey was head of Messrs. Chappell and Company, music publishers; managing director of the Queen's Hall, and chairman of the directors of the Lyric Theatre on London's Shaftesbury Avenue. Chappell and Company had been generous donors to patriotic causes but, nevertheless, Boosey became engaged in a brief public dispute with Sir Arthur Markham, the ultra-patriotic Liberal MP for Mansfield, when the latter criticised the company for planning, in 1915, a series of concerts that were to include German music.

Fighting on tough terrain

The prospect of another contested election attracted wide press interest. The pro-government papers criticised Boosey for forcing a contest and said that Berlin would be hoping for an administration defeat. Conversely, the *Daily Mail* welcomed him as an experienced businessman. Despite the death of Earl St Aldwyn, Boosey got down to campaigning and had his first meetings on 2 May. He announced he was: 'out for the soldiers and sailors and against the muddling of the Coalition Government, which had sent thousands of them uselessly to their death.' He talked about practical issues such as delays in supplying front-line troops with steel helmets and alleged that there was a lack of business ability in war management. He described events in Ireland as showing neglect by the Government which meant British soldiers being sent to kill Irishmen instead of Germans, claiming it was the greatest blunder of the war. The Mayor of Gloucester said it was 'indecent' to contest the election under the tragic circumstances affecting the Hicks-Beach family. Boosey indicated the greatest respect for the previous member but denied that such sentiments should preclude a contest given the widespread dissatisfaction with the Coalition government's performance. The chairman at Boosey's first meeting called on electors to help 'stop such an awful mess as has been witnessed in the fall of Kut, Gallipoli, and in the rebellion in Ireland—three

---

21 William Boosey, *Fifty Years of Music* (1931).
22 *Birmingham Daily Post*, 1 May 1916.

murderous examples, of the mistakes of the present Government (applause)'. Boosey said he was out to reform the Government and make it take measures to protect the lives of those who were fighting. He declaimed: 'They must have a War Council—a soldier, sailor, air member, a politician (not a talker), and one leader of the Labour Party .... Having constructed such War Council ... This is the Council to carry on the war. You politicians retire into the background.'

Billing joined the fray on the Thursday (4 May), speaking at a large meeting in Cheltenham Town Hall alongside Boosey and Boosey's daughter. The Chairman of the meeting described Billing as the man who had arrived and Boosey as the man they hoped was going to arrive. Boosey said the right things in his speech about the late MP and tackled head-on the argument that it was inappropriate to fight, by saying that they owed a debt to the living as well as the dead. He also stated that he was standing as a businessman and a war candidate and would happily resign his seat once the war was won. He picked up on policies included in Hicks-Beach's address, saying:

> '*He has taken the whole of our programme! I don't blame him. Imitation is the sincerest form of flattery. But I will tell you the real difference which still exists between his programme and mine. I am an Independent and if given the opportunity could force my programme through, while my opponent is a Government creature (interruption) who would have to go into the Government lobby whether he wished it or not—who would have to do as he is told.*'[23]

Billing's involvement caused a stir. Writing years later, Boosey described the 4 May meeting: 'Pemberton Billing was then at the zenith of his popularity. Our opening meeting at the Cheltenham Town Hall was absolutely packed. Hundreds were turned away. They told me it was a record political meeting for Cheltenham.' Billing's speech touched on the air situation, but he built a wider attack, reflecting topical circumstances. Talking about the air war he said: 'We must take the gloves off' and argued to defeat the Germans the war had to be carried into their own country and that if they wanted to fight in the air it should be their air. Again, he claimed: 'we have got the men, we have got the money, we have got the resources and we have got the brains. Then

---

23 *Gloucestershire Echo*, 5 May 1916.

what in the name of God was missing? The word Go and the man to say it.' In conclusion, he predicted: 'The aeroplane will make war impossible in the next 10 to 15 years, we will end up with universal peace founded on fear. Then we should have a council of nations and the country that was supreme in the air would sit in the chair and dictate for good or ill the destinies of the world.'[24]

His wider attacks started with 'the recruiting muddle'. A renewed crisis and confusion over conscription was reaching a crescendo. An unintended consequence of the so-called Bachelor's Bill had been effectively to cease voluntary recruitment and increase those seeking designation as essential workers. Consequently, insufficient numbers were coming forward, hence the move to enlist attested married men. The situation was unsustainable but, in late April, the government's first plans to address the issue were withdrawn following universal criticism in a secret session of parliament on 28 April. A revised plan was put forward on 3 May and was to be passed on polling day, 16 May. This finally extended conscription to all fit men aged 16 to 41, whether married or not. Billing said if the initial Bill represented the matured judgement of the government then they should have stood or fallen by it. However, he did not say it was necessary to put the government out to win the war but it was necessary constantly to demonstrate to them that the public were anxious for a vigorous fighting policy; in a neat phrase he said he was not interested in wrecking the government but wanted to 'comb out' those members who were not willing or able to conduct the war aggressively.

The coverage of Billing's speech reflected the fight in Tewkesbury. This election was much less about the air war than Mile End, East Herts or even Wimbledon. One reason was geography. Although Zeppelins had the range to reach Gloucestershire, the west country was not a target destination, and the closest raids were on the midlands; consequently, air defence attracted less interest. Secondly, the country was turning more negative about the Coalition, and its perceived failures and lack of effort in pursuing the war. Problems were occurring across the board. The was no good news to report from the western front while far-flung campaigns like Kut and Gallipoli were disasters; the halting move towards full conscription was satisfying neither the great majority in its favour nor the minority who were opposed; the British

---

24 Ibid.

fleet, the pride of the nation, seemed to have disappeared and was perceived (somewhat erroneously) as failing to implement a successful blockade on Germany; civil war in Ireland was a huge shock; and, finally, Unionists increasingly resented being tied to Asquith. All this provided fertile ground for an opposition candidate but meant that Billing was less of an asset than in Wimbledon, although his presence provided a dramatic start for Boosey.[25]

And Pemberton Billing only remained for a limited time.[26] He spoke again on the following night at another large meeting, this time in Gloucester. He stressed the large amount he had achieved in just six weeks in the Commons. He had asked ministers more straightforward questions in that period than any other member had in the preceding six years. Also, in his opinion, more reforms had been brought about in air defence and the air service since he arrived than in the previous six years. But he pledged to fight to go further and once more supported reprisal raids on Germany and the building of much stronger air forces. He then broadened his attack to the nature of the government, saying that it clearly intended simply to 'muddle through' and so, how well it would do would depend on 'how much ginger was applied'. Consequently, 'if they wanted to strike a blow against Prussianism, Hunnism or brutality he asked them to strike it through the medium of an independent candidate such as Mr. Boosey.'

The Boosey cry was summarised in his advertisement in the *Gloucester Journal*:

Mr William Boosey is the Independent candidate

Mr William Boosey says to the government: 'Stop fooling and get on with the war'

Mr William Boosey says to Mr. Asquith 'Govern or Go'

Boosey explained that he was for business-like prosecution of the war (and would withdraw as soon as peace was declared). He called for a War Council to be in supreme control; equal service and sacrifice for all; comprehensive

---

25 For example, the *Gloucester Chronicle* (6 May) in its section on news from the Forest of Dean, reported 'Numerous trips were arranged to Cheltenham and Gloucester on Thursday and Friday by Foresters who were anxious to hear Mr. Pemberton Billing'.
26 The *Conservative Agents' Journal* later implied this was because of a lack of impact, saying: 'He certainly did not advance the cause of the candidate, and it is understood that his services were not again requisitioned, and we saw him no more'.

re-organisation of the Air Service; a free hand for the navy and a stringent blockade; British trade for the British after the war; removal of all German influence on British commerce and industry; internment of all alien enemies and confiscation of enemy property; value for money in war expenditure and generous provision for the disabled.

He highlighted government failures including Ireland, the withdrawal of the first draft of the Military Service Bill and the surrender at Kut and repeated earlier opposition candidates' pleas that anyone not satisfied with this performance should back 'the Independent Candidate who is pledged to fight in the House Commons for the direction of the war by Soldiers and Sailors, and not Politicians.'

Once the Conservative campaign started it intended to ensure the defeat of this populist programme. Initially, there was concern in Coalition quarters that Boosey had got off to a strong start and was feeding off widespread unease with the government and the progress of the war. However, once a full campaign could begin for the highly popular figure of Hicks-Beach the mood rapidly changed.

On the platform and in handbills and posters, Hicks-Beach stressed four points, starting with his personal philosophy which was: 'My country, first, last and always'. Next, he emphasised that he would be a critical friend to the government, insisting again on 'a free hand' to oppose where necessary. Thirdly, he called for a thorough investigation and attribution of blame for the events in Ireland and, finally, a sustained effort to ensure English supremacy in aircraft. He refused to discuss Kut, arguing that 'In a war of the present dimensions disasters were bound to occur, and an Englishmen was always ready to bear disaster as well as rejoice in victory.'

Much store was put on Hicks-Beach, the man. He, himself, pointed out that the Hicks-Beach family had first represented Gloucestershire in the Commons in the seventeenth century. Others stressed how much he had contributed to the community over a long career and his great knowledge of agricultural matters (easily the dominant local activity); this was contrasted with Boosey of whom it was said: 'certain remarks of which he had delivered himself on agricultural topics suggested that he knew more about pianos than pastures.' The *Daily Mail* acknowledged Hicks-Beach's local strength by reporting that some people, who ideally would wish to register a protest against the government, had decided to take an early holiday to avoid being seen to vote 'against the family'.

A sustained argument by all Coalition speakers was that there was no alternative to the current government. If it suffered defeat, that would be a great fillip to Berlin. Hicks-Beach and his supporters accepted that the administration had made mistakes, no government was perfect but wanted electors to recognise the great achievements that had been made; for example, by now, millions of men had been called to arms when, at the start of the war, the army numbered fewer than 250,000. Hicks-Beach was also conciliatory about the perceived 'conscription muddle'; he argued that a slow progress towards compulsion had been inevitable since, before the war, many Liberals, Radicals, Socialists and some Conservatives were not only opposed to it but would have considered it a distasteful and alien concept.

The hypothetical question of how the government might be replaced was raised. Successful challenges could result in a general election which, during war, would be unthinkable. Linked to this were attacks on the calibre of Boosey and Pemberton Billing and, above all, their key backers at the *Daily Mail*. A senior MP, Henry Duke, the member for Exeter, condemned the 'professional whimperers' and argued that Boosey stood for 'discontent, disunion and dismay'. A different platform speaker asked: 'If not a Radical or a Tory government were they going to have a *Daily Mail* government' whilst another asked: 'did they want a member for Carmelite House or for the Tewkesbury Division?' Arthur Steel-Maitland MP said: 'The whole object of the critics, of course, was to break the Coalition Government. The Government had, he was prepared to admit, made mistakes but Government by these variety artistes would make a great deal more'. Nevertheless, the 'establishment' was not wholly opposed to Boosey. Admiral Rose, a local elector, received a telegram from Admiral Lord Beresford saying: 'I wish Mr. Boosey every success. His return would be a protest against the weakness and mismanagement of the present government resulting in disasters, retreats and surrenders and, lastly, a rebellion in Ireland.' This was followed by a strong attack on the government in the Lords by Lord Loreburn, the former Liberal Lord Chancellor. Boosey capitalised on this, claiming that Loreburn had mounted all the same attacks that he was promoting in Tewkesbury and reproduced the main points from the Lords' debate speech in a leaflet for distribution at his meetings.

Somewhat embarrassingly, Hicks-Beech was Loreburn's father-in-law. Boosey also received a letter of support from the highly popular singer, Clara Butt. By contrast, the local Liberals fully backed Hicks-Beach and distributed a leaflet to all electors, calling on them to unite behind the Unionist.

The mechanics of the two campaigns were very different. Inevitably, Boosey had much less local manpower which limited canvassing. The scale of his disadvantage was clear when nominations were submitted. Boosey produced four papers in comparison with 61 presented for Hicks-Beach. Bereft of a local organisation, Boosey had to rely on the promotional and organisational resources of the *Daily Mail*. He was forced to deny that his campaign was being funded by the *Daily Mail* and claimed that all expenses were coming out of his own pocket. However, if the *Mail* was not providing the cash, the Coalition campaign highlighted how much they were contributing the sinews of war. When the election expenses of the two campaigns were published, it emerged that both had spent heavily but on different things:

	Hicks-Beach	Boosey
Returning officer's expenses	£258	£258
Sub-agents	£198	
Poll Clercks	£28	£24
Clerks	£63	
Messengers	£14	
Printing & Stationery	£300	£249
Advertising and billposting	£269	£418
Postage, telegrams, committee rooms and miscellaneous	£323	£487
Personal Expenses	£6	£100
TOTAL	£1,546 2s 4d	£1,546 2s 4d
Today's value	£110,000	£115,000

Daily Mail support for the Boosey campaign really annoyed the Conservatives. At a meeting in Tewkesbury (11 May), the Conservative agent claimed of the Boosey campaign that:

> 'the advance guard was the advertisement manager of the Daily Mail and he was followed by the circulation manager and since then the countryside had been placarded by the same kind of posters as used in the Daily Mail contests at Wimbledon and elsewhere, and there was a fleet of Daily Mail motors running about the division while Mr. Boosey's address was a series of headlines from the Daily Mail.'

Although he continued to deny finance from the *Daily Mail*, after the campaign, Boosey did acknowledge its help, saying: 'I wish publicly to testify that I owe a very great debt of gratitude for the voluntary help rendered me by that paper', a comment which attracted both cheers and laughter.

One aspect of the *Daily Mail*'s assistance rather backfired, the re-appearance of the 'dummy gun' from Wimbledon. In addition to an actual wooden gun displayed in his main committee room, Boosey also referred to them in his posters. One caused considerable offence; it said: 'Don't send a dummy gun to parliament' and was combined with another that talked about sending a 'live shell' instead. The *Gloucester Journal*[27] noted that 'the plain inference of the two is that the Independent candidate is the explosive force that is going to breach the government ranks while the Coalition candidate must prove to be – well a mere 'dummy'. The insult to Mr Hicks-Beach is palpable and the only possible excuse is that the posters were of a general nature and were issued before he was adopted.' Boosey felt forced to withdraw them, as reported in the *Birmingham Daily Gazette*:

> 'The Northcliffe fly posters are doing their best to paint the constituency red without any squeamish regard for accuracy but Mr. Boosey himself is beginning to realise that sneering at a member of the Hicks Beach family will not help him win this election. He has ordered the withdrawal of the poster.'

---

27 *Gloucester Journal*, 13 May 1916.

Steel-Maitland sought to turn the dummy gun story to advantage against Boosey by arguing that a task of a commander was to mislead the enemy but what, he asked, was to be said of the person who, if he found the dummy gun out, got up and blurted the fact to the very people who ought not to know? Was that folly or knavery?

Despite this hiccup, the Boosey campaign continued to rely heavily on posters, forcing Hicks-Beach to reciprocate. *The Times* (5 May) reported that the constituency was inundated with red posters for Boosey and black ones for Hicks-Beach. The Boosey ones: 'telling the electors he will not be gagged, and denouncing the Irish crime, dummy air guns, wobbling cabinets and party politics and the black posters of Mr. Hicks-Beach declaring that he stands for real independent criticism, a free hand in parliament, a supreme air service and a searching investigation into recent Irish administration'. The *Daily Mail* also reported a complaint in parliament that the Hicks-Beach campaign was using amended recruitment posters (printed at public expense).

Inevitably, there were a vast number of meetings. Having started with major rallies in Cheltenham and Gloucester, Boosey then switched attention to holding smaller meetings in the villages; he drummed up audiences by touring through them by motorcar in the afternoon and returning to speak in the evening. The task was substantial given the size of the constituency, approximately 40 miles long and 20 miles wide. But he was handicapped by having only a small and rather motley collection of platform speakers. Among these were Leo Maxse, editor of the *National Review*, who spoke on 'the crimes of the Coalition'; Arnold White, the sea power expert, who called for 'a free hand for the navy' and a former soldier called the 'Man from Mons' who argued for better treatment of British PoWs. Maxse represented the extreme right-wing of the Conservative party and was eager for a stronger war policy while Arnold White, who had supported Pemberton Billing at Mile End, was a notable anti-semite and in 1917 wrote 'The Hidden Hand'. He was also a leading member of the Navy League. The Man from Mons, James Miles, a former corporal in the 18th Hussars, was an interesting addition to the line-up. He had been injured and subsequently repatriated by the Germans in 1915 as he was unfit for service. A little earlier in May he had written to *The Times*, complaining about the treatment of British prisoners in German camps and government's failure to take any notice. He wrote to Boosey about the issue and the latter undertook to take it up and invited him to speak on his behalf. This he did, at multiple meetings over two evenings. He described 'the terrible story of the bad treatment given to our men in German prison camps' and cited an example of up to 160 men held in a single stable, each with only a blanket to protect against the cold and with insufficient food such that they depended on parcels from home that were often stolen. He condemned the government and said that what ministers had claimed in the Commons was unreliable and that he wanted to see a member returned who would take up the issue, which Boosey would do. *The Times* reported that his intervention had generated considerable interest, especially in the villages.

By polling day, the disparity in scale between the two campaigns was obvious. Although polling hours had been extended to 8am to 9pm, motorcars were considered essential given 'removed' voters; the large number of 'plural' voters who were resident in Cheltenham or Gloucester but eligible to vote elsewhere; and the unwillingness of agricultural workers to leave the land until late in the day. Of this vital asset, it was reported that Hicks-Beach deployed 366 while Boosey was believed to have had only 20 to 25.[28]

A triumph for Hicks-Beach

Hicks-Beach was triumphant by an even greater margin than anticipated; clearly, however much dissatisfaction there was regarding war management, that was insufficient to overcome local loyalty to the family and rural suspicions of an urban 'carpet-bagger':

Dec. 1910			
Hicks-Beach (M)	Conservative	5,699	52%
Lister	Liberal	5,267	48%
Majority		432	
Electorate & Turnout		13,155	83%

---

28 *Gloucestershire Echo*, May 16, 1916.

May 1916			
Hicks-Beach (W)	Conservative	7,127	83%
Boosey	Independent	1,438	17%
Majority		5,689	
Electorate & Turnout		13,818	62%

In addition to loyalty, the victory (which served to 'stop the rot' after East Hertfordshire and Wimbledon) was ascribed to superior forces and highly effective campaigning. Hicks-Beach's literature differentiated between that aimed at Unionists (no mention of the government; stress on the insult to Hicks-Beach and a reminder that no Hicks-Beach had ever been defeated locally) and that destined for Liberal supporters where support for a government led by Asquith was emphasised. Thus, Unionists were voting for Hicks-Beach while Liberals were backing the government.

The Conservative Agents' organisation ascribed success to the combination of selecting Hicks-Beach and an amateur campaign for Boosey. They were scathing about Boosey's supporters from the *Daily Mail* saying they 'degenerated into a disorganised host, and many and frequent were the mishaps, such as abandoned meetings and failure to keep appointments.' Further:

> 'The speakers at their command were either fanatics, or 'cast-off' orators of the political parties, and despite the glorified reports of their meetings the attendance at them was frequently so sparse, that they generally started – if they started at all – long after the advertised time, and then only after the motley audience had been 'whipped up'. They were especially dismissive of Pemberton Billing, saying: 'The redoubtable Pemberton Billing who was speedily styled the 'gas-bag' orator, was on the scene for a brief period during the early stages of the fight.'

The Liberal Agents also evaluated the campaign, saying it had produced 'much weeping and wailing in the camp of the 'all is lost' brigade of snivellers and wailers.' They reported that 'the methods adopted by the Independent

Candidate, consisted of many Meetings, with nearly all imported speakers (of course, one was the exploded rocket, Pemberton Billing), *Daily Mail* motorcars and articles, Dummy Guns, a plentiful supply of posters of the yellow journalistic type; with a large expenditure on advertising, and an endeavour to pose as the Tommies' Candidate.'

The Liberals believed Boosey's votes came almost exclusively from: 'Better Tory types, who read *The Times* or the *Daily Mail* and who were actuated by intense hatred of Asquith and disliked their own party leaders for supporting a Coalition with him as leader.' Conversely, they claimed that 'not one known Liberal was to be found supporting the Independent'. This reflected considerable effort by the Liberals on behalf of the Unionist. Their established candidate, Sir Richard Mathias, had written to all known Liberals asking them to support Hicks-Beach[29] and they claimed that: 'It was generally acknowledged that the Liberals in the constituency were largely responsible for the huge majority obtained in support of the Government.'

Hicks-Beach may have gone to the Commons as a 'critical friend' of the government with 'a free hand' but he failed to make a single speech and stood down at the 1918 General Election. Boosey never stood for Parliament again and returned to the music business.

---

29 This was quite a sacrifice for Mathias. He had been elected for Cheltenham in December 1910 but lost the seat on petition in early 1911 as he had exceeded the expenditure limits and made some illegal payments. He was never to return to the Commons although he did stand, unsuccessfully, in Merthyr in 1922.

8.
HEADS ABOVE THE PARAPET

North Ayrshire, 11 October 1916
Rossendale, 13 February 1917
Stockton-on-Tees, 20 March 1917
South Aberdeen, 3 April 1917
Keighley, 26 April 1918

Few of the 1915-18 contested by-elections were fought on the central issue of war and peace. It took time and the development of war-weariness before the minority opposed to Britain's 'fight to the finish' policy took the difficult decision to put their heads above the parapet.

Because Britain went to war suddenly, it did so without any formal statement of war aims. Patriotic fervour kicked in and government was able to proceed without articulating what might be acceptable terms to end the war by negotiation rather than German surrender. As time went on and sacrifices increased, the dominant rhetoric changed from initial, almost altruistic, arguments ('Protecting small nations', 'The war to end war') to jingoistic and uncompromising positions ('Fight to the finish', 'Smash the Hun'). However, those sacrifices and the absence of any sign of the war ending eventually encouraged some opposed to the pro-war consensus to be more open and to use by-elections as a platform. One analyst concluded: 'By the autumn of 1916 ... domestic-political, military and international developments had begun to provide the dissenters with fruitful opportunities to advance the cause of a negotiated peace.'[1]

The evolving challenges to war

Questioning Britain's participation in the war was difficult. The impact of patriotism was dramatic. In the immediate run-up to 4 August 1914, multiple groups argued for neutrality including significant parts of the ruling Liberal Party, of the Press and of the labour movement. Yet once war was declared, and especially after the invasion of Belgium, nearly all opposition melted away, leaving those who remained as a very small minority. Moreover, that minority was fragmented between disparate groups and motivations; from socialist, Liberal and religious backgrounds.

The labour movement fractured and parts became militantly 'patriotic'. Within the Liberal Party, anti-war sentiment declined dramatically. Fears that the cabinet would be badly split proved unfounded with only three resignations from government. Amongst the churches, too, opposition was a minority position, including among the non-established denominations. In the Anglican church, views were almost unanimously for war and the Anglican Peace League was very much a minority voice while even among the Quakers around one-third of eligible men were to sign up.

Slowly, those with any kind of anti-war perspective began to organise, but largely behind the scenes, recognising, in the early months, that the time was not right to try to change opinion. Eventually, myriad organisations developed. They were small and their aims and motivations diverse, making any challenge to government policy difficult.

The first body to form, amongst the political elite, was the Union of Democratic Control (UDC). This brought together several from the tiny group of pacifist or otherwise anti-war MPs. It united like-minded Liberals and Labour representatives including Edmund Morel (Liberal candidate in Birkenhead but forced to stand down due to his UDC activities), Arthur Ponsonby (Liberal MP for Stirling), Charles Trevelyan (Liberal MP for Elland who resigned from government on the outbreak of war), Ramsay MacDonald

---

[1] A G Gregory, *They look in vain: British foreign policy dissent and the quest for a negotiated peace during the Great War with particular emphasis on 1917*. (Ph D Thesis., McMaster University, 1997)

(The MP for Leicester who stood down as leader of the Labour Party in Parliament due to its support for the war), Norman Angell (author of *The Great Illusion*), Charles Buxton (former Liberal MP) and Philip Snowden (Labour (ILP) MP for Blackburn). The main driving force of the UDC was belief that Britain had become obligated to France because of 'secret diplomacy' and, consequently, it wanted reform to ensure open, parliamentary control of foreign policy and treaties. These were murky waters. In public, Grey and Asquith argued in the Commons that there were no agreements that in any way bound Britain to intervene if France were attacked. But behind the scenes, Anglo-French military discussions, conducted over many years, had assumed the opposite, resulting in the French navy being deployed in the Mediterranean on the assumption that the British would protect the Channel. In theory, Britain was under no obligation; in reality, standing aside was impossible.

Intertwined with opposition to war policy was the question of attitudes to conscription. In November 1914, Fenner Brockway formed the No-Conscription Fellowship which became prominent in the debates regarding the Military Service Acts and the subsequent treatment of conscientious objectors. It had some overlap of participation with the UDC and drew mainly on Labour/socialist and pacifist/Quaker membership.

From the religious world, the Fellowship of Reconciliation held its first meeting at Christmas 1914. This brought together pacifist/ anti-war figures, especially from the non-conformist denominations. However, it never satisfactorily determined real-world objectives and had little impact beyond providing a forum for discussion and support for ministers/clergy who were isolated within their denominations due to their anti-war views and for conscientious objectors after the introduction of conscription.

The war resulted in significant splits within the labour movement as the pre-war commitments of some to international working-class solidarity and opposition to 'capitalist' wars faded away. One exception to this was the Independent Labour Party, the majority of which continued to promote a firm, anti-war stance throughout and actively to support arguments to explore a negotiated peace.

Such a diversity of small opposition groups meant co-ordination would be difficult. They were particularly cautious in the early months of the war.

The UDC emphasised that it was not a 'peace at any price' organisation and focused more on reforms for after the war; it was not until late 1915 that it included in its platform calls to explore whether a negotiated peace might be possible.

The conscription debate of 1915/16 added to the constituency of those willing to challenge government policy but, at the same time, increased the ferocity of the argument; as more lives were lost, the greater the tendency of many to double down in support of a 'fight to the finish'. As one student of the peace movement commented: 'If the British public had abandoned its initial heady Jingoism, it was only so as to adopt an altogether uglier mood, brought on by the growing loss of life at the front and the sinking of the Lusitania.'[2]

However, as 1916 progressed, continuing high casualty numbers (turbocharged by the Somme), greater economic problems (especially price increases) and developing war-weariness combined to create an environment where more (albeit, still a small minority) were willing to question the complete rejection of negotiation. One attempt to co-ordinate dissent was the establishment in spring 1916 of the Peace Negotiations Committee. Instituted by the Union of Democratic Control, this brought together representatives of the Workers' Suffrage Federation, the Independent Labour Party, the No-Conscription Fellowship, the Women's Labour League, the Women's International League, the Fellowship of Reconciliation, the League of Peace and Freedom, the Peace Committee of the Society of Friends, the Church of England Peace League, the Free Church League for Women's Suffrage, and the Peace Society. The Committee was later endorsed by the British Socialist Party after a split in which the anti-war grouping gained control. The Committee's key campaign was to circulate a memorial (petition) which stated: 'That the undersigned urge H.M. Government to seek the earliest opportunity of promoting negotiations with the object of securing a just and lasting peace.' By the time the Memorial was finally presented to the Prime Minister, in August 1917, it had attracted support from just over 221,000 people, despite some instances of police intervention to the prevent collection of signatures. The Committee also distributed pamphlets and formed local committees. ILP branches, particularly, were encouraged to provide active support.

---

2 J Wallis, *Valiant for Peace* (1991).

By September 1916, the pro-government press was concerned about the activities of the Committee. The *Birmingham Daily Post* noted: 'One of the pacifist movements that will need careful watching is the Peace Negotiations Committee, of which Mr. C. R. Buxton, formerly a member of the House of Commons, is the leading spirit ... it desires to hurry up affairs so that, at the very earliest day possible, peace negotiations shall start.'[3] By contrast, the sympathetic *Daily Herald* reported:

> *'the campaign for peace by negotiation is still receiving very enthusiastic support in various parts of the country. Meetings and conferences are being held everywhere. This committee are not asking for a patched or inconclusive peace. Their request is that if the war can be ended by negotiation in such a manner as will secure the safety and well-being of the peoples of Britain and Europe without further slaughter, then the best thing for us all is to urge the Government to negotiate.*[4]

The first election contested on a clear call to consider 'peace by negotiation' was in North Ayrshire.

NORTH AYRSHIRE – October 1916

By October 1916, concern was mounting regarding the military and economic sacrifices being made, and the lack of success achieved. However, although North Ayrshire in west Scotland saw the first candidate standing on a platform of seeking a negotiated peace, it came before wider events (such as the German Peace note, the interventions of President Wilson and the formation of the Lloyd George Coalition) had fully prepared the ground.

The sitting MP was Lt-Col Duncan Campbell. He had enjoyed a long and successful military career, before gaining the seat from the Liberals in a by-election in 1911. On the outbreak of war, he joined up again but was badly wounded at Ypres in November 1914 and only just avoided the amputation of an arm. He returned to the Commons where he was involved in a notable exchange with the (pacifist) Liberal MP for Hanley, Robert Outhwaite, of

---

3 *Birmingham Daily Post*, 8 September 1916.
4 *Daily Herald*, 9 September 1916.

whom Campbell said if he were in his battalion at the front 'he would be strung up by the thumbs before he had been there half an hour.' Asked who would accomplish this, Campbell said: 'I would leave that task to myself, even though I have the use of only one arm.'[5] Campbell's arm recovered sufficiently for him to return to the front in early 1916 but he was to die of pneumonia in September, following severe injuries caused by the explosion of a mine a few weeks earlier.

The constituency was usually closely fought between the Unionists and Liberals and there was also a reasonable Labour vote. Despite this, the party truce held and it was accepted that the Unionists would be unopposed. They considered potential candidates but announced unanimous support for Lt-General Sir Aylmer Hunter-Weston. Described as a local landlord, and 'highly popular as a sportsman', he was a career soldier having entered the army in 1884. He had fought in Flanders and France before taking part in the Gallipoli campaign, during which he was injured. At the time of his selection, he had returned to active service and so would be unable to campaign personally. The selection of a 'militarist' was unpopular among some of the local Liberal party and he enjoyed, at best, a mixed reputation because of the high casualty rate among his forces at Gallipoli. Nevertheless, there was no move to oppose him, and a joint election address was issued by the respective chairmen of the Unionist and Liberal constituency organisations.

Until almost the last minute, it was assumed Hunter-Weston would be unopposed. But just days before nominations the Scottish-born Rev. Humphrey Chalmers, now working as a Baptist Minister in Wandsworth in London, announced that he would be an Independent candidate, promoting a 'peace by negotiation' position. The *Kilmarnock Herald* described him as:

> 'a native of Roseneath and the bearer of a name well-known in fishing and yachting circles on the Firth of Clyde ... He was educated at Larchfield Academy and Glasgow University and is considered one of the finest preachers in the Baptist ministry. His church at Wandsworth is famous for its 'democratic religion' and its minister is a popular figure in the district. Up till recently, Mr. Chalmers

---

5 *Reading Mercury*, 9 September 1916.

was a Liberal in politics, but at present he is not identified with any political organisation'.[6]

The ILP newspaper, the *Labour Leader*, was at the time edited by the pacifist, Fenner Brockway, and declared itself enthusiastic about Chalmers, stating: 'The son of a fisherman, and himself a poor man, Mr Chalmers is in full sympathy with the desire of the workers for self-emancipation.'[7]

Chalmers had long promoted opposition to the war and was active in the No Conscription Fellowship and the Fellowship of Reconciliation. As early as November 1914, when he was a minister in Redhill in Surrey, he had had a letter published in the local press stating: 'There are many of our best who cannot conceive Jesus Christ, whom they revere, thrusting a bayonet into the entrails of a German peasant, and who rightly or wrongly accept the Sermon on the Mount as it stands and therefore would rather die than kill.'[8] A little later, he had written to the *Labour Leader*, stating:

> *'Having received the Householder's Return form from the Parliamentary Recruiting Committee, I have filled it up as follows in the space for the names of those willing to enlist: Conscientiously believing that all war is contrary to the teaching and example of Jesus Christ, I who am the only male in this household will never, under any circumstance, consent to bear arms.'*[9]

During 1915 and 1916, he stood unsuccessfully for the No-Conscription Fellowship Committee and became one of the joint convenors of the Baptist Peace Fellowship.

News of Chalmers' intervention emerged on 2 October, three days before nominations. The first press reports highlighted: 'He favours the Government making a frank declaration of its aims in the war, so that peace negotiations may be possible.' He also mentioned support for improving the treatment of disabled soldiers and soldiers' dependents.[10] That week's *Labour Leader*

---

6 *Kilmarnock Herald*, 6 October 1916.
7 *Labour Leader*, 5 October 1916
8 *Surrey Mirror*, 20 November 1914.
9 *Labour Leader*, 26 November 1914.
10 *Daily Record*, 2 October 1916.

provided a more detailed summary of his platform. It stated that bringing peace to Europe was his primary objective and: 'by that he is prepared to stand or fall'. However, it further noted,

> 'On economic questions he approximates to the Socialist position. He favours national control of food, fuel, and shipping services; desires adequate pensions for those broken in the war and their dependents; wants the franchise extended to permit every man and woman over 21 years of age having a vote; is opposed to the proposed taxation of co-operative dividends; is favourable to Home Rule in the fullest sense for Ireland and Scotland. He also approves of a flat payment of 10 shillings a week, to old-age pensioners, and generally supports the economic policy of the ILP.'[11]

In putting forward such a comprehensive set of policies Chalmers, like many of the independent by-election candidates, could potentially aggregate support from multiple sources and motivations as a 'catch-all' opponent of the government. However, in his primary aim of promoting peace by negotiation, he was either disingenuous or naïve. His claimed 'minimum terms' for any peace were ones that would never be acceptable to Germany as a basis for discussions. According to a meeting report in *The Scotsman*, they included:

> 'Very full satisfaction of all the wrongs done to Belgium; the restoration to France of Alsace and Lorraine, if the inhabitants of these provinces desired it; the granting of independence to Poland if such was the wish of the Poles; and the settlement of the Balkans problem in accordance with the feelings of the inhabitants.'[12]

At a later meeting, he added, 'reconstruction of the damaged parts of France' and 'the Dardanelles, and the Bosphorus to be made international.'[13]

His election address contained further demands. He called for

---

11 *Labour Leader*, 5 October 1916.
12 *The Scotsman*, 9 October 1916.
13 *The Scotsman*, 11 October 1916.

> *'the cessation of the growing militarist domination in our own land, lest, while our soldiers are dying for the liberation of Belgium, they find their own liberties filched from them and theirs... Even in war time let Britain be governed in accordance with British ideals.'*

He also argued: 'to request the Government ... to state immediately, in clear language, the terms upon which they are prepared to bring the war to an end' and further wanted the Government 'to open negotiations with the enemy Powers, either together or separately, as soon as they display willingness to follow this course.'[14]

The election address created immediate controversy. The first signatory on Chalmers' nomination papers, a William E Curle, said he had been assured by Chalmers that he had no connection with the Union of Democratic Control, the ILP or the Socialist party and that none of his expenses were paid by them. He had further been reassured that Chalmers was not a 'peace at any price' man. However, Curle felt that the election address gave a very different impression, and he had telegraphed Chalmers, demanding clarification. Dissatisfied with what he was told, Curle appeared at a meeting on behalf of Hunter-Weston and announced that he was withdrawing his support for Chalmers and would instead be voting for Hunter-Weston.

Chalmers conceded that during the campaign, 'a good deal of abuse had been heaped upon him' but that 'he took that as a sign that his candidature had proved a success far beyond their expectations.' Among policy challenges put to him were how to avenge the Lusitania; shouldn't the war be continued to a finish given the sacrifices already made; and was he aware that Britain could not make peace other than in agreement with its allies? On the Lusitania, (*see chapter 6 for a brief description of the Lusitania controversy*), he argued that the attack had been a crime against humanity, but he didn't know whether it would be possible to punish the perpetrators. If it were possible, well and good, but they should focus on how to make that sort of thing impossible in the future. Regarding a fight to the finish, he claimed that would mean Germany would not have a penny to pay reparations to Belgium and that Britain would have to do so instead. Finally, on being bound to the Allies,

---

14 Chalmers' election address. Bristol University Library: Special Collections.

he said that the government was under a greater obligation to the people of Britain than it could be to any of the Allies. In aggregate, Chalmers offered electors an opportunity to voice economic dissatisfactions, a means to protest against infringements of civil liberties, and a chance to question the 'fight to the finish' approach to the war and the absence of clearly articulated war aims. However, he did so as someone who was openly arguing from a pacifist orientation.

Although the campaign was short, and Hunter-Weston was away on active service, the Unionist and Liberal constituency parties combined to organise on his behalf and brought in multiple speakers to resist the independent challenge. Hunter-Weston's election address was brief and formal. It argued that Party politics were suspended and asked for votes for him entirely as an expression of support for the Coalition in its sole role of bringing the war 'to a victorious end' and to endorse its determination 'to prosecute the war with unflagging energy until our righteous ends are fully achieved.' The address also provided a repost to calls for 'peace by negotiation', arguing:

> *'A premature peace would be a disaster. Only when Germany is brought to realise that her position is hopeless will any negotiations lead to results satisfactory to this country and our Allies. If we were to negotiate peace now, on any terms Germany is yet willing to accept, the brave men who have sacrificed their lives for our cause, would have died in vain.'*[15]

Many MPs came to support the absent Hunter-Weston. On one night alone there were multiple meetings addressed by Sir George Younger (MP for Ayr and soon to be Chairman of the Conservative Party); William Watson (Unionist MP for South Lanarkshire); George Currie (Unionist MP for Leith), John Pratt (Liberal MP for Linlithgow), John MacLeod (Unionist MP for Glasgow Central), Daniel Holmes (Liberal MP for Govan), and Harry Hope (Unionist MP for Buteshire). MacLeod pulled no punches in his speech saying:

---

15 Election address on behalf of General Hunter-Weston, Bristol University Library, Special Collections.

> '*he wished the election day could be postponed for a fortnight to allow Mr Chalmers to go out and read his address to our kith and kin at the front. If nothing else his address would be torn to pieces in front of him ... This was not a question of merely electing General Hunter-Weston. He was only an emblem. But it was a question of the electors of North Ayrshire sending a message to Germany.*'[16]

Powerful, patriotic arguments and the unity between the main parties, carried the day against Chalmers who, of course, was handicapped by the shortness of campaigning time and the fact that he was a total outsider to the constituency. He also had very few resources although he was given some organisational assistance. For example, the UDC, for the first time, became involved in a by-election and sent a key organiser, Egerton Wake (who was later to become National Agent of the Labour Party) to help the campaign.

Dec. 1911			
Campbell	Conservative	7,318	51%
Anderson	Liberal	7,047	49%
Majority		271	
Electorate & Turnout		16,926	85%

11 Oct. 1916			
Hunter-Weston	Unionist	7,149	85%
Chalmers	Peace by Negotiation	1,300	15%
Majority		5,849	
Electorate & Turnout		17,385	49%

Both sides claimed to be pleased with the outcome. The *Pall Mall Gazette* declared:

---

16 *The Scotsman*, 10 October 1916.

> 'The smashing defeat of the peace candidate in the N Ayrshire by-election is very satisfactory. It proves a fact patent enough to all the people of Great Britain; but it is well that the enemy and neutrals from time to time should have clear evidence that the determination of this country to fight the war to a finish remains unabated .... we believe that, comparatively small as was the number of voters who polled for his reverend opponent, not a tithe of 1,300 would welcome an ignominious peace. It is always the fate of Government to make enemies, and a goodly proportion of Mr. Chalmers's supporters may be classed simply as agin' the Government.'[17]

Chalmers' supporters were also content and equally confident that few of their voters wanted any kind of ignominious peace. Chalmers himself claimed that at the beginning of the campaign the expectation was that he would not poll more than 500 votes. Moreover, he felt that the defection of his nominator, too late for him to respond, had cost him dearly. George Lansbury, the strongly pacifist, socialist editor of the Daily Herald (and future leader of the Labour Party), claimed if Chalmers had been allowed a five week rather than a five days' campaign the result might have been very different and even then that:

> 'At the end, without motorcars, canvassers, organisation, newspapers, 1,300 electors went the poll in favour of the programme set out by the Independent candidate. If this is at all representative of feeling in the country, then it means that there is a very considerable and growing body of public opinion in favour of a settlement of the war by negotiation, if this is at all possible, and also in favour of the Government at once, after consultation with its Allies, declaring in detail what peace terms would be acceptable to the Allied Governments.'[18]

In this assessment, Lansbury was whistling to keep his pro-peace by negotiation spirits up.

---

17 *Pall Mall Gazette*, 13 October 1916.
18 *Daily Herald*, 21 October 1916.

ROSSENDALE – February 1917

By early 1917, circumstances had developed to encourage further campaigning in favour of 'peace by negotiation'. The previous year had seen numerous military disappointments, including the surrender at Kut (see chapter 7 for some details on this dramatic reverse for the British army) and the Battle of Jutland. The latter, on 31 May 1916, was to prove to be the only major engagement between the British Grand Fleet and the German High Seas fleet. In a shock to British morale, the country's pride and joy, the Royal Navy, suffered greater losses in the engagement than did the German fleet although, unknown at the time, it was a British strategic victory as the Kaiser's navy did not risk challenging the Grand Fleet again. But the biggest blow of all was the continued failure to break the deadlock on the western front. Worse than that, the 'big push' at the Somme, starting on 1 July, had achieved no strategic gain yet at the cost of an estimated more than 400,000 British casualties of whom around 100,000 died. Inevitably war-weariness was developing alongside increasing home front economic privations, driven by rising prices. At the same time, the collapse of Asquith's government and his replacement as Prime Minister by Lloyd George on 6 December 1916, led those opposed to the 'no stated war aims/knock-out blow' approach to be more despairing of official policy and increasingly motivated to take up public opposition; without doubt, a government led by Lloyd George, Liberal though he was, was going to be distinctly less 'liberal' than its predecessor and much more committed to outright victory. International diplomacy also raised questions about Britain's lack of declared war aims and rejection of negotiation in favour of a 'fight to the finish'. The Germans delivered a 'Peace note' to President Woodrow Wilson on 12 December 1916, to be forwarded to the Allies. In this, they offered to negotiate, albeit from a position of what they saw as strength (for example, they had just enjoyed considerable success in Romania, capturing Bucharest) and an insistence on achieving Germany's main aims. These would certainly include the retention of areas of Belgium and northern France, to provide a 'buffer zone', and the reinstatement of Germany's colonies. Reactions to the note differed; those already supportive of 'peace by negotiation' saw it as a hopeful sign while government, and majority opinion, dismissed it as a ruse designed in part to curry favour with the Americans. They were not wrong as Germany was actively pursuing a dual strategy of exploring to see if a very favourable peace might be negotiated while, at the same time, preparing to commence unrestricted submarine warfare in early 1917. Next, President Wilson, on 18 December 1916, called on all the belligerents to spell out their peace terms as a first step towards a peace conference. Again, reactions aligned with pre-existing positions. Supporters of 'peace by negotiation' were delighted that the concept was moving into the mainstream whereas the government was dismayed that President Wilson appeared to be aligning himself with the German initiative.

Lloyd George rejected the German note but, in January 1917, responded to Wilson's intervention with a first comprehensive statement of the Allies' objectives. These included freedom and full reparations for Belgium; the restoration of occupied parts of France, Romania and Italy; a review of the situation of Alsace-Lorraine; an independent Poland; the 'internationalisation' of the Dardanelles; and a future international organisation to handle conflicts via diplomacy and limit armaments. This gave the 'peace by negotiation' supporters something to work with, and they protested that the stated aims now went well beyond Asquith's original arguments for war. President Wilson moved the debate further with a speech to Congress on 22 January 1917 calling for a 'peace without victory'. Again, peace campaigners welcomed his intervention, which they saw as validating their own arguments, while the Coalition's view was summarised by the *New Statesman*: 'Nothing short of victory will satisfy the Allied peoples, and nothing short of it will secure our aims - and Mr. Wilson's.'[19] Thus, the background to the next by-election featuring a 'peace by negotiation' candidate was one where discussion of such issues was more salient than it had ever been although positions remained entrenched and diametrically opposed.

The by-election in Rossendale in Lancashire resulted from the resignation, on grounds of ill-health, of the First Commissioner of Works and, previously, Secretary of State for the Colonies, Lewis 'Lou Lou' Harcourt. He was appointed to the Lords in Asquith's resignation honours list, which was made public on 22 December 1916.

Immediately after Christmas, the Liberals, both nationally and locally, were contacted by the little-known British Citizens Party (BCP) and requested

---

19 *New Statesman*, 27 January 1917.

not to fight the by-election but to make way for a BCP candidate who would stand on a platform of 'peace by negotiation' alongside 'socialist' economic policies. The BCP, which was a tiny and short-lived socialist and anti-conscription group, claimed:

> '*from Lord Hartington [MP for Rossendale before becoming the 8th Duke of Devonshire; leader of the Liberal party and then Liberal Unionists in the Commons and subsequently leader of the Liberal Unionists and then Conservatives in the Lords] down to the retiring member, the Rossendale division has been the dumping ground for candidates who have been either Lords or knights or have been created Lords or knights, and the time, it contends, has arrived when that great working-class constituency should be represented by a democratic candidate of the British Citizens party.*'[20]

Inevitably, the Liberals declined to withdraw and, indeed, selected a prominent local knight, Sir John Maden. As well as being the current chairman of Rossendale Liberals, Maden was Mayor of Bacup (for the thirteenth time) and had been MP for the constituency between 1892 and 1900. Professionally, he was Chairman of the Bacup cotton manufacturers, John Maden and Son. According to the *Rochdale Observer*, 'he was 'the leading figure in the public life of the Rossendale valley'.[21]

Having failed to achieve a free run from the Liberals, the British Citizens Party also found itself outflanked by more substantial 'peace by negotiation' forces. *The Yorkshire Post and Leeds Intelligencer* reported:

> '*The Socialist party and the No-Conscription Fellowship have been organising their forces, in conjunction with headquarters in London, and it is stated that in a very short time a peace candidate, who will be a Socialist, will be forthcoming ... Mr. Albert Taylor, the secretary of the Rossendale Shoe and Slipper Operatives' Union—the second strongest trades union in the division - has undertaken to lead the fight providing the candidate put forward is satisfactory.*'[22]

---

20 *Burnley News*, 27 December 1916.
21 *Rochdale Observer*, 30 December 1916.
22 *Yorkshire Post and Leeds Intelligencer*, 30 December 1916.

The Union of Democratic Control also decided the time was right, following the advent of the Lloyd George government, to participate in by-elections and they contributed significantly to the Rossendale campaign.

Albert Taylor was soon satisfied with the choice of candidate as, on 11 January 1917, Socialist and Labour representatives met in the constituency and chose to back him. However, Taylor brought complications. As a member of the executive of the BSP and the No-Conscription Fellowship, he was an avowed conscientious objector. He had recently been exempted from combatant service by the Central Tribunal in London but was instructed to undertake 'work of national importance' within seven days, which he refused to do.

Taylor's position highlights the lack of uniformity among conscientious objectors. Some were prepared to undertake roles even within the military (such as being stretcher-bearers) but not to fight; some refused to be under military command but would participate in other work that contributed directly or indirectly to the war effort; but some, of whom Taylor was one, refused to do anything that might assist the war in any way.

Under the Military Service Acts, tribunals had been set up across the country to adjudicate on claims for exemption from military service, including those based on conscientious objection. As was usual, Taylor's case had first gone before the relevant local Tribunal, that in Rawtenstall in east Lancashire. Here he was in an unusual position for he was himself a member of that tribunal. He had several potential grounds for appeal against being called up. He was a widower with two children and his mother was financially dependent on him. Also, his work as a trade union secretary might have given him grounds for exemption. However, he chose to rely on a claim of conscientious objection. The initial ruling of the local tribunal was to adjourn his case for a month and require him to seek work specified by the Pelham Committee, even though he had made it clear he was unwilling to do so. The role of that committee was to identify employers able to offer work of 'national importance' who were willing to accept conscientious objectors and place with them appellants who were unwilling to accept military service if the relevant tribunal accepted that. In practice, the great majority of placements were in agriculture, and they would quite often move people well away from their home areas. Taylor appealed against the decision in his case to the higher tier, Preston tribunal, but that appeal was rejected despite a petition being submitted in his support with more than 1,200 signatures. Following the Preston decision, he was removed as a member of the Rawtenstall Tribunal. In a protest meeting calling for his reinstatement, Taylor said:

> 'he was opposed to the war and to the master class who were living on the labour of his fellows. The workers should refuse to be used as a tool in the hands of the employing class, who bled them white. He would shout for peace and do all he could to get it.'[23]

Taylor's case ended up at the highest level, the Central Tribunal in London. This also confirmed his exemption from combatant duty, subject to his finding 'work of national importance' within seven days. *The Lancashire Evening Post* reported that the seven days had passed, and Taylor had confirmed he had not found such work.[24] Consequently, his selection as a candidate was going to cause the authorities difficulties.

The *Cotton Factory Times* reported him saying at his adoption meeting:

> 'he stood for peace by negotiation as against an enforced peace. If elected as member for Rossendale he would do all he could in the interests of the workers, to whom he might say he was wedded. He was a socialist and held that the war was a capitalist war and if elected to the House of Commons he would try to bring about an international relationship amongst the workers of the world so that they would cease to fly at each other's throats at the dictates of a few men in power.'[25]

The British Socialist Party national paper, *The Call,* provided strong support. They called him a 'gradely Lancashire lad' and claimed: 'there is no other man who could get the same results, as he is absolutely idolised by the members of his Union.'[26]

---

23 *Cotton Factory Times*, 24 November 1916.
24 *Lancashire Evening Post*, 7 January 1917.
25 *Cotton Factory Times*, 19 January 1917.
26 *The Call*, 25 January 1917.

The election writ was moved on 24 January 1917 and Taylor immediately organised a major meeting. Initially, it was to be held at a hall but that booking was unilaterally cancelled by the hall owners so he booked the Haslingden Picture Hall. However, when he and his supporting speakers arrived, they found it locked against them and he was forced to leave the town without speaking. A couple of days later, Taylor received his second calling-up notice and he was ordered to report to the military. His response was: 'I am called upon to go and fight against those with whom I have no quarrel. This I shall refuse to do.'[27]

As a result, on 29 January Taylor was arrested and appeared at a well-attended court hearing. He complained that he had received very short notice of impending arrest and believed that had been orchestrated by his political opponents, the Liberal party. In stormy scenes, one of the magistrates accused him of appealing to an outside mob, to which Taylor responded: 'I don't recognise them as a mob. I recognise them as human beings.' He argued that he should be allowed to continue as a candidate as that itself represented work of 'national interest'.[28] He was fined £2 and instructed to 'await a military escort'.

Despite Taylor being handed over to the military, his campaign, led by Charles Roden Buxton, a former Liberal MP and one of the founders of the UDC, confirmed his 'peace by negotiation' nomination would go ahead. Nor was he inaccurate in seeing the hand of his political opponents in the decision to arrest him so rapidly. As early as 1 February the socialist press was claiming 'the officer who was instrumental in authorising the police to take action was the Liberal agent for the division.'[29] This was Lt. Fred Monks, the local Recruiting Officer, who was the former Liberal agent for Rossendale and had been granted leave of absence to act as agent for the Coalition candidate, John Maden. This lasted a few days, after which the War Office withdrew permission, having been alerted to the situation through comment in the House of Commons. Consequently, Maden acted as his own agent for the rest of the campaign although it did not look good for the government campaign to have its own agent instrumental in the arrest of the opposition candidate.

---

27 *Northampton Chronicle and Echo*, 29 January 1917.
28 *Manchester Evening News*, 30 January 1917.
29 *Labour Leader*, 1 February 1917.

As the campaign began, international events dealt a blow to the 'peace by negotiation' faction. On 31 January, the Germans handed two documents to the Americans. The first was an uncompromising statement of war aims while the second announced the recommencement of unrestricted submarine warfare – something American opinion effectively viewed as a declaration of war on themselves. Suddenly, the apparent momentum towards the possibility of negotiations, supported by the strength of the US, had collapsed.

Back in Rossendale, the campaign would be short with nominations closing on 5 February and polling on 13 February. Despite Taylor's indisposition, a campaign was being put together with the assistance of leading socialist organisers from elsewhere as well as local union activists. Letters of support were publicised early on from leading peace stalwart MPs Philip Snowden, Ramsay MacDonald, and Charles Trevelyan. They wished Taylor success, saying: 'The continuance of the war will never bring conditions out of which a lasting peace can be made' (Snowden); 'I hope that Mr. Taylor may win such a measure of support to show that there is a great and growing opinion that it is time for reason to intervene and end this war, where force can never be a final arbiter.' (Trevelyan).

When nomination papers were submitted, Maden had 34 and while Taylor's agent had prepared 25, only two were accepted. Most of Taylor's papers were rejected because the nominators were required to be present when they were handed in and his were largely working men who could not obtain leave from their employment. Also, as one newspaper noted, Taylor himself was not present, being otherwise engaged in a North Wales military prison.[30]

Maden, meanwhile, was being referred to as the Liberal 'prosecution of the war' candidate and described as 'a popular employer of labour and the advocate of a rational programme' who could be certain of an overwhelming victory.[31] In addition to the expected support from the Coalition parties, Maden also attracted the backing of the Irish Nationalist MP, Thomas O'Connor, who was significant as the constituency contained a sizeable number of Irish voters. In a letter to Maden he said: 'To talk of making peace is an insult, especially at a moment when by proclaiming a policy of piracy and murder Germany has

---

30 *Halifax Evening Courier*, 6 February 1917.
31 *Derby Daily Telegraph*, 7 February 1917

driven the great neutral Republic of the West into hostility. It is an insult to our British and Irish dead.'

In his election address, Maden highlighted the fact that he supported 'prosecuting the war with the utmost vigour until the objectives for which we entered the war and for which we are fighting are finally achieved.' He also stated that the: 'Issues of separation allowances and pensions require investigation and revision' and that 'Provision should be made for more power and discretion being given to local committees.' His campaign slogan was 'Maden for Rossendale and Peace with Honour'.

Taylor's first campaign meeting was on Friday 9 February, the day after he had been court-martialled and sentenced to two years with hard labour.[32] The meeting was organised by a local resident who said he had done so in defence of free speech after Taylor had earlier been refused use of a local hall. The *Manchester Evening News* reported:

> '*Mr. Smethurst said he had been a Liberal all his life and striven for free speech and when he learned last week but one that the use of the Palace for a meeting for Mr. Taylor was withdrawn he offered to take the chair at a meeting called in defence of the rights of free speech, but to get the use of the Palace he had had to give his guarantee that the audience would be decent folks, and he hoped they were not going to ruin him. When polling day came, he would vote for Mr. Taylor.*'

The speakers were David Mason, the Liberal MP for Coventry who was a long-term campaigner for peace and against conscription; the campaign organiser, Charles Roden Buxton of the UDC and the Rev. Herbert Dunnico, the founder of the Peace Negotiations Committee. Each of them was subjected to a continuous fire of interjections, but there was no disturbance.'[33] On the same date, the Glasgow socialist paper, *Forward*, reported that more than 50 meetings had been arranged in support of Taylor and that significant amounts of money had been raised for the campaign.[34]

---

32 Cyril Pearce, *Communities of Resistance* (2020).
33 *Manchester Evening News*, 10 February 1917.
34 *Forward*, 10 February 1917.

Taylor's full election address was reprinted in *The Woman's Dreadnought*, the strongly anti-war Sylvia Pankhurst's weekly wartime newspaper. He led with the statement:

> *'I stand for "Peace by Negotiation." This does not mean "peace at any price," but a peace which will leave to each nation, small and great, independence and freedom of development, and will pave the way for a "League of Nations" to guarantee the world against another War. There is far more chance of obtaining such a peace by early negotiation than by encouraging the idea of a fight to the last shilling and the last drop of blood. If this policy is not adopted, we are informed that the present slaughter may have to be continued for another two years—with the certainty of the peace being brought about by negotiation after all.'*

As a trades unionist and socialist, Taylor also raised the spectre of 'industrial conscription' and argued: 'Notwithstanding the clearest and most solemn pledges, Industrial Conscription is already in operation.' Instead, he stood for 'the conscription of Wealth'. Other issues mentioned included pensions and allowances, female suffrage and 'a solution to the Irish difficulties on democratic lines'.[35] However, despite Taylor's wider, socialist, programme in his absence in detention the campaign was driven by Roden Buxton (who spoke at meetings every night for two weeks) who made it, overwhelmingly, one about peace-by-negotiation.

The Maden campaign, in contrast, began almost determined to ignore Taylor and planned limited activity. However, the mood changed at the weekend before polling day and it was decided to hold major public meetings after all, and to bring in experienced campaigners for a last-minute canvassing push. When polling day arrived, there was no expectation that Maden, who had been backed wholeheartedly by both Liberal and Conservative election workers, would be defeated. However, there was concern that Taylor's detention and the controversy regarding Monks' role would increase the opposition vote. According to the *Manchester Evening News*: 'Sir Henry's

---

35 *Woman's Dreadnought*, 10 February 1917.

supporters feel that Mr. Taylor will receive more votes than will be creditable to the division and to Lancashire, some putting the figure at 2,000.'[36]

Dec. 1910			
Harcourt	Liberal	6,619	56%
Hoyle	Conservative	5,206	44%
Majority		1,413	
Electorate & Turnout		13,217	90%

13 Feb. 1917			
Maden	Liberal	6,019	77%
Taylor	Independent Labour and Peace by Negotiation	1,804	23%
Majority		4,215	
Electorate & Turnout		13,682	57%

As anticipated, the outcome was a clear victory for Maden's 'Peace by Victory' campaign over Taylor's 'Peace by Negotiation'. It was felt that Taylor's vote had been boosted by his imprisonment and the controversy surrounding the role of the Liberal agent and, therefore, somewhat overstated support for any 'peace by negotiation' position.

The Labour Leader, a pacifist ILP newspaper, put a favourable interpretation on the outcome:

> *'To poll 1,804 uncanvassed votes in a constituency so utterly unprepared and apparently barren as this, with the added weight of the unpopularity since the candidate was a 'notorious conscientious objector', is for our cause little short of a triumph. The Government candidate polled 6,019 votes, which gave to our man one in four. In North Ayr, the proportion was only one in five and a half. So, it*

---

36 *Manchester Evening News*, 13 February 1917.

grows. With Rossendale yielding so much, no bye-election in any district should henceforward be allowed to pass unchallenged.[37]

Maden was to remain as the MP only until the 1918 General Election when he was to finish third in the same constituency behind Labour and the winning Unionist candidate. He then retired from political life. Taylor continued to be a problem for the authorities during the war. While in prison he refused to do prison work and was harshly punished and moved from Wormwood Scrubs to Shrewsbury. By January 1918, he risked becoming ill and was discharged and sent home. He was to remain as Secretary of his union until his death in 1947.

STOCKTON-ON-TEES – March 1917

Shortly after Rossendale, another by-election featured a 'Peace by Negotiation' candidate: the result was to be very different. Entirely unexpectedly, the sitting Liberal MP in Stockton-on-Tees in north-east England, Jonathan Samuel, died of a stroke on 21 February 1917.

Again, the by-election campaign coincided with significant developments regarding negotiations and peace. On 20 February, the leading 'peace' campaigners in the House of Commons initiated a major debate. Although still a small minority, they received a better hearing than at any other period in the war. Internationally, once unlimited submarine warfare commenced, President Wilson cut off diplomatic relations with Germany, and it was assumed that America would join the war on the Allied side. This assumption dramatically increased with the shock publication, on 1 March, of the Zimmermann telegram in which Germany incited Mexico to declare war on the United States. On 6 April, the United States entered the war, although it was to be a long time before it became an effective contributor to hostilities.

Back in Stockton, by early March 1917, reports emerged that the Liberals had approached three potential candidates while the Stockton Labour Association had invited Robert Dennison, an official of the Steel Smelters union and a Stockton town councillor, to address a meeting with a view to

---

37 *Labour Leader*, 15 February 1917.

Figure 1: Merthyr: The front page of the *Daily Sketch* (27/11/1915) welcoming Stanton's victory.

Figure 2: A Canadian recruitment poster (1915) highlights prominent British Jewish politicians, including Herbert Samuel, the Coalition candidate at Cleveland.

Figure 3: Cleveland Independent candidate Reggie Knight's long-term claim to fame. Illustration of his dog, Thunder, who was the reference for Knight's codification of breed characteristics for the Airedale Terrier.

Figure 4: West Newington: Socialist firebrand Joe Terrett on polling day in front of a committee room with two of the local councillors who backed him.

Figure 5: Noel Pemberton Billing flying over the hangars at Brooklands on course to gaining his pilot's licence and win a £500 wager with Frederick Handley Page. September 1913

Figure 6: Mile End: Noel Pemberton Billing campaigning in a Rolls-Royce during his first by-election campaign.

Figure 7: Mile End: A voter being taken to the polls in a Pemberton Billing aeroplane. One of Houston's PR stunts.

Figure 8: Mile End: Warwick Brookes being driven around the constituency during the campaign.

Figure 9: Hertford: Brodie Henderson on nomination day, outside one of his committee rooms.

Figure 10: A cartoon sketch of Tommy Gibson Bowles, the founder of *Vanity Fair* and *The Lady* magazines and the 'married men's candidate' at Harborough.

Figure 11: The inveterate showman Horatio Bottomly, addressing a 1915 recruiting rally. He backed several of the independent candidates during the war, finding by-elections almost irresistible.

Figure 12: Wimbledon: Kennedy Jones campaigning, talking to some motor men.

Figure 13: Wimbledon: Sir Stuart Coats and Lady Coats at the formal handing in of nomination papers.

Figure 14: North Ayrshire: The by-election manifesto of the first peace-by-negotiation candidate, Rev. Humphrey Chalmers.

Figure 15: A pre-war illustration of Hunter-Watson who was to be the Coalition candidate in North Ayrshire. He had a rather mixed reputation as a military commander.

Figure 16: Frederick Pethick Lawrence, the peace-by-negotiation candidate at South Aberdeen, in court with suffragette Emmeline Pankhurst in 1912

Figure 17: *Daily Sketch* front page coverage of the engagement of Lord Stanley, who was shortly to be the Coalition candidate at the Abercromby by-election.

Figure 18: A portrait of Edwin Scrymgeour, the Prohibitionist and anti-war candidate who opposed Churchill in Dundee in 1917. The painting dates from 1925, by which point 'Neddy' had become an MP.

Figure 19: East Islington: The National Party's first ever candidate, Edmund Barnard, indulges in traditional campaigning.

Figure 20: East Islington: Christabel Pankhurst, taking advantage of the by-election to continue the campaign for women's suffrage.

Figure 21: The highly patriotic Ben Tillett, the Independent candidate at North Salford, on one of his earlier visits to the front, being shown a howitzer.

Figure 22: Nina Boyle who attempted, unsuccessfully, to become the first ever female candidate at the Keighley by-election. Pre-war she was a campaigning journalist, submitting many pieces to *The Vote*, the newspaper of the Women's Freedom League.

Figure 23: The victor at Clapham, Harry Greer, was a keen golfer. Here he is photographed in 1929 (on the right) with Lord Ashfield at the annual Brigands tournament at Le Touquet.

Figure 24: Large demonstrations in London in favour of the internment of aliens, the inflammatory issue on which Pemberton Billing campaigned vehemently in by-elections towards the end of the war.

becoming a candidate. However, Labour decided not to run, providing the Liberals adopted a candidate supportive of the Lloyd George administration.

At the same time, Edward Backhouse JP, a prominent local Liberal (he was President of the South East Durham Liberal Association) and well-known banker and Quaker, was adopted as a 'Peace by Negotiation' candidate, following a 'well-attended' meeting at which Charles Roden Buxton and a local ILP representative had also spoken.[38] His agent was to be James Standring, who had acted for Taylor in Rossendale. Standring was an ILP activist, and regional organiser in the North-West. He was the author of a 1910 book, Socialism & Peru – in which he argued that the Inca civilisation was socialist in character.

Backhouse immediately started to distribute his election address and by 5 March, the *Yorkshire Post* declared that he had 'already covered the constituency with literature'. The address opened by Backhouse saying that a 'representative Meeting of Electors has done me the honour of inviting me to contest the seat as an advocate of Peace by Negotiation'. Optimistically, he stated: 'I am convinced that negotiation would lead to a satisfactory peace within a very short period, giving to the peoples all for which they entered the War'. He deployed the, by now standard, arguments that the Allies must make it clear they were not fighting a war of aggression and that 'a peace dictated by one side alone would unquestionably be the seedbed for future wars.' Other issues raised in the manifesto were:

- The restoration of British liberties – 'The war has brought to Britain, Conscription, military and industrial. It has deprived us of freedom of the Press, of speech, of trial, and the right of asylum.'
- Opposition to a commercial war after the war
- A levy on capital to help pay back the war debt – 'I have no objection to the conscription of wealth'
- Generous pensions for the dependents of the fallen
- Adult suffrage for men and women
- A policy of reconciliation in Ireland

---

38 *Sheffield Daily Telegraph*, 2 March 1917.

In conclusion, Backhouse exhorted electors: 'In the interests of the men in the trenches I appeal for your votes'.[39]

On 5 March, Backhouse held his first meeting, at the Borough Hall. His key supporters were Edward John, the MP for East Derbyshire and Charles Trevelyan, the MP for Elland and one of the founders of the Union of Democratic Control. According to the *Yorkshire Post*: 'For about three-quarters of an hour, an attempt was made, in face of continuous uproar, to proceed with the meeting, and during Mr. Trevelyan's speech the opposing element in the audience broke from the back of the hall, and took charge of the platform, the meeting ending abruptly'.[40] Other accounts recorded that there were many soldiers and sailors in the audience and that 'scenes of great disorder' occurred. Fortunately, by the next evening, local audiences decided at least to allow Backhouse a hearing, even if by their questions and general reactions they obviously did not sympathise with him.

On the same day, the Liberals selected their candidate Betrand Watson, a local solicitor who had joined the army the previous year while Mayor of Stockton. Watson now issued his manifesto. As with many other 'government' by-election candidates it was highly conventional. He referred to himself as 'The Coalition Candidate' and argued that 'the one dominating matter overshadowing all others is the conduct of the War. Every nerve should be strained and every effort made towards the vigorous prosecution of our cause to a victorious issue.' He further confirmed that he would 'wholeheartedly support the present or any Government in any measure or course of action conducive to the speedy and successful termination of the conflict.'[41]

Labour confirmed they would not make a nomination. In any case, their preferred choice, Dennison, advised them that 'as he was a member of the British Steel Smelters' Association, affiliated to the National Labour Party, which had agreed to the political truce, he could not enter the lists at the present election'. Consequently, 'it was decided to take no further action so far as this election was concerned.'[42] Similarly, the Irish Nationalists' organisation in Stockton resolved to take no part and not to issue a recommendation to

---

39 Backhouse election address. Bristol University Library, Special Collections.
40 *Yorkshire Post*, 6 March 1917.
41 Watson manifesto. University of Bristol Library: Special collections.
42 *Daily Gazette for Middlesbrough*, 10 March 1917.

their supporters. Theirs was a complex position; they were irritated by the government's attitude towards home rule but also wished to see a vigorous conduct of the war. Local estimates were that a clear majority of the Irish vote would back Watson, despite Backhouse's 'forward' position on the Irish question.

In the early stages, the Peace by Negotiation campaign was hopeful of a good result. They had a well-known, and well-liked, local figure as the candidate. Moreover, resources were being drawn from far afield, including the leading lights of the Rossendale election. However, their efforts were to be damaged by a series of missteps, by the candidate and his supporters.

Initially, what were by now the standard arguments were exchanged between the two sides. Watson argued the need for wholehearted support of the government and that Berlin would be watching what the result said about British resolve. He believed no negotiated peace would be durable and, currently, it would be built on the back of German victories. From the Backhouse campaign, it was asserted that indications from Germany were that it should be possible to negotiate a peace that met the primary reasons why Britain had entered the war – namely, the freedom of Belgium and Northern France and reparations from Germany. They claimed the war was now being fought for aggressive purposes such as securing Constantinople for Russia. Moreover, they pointed out that any suggestions of victory in 1917 had been abandoned and that the conflict looked set to continue indefinitely.

One controversy concerned women's suffrage. Backhouse was fully supportive of 'votes for women' and his campaign organised a meeting specifically for women even though they could not vote. The announcement of the meeting was via messages chalked on pavements on the day it was to be held, described as 'a regular dodge of the ILP to save on printers' bills'. However, the local press reported that the suffrage movement was far from united behind Backhouse. Quoting a local suffrage leader, the *Newcastle Journal* reported:

> 'The people connected with the Women's movement in Stockton have no intention officially of entering this contest. ... We officially or unofficially know nothing about the meeting, and none of us will be present. ... I believe it is some of the Manchester men who are supporting the 'Peace-by-Negotiation' candidate

> who have called the meeting. They have done it in other parts, but the women of Stockton are not going to have it. All connected with the women's movement here have relatives fighting or nursing. Can it be expected that we should prove traitors to our brothers and sisters at home or on the fronts?[43]

Yet some national suffrage journals did support for the Backhouse campaign. *The Vote*, the magazine of the Women's Freedom League, which adopted a pacifist position during the war, boasted:

> 'First in the field, as soon as the contest was announced, was the Women's Freedom League. On Friday the streets were chalked, and a fine open-air meeting was held in the Market Place, at which the equal terms resolution was passed with one dissentient. All the week open-air meetings are being held at all the factory gates in the dinner hour and every evening at 6.30 in the Market Place. Miss Sylvia Pankhurst will speak for the League in the Borough Hall on a date to be fixed at 7.30 p.m. Suffrage is one of the leading notes of the campaign.[44]

Sylvia Pankhurst's *The Woman's Dreadnought* also printed messages of support for Backhouse.

As the writ was issued, Backhouse angered the coalition by appearing to say that the government and Watson were lying. On 12 March he said: 'you get nothing but truth from this platform, but you get lies from the other platform. I don't believe they will tell you deliberate untruths, but they don't know the truth themselves'. This caused uproar at the meeting, following which Backhouse tried to clarify his point: 'I say you don't get the whole truth from the other platform, but that is a very different thing to saying that you get lies. The worst thing I have to say about my opponents is that they are blind leaders of the blind.'[45]

The Watson team took strong exception to Backhouse's comments about their campaign and pro-Coalition newspapers argued that they had rather backfired on Backhouse, as demonstrated by the *Newcastle Journal*: 'The heckling which the 'Peace' candidate, Mr Backhouse, is meeting with at every

---

43 *Newcastle Journal,* 13 March 1917.
44 *The Vote*, 9 March 1917.
45 *Daily Gazette for Middlesbrough*, 13 March 1917.

gathering seems to have overcome his temper, and so he has now adopted the non-paying art of personalities and Mr B Watson, the Coalition candidate, has become the chief target.[46]

By nomination day, the peace by negotiation campaign had become downbeat about their chances. However, despite recognising that they were struggling, Backhouse's lieutenants continued to campaign hard, and issued four editions of the *Stockton Elector*, a four-page campaign leaflet/newspaper. When a heckler at a peace by negotiation meeting offered the candidate a one penny to £10 bet that he would not win, much amusement was caused by Backhouse refusing to take the bet, even at the risk of losing only one penny. His campaign was then hit by a further misjudgement. Trouble arose over the distribution of a card which depicted the crucifixion and the words: 'In Christ's Name—Peace'. This significantly offended the catholic community (and so further reduced Backhouse's support from the Irish vote), and the nonconformists. It was said to be the work of 'women agents' of Backhouse although his campaign claimed it hadn't been authorised. According to the *Newcastle Journal*: 'The candidate absolutely denied all knowledge of the matter, but admitted that a lady friend, who was working on his behalf, allowed her enthusiasm to overrun discretion'.[47]

On polling day, all noted the lacklustre nature of campaigning. Posters had been limited due to restrictions on paper, the campaigns managing only one design each. The number of motorcars available to ferry voters to the polls was severely limited by petrol rationing and most were on Watson's side. Commentators acknowledged that Backhouse had fought a committed battle, in the face of very considerable opposition and negativity, but assessed that he was doomed to a heavy defeat. Overall, it was a far cry from the hopeful, early assessment of the *Labour Leader* that: 'there is a large volume of opinion strongly in favour of the ideas put forward by the candidate, Mr. Edward Backhouse.'[48]

---

46 *Newcastle Journal*, 15 March 1917.
47 *Newcastle Journal*, 20 March 1917.
48 *Leeds Mercury*, 21 March 1917.

Dec. 1910			
Samuel	Liberal	5,510	53%
Richardson	Conservative	4,840	47%
Majority		670	
Electorate & Turnout		11,582	89%

20 Mar. 1917			
Watson	Coalition	7,641	93%
Backhouse	Peace by Negotiation	596	7%
Majority		7,045	
Electorate & Turnout		13,882	59%

The outcome was a major blow to the peace by negotiation cause, and widely recognised as such, given a candidate who was known to be popular and respected locally. The *Leeds Mercury* commented:

> 'It is the biggest defeat the Peace party has sustained at any election since the war began, and ought to be sufficient to teach those who live in the cloudy realms of Peace-by-negotiation that they are utterly out touch with the real sentiment of the British people. Mr. Backhouse is an honourable gentleman, whose great local influence as a member of the well-known banking firm, and as a prominent member of the Society of Friends, made him an ideal candidate for the cause he represented. It would be difficult to find one better fitted for the purpose, but the people of Stockton have shown what we believe is the opinion of the British people throughout the world, that it is impossible to negotiate with a nation that treats all its pledges as scraps of paper, or to make peace with a people that would plunge Europe into another war the moment it felt itself powerful enough to do so.'[49]

---

49 *Leeds Mercury*, 21 March 1917.

Some commentators felt that the obviously greater resolve of the new Lloyd George government had made it less likely that people would want to see negotiations entered into 'prematurely'.

Managing reactions, the *Labour Leader* argued that the armaments industry was heavily represented in Stockton and that the ILP was weak there. Moreover, although the paper felt that the campaign had worked effectively, distributing 15,000 leaflets daily towards the end, it recognised the difficulty of overcoming 'misconceptions' that had not been questioned earlier, especially when the mainstream press was talking about 'German retreats' immediately before polling.[50] In the privacy of his (unpublished) diary, Liberal MP Arthur Ponsonby, who had spoken at election meetings in Stockton, conceded that the outcome had been 'a failure, a very small vote'.

SOUTH ABERDEEN – April 1917

During the Stockton campaign, a vacancy arose in South Aberdeen and, again, peace by negotiation campaigners decided to run. The sitting MP, Liberal George Esslemont, resigned following advice from his doctor that for the sake of his health he needed to cease all parliamentary activities; he was to die six months later. There may, however, have been more to the resignation. Esslemont had refused to support conscription and was facing strong opposition from his constituency party.

The Liberals wished to select a candidate quickly but ran into controversy when some in the constituency lobbied to adopt a supporter of Asquith rather than Lloyd George. Early on, Sir James Murray, a former MP, friend of Lloyd George and local benefactor, was put forward as a government supporter who would wish only to serve until the end of the war. Eventually, the Liberals had a list of three potential candidates; in addition to Murray there were two supporters of Asquith, Sir John Fleming and Vivian Phillips but this was reduced to a straight Lloyd George vs. Asquith fight when Phillips, who was Asquith's private secretary, was dropped before the final ballot of Liberal members on 16 March.

Beforehand, the peace by negotiation candidate emerged. On 12 March, Frederick Pethick-Lawrence arrived in Aberdeen, accompanied by his wife

---

50 *Labour Leader*, 22 March 1917.

and supporters. A lawyer from a long-standing Liberal family, Pethick-Lawrence had married the socialist and suffragette campaigner, Emmeline Pethick in 1901 when he also became a socialist. In 1912, he served a prison sentence for his part in the window-smashing campaigns of the Women's Social and Political Union and, after the outbreak of war, became one of the founders of the Union of Democratic Control. On 13 March, a small meeting of UDC and others was held at Aberdeen Central Hall, with fewer than fifty attending, at which Pethick-Lawrence was unanimously adopted. ILP and socialist campaigners were involved at the meeting, but it was decided that Pethick-Lawrence would be named solely as a UDC candidate. He was independently wealthy so there was no doubt that funds would be available, and the *Aberdeen Evening Express* had some fun regarding the likely reaction a pacifist candidate might engender by saying:

> 'By the time the South Aberdeen by-election is over it is pretty safe to say that our Special Constables will have a fair amount of duty put upon them. A political fight means extra work for the policemen. I would not be surprised to learn that the Specials are undergoing a course of dumb-bell exercises to get into what, for want of a better phrase, might be termed "fighting trim" to be ready for all eventualities.'[51]

Pethick-Lawrence immediately detailed his policies. In a substantial press interview he said:

> 'The war at the present time is the paramount issue, and consequently attitudes on that matter take first place. I am convinced that the war could brought to an end on terms favourable to this country by negotiation at the present time. I am not in the least in favour of peace at any price but a peace which will restore Belgium and France and the other countries which are overrun by German troops. I do not think the rights of British men should be sacrificed, and vast treasure expended on vague schemes of conquest, or for the handing of Constantinople over to Russia. I honour the men who have faced injury and death in France, and I think that when they return home they should secure very much better

---

51 *Aberdeen Evening Express*, 14 March 1917.

treatment than they do at the present time. With regard to the future, I hold that it is essential that the people of the country should have a greater control over the House of Commons, and that the House of Commons should have more effective control of the Government. The long fight which I have put up on behalf women's suffrage will be known to everyone ... I am a strong supporter of Free Trade, and an opponent of all the schemes for setting up tariff barriers ... I believe in a system of devolution by which the people of every component part of the British Empire will have self-government for local affairs, while uniting under Imperial Government for the whole; and I particularly desire to see Home Rule granted to Ireland. I am opposed to conscription, either for the Army or for industry, which I think is liable to degenerate into a very serious tyranny. In other particulars, I am also strongly suspicious of the great encroachments upon liberty which have taken place during the last few years.[52]

Another Aberdeen paper, the *Press and Journal*, provided an early sight of the venom likely to be directed at Pethick-Lawrence, saying:

'If he has not come to Aberdeen to tell us he is prepared at this moment to clasp the hands of the bloodstained German murderers, the outragers of Belgian and French women and the slaughterers of innocent children, we shall be glad to know what he is aiming at.'[53]

At the same time, the local branch of the 'patriotic' British Workers National League announced it intended strenuously to oppose any 'peace by negotiation' candidate.

Pethick-Lawrence opened his campaign with a meeting at which Arthur Ponsonby, the Liberal MP for Stirling, and Pethick-Lawrence's wife, Emmeline, also spoke. The meeting passed without much incident, although all the speakers were subjected to heckling and significant questioning. One summary stated: 'Yet Pethick-Lawrence and his hobbyhorse and his motley army are not to be underestimated. The peace candidate has the

---

52 Ibid.
53 *Aberdeen Press and Journal*, 14 March 1917.

field to himself. He had his first canter last night, and seemed to enjoy it, notwithstanding a running fire of interruptions.'[54]

On 16 March, the Liberals came to a surprise decision, and selected the Asquithian, Fleming over Lloyd George's preferred man, Murray, by 63 votes to 27. The discussion had revealed sharp divisions within the party and supporters of Fleming argued that their political opponents were seeking to impose a candidate (Murray) on them. One pro-Murray correspondent summed up the choice that the Liberals had faced: 'One is to bring forward a man who will loyally support the present Government in prosecuting the war to a speedy and successful issue, and the other is supporting the pin-pricking policy of the discredited Asquith party.'[55] Pin-pricking won.

Shortly afterwards, Murray intimated that he would stand anyway, despite not receiving the Liberal nomination while Pethick-Lawrence welcomed Ramsay MacDonald to speak on his behalf. These both turned out to be rather frustrated actions. The MacDonald meeting, estimated to be attended by 3,000 people, was totally wrecked by 'patriotic' protestors howling down the speakers and, although MacDonald persevered for eight minutes, no one beyond the platform and the press table was able to hear him. Furthermore, he and the rest of the platform party were subjected to a barrage of eggs and rotten oranges, onions and potatoes, in between renditions of the national anthem and Rule Britannia. Finally, they were forced to abandon the meeting as 'hundreds' of young men seized the stage. The *Daily Mail* reported this as 'eggs thrown at peace prattle platform' and described it as 'an old-fashioned election'.

As a result of this experience, the next day the peace campaign was better prepared. For that evening's meeting, they decided to refuse entrance to youths. However, the result was a large-scale altercation outside the hall, as described by the *Daily Record*:

> *'A crowd of fully 1000 young men had assembled at the main door of the hall and, thwarted in their efforts to get inside the building, they pelted the windows with rotten eggs and decayed fruit. A large force of police, however ... charged*

---

[54] *Aberdeen Evening Express*, 16 March 1917.
[55] *Aberdeen Press*, 19 March 1917.

the crowd with their batons. A few elderly people and some boys were knocked down... A terrific crash was heard when a piece of metal was hurled through one of the windows of the hall. Thereupon the police made another charge and dispersed the crowd'.[56]

Meanwhile, on the Liberal side, Sir James Murray agreed to withdraw his candidature, following a direct appeal from Lloyd George. In a letter, the Prime Minister wrote:

'My dear Murray,—I understand that you have announced your intention of standing as a supporter of the present Government at the pending by-election in Aberdeen. I have little doubt that, if you persisted in your intention, you would meet with ... success ... It must, however, be remembered that the nation is going through a great crisis in its history, and I wish to give no opportunity for it to be said that I, or any of my friends, are in any way impairing the national unity ... I, therefore, suggest what I know you will agree to, in view of the friendship between us, that you withdraw your candidature... Sincerely yours, D. Lloyd George.[57]

Now, a divided Liberal organisation was under pressure to mount a campaign while Pethick-Lawrence continued, albeit in the face of continuing opposition (the most recent event was the smashing of a window at one of his committee rooms), with a regular programme of meetings. In addition to his main nightly campaign meetings, this also included women's meetings in the afternoon and, soon, both 'dinner time' and 'breakfast hour' outdoor rallies at workplaces. Among speakers who came to support him were the pacifist stalwarts, Charles Roden Buxton and the Rev Herbert Dunnico and the Asquithian MP, Hastings Lees Smith. He was the Liberal MP for Northampton but had joined up in 1915, deciding to serve without a commission and was invalided out in 1917 as a corporal. Despite this, he was one of the founders of the UDC and strongly opposed to conscription. By coincidence, he was, briefly, to be leader of the opposition in 1941 and was followed in that role by Pethick-Lawrence.

---

56 *Daily Record*, 21 March 1917.
57 *Aberdeen Press and Journal*, 21 March 1917.

Fleming issued his election address but that did not end calls from some Liberals (and Unionists) for another candidate to represent the patriotic, pro-government position. The address said little. Fleming claimed: 'My opinions on current political topics are well known to you and are, I believe, in consonance with those of the bulk of the electors'. On the key issue of the war, he stated,

> 'The one thing in the minds of all at present is to hold up the hands of the Government in their strenuous conduct of the War so unjustly thrust upon us, that we may be carried as quickly as possible to a victorious conclusion, and that the demands of the Allies for restitution, reparation, and protection against future assaults may be firmly secured. It will be my duty to support the Ministry in carrying forward these objects.'

Fleming was restricted in his ability to campaign as he was still recovering from quite a long term illness.

The next twist occurred with the arrival of a third candidate: J Robertson Watson, Professor of Chemistry at Anderson's College, Glasgow. Watson had a distinctive political history. He had been a founder member of the ILP and had stood for parliament in Glasgow. He next took up the cause of Tariff Reform, for which he campaigned for many years. With the arrival of war, he adopted a strongly 'patriotic' position and was active in arguing against 'peace' organisations in Glasgow. He opened his Aberdeen campaign in robust fashion, stating he was for two key principles, 'national democratic service' and 'a minimum living legal wage'. He argued that the war was not about Belgium or France; instead:

> 'we are out to save Britain and the British Empire for our children's children and that cannot be done until the German menace has been completely smashed. I believe that Lloyd George is the country's only hope and salvation in the present crisis and if returned by you to parliament will give his government enthusiastic support in the vigorous prosecution of the war to a triumphant issue.'[58]

---

58 *Aberdeen Evening Express*, 27 March 1917.

In his opening speeches, he positioned Fleming as clearly an Asquith rather than a Lloyd George candidate and claimed that he, Watson, was a truer representative of the national coalition of Unionists, Lloyd George Liberals and the 'patriotic' sections of the labour movement. He stood as an Independent National Candidate and advertised his meetings as Citizens' Meetings. These certainly gained attention with one attracting an audience of more than 800.

The press noticed that Pethick-Lawrence was doing much more in terms of distributing leaflets than either of his opponents. It was stated: 'Mr Lawrence is practically flooding the constituency with literature – a phase of electioneering in which his opponents have done little or nothing. But the peace-by-negotiation cause is supported not merely by leaflets and such like, but by the '*South Aberdeen Elector*', a four-page paper expressing the views of the candidate on the war and Free Trade – a repeat of the campaigning approach adopted in Stockton.'[59] Pethick-Lawrence and Watson also held more meetings than Fleming, whose campaigning was still impeded by his ill-health. However, one boost came to Fleming from the local Unionists, who might have been tempted to back Watson. They made a formal statement of their unanimous support for the official candidate, although only following an exchange of letters in which they obtained a personal commitment from him. The Unionists wrote:

> *'I am requested by the executive of this association to ask you to say, whether, in the event of your being returned as member, you will loyally and unreservedly support Mr Lloyd George and the National Government in everything required for the successful prosecution of the war, and in their efforts to bring it to a speedy and victorious conclusion.'*

Fleming, the same day, confirmed his agreement and, in response, the Unionists announced that: 'the association unanimously resolved that, relying on the guarantee contained in the reply sent by Sir John Fleming, and in accordance with the party truce and, further, in order to express its emphatic

---

[59] *Aberdeen Evening Express*, 30 March 1917.

disapproval of the principles of peace by negotiation, it should recommend all Unionists in the division to support Sir John Fleming at the poll'.[60]

As the very brief campaign ended, opposition to Pethick-Lawrence remained strong. At one of his dinner time meetings outside an engineering works he was at first listened to but when his answers to questions were deemed unacceptable, he was then subject to a sustained snowball attack; this only came to an end when one accidentally struck a very young child resulting in the mother turning on the throwers.

All three candidates held meetings on the final evening before polling. Fleming positioned his as a 'great patriotic rally' while Pethick-Lawrence described his meeting as being for 'peace and liberty'. Last-minute appeals also appeared in the Aberdeen press from Unionists dissatisfied with the selection of Fleming and with the Unionist endorsement of him. Instead, they called for support for Watson as a genuine 'win-the-war' candidate. The difference in style between the 'official' and 'unofficial' national campaigns was illustrated by their side-by-side final notices in the *Aberdeen Press and Journal*. The Fleming campaign restricted itself to reminding voters that they could inspect the electoral rolls in their committee rooms to check for which address they were registered. By contrast, Watson, said that voters: 'who wish to give proof of their patriotism and of their desire to strengthen the hand of the current government can do so today by recording their votes for Professor James Robertson Watson'.

Polling day turned out to be quiet and many remarked on a lack of interest in the election. This was confirmed by low turn-out, which fell by much more than in other recent by-elections. Commentators assumed that this was largely a result of dissatisfaction with the Liberals' choice of a candidate who would 'answer to Asquith and not Lloyd George'.

Nevertheless, as the 'official' candidate, Fleming was duly elected, although Watson achieved a respectable result given the extremely limited time available to him to campaign and the slightly quixotic nature of some of his policy positions.

---

60 Quoted in *Aberdeen Press and Journal*, 31 March 1917.

Dec. 1910			
Esselmont	Liberal	5,862	60%
Smith	Liberal Unionist	3,997	40%
Majority		1,865	
Electorate & Turnout		13,657	72%

3 April 1917			
Fleming	Liberal	3,283	64%
Watson	Independent National	1,507	29%
Pethick-Lawrence	Peace by Negotiation	333	7%
Majority		1,776	
Electorate & Turnout		13,791	37%

Despite a strong campaign and a high-profile candidate, Pethick-Lawrence polled very poorly. The pro-government press was delighted to highlight the sustained decline in the 'conchie' vote from the heights achieved in Rossendale. That view was well summarised by the *Aberdeen Press and Journal*:

> 'When Sir James Murray withdrew from the field we concentrated our energies against the peace-by-negotiation candidate in the fear that his persuasions and perversions might possibly give him a vote running towards four figures. Mr Lawrence, with his henchmen and henchwomen, had a week's lead over the other two candidates, he scattered literature throughout the constituency with ... lavishness ... and he worked with an energy which in a better cause would have been admirable. The result was 333 votes and if each vote has not cost him £2 there will be occasion for some surprise. The Peace-by-Negotiation candidate came into Aberdeen like a whirlwind; he may depart from the City in peace, having first received the proverbial flea in his ear. In Rossendale, the Pacifist candidate polled 1,804 votes; in North Ayrshire, 1,300 votes; in Stockton-on-Tees, 596

votes and in South Aberdeen 333 votes. Aberdeen, we may naturally conclude, has given the quietus to the Peace-by-Negotiation cause and no better blow could be delivered.[61]

Other post-election discussion revolved around the impact of the decision of the Liberals to select an Asquithian candidate. The general view was that this had led to considerable dissatisfaction and the sharper than typical fall in turnout was attributed to this, as was the relatively strong polling by Watson, despite his lack of official endorsement and unknown status in the city; some estimated that he received more Unionist votes than did Fleming.

Finally, it is possible that Watson's intervention may have encouraged some Liberals, who might otherwise have expressed a protest through a vote for Pethick-Lawrence, to stick with Fleming out of concern that he might be outflanked from the 'patriotic' direction. But even if that were a contributory factor, South Aberdeen made clear that 'pacifist' campaigns were now striking almost no chord with the electorate. The ILP newspaper, *Labour Leader*, identified several factors to explain the poor peace vote. It argued that news of advances on the Western Front, combined with America's announcement, on the day before polling, that it was entering the war, had together encouraged voters to believe that a successful, and relatively quick, victory might now be achievable. Ponsonby, in his diary, reflected: 'America coming into the war and the hopeless failure of the Aberdeen election made any move on our part out of the question'.

Fleming's stay in parliament was to be short-lived; he stood again in the 1918 election but was heavily defeated by the Unionists. Watson also stood again at that election, finishing third. Ironically, it was Pethwick-Lawrence who went on to have the successful political career. He won Leicester West for Labour in the 1923 election and served as Financial Secretary to the Treasury in the 1929 – 31 Labour government. In the 1945 government he was, from the House of Lords, Secretary of State for India and Burma until independence.

---

61 *Aberdeen Press and Journal*, 4 April 1917.

The rise and fall of peace negotiation hopes

After the setback at Aberdeen, peace-by-negotiation campaigners moved away from by-elections and Edwin Scrymgeour's decision to stand in Dundee in July 1917 was a personal and local one (see chapter 10).

In the year following the Aberdeen election, the hopes of the 'peace by negotiation' factions were to be raised, and then firmly dashed. In July 1917, the centrist parties in the Reichstag succeeded in passing an admittedly toothless 'peace resolution' which said nothing about territorial issues nor indemnities but hinted at support for future 'international organisations' providing any ideas of post-war economic sanctions or exclusions (of Germany) were abandoned. Shortly after, the Pope offered to facilitate negotiations, but that initiative came to nothing. In Britain, the government (and parliament) remained firmly wedded to Lloyd George's 'knockout blow'; an attempt by MacDonald to build on the Reichstag initiative was soundly rebuffed in the House of Commons at the end of July with only 19 voting in favour. So strong was the aversion to any suggestion of negotiations that even a request by Maurice Hankey (Secretary of the War Committee) for permission to begin making administrative arrangements for an eventual peace conference was rebuffed.[62]

In November 1917, the Allied war effort suffered a double blow with the Russian Revolution, which was eventually to precipitate Russia's exit from the battle, and a shattering defeat of the Italians at Caporetto; yet another year threatened to end with gloomy prospects for victory, even despite the arrival of the Americans. This provided the background for the re-emergence of a key figure in the history of arguments in favour of peace negotiations, Lord Lansdowne. Now in his seventies, Lansdowne had stood down as Minister without Portfolio in government with the formation of the Lloyd George administration, in December 1916. Prior to that, he had enjoyed a glittering career in the Unionist party which had culminated in his holding office as Foreign Secretary and then Leader of the House of Lords in the 1900 - 05 Conservative administration. Whilst serving under Asquith, Lansdowne had essayed a first attempt to stimulate consideration of war aims and the potential for negotiations. Depressed by the cost in human lives of Verdun and the

---

62 *Lansdowne: The Last Great Whig* (2017), S. Kerry.

Somme, Lansdowne wanted an attempt at a negotiated peace, in opposition to the ever-growing drumbeats arguing for nothing less than a 'knockout blow'. In October 1916, Asquith asked the War Committee to consider what might be acceptable peace terms. Lansdowne responded by circulating a memorandum questioning whether a comprehensive victory would ever be possible. He hoped to arrange a secret sitting of the Lords to discuss these thoughts but the fall of the Asquith ministry and Lloyd George's appointment as Prime Minister put an end to that plan and to Lansdowne's time in government.

Lansdowne went quietly and made no public statement of his support for exploring possibilities for negotiations until November 1917 when he decided he could remain silent no longer. Dissuaded from raising questions in the Lords, he instead issued a public statement in the press. His first port of call, *The Times*, would have nothing to do with it, but the *Daily Telegraph* was more accommodating, and on 29 November 1917, it published what was to become known as 'the Peace letter'.

The letter came as a total surprise to the public and, generally, a singularly unwelcome one. The *Daily Mail* reflected majority opinion, stating 'if Lord Lansdowne raises the white flag he is alone in his surrender.' In truth, Lansdowne's position was far more nuanced than the jingoes would concede. He doubted a knockout blow could be delivered and, even if it could, he feared the consequence would simply be to set in train future, possibly even greater, conflicts. (In a speech in the Lords in 1918 he reminded the house of the consequences of the crushing defeat of Prussia at the battle of Jena in 1806 which, nevertheless, had been followed by Blucher marching into Paris only eight years later).

The government, and nearly all respectable opinion, responded to the shock of such an establishment figure thinking the unthinkable by doubling down on 'the fight to the finish' and ex-communicating Lansdowne. But his initiative delivered a shot in the arm to the 'peace by negotiation' forces. They sought to build on the accretion to their side of the argument of so august a figure. Early in 1918, discussion of peace prospects moved on rapidly. On 5 January, Lloyd George finally made a speech which addressed Britain's war aims. Three days later, President Wilson outlined his fourteen points, which he envisaged as the necessary building blocks for peace.

Peace-by-negotiation campaigners now pushed to use Wilson and Lansdowne to their advantage. Wilson's speech was viewed as making discussion of peace acceptable while Lansdowne's initiative provided a British focal point that could widen the campaign beyond religious and socialist groups viewed by many as extreme and/or unrepresentative. Forces such as the UDC were delighted but deliberately kept their distance from Lansdowne, so as not to taint his position. A first Lansdowne-Labour conference was held on 26 February 1918 and soon several local Lansdowne Committees had been founded.

But if there had been the potential for momentum towards considering negotiations, it was now sharply reversed. The harsh terms imposed on the Russians at the Treaty of Brest-Litovsk (3 March 1918) provided a difficult background. Also, the Spring of 1918 was a bleak time for allied military prospects, in the face of the major German offensive, which began on 21 March and led to Field Marshal Douglas Haig's desperate Special Order of the Day (11 April 1918) stating:

> *'There is no other course open to us but to fight it out. Every position must be held to the last man: there must be no retirement. With our backs to the wall and believing in the justice of our cause each one of us must fight on to the end. The safety of our homes and the freedom of mankind alike depend upon the conduct of each one of us at this critical moment'.*

KEIGHLEY – April 1918

Consequently, March/April 1918 was not an obvious time to recommence by-election campaigning in favour of peace by negotiation. However, the initiative came from the local ILP in Keighley which had fought the seat in a 1913 by-election and had available the same candidate, William Bland, a local cabinetmaker and long-term activist. He was to stand as 'ILP and Peace by Negotiation'.

As it happens, the 1918 Keighley by-election has its place in history, not only due to the presence of a peace-by-negotiation candidate but also by the attempt of a woman to stand. The Representation of the People Act, which gave some women the vote, received Royal Assent in February 1918 but wasn't to come into force until the next General Election. However, a leading Suffragette campaigner, Nina Boyle, announced she intended to be a candidate. She stated that if her nomination were refused, she would then go to the courts for a definitive ruling on whether women were now eligible to stand as well as vote.

Her plans may have been more devious than that. She submitted two nomination papers, but both contained errors – one included a non-elector and the other had an elector for a different constituency. Therefore, the returning officer declined her nomination although stated that, had the nominations been in order, he would not have refused them as it was not for him to rule on the eligibility of women candidates. These may have been genuine errors but, equally, they enabled Boyle to obtain an indication of the legal position without incurring the expense of an election (At this time, even a candidate who chose to spend no money on their campaign would still be liable for their share of the Returning Officer's expenses). Eventually, the issue of the eligibility of women candidates was taken to the courts which ruled that the Representation of the People Act had not made women eligible to be candidates, only to vote. In response, the shortest-ever British statute (27 operative words) was passed on 21 November 1918 as the Parliament (Qualification of Women) Act 1918 which said: 'A woman shall not be disqualified by sex or marriage for being elected to or sitting or voting as a Member of the Commons House of Parliament.' This made women over 21 eligible to be nominated, even though the voting age for women had been set at 30, in a political compromise to ensure they did not form a majority of the electorate.

The Keighley vacancy occurred due to the unexpected death on 16 March, due to complications following an operation, of the Liberal MP, Sir Swire Smith, who had only entered the Commons at an unopposed by-election in 1915 at the 'advanced age' of 73. Although the ILP were fast to announce they would stand, the Labour Party itself agreed to continue abiding by the truce, as did the local Unionists. The Liberals adopted as their candidate William Somervell, a boot manufacturer from a Westmorland Quaker family. He announced that his aim was to assist Asquith and the Liberal party in supporting the government's prosecution of the war and, as such, that he was the official 'party truce' candidate. Nevertheless, in his initial remarks he also made comments which might find favour with potential peace by negotiation supporters. He said that 'he found very little in Lord Lansdowne's five points with which he could not agree; and he heartily accepted President Wilson's four essentials of a durable peace'.[63]

Meanwhile, Bland, the ILP and Peace by Negotiation candidate, issued a very detailed election address[64] which majored on 'peace by negotiation' although also included key ILP economic demands and policies. He stated that: 'at the request of the local Labour Organisations [essentially the ILP and the ILP-dominated Trades Council] I have agreed to come forward as Labour candidate' and he didn't mince his words in attacking the government, saying 'by its record it stands condemned as unable either to make war or to make peace'. He supported 'every avenue which may lead to peace' and argued that the publication of the 'Secret Treaties' had exposed why the Allied governments had 'rejected all overtures for peace'. Following the Russian Revolution, the Bolsheviks published details of secret agreements that the Allies had made. These included the Treaty of London (1915) in which the Allies promised territorial gains to the Italians in return for their entry in the war and the Constantinople Agreement in which France and England promised Constantinople and the Dardanelles to Czarist Russia in the event of victory. The revelation of the treaties strengthened demands for a clear statement of allied war aims and Bland argued: 'By these treaties they are committed to Imperialist aims which can never be attained without a decisive military victory'.

Other issues Bland raised were opposition to military and industrial conscription; Government incompetence in food supply and shipbuilding which, he argued, threatened the country with famine, and the 'public scandal' of the level of allowances paid to dependents of those serving in the army and navy. He finished:

'I appeal to the electors of this constituency to support this policy for the sake of the millions of brave lads who are daily facing death and danger upon the battlefield and to save the aged men who are now threatened with conscription from having to endure similar dangers and hardship.'

---

63 *Leeds Mercury*, 8 April 1918.
64 University of Bristol Library, Special Collections.

Somervell's election address trod a difficult line between support for the Lloyd George government and his own Liberal and Quaker background.[65] He argued that entry to the war had been 'to uphold our pledge to Belgium and our honour as the neighbour and friend of France, and to guard our national independence' and maintained that the war had now become 'a trial of strength between the forces of democracy and liberty on the one hand, and those of autocracy and military tyranny on the other'. Moreover, he saw the consequences of a German victory to be so awful that 'there is no course open to us but to continue the conflict until such time as we can be assured of 'a clean peace' to use the words of Mr. Asquith.' By contrast, he argued that 'for a patched-up peace, for a German peace, for any peace possible today by negotiation with the deceivers of Russia, we should stand condemned before the bar of history.'

The ILP launched an enthusiastic campaign and mobilised leading external figures including Philip Snowden, Fred Jowett, Arthur Ponsonby and Noel and Charles Buxton.

In his campaign speeches, Somervell, the Liberal Coalition candidate, concentrated on the untrustworthiness of Germany, as evidenced by how it had treated Belgium and now Russia. So far as he was concerned, that ruled out any attempt to negotiate with Germany before its 'dominant military caste' had been defeated, either from without or from within Germany.

The argument was again deployed by the press that the whole world was watching and that a victory, or even a good result, for Bland would be greeted with elation in Germany. And, again, a warning went out from the press against complacency: 'The real danger is overconfidence. Liberals may think that Mr. Somervell enjoying Unionist support, their votes do not greatly matter. Unionists may abstain because they think the Liberal vote will secure Mr. Somervell's return. Patriotic Labour may feel inclined to leave voting to the other two parties for a very similar reason.'[66]

The election was relatively quiet and, on polling day, there were no motorcars taking people to vote or wearing of rosettes. The 'official' campaign had, however, put in effort in the last few days to seek to avoid any

---

65 University of Bristol Library, Special Collections.
66 *Yorkshire Evening Post*, 26 April 1918.

embarrassment. MPs came into the constituency to support Somervell, as did the ever-enthusiastic Horatio Bottomley. The PBN campaign was highly disconcerted by the tactics used against them. In particular, the Somervell people made extensive reference to 'German atrocities' and widely distributed copies of the National War Aims Committee (NWAC) pamphlet 'Murder Most Foul'. This drew attention to many stories of German 'outrages', concluding therefore that, as a nation, they were not to be trusted and consequently that the only solution was full victory. Noel Buxton was furious about free NWAC literature being distributed via W H Smith's bookstalls while another observer claimed to have seen it being handed out, even to children, from Somervell's committee room.[67] They also condemned a Somervell leaflet entitled 'Are we like the Germans?' This seized on comments by Bland that he believed German people were similar to all other peoples worldwide. These comments were used to imply that Bland himself approved of the German actions widely condemned as atrocities and, therefore, that a vote for him was 'a vote for those who seek our destruction'.[68]

The press argued strongly for Somervell. The *Yorkshire Evening Post* summarised:

> *'The question which to-morrow's polling will decide is whether the electors of the division are determined that the Allies shall win the war; or are in favour of a Bolshevist peace. As Keighley is a typical industrial constituency, the result of the by-election will be taken as fairly representative of public opinion throughout the country. If Mr. Somervell heads the poll by a big majority, the Government, and all who value what Mr. Asquith calls 'A clean peace' will be correspondingly encouraged. If Mr. Bland, the I.L.P. and Pacifist candidate wins, or comes anywhere near winning, Germany and all the friends of Germany will feel elated.... Every voter, therefore, who wants to see Germany beaten should make a point of going to the poll'.[69]*

The *Labour Leader* argued that the Coalition campaign was focusing on what would be the 'atrocity' of a pacifist being elected rather than anything

---

67 *New Crusader*, 3 May 1918.
68 Ibid.
69 *Yorkshire Evening Post*, 25 April 1918.

positive. They maintained that Somervell had changed from someone who was 'reasonable' regarding discussions of peace moves to 'a bitter ender'. Possibly whistling to keep their spirits up, Bland's supporters believed that their meetings had been much better attended than those of the Coalition. They were planning thirty indoor meetings in the final four nights of the campaign and the same volume of outdoor ones.[70]

Somervell's final meeting voted to send a message to Douglas Haig, saying that 'the people of Keighley in public meeting assembled in support of the Anti-Pacifist candidature of Mr Somervell, were united in expressing their gratitude to and admiration of the British Army.'

Polling day was quiet. The press reported that there had been no organised canvassing and that motorcars, polling day leaflets and the wearing of party favours were notable by their absence. However, the candidates were out and about; Somerville toured the constituency in his motorcar, accompanied by his wife and daughter while Bland did so in a taxi driven by a woman.[71]

The ILP felt they had run a significant campaign. They had used many posters, in red and green, with the slogans 'Bland and a people's peace', 'No Secret Treaties' and 'Peace Soon' and claimed to have delivered 180,000 leaflets – expensive when during the war the cost of paper had increased twelvefold. Also, all four ILP MPs had attended meetings in the town, as had other leading 'peace by negotiation' figures.

Nov. 1913			
Buckminster	Liberal	4,730	39%
Lascelles	Unionist	3,852	31%
Bland	Labour	3,646	30%
Majority		878	
Electorate & Turnout		14,142	87%

---

70 *Labour Leader*, 25 April 1918.
71 *Yorkshire Evening Post*, 26 April 1918.

26 April 1918			
Somervell	Liberal	4,873	68%
Bland	ILP/ Peace by Negotiation	2,349	32%
Majority		2,524	
Electorate & Turnout		14,400	50%

Bland's supporters had been hoping for a strong result, built on three aspects of the campaign. Firstly, there was an already established ILP position in the constituency, Bland himself having polled more than 3,000 in the 1913 by-election. Secondly, there was a sizeable Irish element, many of whom were expected to poll against the Coalition due to the, eventually abortive, legislation passed on 16 April to extend conscription to Ireland. Finally, they had run an effective campaign, which had seen speakers, volunteers and money brought in from across the country.

Although the campaign had been somewhat lacking in excitement, it was estimated that around 5,000 people assembled to hear the result. When it was announced, Somervell said that across the country there would be satisfaction at the outcome. Bland felt that obtaining one third of the vote was a positive sign for the next general election. Whilst there was pleasure in government quarters at the result, there was concern that so many voters had been willing to back the 'pacifist'. Some put this down to complacency in comparison with the energy shown by the peace by negotiation campaign.

As was so often the experience, the Keighley election had come at a difficult time for those supporting peace by negotiation. The Ludendorff offensive was playing out on the western front with polling day coming two weeks after Haig's dramatic 'order of the day' (see above). German progress was stalling but the final outcome was still unknown and the country was well aware that this could be the crucial event of the conflict, one way or the other. That knowledge served to stiffen rather than reduce the resolve of majority opinion. Consequently, that the 'peace' vote was as high as it was, most likely reflected the existing strength in Keighley of the ILP and Bland, echoing the earlier relative success in Rossendale.

Somervell and Bland were both to stand again for Keighley in the 1918 General Election. However, this time neither of them was successful as a Unionist intervened and was given the coupon in preference to Somervell, who subsequently did not stand for parliament again. Neither did Bland, although he remained a force in local politics and served as Mayor of Keighley in 1928.

9.
TRYING TO WOUND

Abercromby, 28 June 1917

Great Britain was a nation with a small army, and recent experience of conflict limited to the Boer War which ended in 1902. Consequently, it entered the war with poor systems to support discharged servicemen, especially the disabled, and the dependents of those serving. Concern was raised about this from the beginning but provision always lagged behind need; as the sheer numbers grew first of serving men and, in time, of disabled veterans, the inadequacy of support became obvious; a trend that was exacerbated by rapid price inflation.

Additionally, the era of 'total war' saw changes in public attitudes to how dependents and those who had served should be supported. Provision had been mainly through charitable rather than state efforts. Unsurprisingly, the Treasury tended to prefer this but increasingly the public felt those who had served should not be reliant on 'the cold hand of charity'. Concerns about the paucity of support for veterans resulted in the formation of organisations committed to helping them and to campaigning for improved state provision. Eventually, this emotive issue became the focus of a by-election in Liverpool.

The history of support for discharged servicemen and for serving families

Government had long resisted moves to give statutory rights to the families of currently serving rank-and-file soldiers and sailors, or to the widows and children of deceased serving men or disabled or other veterans. Prior to the

First World War, provision was mainly via the charitable Royal Patriotic Fund Corporation, which supported widows and orphans, and the Soldiers & Sailors Families Association, which financed the payment of 'separation allowances' to dependents. Inevitably, this non-statutory, ad hoc support was inadequate for a world war in which more than eight million men wore British uniform.

In August 1914, only a small proportion of the families of those serving was entitled to 'separation allowances' although, within weeks, provision was extended to the dependents of all serving soldiers and sailors. Additionally, soldiers and sailors who were discharged because of disablement were eligible for war pensions, but this was not a statutory provision and there was no right of appeal against the award decisions of the Admiralty or the Chelsea Commissioners.

In practice, the administration even of this level of support was overwhelmed and fell into chaos before the year's end. Even where payments were processed in a timely fashion, a substantial mismatch between military and industrial rates of pay meant that the support offered was inadequate. One detailed review stated: 'a household previously enjoying a weekly income of, say, £3, a figure quoted by Prime Minister Asquith in the Commons, might now have a separation allowance of just a quarter of that, 15s a week. Thus, for many men, other than those in the lowest-paid jobs, joining up could leave their wives and families in severe poverty, and at risk of eviction.'[1]

Aware of the resulting deprivation, local Trades Councils agitated for more generous provision. Many took a leading role in the establishment and activities of War Relief Committees, and Trades Councils were key advocates of the early '£1 a week' campaign, arguing that was the minimum that should be paid to the families of all volunteers. Early campaigning did generate movement by the government, and separation allowances were improved from March 1915.

Initially, most focus was on separation allowances. However, as the numbers of those killed or disabled while serving grew, attention was additionally paid to helping them and their dependents. Further legislation

---

[1] Mike Hally, *Rights not Charity: The Radical roots of the British Legion.* (Edinburgh PhD Thesis. 2021).

was eventually passed in November 1915, requiring the time-consuming establishment of hundreds of local committees to deliver improved pensions and allowances. However, as one historian notes: 'They helped, a bit, but it did seem that throughout the war, the system lagged far behind the needs created by mass enlistment.'[2]

Campaigning organisations & the Review of Exceptions Bill

In 1916, growing casualty numbers and the introduction of conscription, meant that most Trades Councils remained highly attentive to separation allowance and pensions issues. Eventually, the Blackburn Trades Council established a Blackburn Association of Discharged Soldiers and Sailors. They then circularised other Trades Councils and similar organisations soon were being set up elsewhere. The spring of 1917 saw a conference in Blackburn leading to the foundation of the National Association of Discharged Sailors and Soldiers.

Contemporaneously with the Trades Councils' activities, the campaigning MP James Hogge, a radical Liberal, elected for East Edinburgh, was promoting veterans' interests, leading to the birth of a different national organisation. From the beginning of the war, Hogge worked extensively on behalf of individuals with issues about separation allowances and pensions and was also an early advocate of the '£1 a week' campaign. He consistently raised questions in parliament regarding inadequate levels of support and poor administration and was rapidly recognised as the leading authority on the issue. He advertised for people to bring their individual cases to him for help and was soon receiving more than 1,000 letters a week. A new Pensions Ministry was founded in late 1916, but Hogge continued campaigning and established the Naval and Military Pensions and Welfare League in January 1917. Its main aim was 'to remedy the inequalities and injustices in the grant and administration of pensions'.

At the time Hogge established his national organisation, the government started on a path that was dramatically to increase the political force behind his efforts and those of the National Association. Even with conscription, the army was greatly concerned by inadequate numbers of recruits becoming

---

2 Ibid.

available. Options to widen the net were considered in government, including potentially changing the age range for those subject to compulsion. In March 1917, the Military Service (Review of Exceptions) Bill was introduced in Parliament. Drawn remarkably widely, this proposed to cancel all existing exceptions whether granted by government departments, by Tribunals, or under the Military Service Acts. The most incendiary change was that men who had joined on a voluntary basis, and subsequently been discharged because of wounds (or disease), would be eligible to be recalled, should their disabilities have been cured or deemed insufficiently serious. The bill became law on 5 April 1917 and was rapidly met with violent objection. The battle cry became: 'Every man once before any man twice' and the first public protest was on 8 April, organised in London by the Poplar Discharged Soldiers' Club, rapidly followed by other large-scale demonstrations. Anger among veterans was deep and widespread. Even so, they did not totally reject the reassessment of discharged veterans but argued they should not be called again before all able-bodied men had been called once.

At the same time, Hogge, in conjunction with the leadership of the Poplar Club, decided to establish a new national organisation, named the National Federation of Discharged and Demobilised Sailors and Soldiers, which rapidly subsumed his short-lived League. Hogge's motivation in founding an alternative national campaigning organisation to the National Association may have been party political; his Federation was closely aligned with Liberalism while the Association was linked, politically but also geographically, with areas of Labour strength.

Hogge announced a campaign to unite the diverse organisations, including the Association and his Federation, into a single veterans' body to fight against the Review of Exceptions legislation and he organised a major demonstration in Hyde Park in central London for 24 June. However, even prior to the demonstration, government began to prepare concessions. On 20 June the War Cabinet[3] decided to 'make a concession with regard to men who had served abroad during the period of the war and been discharged on medical grounds: such men being in future granted their discharge.' But this was not

---

3 The War Cabinet was the small cabinet committee charged with direction of the war. It had been founded by Lloyd George at the beginning of his premiership.

announced publicly and so the government was subjected to significant attack in a Commons debate the following day. Speeches were savage, expressing repugnance at what was viewed as unjustifiably harsh interpretations by the medical review bodies, in direct contravention of promises that veterans who had been wounded would be treated with due care. The debate was in the traditional form for criticism of the government, a call to reduce the salary of the Secretary of State for War by £100. It was initiated by Liberal MP, William Pringle who was Hogge's usual comrade-in-arms when it came to campaigning on the treatment of veterans. Pringle said: 'The object of this Motion is to call attention to what I think may be described as the scandals in connection with the medical re-examination of discharged and rejected men.'[4] He reminded the House that when the plan for re-examination of discharged veterans had first been proposed: 'it was received with an amount of repugnance such as has seldom occurred in relation to any Bill which has been introduced during the course of the War. Even the sponsors of the Bill did not conceal their dislike for it.' Because of that, they had been promised that the medical boards would act 'with exceptional care and exceptional kindness'. But the actual outcome was instead 'that these re-examinations have been carried out in a harsh, in a cruel, in an unfair, and in a wasteful way.' He described one board examination, saying that: 'There were cripples and hunchbacks, men with curvature of the spine, men who were blind, and men who were suffering from every manner of ailment that can afflict frail humanity. They were marshalled up as if they were a company of convicts; they were sworn at and bullied by the recruiting officer, a man who had never been out of the country.'

During the debate, the ministry now revealed its new policy that 'every soldier who was disabled by wounds or discharged from sickness or ill-health abroad will be excepted under this Act.' The government also offered the establishment of a Parliamentary Committee to investigate how the medical review committees had been implementing the legislation. These were substantial concessions which would inevitably reduce the impact of any opposition.

---

4 This, and subsequent quotations, from Hansard HC Deb 21 June 1917 vol 94 cc1996-2114.

The Abercromby by-election

At the height of the Review of Exceptions controversy, the opportunity of a by-election appeared, and Hogge's Federation immediately decided to exploit it. Abercromby, in Liverpool, was a Unionist seat held since January 1910 by Richard Chaloner, a former serving army officer. He resigned on 18 June ahead of being installed in the Lords as Baron Gisborough. Liverpool's dominant Conservative operative, Archibald Salvidge, recalled in his autobiography: 'That men who had already fought and suffered should be called back to the Colours, whilst for one reason or another thousands of their contemporaries still remained in civil life, was expected to cause some resentment. What surprised the government was the volume and intensity of the feeling aroused'.[5] Frederick (F E) Smith, the Attorney General, asked if Salvidge would put his name forward to be the candidate. He declined for business reasons but suggested Lord Stanley, the son of Lord Derby, the Secretary of State for War and the leading member of the dominant Liverpool Conservative family. In doing this, he hoped that having a well-known name would frighten off any opposition but that was not to be and the by-election became, in his words, 'the cock-pit of the nationwide controversy over the alleged bullying methods of the Medical Boards'[6] and he was worried: 'I have made a false move and have brought round the Stanley family the full force of the present discontents. It is not as though Lord Derby or Lord Stanley was particularly keen on the idea.'

Remarkably, soon after the vacancy was announced, it emerged that there would be a contest between an ex-Eton and Oxford young serving officer, who was unable to take part in his own campaign, and an ex-private, backed by Hogge and his Federation. The Conservatives unanimously put forward the soon-to-be twenty-three-year-old Lord Stanley as their candidate and his acceptance of their offer was made public on 15 June. However, he made it clear that his military duties came first and would prevent him from campaigning. He wrote to the constituency association: 'My first duty is to the regiment, and I cannot undertake any work which will take me away from it as long as the

---

5 A. Salvidge, *Salvidge of Liverpool* (1934).
6 Ibid.

war lasts. I would willingly accept your offer provided it is clearly understood that my political duties, if elected, are entirely military duties'.[7]

Stanley had joined the Grenadier Guards straight from Oxford and had been wounded twice in active service, including while deployed as a Staff Officer under General Horace Smith-Dorrien. He was remarkably well connected, being described as 'a great favourite at court and an intimate friend of the Prince of Wales'. The press noted that he had made his first political speech at the age of 16 in Preston, which was represented in Parliament by his grandfather. Salvidge, meanwhile, sought to deflect attention from his candidate's youth by commenting that: 'the only point I have heard raised was about Lord Stanley's youth, but Bolingbroke and Pitt were both Ministers before they left off playing cricket.'

Salvidge also confided to his diary that the process of getting Stanley to the starting gate had not been straightforward. At first, his Commanding Officer had refused permission for him to stand. Delightfully, Salvidge noted:

> 'Derby is not the sort to use his Cabinet rank to bring official pressure to bear but, luckily, this CO is a family friend, so Derby had him round to his house and used the perfectly legitimate personal touch. After arguing with the stern soldier for hours and explaining the pros and cons of the political situation, the required consent was forthcoming but only on condition that no interference with military duties is entailed'.[8]

That meant there was no prospect of Stanley visiting the constituency during any campaign but, as he did not expect a contest, Salvidge was unconcerned. The other issue was that Stanley had a rather crowded diary. He was currently on what was described as 'a difficult Staff course' at Cambridge with an exam coming up which was to be followed by his society wedding (to Sybil Cadogan, the daughter of Viscount Chelsea) on 7 July.

The writ for the by-election was issued on 19 June and the following day the National Federation of Discharged and Demobilised Sailors and Soldiers at a national conference discussed whether to contest it. The constituency

---

7 *Liverpool Echo*, 15 June 1917.
8 A. Salvidge, *Salvidge of Liverpool* (1934).

was not an obvious one to promote the case of rank-and-file soldiers, since the electorate contained a high proportion (almost two-thirds) of non-resident business voters. Nevertheless, Hogge's organisation resolved to fight. This was the very day that the War Cabinet was deciding, in private, on concessions to the veterans. The Federation announced on 21 June that it would fight the by-election, at the same time the government made public its concession at least for veterans who had been wounded or fallen ill on overseas service.

Initially, it was expected that the Federation's paid organiser, ex-Sergeant Charles Derry, DCM – referred to as one of the heroes of Mons – would be its candidate. Derry had previously been deployed in government recruiting drives and so was very used to public speaking. However, he declined to be the candidate, saying that he was fully occupied working for the Federation and was appointed agent instead. The candidate chosen was a local Abercromby ex-soldier, Pte. Frank Buckley Hughes. Educated in Liverpool he went to sea at the age of fifteen, following which he worked in the United States and South Africa before returning to Liverpool to work in the motor trade. At the time of the by-election, he was Managing Director of the Merchant Service Stores, a Liverpool naval outfitter that he had founded in 1916, and business manager of the Merchant Service Review, a new journal devoted to the shipping industry.

Hughes' military involvement had begun right at the start of the war when he and his five brothers all volunteered. However, his service was limited. He was not sent abroad (and so was not covered by the new concession) and was discharged due to sickness in May 1915. During the election, his opponents were to make much of the fact that he had not been beyond Kent and that he had served solely as a cook in an officers' mess.

A quick offensive

The writ for the election arrived in Liverpool on 20 June and on the following day details of the Federation's candidate and campaign were made public. It was announced that Hughes was standing as the 'soldiers' champion'. He condemned the fact that discharged men were being recalled while there were still men of military age 'hiding themselves in Government offices and munitions factories and the like.' He called for proper provision for the widows and mothers of the fallen; for strong action against food profiteers and for support for the dependents of the men of the merchant navy who had been killed by enemy action. Hogge and fellow MP, William Pringle, announced that they intended to come and campaign on Hughes' behalf.

The Coalition campaign positioned itself as equally strong on the issues raised by their opponents, thereby hoping to nullify their efforts. Lord Stanley was immediately described as Captain Stanley and it was argued that as a serving soldier, twice injured, he would be highly supportive of the interests of veterans. On the conventional political front, in addition to unanimous Unionist support, Stanley gained the firm commitment to the truce of the Liberals and the Irish. When nomination papers were submitted, twelve went in to support Stanley including ones from the local Liberals and one in the name of the United Irish League in Abercromby. Two papers were submitted on behalf of Hughes.

The first controversy came when it was alleged that Hughes was not a properly endorsed candidate for the Federation. The accusation was made by Sergeant-Major George Blythe, who, in a telegram, described himself as founder, president and organiser of the National Federation of Discharged Soldiers and Sailors. His intervention was immediately rejected by Sgt. Derry who told the press that, while Blythe had originally been a member of the Federation, he had since given up any office within it and now had no official standing, other than as an individual member. He said that Hughes' candidacy was backed by Federation branches from across the country and that he would produce telegrams to confirm that. Hughes' first public meeting was on 22 June, reportedly with a large and sympathetic audience. It had been advertised with the slogan: 'Come and show that Liverpool is not a pocket borough belonging to any aristocratic house. Rally up, Workers!'

In addition to his main themes of support for the discharged men, care for the dependents of those lost in the merchant marine and attacks on food profiteers, Hughes also added calls for the restoration of racing and sport as well as 'the liberty to enjoy a glass of beer'. Two of his supporting speakers turned their fire on Stanley's high social standing and inexperience. James O'Connell, formerly of the Liverpool Regiment, held that the nomination of Stanley was servile, unmanly and un-English. He maintained that 'they were asked to put back the hands of time a hundred years and to revert to the system of pocket boroughs' and that 'any working man who voted for his lordship must be a purblind ass, because the interests of the two were diametrically opposed'. Equally strongly, the agent (Sgt. Derry) said they objected to Stanley because 'he belonged to his father and because his father belonged to a party and government that had failed right along the line. What, for example, had they done with their promises to the broken soldier, as well as to the soldier's widow or mother? Picking up on the nature of the Abercromby constituency and the candidate's background, Derry also asked: 'Why was a shipowner not put up for the constituency instead of an inexperienced boy?'[9]

On the other side, unable to deploy his candidate, Salvidge led the attack. He argued that the responsibility of every citizen was to back the government in its pursuit of victory. He conceded that any government would make mistakes and accused the opposition of appealing to and exploiting every man who had got a complaint and that 'the endeavour seemed to be to get all the grumblers and discontented men into one net with a view of striking a blow at the government.' He further claimed that: 'their opponents were trying to bring to the door of Lord Stanley the errors of every Medical Board in the country, so that through him they might hit his father'.[10] So far as he was concerned, as a serving officer Stanley was well able to represent the interests of serving and discharged soldiers and he argued: 'No one was more qualified to speak for the soldiers than Lord Stanley, who had been side-by-side with the privates in France, and faced the bullets and shells of the enemy.'

In a rapid electoral contest, the Federation forces were seriously outgunned by the local strength of the Unionists. Hughes' people had no experience in election logistics, especially in a constituency with such a high proportion of non-resident, business voters and on such an old register. Nor, of course, did they hold previous information on the party allegiance of voters in the way that the Unionists did. Finally, a campaign of only a few days gave them no opportunity to build momentum, especially when the government had largely shot their fox with its concessions on the Review of Exceptions Act.

As the campaign gathered steam, and Hughes' supporters continued to play the 'class' card against Stanley, rumours circulated that the Unionists might have to deploy their candidate after all. Both sides were mustering their campaigning forces. Hogge arrived hot foot from London and pledged

---

9 Speech extracts from *Liverpool Daily Post*, 23 June 1917.
10 Ibid.

to remain in Abercromby throughout the campaign. On the Unionist side, the Countess of Derby attended a meeting of the Liverpool Women's Unionist Federation, supported by Stanley's fiancée, Sybil Cadogan. A meeting of the Working Men's Conservative Association was arranged as was a meeting for businessmen with several prestigious local speakers.

The Unionists, unnerved by unanticipated opposition, campaigned hard. Undoubtedly, Hughes was not a 'peace' candidate, but newspapers sympathetic to Stanley questioned why unremitting prosecution of the war did not form a major part of his campaign (This, even though his agent, Derry, had announced an intention to stand against Ramsay MacDonald when the general election arrived). Another issue raised was the background of Hughes' nominators. The Stanley campaign made much of the fact that of the twenty names, eleven were of aliens, naturalised in the period 1905 to 1914, some assumed to be of Jewish heritage because of their surnames. The Unionists identified that most of them had only been naturalised once the war began and Salvidge went so far as to claim: 'Ten voters' names were needed to nominate a candidate, and if Mr Hughes had been dependent on the nominations of genuine Britishers he would not have been able to stand for Abercromby.' They did not dispute that the signatories were legally British citizens but implied that a candidate for a leading commercial area like Abercromby should have more influential supporters.

The Unionists also cast aspersions on Hughes' military record, comparing it unfavourably with that of Captain Stanley. They recognised that Hughes had volunteered early and 'done his bit'. However, stressing that he had not seen service abroad and had only been an 'acting cook in Tunbridge Wells' they maintained that Stanley would be a much better representative of the discharged soldiers. In response, the Hughes' campaign repeated the claim that the election was between 'the solider of democracy or the soldier of autocracy'.

Other groups took sides or didn't. Leading Liberals came out for Stanley; meanwhile, the local Seamen's and Firemen's Union declared for Hughes. The United Irish League, while noting that some of those who had nominated Hughes were their supporters, made it clear that as an organisation it was staying neutral. Hughes told the press that he had promises of help from 'ex-officers, sailors, and soldiers, and from Conservatives, Liberals, Nationalists and Jews. He had been promised a solid Jewish vote, and a full vote of officers, engineer officers and men of the mercantile marine'.[11] Another group to back him was the recently formed Anti-Profiteering League which claimed a membership of 300 and welcomed his emphasis on food prices and the role of profiteering. That issue had also brought to Hughes' aid the experienced by-election candidate, Joe Terrett, who had fought West Newington (see chapter 3). Terrett supported Hughes on behalf of the British Workers' League and claimed he had strong evidence from the London docks of profiteering.

One Hughes' issue reflected his own merchant marine background. He argued that lives were being lost among merchant sailors due to the delay in arming their ships. The Unionist campaign conceded that on this he had a case. Speaking in support of Stanley, Sir Norman Hill, the Chairman of the Board of Trade Advisory Committee on Merchant Shipping and Secretary of the Liverpool Steamship Owners' Association, said he knew that the arming of merchant ships had been delayed because of demands, particularly from east coast towns, for more guns to protect against air raids. Hill's speech generated an amusing literary debate. He maintained that the east coast towns had won out over the merchant ships in terms of armaments because dwellers on the shore had the votes and more halfpennies to spare for scarce newspapers than 'they that go down to the sea in ships and occupy their business in deep waters'. He was challenged that the correct quotation was 'that do business in great waters'. However, all was well, as it was finally agreed that while the alternative came from the Bible, Hill was quoting accurately from the Prayer Book.

As the brief battle raced to its conclusion, Hughes was noticeable by his absence even though, unlike his opponent, he was in Liverpool. He had already been dubbed 'two-minute Hughes' for the brevity of his speeches (one press report claimed that his longest had been four minutes) but, increasingly, he did not attend his own meetings at all and the, often fiery, speeches in his support were made by others, notably his agent. The explanation was put forward that he was a rather shy and retiring individual, which led the other side to question whether such a character was the ideal person to campaign

---

11 *Pall Mall Gazette*, 25 June 1917.

strongly on the floor of the House of Commons for the discharged soldiers and sailors.

On the final day before polling, the Unionists put out a leaflet emphasising that Hughes had never fought abroad while, by contrast, 'the candidate who is good enough for the trenches is good enough also for Parliament'. Among the MPs coming to assist the government campaign was Ian Macpherson, the Liberal Under Secretary of War, who had been responsible for defending the Exceptions legislation in the Commons. He met considerable opposition when he spoke in support of Stanley. Many Hughes supporters, some wearing their silver badges confirming they had served and been discharged, disrupted his meeting, especially when Macpherson praised Stanley's father, Lord Derby. One notable incident occurred when a discharged soldier, who said he had been wounded at Ypres, told Macpherson that he had been recalled under the Exceptions Act. He demanded that the Under Secretary for War signed his notice paper to confirm to the military authorities that he was free from further service which Macpherson instantly agreed to do.

The two sides continued to trade accusations. Hogge declared that the Unionists had drawn attention to Hughes' nomination papers because names on them were of Jews. The Unionists refuted this, saying they would be the last to offend the susceptibilities of the Hebrew community in Liverpool and that they were simply pointing out that a candidate standing on British issues relied largely on the signatures of men who could not be described as genuine Britishers. They also condemned Hughes' polling card which said that 'he has fought for you and will do so again', re-emphasising that he had not seen combat. In turn, the Hughes camp remained furious at attempts to link them to pacifists.

The Stanley campaign received the traditional supportive telegrams from Lloyd George, Bonar Law and Frederick (F E) Smith. On the other side, Hogge provided a strong final speech in Hughes' favour. He referenced MacPherson's actions in signing the notice papers of someone being recalled and asked the audience how had the Under-Secretary got that power, to which the audience responded: 'You!'. He noted that Bonar Law had accused him of ignoring the law when he had advised people not to agree to be medically re-examined and he asked why Lord Stanley objected to Jews signing Hughes' nomination papers when his father was happy to sit in cabinet with a Jew (Sir Alfred Mond) or the son of a German (Lord Milner). He then 'counselled the audience to get rid of the curse of military despotism in this country, and by their votes in Abercromby to protest against the dragooning by puppets in uniform who ought to be fighting at the front.'[12]

In a final drama, on the eve of poll, Hughes suffered a heart seizure and was described as 'far from well'. On polling day, the Conservative top brass turned out in force, albeit excluding the candidate who remained in Cambridge. The Countess of Derby was present and toured the constituency by motorcar accompanied by Lady Victoria Primrose, Lord Stanley's fiancée and his brother (Major Oliver Stanley) along with leading Tory local luminaries, Sir Charles Petrie, Sir Archibald Salvidge and Alderman Maxwell.

The result, when it came, was a clear victory for Stanley; perhaps not surprising in a largely non-working-class constituency in the heart of a city that, at the previous general election, had returned eight Conservatives plus one Irish Nationalist. The Western Daily Press summarised the result:

> 'The bye-election in the Abercromby Division of Liverpool produced a candidate who apparently tried to secure the votes of all who are agin' the Government for any reason, those who wish air reprisals or do not think much of Food Control, or think the government ought to have insisted on facilities for Ramsay MacDonald going to Russia, or have a grievance of any kind against the War Office. And if the candidate succeeded in getting the support of very different sections, the Government is entitled to regard with more than complacency the result.'[13]

The Hughes campaign was bitter in defeat with his agent, Sgt. Derry, declaring 'We fought something dirty on the Marne, and beat them clean. We have fought something dirty today, and lost clean.'[14]

---

12 *Liverpool Daily Post*, 28 June 1917.
13 *Western Daily Press*, 29 June 1917.
14 *Liverpool Daily Post*, 29 June 1917.

Dec. 1910			
Chaloner	Conservative	3,024	58%
Bowring	Liberal	2,184	42%
Majority	*Majority*	840	
Electorate & Turnout	*Electorate*	6,926	75%

28 Jun. 1917			
Stanley	Coalition	2,224	74%
Hughes	NFDDSS	794	26%
Majority		1,430	
Electorate & Turnout		6,016	50%

Hughes returned to obscurity and did not trouble the political world again. Stanley, by contrast, went on to the prominent career predicted for him. He left Parliament in 1918 when the Abercromby constituency was abolished but re-entered in 1922 and was to remain an MP until his death in 1938. He was appointed to a series of junior government positions before finally entering the cabinet (where he joined his brother, Oliver) as Secretary of State for Dominion Affairs in May 1938; he died of the recurrence of after-effects of a war injury in his leg[15] only five months later.

---

15 *The Argus (Melbourne)*, 17 Oct 1938.

10.
NEMESIS NOT YET

Dundee, 30 July 1917

Winston Churchill, one of Dundee's two MPs, was obliged to submit himself for re-election when he was recalled to government on 17 July 1917, as Minister of Munitions. He was opposed at the election by Edwin Scrymgeour, the founder (in 1901) of the Scottish Prohibition Party. Scrymgeour was a serial candidate against Churchill, having stood in a by-election in 1908 and the two general elections in 1910. In the latter of the 1910 elections he polled six per cent, his highest tally. Churchill's position, in the wake of the Dardanelles fiasco, was highly controversial while Scrymgeour now elevated opposition to the war even above his usual battle cry for total, uncompromising, prohibition of the demon drink. It had the makings of an intriguing contest for which Dundee was a fascinating venue; the divided city had one of the highest levels of voluntary recruitment while also being a bastion of conscientious objection.

A persistent prohibitionist candidate

Scrymgeour was a remarkable figure, remaining steadfast to his beliefs throughout a dramatic career. A committed socialist, his views were founded on strong religious faith as a Wesleyan Methodist. His essence has been described as follows: 'Religion was the root of Scrymgeour's beliefs. But it was a very different religion from that of many others involved in the anti-drink movement. His was not a quiescent, accepting religion. Christianity made

Scrymgeour a socialist and, as socialism was impossible while people drank, drink had to be defeated.'[1]

He never compromised, often turning his fire on churches and temperance organisations willing to support restrictions but not the total eradication of drink. The son of a renowned temperance campaigner, he started his career in the Independent Order of Good Templars, originally a US organisation but which had achieved popularity in Scotland, and soon after joined the Independent Labour Party for whom he was elected to the Dundee Parish Council in 1895. By 1901 he had left the ILP, amicably, shortly before the Scottish Prohibition Party was founded. Kemp argues: 'Scrymgeour was, throughout its existence, the leading member of the Scottish Prohibition Party, and his was probably the inspiration for its creation.'

Although members came from various denominations, the party had a religious backbone, was firmly left-wing and completely unbending in its demands for full prohibition – rejecting alternatives such as public ownership of the drink trade or local option, where the decision whether to licence the sale of alcohol was devolved to councils and local referenda. As early as 1904, the *Dundee Advertiser* said of the party: 'The main contribution the party would make towards the temperance movement would be to make groups that were often accused of being extreme look moderate by comparison.'

Under its auspices, Scrymgeour was elected to Dundee Town Council in 1905, standing as a 'Prohibitionist and Labour' and 'No Licence' candidate. He proved a controversial member, always ready to attack in venomous fashion fellow councillors who had links to 'the trade' but, equally, opposing those who supported temperance legislation that fell short of total prohibition. He remained a member (with one brief interlude) until 1919.

He was employed by the party and travelled widely in Scotland, speaking on its behalf, and in 1908 was sent to the convention of the US Prohibition Party where he became a delegate for Massachusetts. Back home, he had a habit of holding anti-drink street meetings, often provocatively close to public houses and in 1910, because of a conviction for obstruction at one of these meetings, he spent five days in Perth Prison. Kemp reports: 'This spell

---

1 John Douglas Kemp, *Drink and the Labour Movement in Early Twentieth-Century Scotland With Particular Reference to Edwin Scrymgeour and the Scottish Prohibition Party* (PhD Thesis, University of Dundee, 2000)

in prison could easily have been avoided had he paid the 10/- fine he was given as an alternative. Imprisonment was deliberately chosen for publicity value. 2,500 people turned up to hear him talk about his imprisonment on his release.'[2]

As a committed socialist, he did not restrict himself to the issue of prohibition. Kemp summarises that in Scrymgeour's first Parliamentary election in 1908 he covered issues including women's and adult suffrage, home rule for England and Wales as well as Scotland and Ireland and increasing taxation on income to start purchasing the means of production, distribution, and exchange. He invited votes for 'Drink's Abolition and the attainment of Christian Socialism'. By the second 1910 election he had added abolition of the House of Lords[3] and an appeal to vote for him to place at least one member for the poor in parliament. That election also showed Scrymgeour's iron will. In a leaflet to members of the party asking them to attend his first campaign meeting he said: 'Now you either mean business for the Prohibition movement or it has little or no place in your heart and mind. I shall consequently expect your presence ... or intimation of reason for non-attendance then, with promise to help later'.

His attitudes during wartime give a clear indication of the man. On the issue of drink, he did not support campaigns calling for temporary restrictions as they did not measure up to his absolutist requirements. But opposition to the war itself was to overtake advocating prohibition and he campaigned especially strongly against conscription. Yet, although opposed to the war, he was always sympathetic to the soldiers that had to fight it.

To today's audience, Scrymgeour may appear a crank but although his prohibition views were extreme, they were by no means as aberrant as might be assumed: opposition to drink was a strongly held position among sizeable segments of the labour movement and the Liberals. He was also well-established as a local socialist campaigner. He frequently opposed organisations and institutions but had an increasingly positive reputation for working hard to assist individuals; an important example was that although

---

2 John Douglas Kemp, *Drink and the Labour Movement in Early Twentieth-Century Scotland With Particular Reference to Edwin Scrymgeour and the Scottish Prohibition Party*. (PhD Thesis, University of Dundee, 2000).
3 Ibid.

strongly opposed to conscription, he developed a reputation for assisting those struggling to claim service pensions. The area where he ploughed a lonelier furrow was his firm pacifist opposition to the war although, even there, his local reputation gave him some protection against the hostility met by peace-by-negotiation candidates elsewhere.

Scrymgeour's standing in Dundee can be pieced together from an overview of his behaviour on the council. In Autumn 1914, he was opposed for re-election by a 'Business' candidate but safely returned. His council position gave him opportunities to work for residents and he became Chairman of the Ward Committee of the Dundee Executive of the Prince of Wales National Distress Fund, which provided support to the dependents of those who had signed up and to the unemployed. He continued to campaign for prohibition but opposed a motion that called for it during wartime, preferring to introduce (without success) his own in support of permanent prohibition. He did much to advocate for better services including raising concerns about the adequacy of gas supply and access to telephones, calling for 'more penny call instruments' across the town. He was particularly solicitous of the needs of workers and of serving and discharged soldiers. He regularly supported increases in wages for municipal employees; complained about employees apparently being refused wage increases due to their trade union activities and lobbied for support for returning injured soldiers who had previously worked for the council. Nor was he to be bought off by the establishment. His personal papers[4] are full of invitations to municipal dinners and other events, marked as having been declined and when he was eventually invited to be a Commissioner of the Peace, he refused, tersely noting how many times he had been ignored previously. He was a consistent and persistent thorn in the side of the council establishment although nearly always found himself in a minority.

As the war progressed, his opposition to it emerged and this became more important to him even than prohibition. In August 1915, on the war's first anniversary, he tried to hijack a council motion recording full support for the government by adding that the government 'should propound the minimum terms upon which Peace would be declared.' He later expressed

---

4 Scrymgeour archive, Dundee Local History Centre.

concern that the names of council employees might be being passed to the local Recruitment Committee so that pressure could be put on them to volunteer. At a major anti-conscription meeting in January 1916, he was chosen to propose the resolution attacking the passing of the Military Service Act; agreed unanimously it pledged the attendees to work for the repeal of the Act on the grounds that it was contrary to the traditions of British liberty.

Yet, he almost didn't make it into 1914 as a political figure. In 1912, he accused a police sergeant of being drunk while on duty and was sued for slander. Scrymgeour lost and desperately needed to raise money to avoid bankruptcy, which would have prevented him holding any public office. He tried running a sweepstake for an expensive watch until that was declared illegal. Then, he organised an air show, which turned into a disaster; the star pilot had to be substituted, and the display airplane only flew for a few hundred yards, straight into a house, whose owner demanded compensation. These events left him even deeper in debt. Eventually, the plan that did work was to ask readers of his magazine, The Scottish Prohibitionist, to take out annual subscriptions in advance. That generated enough cash for him to meet his liabilities, but it had been a close-run thing.

Churchill had seen off Scrymgeour easily in their previous contests and might have thought that a committed prohibitionist and 'conchie' with a questionable record of failed legal cases (He had also unsuccessfully sued the Town Council) would remain an easy foe but his opponent was establishing a political reputation and base for himself.

Mixed reactions to Churchill

In 1908, Churchill had lost his then seat at Manchester North West when all the stars aligned against him. He was obliged to submit himself for re-election following his appointment as President of the Board of Trade but multiple prominent groups in the constituency decided to oppose him; almost one-third of the electorate was Jewish who were angered by the recently introduced Aliens Act while the sizeable Catholic vote resented his failure to pledge himself to Home Rule. Finally, the growing suffragette movement launched a strong campaign against him. But almost immediate salvation was at hand, courtesy of the Dundee constituency chairman, Sir George Ritchie, who, straight after Churchill's defeat in Manchester, had said to his colleagues:

'We must get that brilliant young man to represent the city and put Dundee on the map.'[5] Consequently, in a by-election only two weeks later, Churchill became the Liberal MP for Dundee. The city elected two MPs in a single constituency and in both 1910 elections Churchill topped the poll, standing as a sole Liberal candidate, effectively running in tandem with Labour who finished a close second. However, by 1917, there were suggestions that Dundee had not entirely taken to Churchill. Complaints were raised that he visited infrequently and paid insufficient attention to local issues. According to the *Dundee Evening Telegraph*: 'Mr Churchill has not been forgotten by his constituents, but a goodly number have been grumbling that Mr Churchill has forgotten Dundee'.[6]

To this background was added intense national debate over his performance as a war minister and whether he should be recalled to government at all. At the start of the war, Churchill was at the Admiralty and received praise for the speed with which he had the fleet ready for war. However, frustrated by the relative inactivity of the navy, he quickly became involved in the first of the controversies to be recalled during the by-election, his behaviour at Antwerp. Churchill had established a new organisation, the Royal Naval Division, and this provided reinforcements (including Asquith's son) to the city of Antwerp in October 1914. Churchill visited the city himself and became actively involved in organising its defence, leaving his cabinet colleagues in London ignorant of what he was doing and when he might deign to return to the Admiralty.

The defence of Antwerp, and Churchill's role in it, was considered either a foolhardy waste of men's lives or a gallant rearguard action that saved vital time for the rest of the British Army; which view was held tended to correlate with the observer's general opinions of Churchill. He certainly became overly excited at Antwerp, even volunteering to give up his beloved role as First Lord of the Admiralty to take over as commander of the British troops there. The issue was directly relevant to Dundee as there was a sizeable number of Dundonians in the Royal Naval Division.

But the largest albatross around Churchill's neck was his role in the disastrous Dardanelles campaign. Once again, assessments tended to reflect

---

5 Quoted in T Paterson, *Churchill: A Seat for Life* (1980).
6 *Dundee Evening Telegraph*, 18 July 1917.

people's existing view of him. The campaign had been launched out of frustration with the static nature of the war on the Western Front. In casting around for potential initiatives, different ideas emerged. Churchill's initial preference was for an attack on German forces in the Baltic. Maurice Hankey, the first ever Secretary to the Cabinet, however, supported an attack on the Ottomans and Jacky Fisher (the First Sea Lord) developed a plan for a naval-only assault on the Dardanelles, using pre-Dreadnought battleships which were relatively dispensable.

Churchill became favourable to such a naval-only assault, but only on a small scale to see if the outer defensive forts of the Dardanelles straits could be forced by naval gunfire. However, Fisher now reversed his position, concerned about possible naval losses and the diversion of assets from the North Sea, and switched to supporting a combined assault aimed at landing army forces. Fatally, an initial naval assault was authorised but without a clear decision whether also to deploy land forces. At first successful, once the fleet moved on to attack the forts further into the straits it suffered heavy losses. Having announced that an attack on the straits was underway it was felt impossible to cut and run and so local commanders decided to deploy troops, attempting ill-prepared landings whilst under attack from strong defensive positions that the fleet had failed to nullify.

As the situation deteriorated, venom, particularly Unionist venom, was directed at Churchill. He was, inaccurately, positioned as being the single figure responsible for the Dardanelles campaign. Conservative antipathy to Churchill was extreme, born of his perceived treachery when he crossed the floor from being elected as a Conservative in 1900 to joining the Liberals in 1904, and his subsequent radicalism alongside Lloyd George. Many Unionists were totally unwilling to forgive him and when Asquith established the Coalition in May 1915, Churchill's demotion was part of the price exacted; he was switched from the Admiralty to the lowly position of Chancellor of the Duchy of Lancaster. Although removed from the centre of the action, Churchill remained in office and was still a member of the Dardanelles Committee (The cabinet sub-committee established under the Coalition initially to consider operations in the Dardanelles and Gallipoli and later to address broader strategic and operational topics). However, in November 1915 that committee was replaced by a new War Committee which excluded him.

Faced with being sidelined and granted continuous Unionist antipathy (and lacklustre support from his own ranks), Churchill resigned his cabinet position and took up a command on the Western Front, becoming one of the 264 MPs who joined the forces, at some point, during the war. He had hoped to be put in charge of a brigade but had to settle for a battalion and was appointed a Lieutenant-Colonel in command of the 6th Battalion, the Royal Scots Fusiliers, remaining at the front from January until mid-May 1916. This period of active service was not typical Churchill; it was neither dramatic nor foolhardy. He faced a difficult task, replacing a much-loved predecessor, and initially did not have the trust of his men. However, he won them over. Famously, when he arrived, he informed his officers that they were going to declare war – on lice – and he did much to improve the living conditions of his troops. Consequently, he left with a favourable reputation and Major Andrew Dewar Gibb noted of the farewell lunch given by Churchill to his officers on 6 May 1916: 'I believe every man in the room felt Winston Churchill's leaving us a real personal loss'.[7] He was now eager to rejoin the political fray and to fight for his reputation concerning the Dardanelles. His biographer, Jenkins, noted:

> *'Churchill was desperate to get rid of the Dardanelles slur on his reputation, or at the very least to spread the guilt. He wanted to do this both in what he saw as the cause of justice and because he realised that, so long as he was regarded as the guilty man, there was a great obstacle to his getting back into the government.'*[8]

Once back in Parliament, Churchill pressed relentlessly to remove the shadow of the Dardanelles from his chances of regaining office. In July 1916, Asquith sought to deflect criticism of the government by establishing the Dardanelles Commission to investigate the causes of the campaign's failure. Churchill feared it was a witch hunt and would find against him. While it was deliberating, he remained persona non grata, outside of government. When Asquith fell and was replaced by Lloyd George in December 1916 there was

---

7 International Churchill Society website (https://winstonchurchill.org/publications/finest-hour/finest-hour-153/in-the-field-churchill-and-northey-commanding-the-6th-battalion-royal-scots-fusiliers/)
8 R Jenkins, *Churchill* (2002).

still no attempt to rehabilitate him; Lloyd George may have wished to do so, but Bonar Law and the Conservatives would have not acquiesced.

Churchill put all his efforts into securing a favourable verdict from the Commission. The public perception, whipped up by the Unionists, was that he had been solely responsible for initiating the campaign and that he had ignored technical naval advice against it. He also incurred some of the blame for the incredibly badly planned landings and the decision to fight on the ground after the naval effort failed. Churchill rejected each of these accusations and hoped that the Commission would exonerate him. When the initial report was published, in early March 1917, it went a long way to counter the more extreme attacks on him. One observer has noted:

> 'On balance, the Dardanelles Report improved Churchill's standing in the eyes of the British public. It was now difficult to sustain charges that he alone was responsible for the disaster ... The report also challenged the popular view of Churchill as a reckless amateur who had brushed aside Fisher's clear warnings of disaster and pressed an impossible scheme on his helpless colleagues. And a careful reading of the document would shift most of the blame for the land campaign from Churchill to Kitchener'.[9]

Partly freed of the Dardanelles incubus, Churchill was closer to being able to return to office. Yet Lloyd George still did not bring him back, fearful of alienating Unionist opinion. Eventually, in mid-July 1917, he took the risk and restored his close colleague to the Cabinet (although not to the powerful War Cabinet). This step was controversial since Lloyd George made the decision to appoint Winston as the Minister for Munitions on his own, without consulting his Unionist colleagues.

There was an immediate outcry on the Conservative benches, front and back, and three committees, the Unionist Business Committee, the Unionist War Committee and the Parliamentary Air Committee, rapidly arranged emergency meetings with the objective of protesting at Churchill's appointment and reversing it. Nor was objection to the return of the 'unsinkable' politician without some justifiable concern regarding the position he was to take up.

---

9 C M Bell, *Churchill and the Dardanelles*, (2017).

Labour relations issues would feature strongly among the responsibilities of the Minister for Munitions and there was fear that 'Mr Churchill's manner and domineering way of doing things may lead to labour disputes'; this was, after all, not so many years after Churchill's role in the Tonypandy riots.[10] To seek to temper the opposition, Lloyd George promised that Churchill would be on his best behaviour.

A ministerial re-election campaign

This rather fraught background formed the start of the Dundee by-election. Churchill was obliged to re-stand for his seat, and it seemed certain he would not be allowed a free run. One desperate for Churchill to be opposed was Howell Gwynne, editor of the Morning Post and a constant critic. He wrote to his proprietor Violet, Countess of Bathurst, that Churchill's return to office was 'an appalling disaster, greater I think than has fallen on us during the whole of the war.'[11] He raised funds to run a candidate against Churchill, even thinking at one point he might stand himself. He reported to Bathurst that he had got enough money together but that the difficulty had been finding a candidate, saying: 'You see all the good men are away and only the scum of military age are left.' He gave up, having been told that there was little chance of success especially as 'the people are on holiday and wouldn't come back to vote.'[12]

Churchill planned an immediate visit to Dundee to kick start a campaign, if one were necessary. However, a complication arose since, as Gwynne had discovered, the Dundee annual holidays were about to begin, meaning that few people would be available, or possibly even interested, in attending a public meeting. It was also likely that the writ would be received at the start of the holiday week which would mean most of the election period taking place while people were away or on holiday at home. In addition to Churchill planning an immediate visit, the Liberals, fearing a Scrymgeour intervention, wasted no time in getting their election machine operational; two MPs, the Scottish Whip, John Pratt, the Liberal MP for Linlithgoshire, accompanied by the author of two biographies of Churchill's career to date, were immediately

---

10 *Aberdeen Press*, 19 July 1917.
11 Quoted in C M Bell, *Churchill and the Dardanelles*, (2017).
12 Gwynne letter to Bathurst, 27 July 1917.

despatched north. The author, Alexander McCallum Scott, the MP for Glasgow Bridgerton, was something of a Churchill acolyte, but also the purveyor of sound advice who guided Winston away from his Dardanelles obsession back towards the social conditions issues relevant to his constituents.[13]

Now a surprise potential opponent emerged. Ruaraidh Erskine, telegrammed from London to announce his intention to stand as a Scottish Home Rule candidate. He was the brother of Lord Erskine and the proprietor of the *Scottish Review*. While Erskine was waiting to see how his offer to run was being received, Churchill arrived on Saturday, 21 July ready for his major meeting that afternoon at the Kinnaird Hall, Dundee's largest and most important venue for political meetings. The meeting, intended to launch Churchill's campaign, had been advertised as non-political and invitations were issued across the political spectrum. He said it was not for him to judge whether he was a suitable person for the role of Minister of Munitions, but he had no doubt that it was his duty, when offered that opportunity to serve, to accept. And now, he called on his audience to permit him that response by ensuring he was returned to be able to do so. He acknowledged there was some opposition to him but implied it came only from long-standing political opponents. He also rehearsed his record, starting with how he had ensured that the Navy was ready for the conflict. He launched an impassioned plea for unity of purpose: 'This was not the time for party politics, still less was it the time for personal feuds.' He drew attention to the fact that 'the might of the United States was coming to our aid, and we only had to hold on until she could throw her whole weight into the struggle to make our victory a decisive and complete one.' In his peroration, he deployed the by now standard appeal to send a message to the world, should there be a contest, calling on Dundee electors 'to secure a majority which would carry the message to Berlin that Scotland was solid and inflexible.'[14]

Churchill did not get through his meeting without challenge. The issue of prohibition was raised, and he said he was not prepared to support it 'at the present time'. Opposing motions were proposed. The Liberal Association Chairman moved that 'the citizens of Dundee, resolute in their determination

---

13 Paul Addison, *Churchill on the Home Front* (1992).
14 *Dundee Courier*, 23 July 1917.

to defeat the attempt of German militarism to subjugate the free nations of Europe, resolved to support the election of Mr Churchill'. This was passed by overwhelming acclamation while a counter motion that 'Mr Churchill was not a fit and proper person to represent the constituency' was drowned out by the sound of stamping feet.

On the possibilities of an opponent, things moved at pace. The Unionists met and, despite hostility to Churchill, announced they would not stand; the same position was taken by the local Labour Representation Committee. It was reported that a deputation from Dundee had visited David Davies, the defeated Attested Men/Trade/Bottomley candidate in Hyde (see chapter 6) to ask him to oppose Churchill, but he had refused. It was also recounted that a mysterious group of 'businessmen' had visited Dundee to assess whether to bring forward a candidate. Then it was revealed that Scrymgeour had been promised the necessary funds to stand, in the light of which Erskine said that he would not come forward as a candidate, after all. Erskine expanded on his position in a letter to the local ILP, saying: 'I quite agree that it would be a pity to allow the place-man Churchill a walk over. That Dundee could ever have been about to elect such a characteristic complement to his friend, Lloyd George, fair beats me.'[15] The die appeared cast for a straight fight between Scrymgeour and Churchill although on nomination day a Major Frederick Scott arrived in Dundee, hoping to stand as an independent Unionist. Scott had fought with distinction in the Boer War and had volunteered at the start of the current one, serving until he was invalided out in 1915. He then undertook significant administrative roles, including as Director of Release from the Colours where he organised the return from the forces of highly skilled workers; for this work, he had been praised, by name, by Lloyd George in the Commons. He was again praised in the Commons for work for the National War Savings Committee and, later, had been transferred to the Department of Information, by special request of the Prime Minister. However, Scott 'learning the local situation and owing to lack of time, decided to withdraw.'[16] It is likely his prospective candidature was related to the earlier mysterious visit to Dundee of people assessing the situation. However, lack of organisation caught him out. He

---

15 Quoted in *Dundee Evening Telegraph*, 24 July 1917.
16 *Lincolnshire Echo*, 25 July 1917.

revealed that he had only received 'an invitation to stand' in London at 7pm the night before nominations closed and arrived at 9am; nominations were open between 10am and Noon. He went to the Sheriff's Office and collected a nomination paper but only then discovered that he was legally obliged to have an Agent. Finding one proved impossible since the local solicitors were closed due to the holiday week. He told a local paper: 'It was not a question of funk. I was to have stood as an Independent candidate, and I would have opposed Mr Churchill simply and solely on his past war record.'[17] Had Scott been nominated he would undoubtedly have drawn a sizeable number of votes from disaffected Unionists.

Meanwhile, Scrymgeour had needed a promise of cash, simply to be able to proceed with a nomination. In a contested election, the candidates would, between them, be required to pay the returning officer's expenses, which were set at £500, meaning in a two-horse race, each candidate would need to lodge £250. Scrymgeour announced that the funding had come from a friend who had put forward almost his entire life savings as a loan. His first meeting in Dundee was attended by around 100 people and included, not only stalwarts of the Scottish Prohibition Party but also a senior representative of the Union of Democratic Control, although they were not to take an official role in his campaign. Scrymgeour announced that he would be standing in the interests of 'Prohibition and Labour' and, even prior to this formal 'launch' meeting, he had held some open-air meetings pursuing holidaymakers in Carnoustie.

Two very different campaigns

The stage was set for a rapid contest, fought in very different styles. Churchill had returned to London and his new ministerial responsibilities, leaving the campaign in the capable hands of his wife, his two MP colleagues (John Pratt and Alexander McCallum Scott), and a highly loyal constituency chairman, although it was expected, should a contest go ahead, that he would return for the final weekend.

Clementine Churchill's speaking efforts on her husband's behalf, including at open air meetings, were well received in the press. She was described as delivering 'a short speech in neat style' and deployed the usual argument

---

17 *Dundee Evening Telegraph*, 25 July 1917.

of the need to deliver a result that would send a message to Berlin as to the country's continuing resolve. She said:

> *'I hope very much that you are going to give my husband a very big majority, not only for his sake ... but for the sake of the government which he had been invited to join, so that a message would be sent to Germany to show them that over here we had no dissension.'*

She also argued: 'However sincere Mr Scrymgeour might be, I do not think any sensible man or woman could say that a vote given to Mr Scrymgeour was a vote to carry on with the war.'[18]

Regarding her next meeting, it was recounted that 'despite the rain, Mrs. Churchill pluckily mounted to the driver's seat of the cab and spoke to the large gathering.' She, and her fellow speaker, the MP McCallum Scott, found the reception quite lively and they were often interrupted. According to Scott: 'This was in no small measure due to the fact that amongst the audience, Mr. Scrymgeour could find excellent arguments for his Prohibition campaign.'[19] Clementine faced challenging questions about her husband and his record. What had Churchill done for Dundee? In response, she reminded them of his actions in ensuring the fleet was ready for war and she knew that everyone in Dundee 'cared very much for the fleet'. She was also challenged about the low separation allowances paid to families and responded by saying she wished that they could be higher, but the army was very big and, also, that the British troops were better paid than the French or Germans.

Churchill's election address was now issued, emphasising that this was no time for political disputes and that all parties had laid aside their strongest convictions: 'Liberals have voted for conscription, Unionists have laboured for an Irish settlement, trade unionism has laid upon the altar of public duty its deeply valued customs and privileges.' It also eulogised the contributions made, specifically by Scotland, to the fight against Prussianism. One thing it did not do, was endorse prohibition although, in early statements, Churchill had paid some lip service to the issue, having said: 'I shall not support any

---

18 *Dundee Courier*, 27 July 1917.
19 Ibid.

legislation which, in my opinion, weakens the rights of the public and the interests of temperance as established by the Scottish Licensing Acts.' Under Scottish law, a provision had been introduced in 1913 for voters in local areas to be able to request a ballot on whether their area should be 'dry' (banning the sale of alcohol). The first opportunities to hold such ballots were not until 1920.

He also collected endorsements to balance some continued griping about his mercurial track record. His fellow MP, Alexander Wilkie (Labour), was fully supportive, saying 'Never mind a contest now, get on with the war.' Another Labour MP, Stephen Walsh, stressed Churchill's work at the Admiralty saying: 'The unchallenged supremacy of the British navy from the very outbreak of the war proves ... your services to the nation were invaluable.' From the Unionist side, the Chairman of Dundee Unionists (and Churchill's former opponent) called on supporters to back him. Nevertheless, there was animosity to Churchill and his track record. Churchill tried to shrug it off, saying: 'There is always a certain proportion of people who like to deal only with what went wrong and invariably ignore what was achieved.' But the attacks were harsh. Views expressed in the local press included: 'Mr Churchill is no untried man; his opportunities have been manifold, and his failures have been disastrous.' The Secretary of a key union (Dundee and District Jute and Flax Workers' Union) was scathing, saying that he had requested Churchill's assistance to get the jute and flax trades onto the list of protected occupations, but Churchill had ignored the request, in sharp contrast to the support received from Wilkie. Another correspondent to the papers described Churchill as 'erratic and wilful' and that he had been 'far from attentive to local interests'.

Scrymgeour also attracted a combination of strong support and antipathy. But this campaign was different to his previous tilts against Churchill. Firstly, he was now better known, and genuinely better liked (or at least appreciated). In particular, he was to reap benefits from his efforts as a local councillor. One letter writer to a newspaper said he

> 'appeared a great, large-hearted person, bubbling over with the milk of human kindness; one who has been guide, philosopher, and friend to thousands, and who has given the best years of his life in serving faithfully and well the proletariat.'

That may have been over the top, but Scrymgeour did by now have a record of service, to set alongside his unbending commitment to Prohibition. For example, by this stage in the war, the cost of food was of great concern and Scrymgeour was actively involved in that area. He was also able to tap into a seam of anti-war feeling among parts of the Dundee working class. The local ILP took a firm stand and, by November 1915, there was a Dundee branch of the No Conscription Fellowship followed, immediately after the passage of the Military Service Act, by the establishment of a Dundee Joint Committee Against Conscription. According to *Forward* (April 1917), the city was 'fair hotchin' wi conchies.'[20] Scrymgeour's anti-war position emerged under his editorship of the *Scottish Prohibitionist*. At the outbreak of hostilities, the 8 August 1914 edition revealed a switch of views matching that of most of the left. The paper commented: 'We sincerely took part in the Prohibitionists' appeal for neutrality made on Sunday night', but then explained that the treatment of Belgium required a sharp change of view leading the paper to announce: 'Britain, for whose government we have certainly no admiration, could not possibly in such circumstances have done other, on the grounds of sheer self-defence alone, than challenge sooner or later a force so completely given over to bullying.' Subsequent editions of the paper continued to show no antipathy to Britain's involvement in the conflict; there were headlines celebrating victories and news from prohibitionists who were serving at the front. Yet, in early 1915, Scrymgeour asked, why not demand peace and used as his text Psalm 49 v.6: 'He causes wars to cease to the end of the earth'. In May 1915 at a mass meeting he proposed a motion calling upon Government to now definitely proclaim the minimum terms upon which peace could be declared. He also capitalised on some disapproval of Labour entering the Coalition and declared his total rejection of conscription. By December 1915 he was supporting the view of the Union of Democratic Control, that the war was a result of secret diplomacy, stimulated by capitalist considerations.

Yet, it was conscription that drove Scrymgeour to make opposition to the war his dominant policy, and to make common cause with those forces on the left doing likewise. In January 1916, he was speaking at anti-conscription meetings and later his newspaper was carrying harsh criticisms of the Dundee

---

20 Quoted in C Pearce, *Communities of Resistance* (2020).

Tribunal and fulsome support for the conscientious objectors appearing before it. By June 1916, the paper was claiming that: 'The Scottish Prohibition Party not only leads the nation regarding drink's abolition but is also to the front in the peace movement.' By the end of 1916, Scrymgeour was immersed in the anti-conscription/peace movement speaking, for example, at the No Conscription Fellowship Scottish conference and was appearing in support of conscientious objectors at tribunals, while his paper was carrying more news about anti-war opinion and activities than it was about prohibition.

Scrymgeour also increasingly used the *Scottish Prohibitionist* to attack Churchill. He published a report claiming that Churchill was notorious in the constituency for completely ignoring communications and, in a long piece on the Dardanelles, argued that 'Churchill's gamble' had resulted in 112,000 casualties. By summer 1917, the *Scottish Prohibitionist* was also celebrating Scrymgeour's actions, as a councillor, to address local scandals regarding the supply of milk and meat, playing into concerns about the rising cost of food, and contrasting this with Churchill's inactivity.

By the time the by-election was approaching, Scrymgeour was fully integrated into the anti-war left and accepted by organisations such as the ILP that, before the war, had ignored or rejected him. This transformation was providing the building blocks that would eventually make him a serious opponent. In March 1917, he had been invited to speak at an ILP conference in Glasgow, attended by over 1,000, and in May he (unsuccessfully) moved an amendment at the Dundee Labour Conference which 'calls on Labour members of Parliament to urge the opening of negotiations for peace and to vote against the granting of credits in continuation of the war.' Most notably, he attended and spoke at the Leeds Peace Conference as a delegate and welcomed its decision to call for workers' and soldiers' councils. So, as he was about to take on Churchill again, Scrymgeour was fully a member of the socialist peace movement. He was also a well-regarded local activist, renowned for conscientious and hard work for the Dundee working class. And, despite his views on the war, this extended to support he gave to individual members of the forces and their families. Indeed, at the beginning of the by-election, he received a donation of £10 from the local branch of the Discharged Soldiers' and Sailors' Association (DSSA). The pacifist Scrymgeour's relationship with the DSSA dated from its first demonstration in Dundee when he had led the meeting in prayer and seconded the main resolution complaining about inadequate pensions and support; in his speech, he claimed those who had been in favour of conscription now didn't care about the men who were discharged. Explaining their decision to back Scrymgeour, Sgt. John Bowman, President of the DSSA said they had decided to support him 'as a matter of self-interest'. He disagreed with him on several matters, but from the point of self-interest they were bound to back him up. They all knew what Mr Churchill was.'[21] Unsurprisingly, their decision raised controversy, with a correspondent to the local newspaper saying:

> *'The committee may consider the financing of pacifist candidates one way of advancing their own interests, but the average man will be inclined to the conclusion that they are acting the 'traitor part' to their comrades in the trenches.'*

The DSSA certainly made a strange bedfellow with the various 'peace propaganda societies' from across the country which were reported to have sent telegrams offering support.

At Scrymgeour's launch meeting, he confirmed that he was standing as a Prohibition and Labour candidate. It was in the nature of the man that he welcomed the chance to stand because it would 'test the sincerity of the Churches and temperance organisations in the city which had been agitating for prohibition' although, beyond that, it would 'also afford those who had so much to say against the Government the opportunity of expressing their opinions.'[22] Scrymgeour continued pursuing the prohibition 'faint-hearts' among the churches at his next meeting, the following evening, Tuesday 24 July. This was outside, in Albert Square, with a crowd estimated to be around 800. He relished informing his audience that had just come from asking the Rev. Thomas Templeton to sign the nomination paper of a Prohibition candidate, but Templeton had declined. Scrymgeour said that:

> *'one of the main objects of this contest was that some people were going to be revealed. Mr Templeton and his crowd were to be made to stand out in their true*

---

21 *Scottish Prohibitionist*, 4 August 1917.
22 *Dundee Courier*, 24 July 1917.

> light. The Churches had identified themselves with petitions and memorials, and they had spoken out with apparent courage, and in this contest the Government was going to realise that either these people never meant business, or they were going to come out like men and stand by the Prohibition candidate.'[23]

Scrymgeour's habit of challenging those on the same side of the argument as himself was not restricted to the church as he said the contest was also:

> 'to test the workers who had declared their dissatisfaction with the government. On Monday, they would have the chance to choose between democracy versus autocracy, Prohibition versus the drink traffic. If they wanted to vote for their own interests and the interests of the people as a whole and for the advancement of progress, they would support him.'

Views were divided on how much attention locals were paying to the election, alongside the competing attractions of annual holidays. They were described by a visiting London journalist as treating the numerous meetings, mostly outdoors, as additional holiday entertainment. He provided 'colour' for his readers:

> 'The natives of this place seem to spend the greater part of their time in learning the piano and having their teeth drawn for all over the centre of the town there are advertisements for music teachers and dentists. Assuredly, the teeth of Dundee are not good. I am told it is the water which, however, is not always taken neat.'[24]

The *Dundee Evening Telegraph* referred to indifference by describing it as the 'By-the-by election'. But, according to *The Post* newspaper:

> 'Interest in the election is growing because holiday makers are on the trek home. In former years it is generally in the last train that folks left their summer quarters for home, but many were constrained to start earlier to see what all the row

---

23 *Dundee Courier*, 25 July 1917.
24 Quoted in *Edinburgh Evening News*, 27 July 1917.

was about in Bonnie Dundee. Not a few 'dumped' their luggage some place and hurried to the meeting'.[25]

Although an easy victory was anticipated, the Liberals worked hard. Churchill returned to campaign for the weekend before polling day. And strong Labour support was mobilised to shore up his position in working-class areas, alongside the endorsement from Wilkie. William Brace, the Labour MP for South Glamorgan and Under Secretary at the Home Office, was brought up as a speaker and George Barnes, the pensions minister, sent a letter of support. From the other side of the political spectrum, Sir George Baxter, his former Unionist opponent, called for backing for Churchill 'at the time of the country's need'.[26]

In his final speeches, Churchill made fun of Scrymgeour saying that he 'proposed to seek peace with Germany in order to suppress the liquor traffic in Scotland.' Heckling meant he was obliged to address his role at Antwerp. One question put to him was: 'what part had he played in the tragedy of Antwerp when hundreds of young lads, many of them belonging to Dundee, not much over school age, without proper equipment, were sent across to provide a target for German guns?' Churchill responded robustly. He argued that it had been vital to prolong the defence of Antwerp for a few days to protect other parts of the army and that he had used the Naval Division because no other forces were available. He maintained that the action had provided an eight-day window which had been vital to saving Calais, Boulogne and the channel ports. In summary, he argued:

> *'There is no subject which has been made more a parrot cry by people whose brains are smaller than those of the smallest parakeet than the subject of Antwerp, but there is no word in the vocabulary that I am more proud to be associated with than the word Antwerp.'*

The main thrust of Churchill's attack on Scrymgeour was to paint him as the most extreme of pacifists. He seized on a statement in his opponent's election

---

25 *The Post*, 28 July 1917.
26 Quoted in *Dundee Courier*, 27 July 1917.

address that he would match the German Socialists by refusing to vote for a continuation of war credits in order to force a peace settlement; Churchill characterised this as risking the safety of those at the front: 'He proposed if he were returned actually to cut off the credits on which the supply of everything necessary to our soldiers and sailors depended, and he proposed to do this in order, by producing great catastrophe on the fighting fronts, to force peace at any price and on any terms.' In a jibe, Churchill noted that this section came from 'the more coherent portion of his address' but argued strongly that 'every vote for Scrymgeour is a vote for a shameful peace with Germany.'

He condemned Scrymgeour for being completely beyond the pale, even for the peace- by- negotiation faction. He said that there were currently about nineteen MPs who might be called a peace party, whose views were extremely unpopular and, he felt, extremely unwise and untimely. However, he maintained even they would not endorse opposing what Scrymgeour described as the 'insanity' of continuing war credits, in other words, funding for the war.

To sum up his assessment of Scrymgeour, Churchill produced a comparison that, in time, came to be worn as a badge of honour by his opponent. He asked if the electors were going to vote for the candidate in favour of the vigorous prosecution of war waged in a righteous cause or whether they would vote for 'a candidate whose doctrines are the dirty and degrading doctrines of Lenin.' Churchill continued:

> *'The views of the Prohibitionist candidate were not the views of Ramsay MacDonald... They did not find a single responsible exponent in the House of Commons. They had got to leave their country altogether in order to find a prominent name associated with the views placed in the Prohibitionist candidate's election address ... It was the notorious name of Lenin, that criminal agitator who was causing the utmost disorder and paralysis in the Russian capital.'*

He said of Scrymgeour, 'The policy which he stood for was not pacifism, even; it was Leninism.' Thus was the 'Scottish Lenin' born. But this became a badge of pride and, according to one researcher, 'being hailed the Scottish Lenin by his peers epitomised Scrymgeour's transformation from a somewhat intolerable politician (even among his allies) prior to 1914, to a key figure in the radical Left movement in Scotland.'[27]

Churchill now attracted highly assertive trade union support. Several members of the Executive Council of the Sailors' and Firemen's Union hot-footed it to Dundee to speak and campaign in his favour and against a detested 'pacifist'. The union Secretary, Captain Edward Tupper, whom we last saw leading his members in the attack on the 'pacifist' meeting at the Battle of Cory Hall in 1916 (see chapter 2), said that they were there to present to the electors the views of men who in their daily calling had to face the submarine peril. He said: 'In view of the German outrages on sailors and firemen in open boats they were opposed to the return of a pacifist' and he pointed out that 'the people of this country – even the pacifists – owed their very existence to the seamen in keeping up the supplies of food'.

The last shouts of Scrymgeour's campaign comprised ripostes against Churchill's accusations and further adamantine criticisms of faint-hearted churchmen and so-called prohibitionists who countenanced compromise. The focus on his call to oppose war credits particularly stung, given Churchill's interpretation that this would harm all those serving. Scrymgeour was at pains to clarify that he would in no way allow the withdrawal of credits while fighting was continuing; instead, he intended such a vote to trigger negotiations such that all fighting would cease. He told an election eve rally:

> *'Contrary entirely to the deceptive and rather discreditable tactics of Mr Churchill, he was not proposing in any way to endanger anybody at the front. He was proposing what Mr Churchill knew very well, that the first step to be taken was a truce, a cessation of war, and that in the interim the representatives of the democracies of the belligerent nations ... would come together and make their minds to settle the question.'*

The association with Lenin brought arguably an equal retort when Scrymgeour responded that he placed Churchill alongside Sir Edward Carson. There was

---

[27] S Bannerman, *The Scottish Lenin or Reluctant Resister*, (University of Dundee dissertation, 2011).

a sizeable Irish vote in Dundee and this comment may have played well with them, but Scrymgeour was making a wider point. He told a meeting:

> 'Sir Edward Carson, along with Sir F. E. Smith, actually took up an attitude of direct defiance to the King and to the Houses of Parliament. They unquestionably took into their hands the direct leadership of armed rebellion. That such men should be given appointments, in the face of all these facts, showed that they were face-to-face with a Government, whether headed Mr Lloyd George or Mr Winston Churchill, which, behind their backs, carried out a conspiracy instead of looking to the interests of the people.'[28]

While Churchill had the highly patriotic seamen's union at his back, Scrymgeour was aided by two, very different, groups. As already noted, the Disabled Sailors and Soldiers were supporting him, out of 'self-interest'. One local vicar, Rev William Paxton, expanded on that position by telling a meeting that

> 'he was in favour of prosecuting the war, but was going to vote for Mr Scrymgeour. They in Dundee had had quite enough of the swashbuckler adventurer and they wanted a man they knew. He had had something to do with pensions, but was there a single man in the meeting who had been in difficulty about his pension who had got any sympathy or help from Mr Churchill? (Cries of 'No').'

The contrast with Scrymgeour's record was clear and was referenced by the DSSA President who described Scrymgeour as the man who would back them up in Parliament in contrast to Churchill whom he maintained was 'probably the most brilliant failure produced in modern times.' The DSSA's support extended to 40 discharged soldiers and sailors joining Scrymgeour's platform at his final election meeting. The second group, who arrived to provide much-needed canvassing manpower on polling day, were a completely different kettle of fish. Drawing on Scrymgeour's now strong links with the left, these were referred to as 'Clyde agitators'; the prohibitionist extremist had managed to bring together a wide-ranging coalition.

---

28 *Dundee Courier*, 28 July 1917.

As Dundee prepared to vote, the many cross-cutting arguments were confusing. Scrymgeour opposed the war but had shown himself solicitous of those serving while Churchill backed the war but was accused of ignoring constituents badly affected by it. Churchill argued that prohibitionists could safely back him, as he fully endorsed the temperance legislation in Scotland, and that there was every case for a sincere prohibitionist voting against the prohibition candidate because he was a pacifist, while Scrymgeour did not soften his position in any way to offer a warm embrace to fellow prohibitionists who would brook compromise. Consequently, the Scottish Temperance League, for example, did not advise its members which way to vote saying only that they were 'opposed to State purchase and are strong for the Temperance (Scotland) Act and for prohibition during the war'.

The election had not raised intense interest locally, due to the holidays, but the final weekend and polling day saw more activity. Scrymgeour held two large outdoor meetings on the Friday evening at one of which he revealed himself as surprisingly sensitive to heckling. Having been interrupted a couple of times, he turned to the police constables present and asked them to remove the perpetrators. They declined to do so until Scrymgeour, more in character, threatened to stop the meeting and go directly to the Chief Constable's office; that had the desired effect, and the interrupters were quickly neutralised. Churchill closed his campaigning on the Saturday and headed back to the Ministry of Munitions, leaving Clementine in charge. No fewer than five meetings were held in the Albert Square on the Saturday evening where 'Mrs Churchill and Mr McCallam Scott MP perambulated from gathering to gathering, arriving at Mr Scrymgeour's crowd just in time to hear a vote of confidence carried for the Prohibition candidate.' The Coalition did little on the Sabbath while Scrymgeour carried on campaigning via a large demonstration in the Kinnaird Hall since, as the *Dundee Courier* wryly noted, 'as usual, The Sabbath was Mr Scrymgeour's great day'.

A win, but a trend confirmed

Polling was on the Monday, 30 July, the first day back after the holidays, and voting was brisk from early morning as people cast their ballots on the way to work. Clementine motored around the city, visiting many of the industrial areas while the Sailors and Firemen's Union members were busy at the docks drumming up support for her husband. Press expectations were for a 'thumping' majority for Churchill. A majority was delivered but it came with a tinge of disappointment for the government as the vote for Scrymgeour, at over one-fifth, was greater than anticipated, and much higher than he had managed previously.

Nov. 1910[1]			
Churchill	Liberal	9,240	
Wilkie	Labour	8,957	
Baxter	Lib Unionist	5,685	
Lloyd	Conservative	4,914	
Scrymgeour	Scottish Prohibition	1,825	
Majority			
Electorate & Turnout		19,118	84%

(2 members elected after Dec 1910).

30 Jul. 1917			
Churchill	Liberal	7,302	78%
Scrymgeour	Scottish Prohibition	2,036	22%%
Majority		5,266	
Electorate & Turnout		21,953	43%

A crowd of around 5,000 waited for the result, which was declared just after 10pm. Clementine Churchill moved the vote of thanks to the returning officer. She was emollient in tone commenting that it had been a clean contest. Nevertheless, she welcomed the result as a great mandate for the government to get on with the war and went out of her way to record her husband's gratitude to the Unionists for backing him. Scrymgeour declared his pleasure at seconding her motion but was more political in his comments, saying: 'He considered that the contest ... had been thoroughly warranted by the magnificent vote which had been given against the Coalition forces in the city of Dundee. To say that a Cabinet Minister had had to be dependent upon the votes of Unionism in a constituency marked in its Liberal tendency was a stimulus to them.'[29] Scrymgeour also reinforced his pacifist credentials, thanking Churchill for pointing out that he stood ahead even of the pacifist party in the House of Commons and claiming that:

'This was the most magnificent vote that was ever on a peace issue and he was quite satisfied when the real truth of affairs was made known this record would stand in history, not only in the Prohibition movement, but as regards all the rottenness that lay behind deceitful diplomacy'.[30]

Press comment endorsed the opinion that Churchill's opponent had done better than expected or hoped by the government. The *Daily Record* noted: 'The only speculation anyone made was the probable number of votes Mr Churchill's opponent would secure, and it must be admitted that this was more than was generally anticipated here'[31] while the *Western Daily Press* opined: 'Mr Winston Churchill has won by a handsome majority at Dundee, but we do not consider it satisfactory that his opponent received more than two thousand votes.'[32] They were of the view that as Scrymgeour was now standing as a Pacifist, he should have gained fewer, not more votes than in December 1910. In similar vein, the *Aberdeen Press* (same date) felt Dundee should have

---

29 *Dundee Courier*, 31 July 1917.
30 Ibid.
31 *Daily Record*, 31 July 1917.
32 *Western Daily Press*, 31 July 1917.

followed the example of South Aberdeen where Pethwick-Lawrence received only 333 votes. (see chapter 8)

Tireless opponent

Even as the votes were being cast and counted, Churchill was in harness at the Ministry of Munitions, an appointment which turned out to be more successful than many, especially Unionists, had expected. His later emergence as the country's pre-eminent statesman needs no retelling here.

Scrymgeour returned to local activism, in support of prohibitionists, conscientious objectors and the wider Dundee working-class. In his concession speech, ever pugnacious, he noted: 'This vote would stimulate them to go forward and one day, if spared, he should have the opportunity of standing there as the successful and returned member for Dundee.'[33]

The 1918 General election was not to fulfil his prediction and Scrymgeour now came third behind Churchill and sitting Labour MP, Wilkie, but polled over 10,000 votes, despite his appearance in Horatio Bottomley's Political Blacklist in the popular *John Bull* magazine (a list of candidates people were enjoined not to support). But his reputation as a seer was made at the 1922 General Election when, at the sixth time of asking, he emerged victorious, and Churchill was removed as one of Dundee's MPs. At this election, all the fates conspired to bring 'Neddy' success. The Tory backbenchers had finally brought down the Coalition government rendering it a disastrous time for its National Liberal members to face the country such that more than half of them lost their seats. Churchill was ill, recovering from appendicitis, and largely unable to campaign. After the result, he ruefully reflected: 'In the twinkling of an eye, I found myself without an office, without a party and without an appendix'. Vitally, Scrymgeour now reaped the benefits of his close identification with the more radical wing of Labour. In Dundee, Wilkie announced in 1920 that he would stand down at the next election and he was replaced by a leading figure from the Union of Democratic Control, Edmund Morel. More significantly, Labour again decided to run only one candidate, opening a major opportunity for the Prohibitionist. Their election literature did not overtly call for supporters to give their second vote to Scrymgeour, but

---

33 *Dundee Courier*, 31 July 1917.

the implication was clear, and this gave him the space finally to benefit from his local activism as people said it was time 'to give Eddy his chance'.

Scrymgeour topped the poll with more than 32,000 votes, closely followed by Morel. Churchill did not even finish third, coming narrowly behind his National Liberal running mate. Observers at the time joked that one of the reasons for Scrymgeour's success had been that everyone associated with the liquor trade had backed him, on the basis that all the other candidates planned to support some restrictions on alcohol while Scrymgeour's position was so extreme it would never come into effect.

Churchill went off to further election defeats in 1923 (Leicester West, as a Liberal) and 1924 (Westminster Abbey, as an Independent) before returning to the Conservative Party and being elected at the 1924 General election for Epping, a seat he was to hold until his retirement from the house in 1964. [34] Scrymgeour did not disappoint his labour movement backers, promptly making his maiden speech on unemployment and poverty and the need for drastic action on both. He was re-elected three times, in 1923, 1924 and 1929 before finally being defeated at the 1931 General Election. True to his life-long Christian principles, he spent his years after Parliament working as an evangelical Chaplain. He died in 1947.

---

34 The seat changed boundaries and name, from Epping to Woodford at the 1945 General Election.

11.
LABOUR PAINS

North Salford, 2 November 1917
Prestwich, 31 January 1918
Wansbeck, 28 May 1918
Gravesend, 7 June 1918

Labour in parliament was an equal signatory to the truce, alongside the Unionists and Liberals, and stood staunchly by it, as did their national organisation. However, as the war continued, there was increasing unrest among their rank and file about being prevented from flexing their electoral muscles and unofficial candidates began to be adopted. The pressure became too much, and Labour eventually abandoned the truce in June 1918 although ironically from that point on, renegade Labour candidates ceased to appear.

NORTH SALFORD – November 1917

The unexpected death of the Liberal MP for Salford North, Sir William Byles, in October 1917, opened the way to the first independent Labour candidate standing against the chosen Coalition nominee since Merthyr in 1915 (see chapter 2). Byles had long been on the Liberals' radical wing. He was strongly supportive of the labour movement and, at each election in Salford from 1906 when he first won the seat, he had been endorsed by the local trades council and described as a Lib-Lab candidate. He was a pacifist and voted against conscription. Initially, there was no expectation of drama after he died on 15

October following complications from bronchitis. Although Salford North was marginal, the established Unionist candidate was on active service, and it was quickly stated they would stand by the truce. Likewise, despite Salford's highly industrial nature, the national Labour party agreed not to intervene.

The local Liberals proceeded to choose a candidate. Their selection committee put forward a single name, Sir Charles Mallet, the former MP for Plymouth. Mallet had first stood for parliament in Salford West in 1900, when he was unsuccessful, but he was then elected in Plymouth in 1906 and remained an MP until defeated in December 1910. He had briefly held office as Financial Secretary to the War Office.

Mallet's unopposed selection was made on 24 October 1917, and it was decided that nominations would be on 31 October and polling, if necessary, on 2 November. Yet even with this break-neck timetable, news emerged that there would be a contest. A possible National Party intervention was rumoured, but on 27 October (the same day that Mallet travelled to Manchester to begin his electioneering) Ben Tillett, a longstanding trades unionist and maverick, announced himself as an Independent workers candidate.

In reply, Mallet quickly laid out his case. He emphasised that he was the Coalition flag-bearer, with the support of Liberals, Unionists and Labour alike. He maintained that no-one in the country was more committed than he to the strongest possible prosecution of the war and that consequently the electors of Salford should not be troubled with a contested election. Mallet was undoubtedly a well-regarded scion of the establishment, holding a first in history from Oxford, called to the bar, a former MP, and knighted earlier in the year. However, in Tillett, he was up against a true aristocrat of the labour movement.

Tillett's was a long and colourful history. In the words of his biographer: 'there is scarcely a position he took up which he did not later directly contradict.'[1] A key founder of 'new unionism', Tillett had been celebrated and feared alike as a hard-line socialist. However, over the years he zig-zagged between right and left-wing positions. From a poor background and an unhappy home, he had run away twice by the age of seven and joined a circus, where he learned to be an acrobat. At thirteen, he entered the navy

---

[1] J Schneer, *Ben Tillett* (1982).

and, when invalided out, joined the merchant navy; after that, he sought work in the docks. Here, Tillett's trade union and political career began. He saw the need for a union that would unite all dockworkers, including the unskilled. In this he was opposed by the established 'craft' unions but pushed forward and became a major force through the foundation in 1887 of his Tea Operatives and General Labourers Association, to be renamed in 1889 as the Dock, Wharf, Riverside and General Labourers' Union.

The first strike he led, in 1888, was unsuccessful but he was a prime mover in the ferocious 1889 London docks strike where the union was victorious. In the following years, industrial conflict in the docks continued unabated as the employers organised and fought back against Tillett. At the same time, he broadened his political activism, becoming a strong supporter of independent labour representation. He stood unsuccessfully against the Liberals in Bradford in 1892 and in 1893 was one of the founders of the Independent Labour Party.

In the next period, Tillett drifted to the right. Now he backed arrangements with the Liberals. He spent time in Australia becoming a supporter of arbitration in industrial disputes and later he formed a friendship with Horatio Bottomley. Nevertheless, at the 1906 election he stood as the ILP candidate in Eccles, again unsuccessfully. Tillett now moved to the left again. He became a member of the Social Democratic Federation and declared in 1908 that there was no solution but revolution and that he was against 'the wage system'. In the January 1910 election he stood in Swansea as an independent labour candidate (against the wishes of the national party which had wanted the seat left as a clear run for the Liberals) but again finished third.

The period from 1910 to 1914 was one of increasing labour militancy in which Tillett became a leader who was well regarded by the left. According to Schneer: 'Tillett came in the public mind almost to personify the aggressive class consciousness of the syndicalist movement'.[2] He was involved in the foundation of the National Transport Workers Federation and led another successful London docks strike, in 1911. However, a further strike the following year failed and Tillett declared: 'Sedition or no sedition, I want to say that if our men are to be murdered, I am going to take a gun and I will shoot Lord

---

2 Ibid.

Devonport.'³ Devonport was the head of the Port of London Authority. At one mass meeting during the strike, Tillett said 'Repeat after me: Oh God, strike Lord Devonport dead'.

By the outbreak of war in 1914, Tillett was a member of the British Socialist Party and had been selected as their candidate for Northampton. Initially, it looked as if he would back the strongly 'internationalist' position for which he had argued previously; for example, he had moved a resolution at a Council meeting of the National Transport Workers Federation, stating: 'In the event of international war being imminent .....we recommend a general stoppage of work among all transport workers who are engaged in the transportation of troops and munitions of war.' He had attended the 2 August 1914 Trafalgar Square demonstration against Britain entering the conflict.

Yet, once war was declared, he switched to the extreme patriotic wing of the labour movement, alongside figures such as Havelock Wilson of the Seamen's Union with whom Tillett had co-operated in the foundation of the National Transport Workers Federation and Henry Hyndman, the founder of Britain's first socialist party, the Social Democratic Federation, and in 1911 of the British Socialist Party. Tillett condemned the early anti-German hysteria but argued that British soldiers must be supported because they were workers. He now threw himself wholeheartedly into support for the war and made trips to the front to back the troops and undertook multiple speaking tours (totalling over 600 meetings in 16 months), rallying support for the armed forces and the war. As with Bottomley, there were rumours, by his political opponents, that he was well-remunerated for his efforts with estimates that he was receiving up to £20 a week for his musical recruitment performances.⁴

So radical was his switch of position that he now feared the possible outbreak of revolution and 'he demanded that workers be given guns, that Conscientious Objectors be imprisoned, that dissident newspapers be censored, and that air raids be launched against German civilian centres.'⁵ At the 1916 Annual Conference of the British Socialist Party, the majority

---

3 Ibid.
4 D J Swift, *Patriotic Labour in the Era of the Great War (PhD Thesis: University of Central Lancashire*, 2014)
5 J Schneer, *Ben Tillett* (1982).

came out against the war and, as a consequence, a breakaway group including Tillett left to found the National Socialist Party.

Following Byles' death, Tillett received an invitation from his union branch to stand as an independent candidate, regardless of the decision of the parliamentary Labour party to abide by the truce. Local newspaper reports argued that, although the dockers union was well-represented in Salford, the vast bulk of the port employees (and so their members) were in Salford East rather than Salford North.

A battle between two committed warriors

In his opening campaign salvo, Tillett aimed to outflank Mallet in terms of support for the strongest possible prosecution of the war. He placed particular emphasis on air retaliation against the civilian population of Germany. As the *Manchester Evening News* reported: 'Mr. Tillett said that one of the points of his programme would be a gigantic scale of air reprisals on Germany, he holding the view that if the German people came to realise what had been done to the civilians of this country their views would be altered.'[6]

Alongside his strident militarism, Tillett could deploy a credible commitment to campaigning to improve the living standards of workers and members of the armed forces alike. He argued: 'I shall advocate a ruthless crusade against profiteering, the more efficient control of foodstuffs and their more adequate distribution, and a larger measure of popular government control in the handling and control of shipping and transport generally.'

From a stalwart of the labour movement, these pledges were more credible than those Mallet could offer. Nevertheless, press speculation suggested that the local Liberal machine would be strong enough to overpower the blandishments of the maverick. As the *Manchester Evening News* said:

> 'The electorate is largely a working class one, but it is doubtful whether a candidate even as strong as Mr. Ben Tillett can make an appreciable impression against the nominee of the Coalition, which, of course, includes the Labour party. By coming forward as an Independent candidate Mr. Tillett obviously does not consider himself bound by the party truce which has been faithfully

---

6 *Manchester Evening News*, 27 October 1917.

observed by the three political organisations in every war-time election... his main plank is vigorous prosecution of the war and the restoration of industrial principles after victory has been won.'

However, they went on to argue:

'Polling day (Friday next) will find the Liberal organisation well equipped for a fight. The division has been carefully 'nursed' in view of even as unlikely a contingency as the abrupt termination of the party understanding. It should also be remembered that on this occasion the Liberals will have the active co-operation of the Unionists, who have promised the fullest support to Sir Charles Mallet. Against a combination so strong the supporters of Sir Charles feel that Mr. Ben Tillett, with all his exceptionally good fighting qualities, is hardly likely to make much headway.'[7]

The contrary view was expressed, on the same day, by the *Derby Daily Telegraph* in a leader column:

'If Mr. Ben Tillett complies with the wishes of his local admirers and consents to woo North Salford as an Independent, poor Sir Charles' chances of election will be remote. The organiser of the Dockers' Union is a formidable opponent ... His views on social questions may be too advanced for the average Democrat, but in this conflict he would be known, not as Ben the Socialist, but an Independent, pledged to what our Correspondent describes as a vigorous war programme with the interests of sailors, soldiers, and the discharged at the forefront of the campaign'.[8]

Both campaigns launched intense programmes of 'dinner time' meetings outside factories and then evening meetings with a multitude of supporting speakers. Mallet's first public meeting included speeches and endorsements from leading Unionists, as well as Liberals, and he reinforced the Coalition argument that Tillett's campaign was unnecessary. Speaking about air reprisals, Mallet said: 'If the Germans bomb our towns, we must bomb theirs....

---

7 Ibid.
8 *Derby Daily Telegraph*, 27 October 1917.

Our airmen must have a free hand.... and if they do happen to hit a palace at Potsdam or even a cathedral at Cologne, well, with the bitter memories of these years behind us, I, for one, cannot and will not interfere.'[9]

Mallet's early supporting cast was drawn from across the country. Visiting speakers included John Robertson MP (Liberal; Tyneside), Aneurin Williams MP (Liberal; NW Durham), George Hay Morgan MP (Liberal, Truro), Thomas Dobson (Liberal; former MP for Plymouth). He was also backed by the Chairman of the North Salford Conservative Association. Later in the campaign, three Unionist MPs visited to speak on his behalf – Sir Stuart Coats, MP for Wimbledon, Ronald McNeill, MP for St. Augustines, Kent, and Lieutenant-Colonel Percy Clive, MP for Ross, Herefordshire.

Tillett also brought in an impressive cast, including Councillor Charles Taylor (Shoreditch), Rev. Arthur Waldron (London), Alf Pursell (Furnishing Trades Union), and Joe Terrett (London). Terrett had, of course, stood as an independent in the West Newington by-election (see chapter 3). Tillett was also supported by one sitting Labour MP, James O'Grady (Leeds East) who was a leading trades unionist.

Two potentially influential organisations made early decisions regarding the contest. A meeting of the United Irish League branches in the constituency decided not to endorse either candidate. The local Catholics, however, came out in support of Mallet. The Manchester and Salford Executive of the Catholic Federation put questions to both candidates, regarding their views on the Education Bill. The Federation asked: 'Having regard to the fact that the Coalition government has violated the war truce by introducing an Education Bill which is controversial and unacceptable to Catholics, are you prepared to demand that the Bill is withdrawn?' Catholic opinion on the Bill was negative because, although they recognised good things in the proposed legislation, they also feared that it would give local authorities much greater power over denominational schools. They welcomed the proposal to increase the school leaving age from 12 to 14 and also the concept of part-time continuation education beyond that. But they believed the financial arrangements would put them at a major disadvantage as they would not be entitled to the same level of state assistance as that provided to non-denominational schools. They

---

9 *Manchester Evening News*, 30 October 1917.

also read the Bill as meaning they could not ban non-Catholic teachers from appointment in their schools. In the event, the local Catholics found Mallet's responses more to their liking than those of Tillett and so advised their supporters to back the Coalition man. Tillett's attitude was likely to have been aligned with that of organised labour in general which was overwhelmingly in support of the legislation.

The short campaign gathered pace but was strongly impacted by the ever-greater privations of war-time. Regulations now meant that motorcars could not be used for campaigning nor the conveyance of voters to the polls. Also, the use of large-sized posters was banned under Defence of the Realm Act regulations and the candidates were restricted to limited numbers of bland, small posters. The nature of campaigning also changed, in response to the very few days available. Both candidates made little attempt at canvassing. Instead, the main efforts were put into as many meetings as possible and unprecedented levels of leafleting.

Since both candidates supported maximising the war effort, the contest came down to a choice between Tillett stressing his working-class roots and commitment to protecting and enhancing the rights of workers and Mallet's appeal to loyalty to the Coalition government. The Unionists did their bit to bolster Mallet's argument. Their local leaders issued an appeal:

> *'Let us forget that there is such a thing as party. Let us think only our country, of its need, of its perils and let us give our votes through Sir Charles Mallet to the Government which represents all parties, and which is honestly doing its best in the face of enormous difficulties to secure for us that speedy victory for which we are praying'.*

In opposition, Tillett claimed his right, as a working man, to represent working men. He argued that while he spoke no ill of Mallet, the latter could not adequately represent the workers of Salford, and that the establishment must learn that it could not dictate whom the workers should choose to speak for them. Tillett laid great stress on how he would act against profiteering in food and munitions. According to the *Manchester Evening News*: 'He would put it down ruthlessly, he said, and raised a cheer when he declared that he would see to it that the cost of living was not inflated by these sordid food profiteers.'[10]

Right to the last minute, the *Manchester Evening News* continually informed its readers that, while Tillett had put up a good fight, he could not overcome the combined might of the Liberals and Unionists. However, on polling day itself, the paper began to concede the strength of Tillett's campaign. It commented that:

> 'Literature has been distributed throughout the division in lavish fashion during the closing days of the contest... The hoardings in the division were freely plastered with literature to-day, but in this respect Mr Ben Tillett had a big advantage over his opponent, many reasons being given why the Independent candidate should be given the electors' vote in preference to that of Charles Mallet. One bill read: 'If in Parliament you put Ben Tillett you send a bullet to its billet in Kaiser Bill.... Particularly in the working-class district did Mr. Tillett meet with a warm welcome, large crowds of children cheering and singing popular ditties parodied to suit the situation in his favour.'

Against this, they commented on the Mallet campaign: 'Sir Charles Mallet's supporters have not made the theatrical display of the other side, but notwithstanding, a great deal of hard work has been put in on the Coalition candidate's behalf. They are not at all dismayed by the flood of literature poured out by Mr Tillett and his friends.'[11]

The *Liverpool Daily Post* also provided a final campaign summary which although designed to be supportive of the Coalition man in practice highlighted Tillett's strengths. It noted that there was nothing to choose between the two candidates in terms of support for the war effort. As a result, Tillett was stressing other campaign points. First, that Mallet was not a local man. On this, the paper highlighted the irony that at least Mallet had previously fought in Salford whereas Tillett was from Bristol and had no local connections. Secondly, they pointed out that Tillett was seeking to make much of his opposition to food price rises. The paper commented:

---

10 *Manchester Evening News*, 31 October 1917.
11 *Manchester Evening News*, 1 November 1917.

> 'he has seized upon profiteering, and worked the food ticket for all it is worth. His virility and gift for denunciation have secured him highly successful meetings, and it is obvious he has made considerable headway with his whirlwind methods. He asserts that North Salford, being a working-class constituency, should be represented by a working-class member, and has been comparing his own services on behalf of the workers with those of Sir Charles Mallet. Mr. Tillett has a loud trumpet. He has been generous with promises, and in one handbill issued on his behalf by the Manchester and District Furnishing Trades' Federated Committee it is stated: 'Ben Tillett has also declared his determination to criminally convict all food profiteers.' This is a noteworthy determination since even a seat in the House does not carry with it a seat on the judicial bench.' [12]

Certainly, food price rises and allegations of profiteering had become key issues on the home front during 1917 and contributed to a marked increase in industrial unrest. Early in the war, little action was taken by the authorities despite shrinking food supplies caused by the reduction in available home front agricultural labour and the disruption to imports. Consequently, it was estimated by the Board of Trade that food prices had risen by 61 per cent between July 1914 and July 1916. Poor harvests in 1916 exacerbated the situation and, at the end of the year, the government appointed Lord Devonport as Food Controller. Devonport still relied on voluntary restraint but the dramatic increase in sinkings by U Boats produced ever greater problems and, in May 1917, he was replaced by Lord Rhondda who commenced more interventionist policies.[13] Despite the change of management, rationing (which was to prove to be popular and effective) was not introduced until shortly after the North Salford by-election and so the problems were still felt acutely at the time of the campaign, especially as food prices had now more than doubled since the start of the war. Industrial unrest led by the unions was increasing markedly;

---

12 *Liverpool Daily Post*, 2 November 1917.
13 At its peak effectiveness, the German U Boat fleet was sinking one-third of merchant ships attempting to sail to the UK.

so much so that eight regional commissions were established in May 1917 to investigate the causes. They found that 'food was at the root of the discontent.'[14]

Reports of election day were of a subdued turnout. However, one event livened up proceedings – the Salford magistrates remanded a young man in custody, charged with having in his possession thousands of copies of what the police termed 'peace literature', which it was alleged he intended to distribute among the voters. He was not, of course, connected with either candidate. North Salford prided itself on delivering election results quickly and the outcome was declared just 45 minutes after the polls closed. The notional electorate was 10,623 but observers calculated, with deaths, absence on active duty and 'removals' the true number was probably around 8,000. Even allowing for that, the turnout was low at 4,367 (41 per cent of the nominal electorate and approximately 55 per cent of the true voter base. This compared with an 87 per cent turnout in December 1910).

The result was a dramatic, and emphatic, victory for Tillett and so the second wartime defeat for the government, following Pemberton Billing's success in 1916.[15]

Dec. 1910			
Byles	Lib-Lab	4,402	51%
Potter	Conservative	4,163	49%
Majority		239	
Electorate & Turnout		9,850	87%

---

14 Commission of Enquiry into Industrial Unrest, G N. Barnes (Chairman), Summary, Cd 8696 (1917—18). Recorded in: M Barnett, *British Food Policy During the First World War* (1985).
15 Although Merthyr was also strictly speaking a government defeat, it was a victory over an 'official' candidate that was, on balance, probably welcomed by the administration.

2 Nov. 1917			
Tillett	Independent	2,822	65%
Mallet	Liberal-Coalition	1,545	35%
Majority		1,277	
Electorate & Turnout		10,623	41%

The outcome was a surprise to many who had anticipated that the allegiance to the truce of the Unionists and the official Labour Party would have seen Mallet home. Several reasons were identified and discussed. It was noted that the previous MP, Byles, had been both assiduous and very popular, among Liberal and Labour supporters alike. Next, that the selection of Mallet as the Coalition candidate had not adequately reflected the strong working-class nature of the constituency and that he was not seen as a local man. Instead, it looked to some like an establishment 'stitch up' to get a 'carpet-bagging' former MP back into the House, regardless of the feelings of Salford residents. There were suggestions that many Unionists stayed at home and that some Liberals also abstained as they would have preferred a local candidate.

Tillett's strengths were attributed to his militantly pro-war stance, his reputation as a long-standing campaigner for the interests of the working class, and the predominantly working-class make-up of the constituency. It was recognised that he had put together a highly effective campaign, despite the restrictions of time and resources and his triumph was not felt to rest on his standing among dockworkers, few of whom were believed to be registered in the Salford North constituency.

Speaking after the declaration, Tillett said that the result justified his opinion that the country was ready for more strenuous representation to give confidence, not to the Government, but to the Army and Navy, the maritime workers, and the public generally. Every day brought its crises, and there was more need than ever for fortitude and determination. After all, however, he was going to represent many of the causes which Charles Mallet would have represented, and what Sir Charles wanted to do for the public, he in his humble way would try his best to do.

Tillett's previous electoral failures were due to his socialist positions being well in advance of those held by most members of the working class who were electors. However, his commitment to the war, and the home front crises, were now sufficient to overcome any squeamishness about the positions he had adopted in the past. His 'home' newspaper, the *Western Daily Press*, reflected this clearly:

> *'The success of Mr Ben Tillett in winning the seat at North Salford against an admirable supporter of the Coalition is a triumph of personality that cannot surprise Bristolians who know Mr Tillett well and appreciate his great power on the Platform. If Tillett had been a follower of Mr Snowden and Mr Ramsay MacDonald, congratulations would have out of place, but throughout the war he has done splendid national work, cheering our soldiers and getting recruits, and he is utterly free from the taint of Pacifism. ... And so, although we might not care to endorse all Mr Tillett's social and economic ideas, his election just now is a sign that a popular electorate is 'more Royalist than the King' in urging a whole-hearted prosecution of the war'.*[16]

Another paper, the *Derby Daily Telegraph*, described the result as 'remarkable'. It, too, attributed Tillett's success to his personality and track record. However, it also saw the outcome as a harbinger of more assertive demands for working-class representatives in the future: 'To old party managers his return is instructive as a hint that the working classes mean to obtain a much larger share parliamentary representation than they have hitherto possessed.'[17] Certainly, the Salford Liberals had judged poorly when they decided to replace a strong supporter of working-class issues like Byles with an outsider with no such hinterland or reputation.

Nevertheless, the Coalition government accepted Tillett's victory with equanimity since his aim was to encourage rather than threaten it. Mallet's defeat was also a reminder of the serious divisions within the Liberal Party. He was very much from the Asquith wing of the party and some Liberals may have felt him insufficiently supportive of Lloyd George.

---

16 *Western Daily Press*, 3 November 1917.
17 *Derby Daily Telegraph*, 3 November 1917.

Tillett was to enjoy a long political career as the representative of Salford North and of the dockers. Yet, as the labour movement grew in political and industrial importance, he did not attain the heights that he might have expected. In the 1918 General Election, he was returned with a massive majority in a straight fight with the Liberals. He was then narrowly re-elected in 1922 and 1923, only to be defeated in 1924. He came back in 1929 only to lose again, in his final parliamentary election, in 1931. He remained on the backbenches during both Labour governments. In the trade union world, his career was fading. His dockers' union was a driving force behind the formation of the powerful Transport and General Union in 1922, but he was eclipsed by his former deputy, Ernest Bevin, who was elected as General Secretary of what rapidly became the country's most powerful union.

Mallet did not contest the 1918 election but busied himself as Honorary Secretary of the Free Trade Union which had been founded to fight Chamberlain's Tariff proposals. Future unsuccessful parliamentary campaigns followed in Aberdeen South in 1922 and 1923. He wrote a biography of Lloyd George, which was wholly negative.

Labour in Parliament were not unduly concerned by Tillett's success, even though it had broken the party's firm adherence to the electoral truce. However, it was an indication of a growing desire for working-class representation (which was only to increase as the focus moved from war to peace and the prospect of universal male suffrage) and of the parliamentary Labour Party's sporadic inability to impose its will on the labour movement locally.

PRESTWICH - January 1918

The impact of North Salford reverberated just up the road in Prestwich. There, the sitting Liberal MP, Frederick Crawley, was elevated to the peerage in the 1918 New Year's honours list. The Manchester and Salford Labour party was keen to contest the seat, notwithstanding the truce, and made a request to the national party to do so. Anticipating refusal, it explored running a candidate backed by the co-operative movement which was particularly strong in the Prestwich area. The co-operators felt hard done by during the war. They had worked to limit cost of living increases for their members and campaigned against profiteering. However, they believed that fewer of their staff were being protected from conscription by being 'starred' than was the case for other retailers and they particularly resented their dividends being subject to the Excess Profits tax. Consequently, in October 1917 they held an emergency political conference which decided to abandon political neutrality and to work to see co-operators elected to the Commons, effectively forming the Co-operative Party.

The Liberals appeared unconcerned about the possibility of a fight with Labour, in whatever guise, and proceeded to choose their MP's successor. Initially, the only name discussed was Cawley's eldest son, Robert. Yet, in a surprise development, the Liberals then plumped for Oswald Cawley, the youngest son, Robert having ruled himself out due to heavy business commitments. Oswald was 33 years old and had been employed in his father's business, the Heaton Mills Bleaching Company. Previously educated at Rugby and Oxford, at the time of his nomination he was serving in Palestine as an officer in the Shropshire Yeomanry. In response to the offer of the seat, he said 'I agree to my name being brought before the Selection Committee, conditionally, that I shall not be obliged to remain in England permanently during the war. The regiment has lately been serving as infantry and has taken a gallant part in recent battles.'[18]

The writ could not be issued quickly as parliament was not sitting, leaving time for further developments regarding potential candidates. There were rumours of a movement to run a candidate 'who will be in complete sympathy with President Wilson's latest views of peace, Lord Lansdowne's ideals of stating our war aims, and the views so recently expressed by the Speaker in the House of Commons.'[19] Also, the One Man Business Association, an organisation for small traders, resolved that its chairman, Sam Bloor, would be put forward while, on the other hand, the National Labour Executive confirmed they would abide by the truce. In response, the Manchester and Salford Labour party decided, nevertheless, to support Joseph Binns, a local councillor and the district organiser for the Amalgamated Society of Engineers, provided the union would bear the expense of the election; it was also expected that he could well attract the backing of the Co-operators. Only days later, there was a dramatic Labour reversal. The Amalgamated Society

---

18 *Manchester Evening News*, 9 January 1918.
19 *Manchester Evening News*, 4 January 1918.

of Engineers was not able to provide financial backing for Binns while the Co-operators selected Henry May from London, who was the Parliamentary Secretary of the Co-operative Union. It was now expected that were he to be nominated he would also receive the backing of the local Labour party. Meanwhile, the prospect of a One Man Business Association campaign disappeared as Bloor announced he would not stand after all, given that the seat was due to disappear under redistribution and that there would soon be a General Election on new boundaries.

At the close of nominations, a straight fight emerged between Cawley and May, with the local Labour forces aligning behind the Co-operative nominee. May was accompanied to the nomination by his agent, Councillor Joseph Whiteley, and his assistant agent, James Standring. Both campaign activists were ILP members and Standring had already been agent for two peace by negotiation candidates, Albert Taylor in Rossendale and Edward Backhouse in Stockton (see chapter 8).

Cawley was an absentee candidate, but truce-based support was provided by the Conservatives who issued a letter to electors reminding them that

> 'The Empire is at war and there can be only one dominant question at this election and that is to support the Prime Minister and the Government in all measures necessary for the vigorous prosecution of the war. Let us think only of our country and its perils, of its needs, of its war aims, and give our vote through Lieut. Cawley to the government which represents all parties, and which is honestly doing its best in the face of enormous difficulties.'

In discussion with the returning officer, it was agreed that the polls would be open for an hour longer than usual, until 9pm, to accommodate late workers. However, the use of motorcars would be restricted to one for each campaign, for the use of candidates and agents, and posters would be limited to 'double royal' size (25 inches x 40 inches).

May was guaranteed his place in history, as the first ever Co-operative party candidate, but he struggled to make an impact. Although the movement was strong locally, its supporters included many who were committed Liberal or Conservative voters and so he was not guaranteed their backing. As in other by-elections, a major campaigning problem was the large number of 'removals'; to trace these and encourage them to vote required an experienced electoral organisation which the Co-operators lacked. Again, as in other campaigns, the government side sought to nullify the impact of any opposition by claiming to support similar policies, in this case on the topic of food distribution and prices.

May also managed to adopt positions that may have reduced his appeal on both the left and right of politics. Though receiving the unofficial backing of local Labour forces, he announced that if elected he would not associate with Labour or any other party but would sit as an Independent. Despite this, he also said that he was in absolute agreement with US President Woodrow Wilson's 'Fourteen points' and with the statement of war aims issued by the Trade Union Congress Parliamentary Committee which the Spectator reported as follows: 'Mr. Henderson summarized the proposals as requiring a speedy settlement 'founded on the principles of democracy and security,' and as excluding either annexationist or Imperialist designs for territorial adjustment or an economic war after the war against the German people.'[20]. May was reported as arguing: 'The time was long passed ... for a meeting of all belligerent countries in some neutral centre'[21], thereby setting himself at odds with the 'knockout blow' school and perhaps dangerously near 'peace by negotiation'

If the Co-op campaign hoped that Cawley's absence might assist them, drawing attention to it proved a double-edged sword since it served to emphasise how he was 'doing his bit'. Both sides held numerous meetings, with a star-studded roster of outside speakers being brought in to support Cawley. But the campaign largely failed to capture the interest of the electorate, and this would result in a particularly low poll. A clear Coalition win was anticipated especially, as a non-local candidate, May had failed to generate enthusiasm. The by-election was described as 'one of the tamest election contests that have ever taken place in this part of the country'[22]

The declaration, held the day after polling, attracted only a small audience of twenty or so people. They would not have been surprised by the outcome, which was an emphatic victory for the Coalition, although the turnout was greater than expected. The Co-operative Party was disappointed by the result

---

20 *The Spectator*, 5 January 1918.
21 *Manchester Evening News*, 24 January 1918.
22 *Manchester Evening News*, 31 January 1918.

and felt let down by Labour. Accusations were made that promised support from leading Labour figures had not materialise and it was wondered, in Co-op circles, if the Labour party had adopted a deliberate approach of not assisting, in order to push home the message that all working-class political activity needed to be channelled through them.

Dec. 1910			
Crawley, F	Liberal	10,355	59%
Brocklehurst	Conservative	7,189	41%
Majority		3,166	
Electorate & Turnout		22,123	79%

31 Jan. 1918			
Crawley, O	Liberal	8,520	75%
May	Co-operative	2,832	25%
Majority		5,688	
Electorate & Turnout		26,523	43%

Cawley eventually returned from the Middle East and took his seat on 21 June. He was unable to stay long and was soon back on active service in France, where he was killed in action in August 1918, aged 36. May was to have one more attempt to be elected, in Clackmannan and East Stirlingshire at the 1918 General Election where he lost by just over 1,000 votes. In later life, he was President of the Co-operative Congress in 1929 and served on the National Peace Council and attended the World Disarmament Conference.

WANSBECK – May 1918

The next example of Labour nationally losing control was the combined Peace by Negotiation/ ILP campaign in Keighley in April 1918 (see chapter 8). But tensions really came to the fore with the Wansbeck vacancy which followed shortly after. A similar scenario to that of Salford arose in this north-eastern constituency. Again, a much-respected Liberal MP, Charles Fenwick, who had worked assiduously for the interests of labour (mainly the miners), had passed away in April 1918. A former miner himself, Fenwick was consistently elected by large majorities (even in the dark days of 1900). Alongside being an MP, he spent a lot of time on trade union activities, but always resisted any suggestion that he should migrate from the Liberals to Labour.

His local association was a Liberal – Labour Association and this immediately claimed the right to the nomination. But the area now also had a newly established local Labour Representation Committee which argued that the nomination should rest with the miners. Into this unprecedented situation, the Unionists did not step, promptly announcing they would not nominate a candidate. There were hints that Nina Boyle, the suffragette activist and leading member of the Women's Freedom League, might come forward and seek to improve on her failure to be nominated at Keighley (see chapter 8) and some looked forward to the prospect with relish:

> 'The threatened invasion of a woman candidate has not yet materialised, but inquiries on Saturday elicited the fact that some women have been in the division spying out the land ... If a woman would come forward, said one aged miner, she would have a sporting chance of being elected. Hundreds would vote for her, if only for the fun it would cause.'[23]

Both the Liberal-Labour Association and the Labour Representation Committee failed to reach decisions about candidates at their first meetings and the initial sense was that the LRC would, after all, abide by the national truce. There were rumours of communications between the two bodies, to see if agreement could be reached on a mutually acceptable candidate. But the Liberals then moved ahead and put forward a single name for ratification by their association. This was County Alderman Robert Mason, of Whitley Bay, who was president of the association, and a well-known member of the shipping community in Newcastle. Meanwhile, the national Miners Federation of Great Britain sent a telegram to the Northumberland Miners Association saying that it considered Wansbeck to be a miners' seat and so

---

23 *Newcastle Journal*, 6 May 1918.

would support the local Labour Party in contesting the division. It asked to be told the name of the candidate. With relations between the two 'progressive' organisations becoming more strained, the Unionists chose this moment to add to the drama by suggesting that, since the Liberals and Labour could not agree on a single candidate, both should stand aside and make way for a Unionist coalition candidate. This 'overture' was swiftly rejected.

With the Liberals close to adopting their man, word was that the local LRC was considering three possibles. Of these, the favourite was William Straker, secretary of the Northumberland Miners Association; the other two were William Hogg, Treasurer of the Association, and Ebenezer Edwards, an anti-war activist from Ashington and member of the management committee of the Northumberland Miners Association. Edwards had opted to continue working as a miner rather than be called up; a confirmed Marxist, he had attended Ruskin College although was forced to leave after ten months as his finances ran out.

But the LRC was soon in an impossible position. The Miners Federation of Great Britain was adamant there should be a miners' candidate while the national Labour Party Executive wished to abide by the party truce and did not want a nomination. In line with that wish Straker, the favourite, announced that he would not run. Strictly speaking, the LRC branch fell under the authority of the national executive and so should have decided not to fight. Between this rock and the hard place of the miners' organisation (the dominant force locally), the LRC decided to call a special conference to decide what to do.

The Liberals meanwhile unanimously adopted Alderman Mason while simultaneously the writ was moved in parliament and nominations were fixed for the Tuesday following the proposed Saturday date of the LRC meeting. It was rumoured that the LRC would run a candidate, as a 'preliminary canter' before the general election, and that Hogg was now the favourite. At the crucial special conference, a representative of Labour's National Executive argued that the truce should be observed this time but that the seat should, outside of wartime, be a 'miners' seat'. The position that the truce should be respected was rejected by a four-to-one majority, in a meeting dominated by miners' delegates. That opinion was strengthened, as in Salford, by the Liberals having selected a businessman and not a local worker. When it came to candidate choice, the overwhelming strength of the miners' representation prevailed. Many of the miners' lodges in the constituency had strong pacifist or anti-war elements within them and the final vote, by a large majority, came out in favour of Edwards, a miner but also an anti-war activist.

Thus, the battlelines were drawn between a strong 'fight-the-war' businessman (Mason was managing director of Messrs L. S. Carr and Co., shipowners, Newcastle) who also had the backing of the Unionists, and a left-wing, pacifist miner (a strong supporter of Robert Smillie) who enjoyed considerable strength of support in the Ashington area of the constituency but possibly less elsewhere. The result would turn on whether the 'miner' vs. 'shipowner' issue would be stronger than the 'pacifist' vs. 'win the war' one.

The submission of nomination papers seemed to confirm that Edwards was at a significant disadvantage. Four papers were put in for him, all bearing signatures from the Ashington area. In contrast, Mason had fifteen papers from across the constituency; one of these was filled out by prominent Unionists and he also had support from labour representatives. Press speculation was that many miners would not vote for Edwards but would probably abstain so as not to vote against a miner in a contest with a 'shipowner'. It was also expected that the sizeable farming vote would go to Mason.

The *Newcastle Journal*[24] saw little hope for the Labour man. Firstly, even the party's activists felt they had much to learn about electioneering and did not believe they were ready to run a proper campaign. There was also real confusion about whether Edwards was standing as a 'pacifist'. The newspaper summarised the election: 'Edwards denies that he has pacifist views or that he believes in the isms of MacDonald and Snowden. Yet in Ashington he was referred to as the Socialist candidate.' It noted that the Ashington area was said to be solid for pacifism and that was why Edwards was chosen, but the paper's reporter failed to unearth a single pacifist. The Liberal agent said that so far, they had found only one.

At his first formal meeting, Edwards claimed not to be standing on a pacifist platform: 'I stand here, declared Mr Edwards, to support the Labour Party War Aims programme, believing that it is the only consistent, the only logical, and the only correct basis to secure us a lasting and permanent settlement.

---

24 *Newcastle Journal*, 23 May 1918.

I do not stand for a peace-at-any-price.'²⁵ In the midst of the campaign, the annual council of the Northumberland miners was scheduled to consider a motion calling for peace negotiations, but it was withdrawn before any debate could be held.

A significant organisation in the constituency was the local branch of the Federation of Discharged and Demobilised Sailors and Soldiers, the largest in the country. Edwards' people tried to influence them, but its vice-chairman presided over Mason's meeting in Ashington and there seemed to be little support for a perceived anti-war candidate among those who had done their duty at the front. Edwards' election address claimed that a contest had been forced on the miners while Mason's took the standard Coalition line that: 'In this grave crisis of our nation's fate ordinary political strife must be put to one side, and all our energy devoted to securing such clean and victorious peace as will assure the safety of future generations from the curse of German militarism.' He argued: 'This, in my opinion, can only be accomplished by the defeat of the enemy and the opening of a pathway leading to the formation of a league of nations to prevent the repetition of the present carnage.'²⁶

As a brief campaign reached its end, the feeling grew that Edwards would not gather the wholehearted support of the miners and therefore Mason would be safely elected. On polling day, Edwards concentrated in Ashington, his area of strength, while Mason was out and about firstly among the farming areas, from which he expected support, and then among the other mining areas in the constituency. Edwards' election workers felt that the old register was working strongly against them as it disenfranchised their young, enthusiastic backers. In addition to the Unionists, Mason also received help from 'patriotic Labour' in the form of the British Workers League.²⁷

The result, when it came, was a shock. The turnout was greater than an apparently rather apathetic response to the electioneering had led observers

---

25 Ibid.
26 Quoted in *Newcastle Journal*, 25 May 1918.
27 The British Workers League was formed from the split on war policy in the British Socialist Party in 1915. It was originally known as the Socialist National Defence Committee and went on to run candidates in the 1918 General Election as the National Democrat and Labour Party.

to expect, and Edwards came, from a Coalition point-of-view, uncomfortably close to a shock victory.

Jan. 1910[1]			
Fenwick	Lib-Lab	10,872	70%
Percy	Conservative	4,650	30%
	Majority	6,222	
	Electorate	19,028	
	Total Vote	15,522	82%

28 May 1918			
Mason	Liberal	5,814	53%
Edwards	Independent Labout	5,267	47%
Majority		547	
Electorate		21,602	
Total Vote		11,081	51%

---

1 Fenwick was unopposed in December 1910.

There was relief on the Coalition side that Mason had won while Edwards' supporters were delighted by a result that exceeded expectations. The general interpretation was that the result reflected a widespread wish among the miners to be represented by 'one of their own' and that it was not an endorsement of Edwards' position in favour of peace negotiations. Mason was furious that he had been characterised as a 'shipowner' and felt this had done him real harm while Edwards was also angry about how he had been described and felt that this had done the greatest damage to his chances. However, although at times he had been somewhat opaque regarding his 'peace by negotiation' position, on which he had been attacked relentlessly in the press, in his concession speech he said that 'the result showed the right of the miners to claim the seat and also that an avenue should be opened for a satisfactory settlement of the crisis.'[28] One other possible influence had been dissatisfaction at the government's more aggressive policy on 'combing out', which the Miners Federation of Great Britain opposed. The timing of the election may have made Edwards' position on negotiations less damaging than it might have been as the campaign came after the April crisis of the great German offensive had somewhat subsided. Taking a strategic overview, Labour drew the lesson that it needed to learn more about the arts of electioneering while the Liberals needed to take note of the real threat to their position from the rise of a robust labour movement.

The 1918 General Election was to be a straight re-run between Mason and Edwards; there was again no Unionist candidate, and Mason received the Coalition coupon. This time, he won easily with a majority of more than 3,000 votes. He stood down from parliament in 1922, but Edwards went on to enjoy a substantial career. He finally reached parliament in 1929 (elected as a Labour MP for Morpeth to replace his own political hero, Robert Smillie) although he lost the seat two years later. However, he was to be President and Secretary of the Miners Federation of Great Britain and the National Union of Mineworkers' first secretary in 1945, following which he served on the National Coal Board.

GRAVESEND – June 1918
Hard on the heels of Wansbeck came a very rapid by-election in Gravesend in Kent. The seat had been held since 1900 by Sir Gilbert Parker. Born in Canada and married to an American heiress, Parker was a popular romantic novelist as well as a Unionist MP. He played a significant role in the war, being responsible, via Wellington House, for the British government's propaganda efforts in the United States. Early in 1917, with the US about to enter the war, he resigned from Wellington House due to ill health. He remained an MP but, unexpectedly, suddenly announced in May 1918 that he would not be standing at the General Election. But there was more to this than met the eye. Within days of the

---

28 *Newcastle Journal*, 30 May 1918.

announcement, the local Unionists had selected Alexander Richardson, from London, as their prospective general election candidate. Less than two weeks later, Parker resigned his position in the Commons 'under urgent medical advice' although, whatever the health issue was, Parker lived until 1932. The by-election writ was moved immediately on 29 May with nominations set for 3 June and polling day, if required, for 7 June. As the *Kent Messenger* wryly observed of the timetable: 'It means probably, therefore, that the side that is best organised will have an advantage.' If the ploy was intended to usher in a new Unionist MP quickly and without fuss, it backfired spectacularly. A local leading Unionist, Alderman Henry Davis, a current county councillor, five times mayor of Gravesend and a town councillor of 21 years standing was furious and immediately announced he would stand. Given his local reputation, compared with the complete lack of knowledge of the new man from London, this could represent a significant risk to the Coalition candidate, even though the Liberals immediately agreed to stand by the truce. Davis stated that he was a patriotic 'win-the-war' candidate, thereby clearly splitting the vote, and that he would fight as an Independent Coalition candidate. In the press, he attacked what he saw as the chicanery of the rapid by-election and declared:

> *'This is, I am convinced, nothing more than a deliberately arranged trick to take the constituency by surprise and to foist upon the borough an outsider, with no record of public life behind him, without giving others a chance of the fair stand-up fight which every Englishman and sportsman willingly grants to his adversary.'*[29]

There is also something of a mystery as to why Richardson, the beneficiary of such Unionist manoeuvring, had been selected for Gravesend for he did not appear to be an outstanding candidate. Born in Scotland, in his early career he had been a journalist. However, he became a specialist in naval issues and particularly naval architecture and perhaps that explained his attraction to Gravesend which was still a major shipbuilding centre.

---

29 *Kent Messenger*, 1 June 1918.

Davis, originally a Conservative, had already stated in January his intention to stand in the next general election as a non-party Independent. He argued that party allegiance consistently held back sensible decision-making and pointed out that Lloyd George himself had found it necessary to bring in many non-party businessmen to progress the war effectively. He now said that having promised local people he would stand he was not going to go back on that pledge even if a snap election was being forced upon them.

He stood on a comprehensive programme. On the war he demanded 'a fight until we have the German on his knees and are able to dictate terms of peace which will keep him from threatening the safety of our Empire for a hundred years to come'. He was also harsh on resident aliens, demanding laws that would 'make it impossible for the foreigner to obtain a strangle-hold upon our commerce and finance'. Linked to that, he wanted trade protection for British industry against unfair foreign competition and also backed agriculture saying that the war had taught the need for Britain to grow more of its own food requirements. Finally, on 'social conditions' he advocated more sympathy between employer and employed and cooperative working with good wages and reasonable hours of work. He further called for better housing on sound and sensible business lines and improved education, 'aimed at the sending out into life of every boy and girl fully equipped for an employment which will make them self-supporting and self-respecting citizens'.[30] Finally he noted that the external candidate had just said that he supported a local scheme for Deep Water Wharves. Unimpressed, Davis' riposte was: 'I gave the Town Clerk a cheque for £100 to support it months and months ago'.

There were rumours of two more potential candidates. One, who in the end did not come forward, was Stanley Cousins, a director of Imperial Paper Mills in Gravesend, who had talked of being a patriotic Lloyd George candidate. He based his decision not to stand out of a wish not to oppose Davis. He sent a telegram to him, stating: 'Politics should be dead today and the borough should be represented by a member who has strong interest in local affairs. You for years have faithfully and loyally done your best for the town. Immediately I definitely heard of your candidature I retired in your favour. Work hard and win.'

---

30 Ibid.

The candidate whose nomination did go forward was another well-known local political figure, Harry Hinkley. Also originally a Conservative, Hinkley had been an active, and garrulous, member of the town council since a by-election in 1912. At that election, he had stated:

> *'I am strongly in favour of the abolition of slum and insanitary dwellings, which are a standing disgrace to our borough. I am also in favour of the Council, wherever possible, doing its own work in the borough, and of the payment of Trade Union rates of wages, and the observance of Trade Union conditions in all work .... I am also in favour of Evening Sittings of the Council.'*

By the time of the by-election, his political migration had taken him as far as to be chairman of the local British Workers League. The League was standing by the truce, but Hinkley still came forward as an Independent Labour candidate, once the necessary £100 to be paid to the returning officer had been provided by a friend.

Richardson, faced with two well-established local candidates who were both fully supportive of the war effort, had little to fall back on other than conventional statements of 'red, white and blue' sentiment and appeals for loyalty to Lloyd George and the government. He wrote in the local press that he should be supported since he had been chosen by the Unionists and was not to be opposed by the Liberals and that his sole objective was 'the attainment of complete naval and military success by the Allies'. On peace terms he argued 'details cannot be discussed until the military yoke of Germany has been broken.'[31]

He outlined some aspirations for the future: improving education, delivering equal opportunity for the poor as well as the rich; the encouragement of agriculture; re-organisation of industry to deliver higher efficiency; mutual understanding and sympathy between employers and workers; a stop to undesirable aliens to prevent 'the sweating of labour' and the provision of 'liberal pensions' to veterans.'[32]

---

31 *Kent Messenger*, 1 June 1918.
32 Ibid.

Richardson organised, in the brief time available to him, a series of public meetings. He also received the customary government telegram, this from Bonar Law, stating: 'I sincerely hope that in the present critical position all patriotic electors will strengthen the hands of the Coalition Government combining to return you for Gravesend by an overwhelming majority'. There was also one in similar vein from Lloyd George.

The timings meant that there was virtually no campaigning, and the result was anticipated with some concern in government quarters. In the end, loyalty meant that Richardson came home but with a majority of only just over 200 ahead of the local stalwart, Davis. Hinkley trailed behind but it is likely that, had he not stood, enough of his voters might have turned out for Davis to see him successful.

Dec. 1910			
Parker	Conservative	3,108	55%
Jenkins	Liberal	2,506	45%
Majority		602	
Electorate & Turnout		6,731	83%

June 1918			
Richardson	Unionist	1,312	44%
Davis	Independent Unionist	1,106	37%
Hinkley	Independent Labour	562	19%
Majority		206	
Electorate & Turnout		8,142	37%

Richardson was to be re-elected in the general election and again in 1922 but lost the seat to Labour in 1923. Davis was as good as his word and stood again in the 1918 general election and in 1922 (as an unofficial Anti-Waste candidate) but was unsuccessful on both occasions.

The Gravesend result was not seen as having policy significance, since it was fought by three candidates all determined to emphasise their support for Lloyd George and a strong commitment to winning the war. It did seem, however, to be a clear sign that Labour was finding it increasingly difficult to enforce the support for the truce onto their disparate supporters across a range of constituencies. Salford and Gravesend had seen independents claiming some allegiance to Labour standing on a 'patriotic left' position while Keighley and Wansbeck had been contested by Labour-related candidates who aligned with the peace-by-negotiation/ pacifist wing of the movement. Moreover, as a general election came nearer, a majority in the party nationally was becoming frustrated at being unable to stand in their own right. But the problem remained of how Labour could oppose Coalition candidates in by-elections when they had eight ministers in the administration.

On polling day in Gravesend, the Labour National Executive, influenced by the events in Keighley and Wansbeck, resolved to present a motion to the forthcoming party conference to pull out of the truce. The expectation was that Labour would aim to keep its representatives in government and continue to support the war wholeheartedly while gaining the option of projecting its own identity at by-elections. Both factions in the party could see advantages to this; the majority pro-war element expected to be in a stronger position to stop unofficial 'pacifist' candidates from being nominated, while the more pacifist wing also hoped greater opportunities would arise for them.

The Executive could see only benefits in putting the question to the conference. If withdrawal from the truce were accepted, it would be spared the problems caused by sporadic, local action in contravention of the agreement. Alternatively, if the conference endorsed the continuation of the truce, then that would significantly strengthen the hand of the Executive against local attempts to circumvent it.

Nevertheless, in the run-up to the conference, the Labour ministers issued a statement calling on the movement to maintain its support for the truce and, through that, for united national action to win the war. They complained:

> *'Our position, however, is being rendered very difficult by incessant sniping on the part of anti-national factionalists who ... attack us through the Labour Press, and other means open to them ... It is, manifestly of supreme importance*

> *that national unity should be maintained. Even the appearance of weakness or division would have the most disastrous effect on our Allies... But there is another consideration present in our mind. We are Labour representatives. We are desirous of maintaining the solidarity of Labour. We look forward to the time when there must be rebuilding of the social and industrial fabric. In order that Labour may then exert its due influence it is necessary that Labour should be a united body.*[33]

With groups like the miners in support, it was recognised that the resolution to withdraw from the electoral truce would be passed. To seek to minimise any damage, the Labour leader, Henderson, stated that the decision related only to by-elections and, therefore, there would be no reason for Labour ministers to withdraw from the Coalition government. The final card vote result was 1.7 million in favour and 950,000 against. The impact of the decision turned out to be negligible. The Labour men remained in Lloyd George's government while the Labour Party, now having the power to nominate by-election candidates, never used it in wartime but nor were they troubled again by unofficial Labour candidates coming forward. A political fudge had achieved its objectives.

---

33 *Daily News*, 24 June 1918.

12.
BILLING'S FINAL MISSIONS

East Islington, 23 October 1917
Clapham, 21 June 1918
East Finsbury, 16 July 1918

Noel Pemberton Billing's parliamentary and political career from spring 1916 to autumn 1917 continued in controversy. His themes remained inadequate management of the country's air forces at the front and of air defence at home. However, he did not restrict himself to that narrow brief, becoming involved in many other issues. In early October 1916, he launched what he called an 'independent viewspaper', entitled *The Imperialist*, and next appeared in the public eye when a libel action he launched against *The Globe* newspaper came to court. In April 1916, *The Globe* had used advertising placards saying: 'Spying for Pemberton-Billing: Airman arrested'. It referred to an arrest under the Defence of the Realm regulations of someone for seeking information from Royal Naval Air Service officers. Allegedly, the detainee said he was trying to 'do a spot of spying for Mr. Pemberton-Billing'. Billing considered the placards libellous and initiated proceedings. The case was heard before Mr Justice Darling who was highly unimpressed with the complaint and the jury found against Billing whose response was to announce that he would resign and fight a by-election to prove he retained the support of the people of Hertford. However, he soon thought better of this and instead held meetings across the constituency seeking 'votes of confidence'. Unsurprisingly, Billing assessed that these meetings had supported him and so didn't resign.

In the House, he concentrated on calling for massive air reprisals. He was also charged by another MP, Major Martin Arthur-Shee, of being 'caddish and most offensive' for claiming that officials had been publishing false casualty figures following air raids. The two of them continued their disagreement outside in Palace Yard and a scuffle resulted that had to be stopped by police. Billing then challenging Arthur-Shee to a 20-round contest under the Marquis of Queensberry rules, the loser of which would donate £200 to the British Red Cross. The challenge was ignored.

In the various editions of *The Imperialist*, Billing called for transparency in Liberal Party funding; said that conscientious objection should be outlawed; boasted that he had asked more than 200 questions in parliament; attacked US President Wilson for 'playing Germany's game'; called for the 'purification' of politics (ending corruption); and argued that, by summer 1917, the most important issue was food difficulties. Then, in July 1917, he set up a new organisation, the Vigilante Society, to 'promote purity in public life'. His target was corruption in politics, widely defined, and he announced a plan to adopt nine Vigilante Parliamentary candidates who, if elected, would not accept 'any honour, title or dignity, or any office or place of profit in the disposal of the Government'. In the magazine he called on readers to sign up for the Vigilantes, paying one shilling immediately and then one shilling for each by-election that it was decided to fight. The first of Billing's proposed nine candidates turned out to be Alfred Baker, the Town Clerk and former Mayor of Hertford in Billing's own constituency.

EAST ISLINGTON – October 1917

This election came when, once again, Billing's profile was high in London due to his assiduous campaigning on home defence against Zeppelin and bomber raids. Early in June 1917, Billing had condemned the weakness of fighter cover for London and the continued refusal of the authorities to issue warnings of attacks. He sought an adjournment debate in the Commons on London's air defence but was refused and caused such a commotion in response that he was ordered to withdraw from the chamber. He was soon to be vindicated on both counts. The shortage of fighter cover had become even worse in recent weeks since Field Marshal Douglas Haig, the British army commander-in-chief, had persuaded the government to move aircraft away from London to bolster his resources on the Western Front.

There now followed a dramatic period of raids which shook Londoners' morale. On 13 June 1917, more than ten German Gotha bombers arrived over the capital during daytime and conducted a devastating attack out of range of defensive guns. This was the most lethal raid of the war, the brunt of which was borne by Poplar in the East End of London. There were 145 fatalities and 382 injured including terrible loss of life at the Upper North Street school where eighteen infants died and 34 were wounded. Billing immediately renewed his campaign for widespread reprisals against German cities to deter further attacks. Speaking at the London Opera House on 17 June he proposed using 500 aircraft for reprisals, suggesting that 'In fifteen minutes, the German nation, for the first time since August 1914, would know what it was to let loose the dogs of war on Europe.'[1] He carried this appeal to a series of public meetings, in locations such as Dover and Folkestone, and unsuccessfully asked Bonar Law for a debate in parliament on the issues of air raid warnings and compensation payments to victims.

The next major raid, again in daylight, on 7 July comprised more than twenty Gothas which were unchallenged until the last minute. This attack occasioned less loss of life but much more damage than that on 13 June. Further, it was seen as a great blow to British pride and generated fury at the obvious inadequacy of defensive arrangements, culminating in attacks on 'alien' businesses in the capital, several of which were looted. The raid prompted a secret session of parliament to discuss air defences which, Billing argued, should be held in public.

The July raid resulted in sharp changes in policy regarding air-raid warnings. Despite widespread public agitation, the government had been refusing warnings but now decided to introduce them, although only in daytime. This policy change, however, had no relevance to the next series of attacks. These were the 'Harvest Moon' night-time raids by Gothas (and the new Giants) between 24 September and 1 October. The outcome of these was 47 deaths with 226 injured. Also, London suffered under the night-after-night strain of raids – or the fear of raids. Many residents adopted a policy of heading

---

1 *Taunton Courier*, 20 June 1917.

to the underground stations every evening and increasing numbers decided to evacuate from the capital. Although there was then a lull after 1 October, the continuing fears of air raids provided a strong background for Billing to run his candidate in the Islington by-election which was about to take place.

The death of the Liberal MP for East Islington, Sir George Radford, on 5 October 1917 opened the possibility of a contested by-election. Perhaps because it was conveniently located in London, there was rapidly talk of potential unofficial candidates. The seat had been a surprise Liberal gain in the 1906 landslide and was narrowly held in both 1910 elections. Despite this, the Unionists stood firmly by the truce. However, the newly formed National Party was quick to announce that this would be their electoral debut and, at their National Council meeting on 12 October, they decided to run Edmund Barnard, the former Liberal MP for Kidderminster and current Chairman of the Metropolitan Water Board. Barnard had gained the Kidderminster seat in 1906 (winning against Stanley Baldwin) but then switched, in January 1910, to fight (unsuccessfully) the Hertford seat that was to be won by Pemberton-Billing in 1916. He then returned to Kidderminster in the December 1910 election, again without success.

The National Party had been founded two months earlier, at the initiative of the Unionist MP, Henry Page Croft. Throughout his career, Page Croft had been an extreme supporter of Conservative Joseph Chamberlain's campaign for protectionist 'tariff reform'. His first unsuccessful parliamentary outing, in 1906, had been as a Conservative standing against a sitting Liberal Unionist MP who had chosen to fight as a Free Trader. Croft became a member of the 'Confederates', a somewhat secretive group pledged to rid the Unionist party of its free traders, and he was elected MP for Christchurch in Dorset in 1910.

Before the war, Croft had been frustrated by the failure of the Unionist party to give consistent and wholehearted support to the cause of tariff reform. When war began, as a member of the Territorial Army, he volunteered and was to spend twenty-two months at the front. Although Lloyd George's more forceful prosecution of the conflict was welcomed, Page Croft and other right-wingers in the Conservative ranks could never bring themselves to forgive his radical roots and frustration abounded at being tied to him in the Coalition. Key drivers of Page Croft's frustrations, with both Liberals and Conservatives, were perceived abuse of the honours system, wartime profiteering, failure to adopt strong measures towards enemy aliens in the country and the willingness of the trades unions to strike; all of these were to find a place in the National Party's programme. However, he reserved his harshest words for the honours system: 'What exasperated us more than anything was the bestowal of honours right and left upon men whose services to the State were unknown and whose sole claim to fame was that they had amassed recent fortunes.'[2]

Croft bided his time to launch the new party and, initially, anticipated that as many as twenty MPs might join. In fact, only seven did so alongside a greater number of peers. All the MPs and the great majority of the Lords were Unionists, largely from the extreme right of the party; consequently, Barnard was very much an untypical supporter. In his autobiography, Page Croft revealed that such was his disappointment that only seven MPs had adhered to his cause that he would have abandoned the party launch, had he been able to do so – it was hardly an auspicious beginning.[3]

The National Party's initial 'statement of aims' was published in *The Times* on 30 August. Policies included: complete victory in the war and after the war; the eradication of German influence; honest administration .... No sales of honours; class unity and confidence between employer and employed; and, the unity of the Empire.[4] The first major event involving the new force was an attempt at the Tariff Reform League's annual meeting to merge the League into the National Party. A motion welcoming National Party support for tariff reform was accepted but moves to merge were 'referred back'.

Early in October 1917, it was announced that the inaugural meeting of the Party would be 25 October in London for which admission was to be free and 'special seats will be reserved in the Grand Circle for wounded men to avoid the necessity of climbing the stairs.'[5] The by-election arrived before the full organisation could be validated at this meeting but on 15 October *The Times* was able to speculate there might be four candidates; Barnard for the National Party; Edward Smallwood, a local coal merchant and the Progressive member for Islington on the London County Council, as the Coalition Liberal; Councillor Robert Forsyth from Folkestone as a 'Patriotic' candidate and Allen Clark, standing as a candidate for discharged soldiers and sailors.

---

2 Lord Croft, *My life of strife* (1948).
3 Ibid.
4 *The Times*, 30 August 1917.
5 *The Times*, 4 October 1917.

In an early indication of likely issues, Clark mentioned air defence, internment of enemy aliens, profiteering and opposition to the Review of Exceptions Act (see chapter 9). First comments from the National Party stressed that they were out to stop 'peerage-mongering' and 'seat selling' and called on people to back their 'crusade against the sale of honours'.[6]

Pemberton-Billing now arrived in the constituency and confirmed that he would be putting forward a Vigilante candidate. Given this news, Clark immediately stood down to back the Vigilante – whomever that might be. Billing had first raised the suggestion of intervening in East Islington when speaking in Liverpool on 12 October at a large meeting on the themes of 'Victory Through the Air, Purity in Politics, and the Politician of the Day'. In this speech, he had once more stressed the need for air reprisals against Germany. The involvement of Billing immediately revitalised the interest of the popular press in by-elections and wide coverage ensued in the *Mail* and *Mirror*.

Billing announced that the Vigilante campaign platform would be 'a great air offensive and the purification of politics'. His candidate would be the first of the nine he would seek to get elected, each with 'an intimate knowledge of a particular department of state'. Billing's own paper reported: 'In accordance with the constitution of the Vigilantes, the Council of Parliamentary Lodge Number One (British) have formally applied to all members of the 'Vigilantes' to send to the Treasurer the first election levy of 1s towards the expenses of contesting the seat.'

There was further rationalisation of candidates when the putative 'patriotic' flag-bearer, Councillor Forsyth, decided to withdraw, in favour of the National Party. Page-Croft thanked Forsyth:

> *'I am writing on behalf of the Provisional Council of the National Party to express their grateful thanks to you for the patriotic course you have taken in connection with the East Islington by-election... you generously decided to withdraw from the contest in order that the party for victory might not go to the poll with a split vote.'*[7]

---

6 *The Times*, 15 October 1917.
7 *The Globe*, 16 October 1917.

Readying for the fight, the National Party put out a plea: 'The contest will be very short and sharp, and canvassers are earnestly needed. Those sympathisers who are unable to canvass are warmly solicited to report to the Chief Committee Room with a view to addressing envelopes, distributing literature, etc.'

There had briefly been a suggestion that the Unionists, in the face of multiple candidates already announced, would no longer feel obliged to stand aside. The temptation must have been great since their established candidate, Philip Pilditch, had previously lost to the Liberals by only 125 votes in December 1910. However, they dutifully stood by the agreement after having been fully assured that Smallwood would support all government policies for the strongest possible prosecution of the war.

Early speculation was that the main battle would be between the Coalition candidate, Smallwood, and Barnard on behalf of the new National Party. Both swiftly issued election addresses. Barnard's said that he had hoped for much from the Coalition and the party truce but felt let down. Despite the replacement of Asquith by Lloyd George, he claimed that the 'coils of politics' were still preventing a vigorous prosecution of the war. Instead, he:

> 'looks with hope at the young National Party which has honestly set itself to provide a new and better system, founded upon higher principles and he appealed to electors to insist that the nation's interests should no longer be the battledore and shuttlecock of politics.'

Smallwood's address stated that he had been in business in the constituency 'for 30 years, and resident for 27, been for years on the Borough Council, and eight years on the London County Council.' He promised loyal support to the Government on all war measures and 'as one who has served in the Royal Naval Air Service, strongly supported exemplary punishment for the enemy who murders women and children in residential districts.'

Next, Pemberton-Billing revealed Alfred Baker, the current Town Clerk of Hertford in Billing's own constituency, as his man. Baker was described by the *Pall Mall Gazette* as 'one of the hardest fighters in the Conservative cause in the district'. His election address fully echoed Billing's 'Vigilante' programme. The main pledge was that he had executed a bond, 'in the penal sum of £5,000' which involved him solemnly declaring that:

> *'if elected to represent the aforesaid constituency I will not at any time within a period seven years from this date accept any honour, title, or dignity, any office or place of profit in the disposal of the Government, nor do any act which would in any way place me under any obligation to the Government or to any political party, nor use my position as a member of Parliament for the furtherance of my personal interests, but will at all times use my best endeavours to further the object of the Vigilantes, which is purity of public life.'*

He continued: 'I ask you to send me to the House of Commons to support Mr. Pemberton Billing in his repeated and persistent demand for a great air offensive over Germany, and in his single-handed fight against inefficiency, political corruption, profiteering, and all other attendant evils.' Baker summarised his programme as 'Bomb Germany and purity in politics', while Pemberton-Billing promoted the slogan: 'Purify politicians, pulverise profiteers, petrify Huns.'

On nomination day, Baker arrived with a single paper. But that was declared invalid due to a missing signature and for having been signed by his nominators while missing some information. Thus, he had to undertake a desperate rush to get another paper completed accurately before the noon deadline. He managed it with only minutes to spare. Billing made light of the situation, saying: 'If it had not been for my car, I should not have won East Herts, nearly won Wimbledon and shall win East Islington.'[8] Smallwood submitted two nomination papers, one signed by Liberals and the other by Unionists while the National Party candidate, Barnard, submitted a single paper.

The next intervention came from the Suffragettes. Christabel Pankhurst of the Women's Social and Political Union started an hourly series of open-air meetings. She was not 'for' any one candidate but was determined to raise the spectre of the possible return of Asquith. The former Prime Minister had stood firmly in the way of women's suffrage throughout his political career

---

8 *Gloucestershire Echo*, 19 October 1917.

and so was a totemic opponent for Christabel although, ironically, he was now changing his opinion. She claimed there was a plot to restore him as Prime Minister and so challenged Smallwood to say whether he would pledge himself, if elected, to vote and work against such a plan. She accused Asquith of having wanted a compromise peace and suggested that his incompetence in office had delivered the munitions scandal, the Gallipoli gamble, the crushing of Serbia, and the Mesopotamia fiasco. She argued that there was nothing in Smallwood's election address which guaranteed he would oppose another Asquith Premiership.

But the war now intervened in the form of another air raid on London. The attack was by a single Zeppelin, one of 11 German naval Zeppelins that raided England on the night of 19/20 October in what was to prove the last large-scale Zeppelin mission of the war. The sortie was intended for the Midlands and North, but Zeppelin L.45 was blown off course and eventually saw the lights of London ahead of it. This became known as the 'silent raid' since the airship operated at very high altitude, rendering it unseen and meaning that no defending guns were turned on it. Bombs were dropped almost randomly on Hendon, Cricklewood, Piccadilly Circus (where seven were killed), Southwark (where ten died) and Lewisham (where 15 more were killed, including 12 children). The King and Queen toured affected areas in the aftermath of the raid, including to the scene of the reported deaths of eight children in a single property. The two opposition candidates made much of the incident. Barnard, for the National Party, firmed up his position by issuing a poster proclaiming: 'Be British - and bring in Barnard. Bomb the brutes who bombed the Babies.' Meanwhile, Baker, for the Vigilante Party, employed twenty sandwich-board men to demonstrate in the Islington streets with placards stating: 'Bomb Germany through the Ballot-boxes. Vote for Baker, and all's clear.' For the Coalition, Smallwood was more measured but maintained that the government was doing everything possible to win the war and implement reprisals. The general belief was that the raid would assist the Vigilante candidate the most, especially since the 'powers that be' had been so confident that further raids would be prevented. Smallwood's response was considered unsatisfactory. One of his (Unionist) nominators wrote to the constituency secretary, resigning as ward chairman and saying that he no longer intended to vote for the Liberal. He followed this by writing to Barnard:

> 'Having severed my connection with the Unionist party owing to the unsatisfactory conduct of the Government on the question of reprisals, I have great pleasure in giving you hearty support in the election to-morrow, Tuesday, and I advise my Unionist friends to do the same. Good Canvass.'[9]

The issue set the election agenda through speeches in the constituency and in the House of Commons. Lord Beresford, one of the peers who had joined the National Party, came to Islington to support Barnard; although now somewhat superannuated, he was a significant figure, having served in the Commons for almost twenty years during which time he represented five different constituencies while simultaneously pursuing a naval career that saw him appointed as commander-in-chief successively of the Mediterranean and Channel fleets. He argued that he would bombard with a thousand aeroplanes, when they were available, four towns in Germany for every town attacked in this country. The voters could depend upon it that when Sir Douglas Haig was properly supplied with machines, 'he would punish the enemy by knocking about their towns, bridges, railway stations, and lines of communication.'[10]

Such was the mounting controversy that Smallwood was forced into a stronger position on reprisals, but his heart wasn't in it and he noted: 'There is too much bomb about this election; any mountebank can say, 'bomb, bomb, bomb,' but it is not the cry of a politician'.[11] At the same time, he was cultivating the nonconformist vote, with which he was in good standing because of work he had done on the County Council. However, for doing so he was criticised by his opponents. Specifically, Barnard claimed:

> 'Mr. Smallwood's people made a great feature of doing nothing on Sunday, but this would seem to have been pure cant and theory. Early on Sunday morning, when I was walking round the constituency, I saw a man posting the Smallwood bills over those of another candidate. Soon afterwards I heard that a Dissenting minister had been preaching a strong sermon against patriotic candidates and in favour of Mr. Smallwood.'

---

9 *The Globe*, 22 October 1917.
10 *Birmingham Mail*, 23 October 1917.
11 *The Globe*, 23 October 1917.

Meanwhile, PB's campaign on behalf of Baker was assisted by the fallout from the Zeppelin raid. Summarising the electoral consequences, the *Liverpool Daily Post* commented:

> 'Friday's raid has been a perfect godsend to Mr Billing's protégé in the East Islington by-election and his sponsor is now fondly hoping to see him at the head of the poll. Electoral forecasts are difficult at a time when half the electorate is away, and no one knows exactly what influence recent events have had on the voters who remain. The Coalition candidate will certainly be harder pressed than was at one time expected. Mr Barnard, the National Party candidate, is a shrewd electioneer, and Mr Billing's candidate can play on natural resentment and popular fears and ignorance. It is the liveliest by-election we have had since the war began. 'Reprisals' and 'Bombs on Berlin' are hurtling through the air and Miss Christabel Pankhurst's wild harangues would arouse the most apathetic elector. All the candidates seem to think they are going to win, but despite all the disturbance the chances still seem to be in favour of the Coalition candidate.'[12]

The Daily Mail was in no doubt that Billing's man would be the main challenger, claiming 'Surface indications yesterday pointed to the return of Mr Pemberton Billing by the unanimous vote of the constituency.' It recognised that he was not actually a candidate and also that the Coalition parties were working strenuously behind the scenes. However, it claimed that in reality 'It is his election. He makes all the speeches that the crowd will listen to. Nobody else can collect an audience, and an open-air meeting if he does not dash up in his motorcar is not a meeting.'[13] *The Daily Mail* 'boomed' that it expected a Vigilante victory because 'Reprisals is the one topic that counts... The crowd wants reprisals and they want to listen to the man who talks reprisals most fiercely.'[14]

Meanwhile, Billing's own magazine exhorted its readers to vote for Baker to 'Hinder the Huns, Paralyse Profiteers, Purify Politics, Win the war'. From the sidelines, the Women's Social and Political Union continued its daily campaign of insisting 'that a vote for Mr Smallwood means a vote for

---

12 *Liverpool Daily Post*, 23 October 1917.
13 *Daily Mail*, 23 October 1917.
14 Ibid.

the return to power of Mr Asquith, the ex-Premier having not yet received forgiveness from the [Women's Social and Political Union] for his opposition to votes for women.'[15]

In the event, despite all the fireworks and strong rhetoric of the short campaign, the Lloyd George government safely negotiated the test.

Dec. 1910			
Radford	Liberal	4,503	51%
Pilditch	Conservative	4,378	49%
Majority		125	
Electorate & Turnout		11,118	80%

23 Oct. 1917			
Smallwood	Liberal	2,719	57%
Baker	Independent	1,532	32%
Barnard	National	513	11%
Majority		1,177	
Electorate & Turnout		12,874	37%

Immediate reactions were that the Coalition had done well, against the concerted attack of two 'ginger' candidates, since Smallwood had secured a majority of the vote. The first outing of the National Party was seen either as disappointing (given that it had a highly credible candidate) or unlucky since it faced competition from Billing and had little time to get its message across to the electorate. Baker's failure to win was viewed as a major disappointment for Billing, especially as he had been loudly confident of victory in the run-up to polling day. Billing's response was to allege that there had been electoral irregularities and that more votes had been counted than ballot

---

15 *Aberdeen Press*, 23 October 1917.

papers issued. The next edition of *The Imperialist* offered a £500 reward for evidence of malpractice with Billing writing: 'We, at least, leave the ring with clean hands.' One of his organisers, Harry Biner[16], who was Secretary of the Fairplay League, had been arrested at the count after protesting that 'It's a fraud, a swindle' and was bound over by the magistrate the following day. Billing, himself, raised the issue of possible electoral malpractice with the Home Secretary who replied that he was unaware of any irregularities.

Billing's court 'triumph'

As 1918 began, Billing continued agitating on multiple subjects and changed the name of *The Imperialist* to *The Vigilante*. In January, he took an unwise step when he appointed Harold Spencer as his assistant editor. Spencer was an American who had volunteered for the British army and claimed he had worked with the Secret Service in the Balkans until being invalided out. In fact, although Billing was unaware of this, Spencer had been discharged from the army suffering from 'delusional insanity'. Thus, the ground was laid for the most dramatic event of Billing's public life. The trigger was an article, written by Spencer but published in Billing's name, which appeared in one of the last issues of *The Imperialist*, before its name change. Called 'The First 47,000' the piece claimed that the Germans had a book listing 47,000 leading British citizens who were vulnerable to blackmail, largely due to homosexuality, and that this threat was the reason for incompetent prosecution of the war. It further claimed those involved included: 'Privy Councillors, youths of the chorus, wives of Cabinet Ministers, dancing girls, even Cabinet Ministers themselves' and that those named 'were prevented from putting their full strength into the war by corruption and blackmail and fear of exposure.' It added that German agents had infiltrated the navy, such that 'the stamina of British sailors was undermined', and the world of high politics where 'wives of men in supreme position were entangled and in Lesbian ecstasy the most sacred secrets of state were betrayed', while 'the sexual peculiarities of members of the peerage' were also exploited for espionage purposes.

---

16 This was the same Harry Biner who had briefly been mooted as an anti-Liquor Board candidate for Mile End. (see chapter 4).

Billing expected this explosive piece to generate a libel case and even circulated copies to Cabinet ministers in the hope that they might indirectly implicate themselves by taking the journal to court – but none did so. The story developed when a reader drew attention to a planned private performance of Oscar Wilde's Salome in which the leading role would be taken by Maud Allen. It was rumoured that she was a lesbian and it was known that she had been invited to Downing Street during Asquith's time there. Spencer immediately saw a conspiracy since there were also rumours put about by Margot Asquith's enemies that she too was a lesbian. Consequently, on 16 February, Spencer published in *The Vigilante* (previously, *The Imperialist*) an item headed 'The Cult of the Clitoris'. This hinted that if the police seized the names of those planning to attend the salacious performance, they would no doubt 'secure the names of several thousand of the 47,000'. Billing realised the dangers of this follow-up article and immediately stopped Spencer from expanding the story. But the damage was done. Maud Allen, and the owner of the Independent Theatre Society, Jack Grein, started criminal proceedings against Billing for 'obscene libel' and 'defamatory libel'. After two initial appearances before Magistrates, at which Billing conducted his own defence, he was committed for trial at the Old Bailey.

As the case commenced on 29 May 1918, the war, and the standing of the government, had taken serious turns for the worse. The failure of the Passchendaele offensive and the release of German troops from the Eastern Front following Russia's surrender had set the stage for a German military renaissance. During 1918 to date, aircraft and Zeppelin raids had continued, food rationing had been introduced and the Manpower Act had raised the maximum conscription age and introduced more 'combing out' of reserved occupations. Above all, Germany now launched what were to prove her final offensives which genuinely seemed to threaten British defeat. Ludendorff's initial attack, towards the end of March, was eventually halted but not before the British lost 160,000 casualties in a week. On 11 April, Haig issued his dramatic 'backs to the wall' order of the day (see chapter 8 for the full text), which was subsequently published in the newspapers. Then, on 27 May (immediately before Billing's trial), a further German assault resulted in a breakthrough on the Aisne. All in all, this was a fevered atmosphere and not one likely to instil strong support among observers (or jurors) for the forces of the British establishment. War fatigue was extreme and, despite the participation of the Americans, expectation was that the conflict would continue into 1919 or 1920. Consequently, it has been argued that:

> 'By 1918, Britain in late war crisis was ripe for a new demagogue, and Noel Pemberton Billing was more than a suitable candidate for the job. Building on his flamboyant reputation and the precedent set by Bottomley, he seized the opportunity to pursue political fame.'[17]

As the case opened, Billing could have been forgiven for suspecting an establishment conspiracy against him. The prosecuting counsel was a Conservative MP while the rota of judges had been modified so that Judge Darling would be presiding – the very judge with whom Billing had clashed so strongly in his case against *The Globe* newspaper. Billing made a formal objection to Darling's appointment, but to no avail. Early in his defence, Billing sought to 'prove' the existence of the 'Black Book', allegedly held by the Germans. He did so in a most remarkable way. The first witness he called was Eileen Villiers-Stuart. Her's, in relation to Billing, was a remarkable story. Until 1917, she had been the mistress of Lord Rosebery's son. She had written to Billing claiming to have information she could share regarding homosexuality among men 'high up in military and naval circles' and asking to meet. She claimed later that the meeting was the idea of 'certain Political Associations in London', with a plan that she should take Billing to visit a male brothel where he would be photographed. However, she switched sides, becoming Billing's mistress. Consequently, she was prepared to perjure herself in dramatic fashion. She claimed to have been shown the Black Book with the list of the 47,000 in 1915 by Rosebery's son. Billing asked her, in turn, whether Judge Darling's name and those of Mrs Asquith and Mr Asquith and Lord Haldane were in the book and to each she confirmed that they were. Spencer was the next witness, and he also claimed to have seen the book, in the possession of a German Prince in 1914.

The judge had decided to split the hearing, commencing with only the point as to whether Maud Allen had been defamed. Despite the weaknesses

---

17 Philip Hoare, *Wilde's Last Stand* (1997).

of his case being dissected by prosecution counsel, remarkably, and even somewhat to Billing's surprise, the jury found him not guilty, following which the prosecution decided not to bring any evidence on the other points. On the steps of the Old Bailey, he was met by a large crowd of well-wishers and police had to clear the way for him. Despite the nonsense of his claims, Billing appeared to have come away from the case with his standing yet further enhanced in the fevered atmosphere of war-weary London.

CLAPHAM – June 1918

On 3 June, the day before Billing's acquittal, the Clapham constituency in south London fell vacant, following the elevation to the peerage of George Denison Faber. Immediately after his acquittal, Billing threw himself into working for the election of a Vigilante candidate in this by-election. The campaign was to focus almost exclusively on the vexed issue of the treatment of 'enemy aliens'. A running sore throughout the war, this question was frequently fanned by extremists, coming to a crescendo at different times in response to specific events, war-weariness and the general state of the conflict. In the run-up to August 1914, there had been outbreaks of 'spy mania', reflecting ever deepening British concern about the rise of Germany. Then, during the conflict, in the words of one researcher:

> *'Few domestic issues in Great Britain during the First World War proved more politically sensitive or more difficult to resolve than the question of how to deal with the generally perceived threat posed by enemy alien residents.'*[18]

Action was taken immediately war broke out with the passage, on 5 August 1914, of the Alien Restrictions Act. This, with other legislation, gave the government extensive powers in particular over aliens from enemy countries. It became a question of how to allocate people between internment, repatriation and 'freedom'. Equally, for those who were to be allowed to remain 'free' there were decisions to be made regarding what level of restrictions should be imposed on them. At the commencement of hostilities, these options covered

---

18 John Clement Bird, *Control of Enemy Alien Civilians in Great Britain 1914-1918* (PhD Thesis – University of London 1981).

approximately 70,000 enemy alien residents, excluding British-born women who had acquired enemy nationality by marriage, and children younger than fourteen.

Levels of xenophobia had been growing, so it is unsurprising that treatment of aliens became a high-profile issue. Certainly, much of the public disquiet was generated and exploited by various political extremists and by elements of the media. But the government itself carried some of the blame through the unintended consequences of its propaganda efforts to demonise the Germans for their 'frightfulness' and sole responsibility for the war. Public concern on the subject waxed and waned but was often sufficient to force government action. The gap between (more extreme) public demands and (less extreme) government policy preferences partly reflected the failure of the public to appreciate the realities facing the authorities. Thus, calls to 'intern them all' were entirely impractical given accommodation capacity; indeed, this was a problem even for the government's far more moderate internment targets.

Policy went through phases, often reacting to public disquiet. Initial plans were aimed only at enemy aliens believed to be a genuine threat. But, as the first weeks of war went by, public clamour for more stringent action grew. Thrown into a frightening conflict of uncertain outcome, people could not see why 'the enemy' should be allowed to move freely among them or German-owned or named businesses be permitted to continue trading. By October 1914, nearly 10,000 male enemy aliens of military age were in custody, but around twice as many remained free. Some in government recognised the danger this caused by allowing extremists to campaign for harsher policies. But the War Office simply could not provide the necessary accommodation to implement more extensive action. The cabinet agreed to general internment of men of military age, but the accommodation shortage meant that this was impossible, especially in the London area. The outcome was continuing public annoyance at a 'soft' policy, but by late Autumn 1914, the accommodation problem was so severe that the War Office even began releasing some people from internment, which stirred further public concern.

Early in 1915, Asquith's cabinet became concerned that failing to pursue 'harsh' policies was weakening the government's standing, however irrational and impractical they considered such policies to be. Events then escalated dramatically after the sinking of the Lusitania on 7 May 1915. In response, there was rioting and attacks on homes and businesses believed to belong to enemy aliens, accompanied by calls for comprehensive internment. Asquith responded almost immediately. Now, all adult male enemy aliens were to be interned or, if over military age, repatriated. Some women and children would also be repatriated. Exemptions from the policy were to be decided by judicial-style committees. As soon as the military authorities had provided the necessary accommodation those who did not secure exemption would be interned (although the assumption was that those who had been naturalised would remain at liberty).

Implementing the expanded policy resulted in few enemy aliens remaining free. Between May and November 1915, the number of men in captivity increased from almost 13,000 to over 32,000. However, this was not the impression held by the public, and the government continued to be harried. When Lloyd George replaced Asquith, yet tougher measures were expected but little changed. Lloyd George was, however, happy to deploy harsh rhetoric on the topic and implement the occasional token gesture, such as instructing the Home Secretary to conduct a review of all those who had been exempted from internment or repatriation.

Ginger groups, especially among the Unionists in parliament, constantly called for stronger measures and public opinion again came to a crescendo as spring moved into early summer 1918 and in the face of the ongoing German offensive. Bird summarised the situation:

> *'Demonstrations in Hyde Park and elsewhere, petitions to the government and resolutions by local councils, patriotic groups and other organisations demanded sterner measures against the enemy alien population. With stridently anti-alien groups such as the nationalist (sic) Party – formed by right wing Unionists under General Croft's leadership – and the British Empire Union*[19] *fomenting agitation, urged on by the Northcliffe Press, Lloyd George and his cabinet colleagues accepted that changes in aliens' policy were a political if not a practical necessity.'*[20]

---

19 The British Empire Union had been founded in 1915 as the Anti-German Union and changed its name in 1916.
20 Bird ibid.

Thus, by the time of the by-election, the scene was set for the treatment of enemy aliens to be the major feature.

On the day the writ was moved (13 June), Harry Greer was announced as the Conservative, Coalition candidate. His selection was a surprise since the sitting MP for Hastings, Arthur Du Cros, had already been adopted as the prospective candidate for Clapham for the next general election. Some commentary implied that Du Cros had not come forward since the seat was to undergo boundary changes. However, the more likely reason was that Du Cros would have had to resign his seat in Hastings in order to stand at Clapham, resulting in another by-election.

Assuming this pattern of events was anticipated, then the selection of Greer ceases to be a surprise as he was a long-standing friend, business partner and political colleague of Du Cros who also held ambitions to enter the Commons. The links between Du Cros and Greer were extensive. They had been Unionist activists together in Bow in the 1900s and they were both Directors of the same bicycle and car manufacturing company. Also, Du Cros was managing director of Dunlop Rubber while Greer, with his brother, had established a company in China which distributed Dunlop products. It appears, therefore, that Greer was put forward simply to keep the seat warm for Du Cros.

No policy issues lay behind Greer's selection. He was described as follows:

> *'His has been an active and prosperous career. The firm of H. and W. Greer Ltd., merchants, manufacturers, shippers was founded by him, and he is its chairman and managing director. It is closely identified with our colonies ... It is scarcely necessary to say he is a sound and whole-hearted imperialist. His Imperialistic ideals have been strengthened by extensive and world-wide travel. Mr. Greer 's patriotism manifested itself in an offer of his services to the Ministry of Munitions an offer which was readily accepted.*[21]

Other reports expanded on his travel, claiming that he had been round the world 'seven times'. But Greer was not to have a clear run since Billing was determined to put forward a candidate, concentrating on the treatment of

---

21 *South Western Star*, 14 June 1918.

enemy aliens. Nominations were fixed for Monday 17 June and, two days prior to that, Billing held a mass meeting of his Vigilante Society at the Royal Albert Hall specifically on the 'alien question'. At that meeting he put forward an extreme resolution:

> *'That this meeting of citizens of the British Empire, assembled at the Royal Albert Hall today, views with dismay and alarm the influence of the naturalised and unnaturalised enemies in our midst, and calls upon His Majesty's Government to take immediate steps to denaturalise all enemy born subjects and intern them forthwith; and, further, to take power under the Defence of the Realm Act to provide that all aliens shall, for the duration of the war, exhibit on the lapel of their coats an emblem of their nationality.'*

The Billing motion draws attention to two aspects of the 'aliens' issue. Firstly, it argued that no constraints on the rights of enemy aliens would be sufficient, short of incarceration. In fact, from early on, considerable limitations were introduced on their freedom of action. These included restrictions on where they could live (they had to be outside of extensive 'prohibited areas' which included all the North-East and substantial parts of the South coasts), where they could travel (permits could be required for journeys of greater than five miles), and what kind of employment they could undertake. They were also not allowed to change their names, restricted as to which newspapers they could read (German newspapers were closed), and banned from owning items such as firearms, cameras, motor cars, motorcycles, military maps, homing pigeons and telephones. In some areas, curfews were imposed on them.

Secondly, it turned fire on those of 'enemy origins', regardless of whether they had been naturalised. The position of naturalised citizens had been of concern to those agitating. The lack of restrictions on them was seen as a potential gap in the country's defences against the 'hidden hand' of 'traitors in our midst'. At the Royal Albert Hall, Billing claimed so-called 'friendly' aliens were able to buy up the businesses of loyal Britons who had put them up for sale so that they could 'answer the call'. Bird summarised:

> *'The status of naturalised subjects proved to be a mixed blessing for those born in enemy countries. While they were not subject to the same stringent restrictions*

or to the internment and repatriation policies imposed on enemy aliens, they were a target of popular suspicion and abuse. Some politicians and newspapers insisted that such subjects were a greater danger to the state than enemy nationals because of their much greater freedom to engage in subversive activity.[22]

The resolution was passed unanimously, and Billing further used the meeting as a rallying cry for Vigilante members to campaign in the forthcoming by-election. He announced that after the meeting he was going to Clapham to help the Vigilante candidate, whom he revealed as Henry Beamish who he said was standing for 'the internment of all Germans, the registration of aliens, and the preservation of this country for its own people. It would not be an easy fight, but if Mr Beamish was successful every German would be interned inside a month.'[23]

Billing appealed for help for his cause. He said that he had asked more than 1,400 questions in the Commons in the last session, but he needed the voters to send someone to help him and so invited all those who could, to go to Clapham that very day. He finished with his most incendiary comment on the aliens' issue, proclaiming about Germans in the country: 'There is only one place for those traitors – that was with eyes blindfolded up against a brick wall.'[24]

Billing's candidate, Captain Henry Hamilton Beamish, was an ex-officer who joined the Vigilantes and became a regular contributor to the group's magazine; he had also, unfortunately, been the person who introduced Billing to Harold Spencer. (Soon, Beamish's contributions to the Vigilante magazine became too extreme, even for Billing, who would not accept their increasingly anti-Jewish tone). By the time of the by-election, Beamish was Treasurer of the Vigilantes. He was also the originator of the policy for all aliens to 'exhibit on the lapel of their coats the emblem of their nationality', a policy which Billing initially had opposed as he feared it might mean innocent people could be attacked by those with extreme anti-German feelings.

Beamish had enjoyed an exotic career. He started as a fur trader in Canada then worked on tea plantations in Ceylon, fought in the Boer War and

---

22 Bird ibid.
23 *Sunday Post*, 16 June 1918.
24 Ibid.

subsequently settled in South Africa where he ran a company called Empire Tea Rooms and founded a newspaper, the *Farmer's Advocate*. At the start of the war, he founded in South Africa the British Citizen Movement, which was dedicated to promoting the purchase of British goods and rejecting anything German. He then served in the Natal Regiment of South African Infantry, after which he relocated back to Britain. He arrived convinced that he had discovered the existence of a world-wide Jewish conspiracy, a view which was to dominate his future political activities.

At nominations on 17 June, there were no surprises. Three papers were submitted in support of Greer and two for Beamish. As the campaign began in earnest it was to do so under continued straightened circumstances. Petrol rationing meant that only the candidates themselves were permitted to use motor vehicles and paper shortages and restrictions essentially precluded the widespread use of posters. Consequently, there was an even greater emphasis on meetings. On one day, Beamish held thirteen meetings, including eight outdoors. Greer also relied heavily on them and was able to call on outside speakers, such as John Hodge MP, the Labour Minister of Pensions.

Beamish opened his campaign saying that his special policy was to 'intern every German in the country, denaturalise every German and to deport the brute'.[25] He said: 'He did not know about politics, but if he were returned to the House of Commons, he would make just such a row in the House regarding the internment of Germans as Mr Pemberton Billing had done with regard to the Air Service.'[26] The Times reported that Beamish stood for 'denaturalisation and internment of all enemy-born subjects in the country; the closing of all enemy banks and businesses and the badging of all aliens.'[27]

The potential effectiveness of the 'intern them all' policy was spelt out during the campaign by press observers. One noted: 'As long as the Home Office shields these men the government will be liable to such attacks as are coming from Mr Pemberton Billing and his nominee at Clapham, where a by-election is being conducted on the cry of 'Intern them all'. Why should the government oppose such a policy?'[28]

---

25 *Exeter & Plymouth Gazette*, 18 June 1918.
26 *Aberdeen Press & Journal*, 18 June 1918.
27 *The Times*, 18 June 1918.
28 *Western Morning News*, 18 June 1918.

Why indeed? As in several other by-elections, the government's response to a difficult situation was, as far as possible, to steal the thunder of the ginger groups. Thus, Greer rapidly adopted a similar line. He outlined a series of strong positions in his election address and summarised his aims as being: 'Win the war, Intern all enemy aliens'. The detail of his position on aliens was that:

> *'Stronger measures are necessary when dealing with enemy aliens ... I would compel all Naturalised Enemy Aliens to publicly renounce allegiance to the country of their birth, to reaffirm their pledge of loyalty to King George, to express horror and indignation at the conduct of the Central Powers, and to place their services unreservedly at the disposal of the country of their adoption. No naturalised person of enemy origin should be allowed to sit on our Privy Council; to hold a Commission in our Army or Navy; to be employed as a Pilot or a Master on a British ship; or be entitled to acquire or hold land here, or a residence in a prohibited area.'*[29]

He also tackled other issues of the day. In harsh words, he argued: 'There are far too many shirkers in Government offices, and among farmers' sons. It is our duty to get these people to the front at the earliest opportunity. Every fit man should go once, before any man goes twice.' Further, he advocated that 'adequate pensions must be granted to every Soldier, Sailor or Widow, and a full education given to fatherless children'.[30]

Greer also deployed the standard government line supporting unity. A Liberal leaflet stated:

> *'any parliamentary contest at this time is a betrayal in the face of the enemy. A Billing candidature will create feelings of distrust and discontent among people, thereby causing confusion and weakness and opening the road to ruin. It would cheer the heart of Berlin while 'Every vote given for Greer will be a vote for the Empire'.*[31]

---

29 *The Globe*, 18 June 1918.
30 Greer election address. University of Bristol Library Special Collections.
31 *The Times*, 18 June 1918.

Such was the concern in ministry circles that a revitalised Billing might succeed if he annexed the 'aliens' issue, that interventions from both Bonar Law, Leader of the Conservative Party and Leader of the House of Commons and Lloyd George, the Liberal Prime Minister, were organised. Bonar Law sent a telegram to Greer saying: 'The greatest need of the present hour is a united home front to support the men risking everything in face of the enemy'.[32] Lloyd George initially restricted himself to the usual open letter from the premier to a by-election candidate, calling for voters' support in the cause of national unity:

> 'The Germans have concentrated their whole army to-day in an attempt to destroy, in one supreme attack, our armies in the field. They are not less bent on undermining the moral of the allies by promoting dissension and distrust behind the lines. We have got to show ... nothing can turn us aside from our goal. .... I sincerely trust, therefore, that the electors of Clapham can be relied upon in order to emphasize the national unity at this grave juncture to return you as Coalition candidate at the head of the poll'.[33]

However, concerned this might be insufficient, twenty-four hours later a more dramatic and unusual intervention was made by Downing Street. In this Greer received a further communication, for publication, from the Prime Minister's secretary, William Sutherland, saying:

> 'In answer to an inquiry, I am desired by the Prime Minister to say that he is himself examining into the whole question of the position of persons of enemy alien birth or connexion in this country, and that he is determined to take whatever action is shown to be necessary.'[34]

Perhaps stung by this attempt to nullify Beamish's push on 'enemy aliens', Pemberton Billing claimed to have sent a reply-paid telegram to Lloyd George and published copies of the text as a polling day poster. The wording was:

---

32 *Daily Gazette for Middlesborough*, 19 June 1918.
33 *Aberdeen Evening Express*, 19 June 1918.
34 *Evening Mail*, 21 June 1918.

> 'David George, Prime Minister. If you are prepared to give a written undertaking this day to intern all enemy-born subjects in this country within thirty days from this date and close all German and Austrian banks forthwith we are prepared to concede this seat to the Government nominee. In sending you this message we feel we are voicing the considered view of the Clapham electorate and the opinion of all British subjects throughout the Empire. (Signed) Pemberton Billing, President of the Vigilante Society. God save the King!'

Although this was clearly an election stunt, the Greer campaign responded. They announced they had checked with Downing Street and the Post Office and that no such telegram had been received, or even sent. Greer's supporters displayed posters of their own about the telegram stating 'Downing Street knows nothing of it. The receiving post offices for 10, Downing Street know nothing of it. Was it ever sent? What do you think?'. Whether it was smart election tactics to draw attention to Billing's agitation is debatable.

Commentators reflected on two key aspects of the conflict. That it was one of the quietest campaigns people could remember but, paradoxically, it had been focused exclusively on the issue of enemy aliens on which strong views were held. The quietness of the electioneering reflected the now tough restrictions on motor vehicles and shortages of paper. However, the Billing campaign was well provided with enthusiastic canvassers who seemed to be effective in the areas they were able to cover in the limited time of the campaign.

All agreed that the election would turn on each candidate's position on the enemy aliens. An accurate summary of the relative positions, and the reasons for them, was provided in the press:

> 'When, in spite of the party truce we have by-elections, they are generally rather feverish contests over a stunt. Clapham is no exception. The alien peril is the immediate question, and just as the air-raid scare brought Mr. Billing into Parliament, there is always the possibility of some similar agitation being successfully exploited by one his nominees. That there is strong feeling at present on the position of aliens is obvious, and the extent to which the Coalition candidate has thought it worthwhile to steal his opponent's thunder is an indication of it. Mr. Greer is avoiding some of the more ludicrous of the Vigilante proposals, such

> as the labelling of aliens, but is for gingering the Government on the subject. Successive Home Secretaries have been embarrassed by campaigns of this kind, and there is always a danger of a policy being practically forced on the Government which calm reason does not approve'.[35]

There was fear among government supporters that victory would go to the candidate who adopted the more extreme policies, namely Beamish. Concern about the aliens' issue was particularly great in London and a few councils there, including Stoke Newington and Stepney, had passed strident resolutions demanding that all enemy aliens over 18 should be interned, repatriated or employed on national duties and should not be allowed to acquire British businesses. Reasons identified for the strength of feeling at this stage in the war, in addition to the recent German offensive, were summarised in the press:

> 'The new-born antipathy to the alien arises partly from the persistence with which respectable British tradesmen have to protest to Appeal Tribunals that while they are called up for military service, Germans and sons of Germans are permitted without hindrance to snatch their businesses; and partly from a belief that highborn Huns are permitted privileges quite inconsistent with the safety of the country in a state of war.'[36]

The *Pall Mall Gazette* expanded on the theme stating:

> 'Nothing did more to destroy public confidence in the late Government than the pampering of German prisoners, and the general laxity displayed in the official treatment of the enemy in our midst. The same follies and the same resentment of them will end the career of their successors unless there is a very sincere repentance and a very definite reformation ... The Clapham election shows that on no other subject are plain people so deeply moved; and the degree of exasperation is becoming very dangerous to a Government which more than ever requires to have the country behind it.'[37]

---

35 *Cambridge Daily News*, 20 June 1918.
36 *Western Daily Press*, 21 June 1918.
37 *Pall Mall Gazette*, 21 June 1918.

The result, when it came, was another close win for the Coalition.

Dec. 1910			
Faber	Conservative	9,560	56%
Benn	Liberal	7,639	44%
Majority		1,921	
Electorate & Turnout		22,611	76%

21 Jun. 1918			
Greer	Conservative	4,512	58%
Beamish	Vigilante	3,331	42%
Majority		1,181	
Electorate & Turnout		23,526	33%

Greer, and the Coalition, declared themselves delighted but there was concern that the Billing candidate came so close. As one newspaper put it: 'That more than three thousand British voters should have been found ready to support a follower of Mr. Billing is assuredly not an encouraging sign'.[38] Similarly, the *Pall Mall Gazette* described the result as 'a warning bell' which demonstrated the extent of public concern. The newspaper concluded that 'The Cabinet must be up and doing!'.[39]

Clapham did have a long-term impact. Lloyd George, having promised action on the enemy alien issue, now established a new committee of six MPs, most of whom had already advocated harsher measures, to investigate current policy and recommend changes. The committee reported (the Dalziel report) in July and proposed:

> 'the wholesale internment of all enemy alien men over the age of 18, with exceptions on 'national or medical grounds' within the discretion of the Home

---

38 *Derby Daily Telegraph*, 22 June 1918.
39 *Pall Mall Gazette*, 22 June 1918.

> Secretary; the repatriation of alien women of enemy origin, again with provision for exceptions on grounds of justice and humanity; the review of naturalisation certificates granted to persons of enemy origin; the discharge from government offices of men and women of enemy origin; the invalidation of name changes by persons of enemy origin since 1 August 1914 until six months after the armistice, and the immediate winding up of enemy businesses and the closing of enemy banks still in operation.[40]

The proposals were well received, and government established a reconstituted aliens advisory committee for England and Wales to sift through all cases of enemy aliens at large, especially Germans. By the end of October, the committee had considered about 3,200 people of whom some 300 were interned and about 220 recommended for repatriation. Thus, although Billing had been unsuccessful electorally in Clapham, his intervention swayed policy. The low extra numbers interned or proposed for repatriation reflects the reality that the state had, in any case, already been much harsher on enemy aliens than Billing acknowledged. There was one further historical feature of the Clapham by-election: it was the first at which women were employed as polling and counting clerks.

The successful candidate, Greer, did give up his place at the 1918 General election to his long-standing friend Arthur Du Cros and moved to become the MP for Wells. He stood down in 1922. Beamish continued his quixotic and extremist career. He stood again as an Independent candidate in Clapham in the 1918 General election, finishing second ahead of the Liberal. The following year, he established The Britons, an organisation dedicated to circulating antisemitic literature. Shortly after he fled the country following a conviction for libel and travelled widely, promoting the antisemitic cause; he spoke at one of Hitler's meetings in 1923. He settled in Rhodesia and, ironically, was interned during the second world war due to his pro-Nazi views.

---

40 John Clement Bird, *Control of Enemy Alien Civilians in Great Britain 1914-1918* (PhD Thesis – University of London 1981).

EAST FINSBURY – July 1918

Billing was somewhat quiet after Clapham although he wrote in *The Vigilante* that the close result meant that despite 'the mean and dirty tricky employed by the opposing Coalition candidate; support for the Vigilante Party was growing'. He remained active in parliament, seeking debates on the aliens' issue; so much so that he refused to obey the Speaker and was forcibly removed from the chamber, shouting 'Intern the aliens'. Soon after his expulsion, he nominated a candidate for the forthcoming East Finsbury by-election in north London and again telegrammed Lloyd George offering to withdraw if the Vigilantes' policies on aliens were adopted.

The East Finsbury campaign occurred at a difficult time for Billing. Firstly, all three members of the Vigilante finance committee resigned, claiming he had been spending large sums without permission. Secondly, an article appeared in the *Daily Chronicle*, stating: 'It is a curious coincidence that the real director of the Prime Minister's Advisory Committee, the Chief Vigilante – Mr Pemberton Billing – should himself be married to a lady of Prussian origin'. The paper felt there was nothing unpatriotic about Billing's wife but wondered why the Vigilantes had not wanted her investigated. Against this background, and still barred from the Commons, Billing set about orchestrating the by-election campaign. He continued to believe Spencer's remarkable tales and so happily chose him as the Vigilante standard bearer in East Finsbury.

The vacancy was caused by the unexpected death of the Liberal MP, Joseph Allen Baker, who suffered a seizure at the Commons on 2 July 1918 and died early the next day. The Unionists quickly announced that they would put up a candidate unless the Liberal nominee committed to supporting fully the Lloyd George government. This was judged by some to represent a re-negotiation of the party truce. This was also the first by-election since Labour had withdrawn from the party truce the previous month. Consequently, comments were made about the Conservatives heavily criticising the Labour party for withdrawing from the truce while at the same time implying they would break it themselves unless the selected Liberal candidate agreed to follow Lloyd George, which conceivably might require him to vote against the leader of the Liberal Party, Asquith.

Word was soon out that the coalition candidate would be Evan Cotton, the Progressive member for East Finsbury on the London County Council.

His keenest area of interest was India (where he was born) and, following his return from there in 1906, he had been the editor of the London journal of the Indian National Congress. It was felt understandable that he might want to join the Commons since the future governance of India had risen to prominence on the political agenda, following publication of the Montagu Report. That addressed mechanisms for a gradual introduction of self-government in India and formed the basis of what became the Government of India Act, 1919.

Cotton also had a track record on British social issues. Even while an undergraduate at Oxford he supported Joseph Arch in setting up branches of the Agricultural Labourers' Union. He gave the Unionists the assurances of loyalty to the Lloyd George government they requested and so they stood by the truce and his first campaign meeting was chaired by their prospective general election candidate. Newly elected Harry Greer was one of the supporting speakers, attending as thanks for the substantial efforts on his behalf by the Liberals in Clapham.

Nominations were to be submitted on 12 July and polling day was set for 16 July; yet another campaign period designed to be too short for any 'irregular' candidate to have an impact. This, however, was insufficient to demotivate not just one anti-government campaigner, but two. First to emerge was Allan S Belsher, a solicitor's clerk and chairman of the Licensed Victuallers Central Protection Society of London. He set up committee rooms directly opposite Cotton's and quickly issued an election address. He said the only acceptable terms of peace were victory and the overthrow of the military and commercial domination of Germany and that he was in favour of the seamen's boycott, whereby British sailors would refuse to carry German goods or visit German ports for six years after the end of the war, the internment of aliens and the shutting up of enemy businesses. Billing also rapidly announced Spencer's candidacy and their campaign began working not from a committee room but from a cart, located outside Cotton's headquarters. Billing continued to campaign on the cry of 'intern them all', while the Vigilante literature highlighted this theme, oddly, with an illustration of four men being hanged. This, apparently, 'seemed to be interesting the youth of Finsbury.'[41]

---

41 *Daily News*, 10 July 1918.

At the first night's meetings, Unionist Sir Kingley Wood declared that: 'this was a time for national unity, not Old Bailey antics and freak candidatures' while Belsher claimed he was the patriotic candidate, coming forward because people were not satisfied with the Coalition choice and Spencer announced he desired to support Mr Billing in parliament as he had done at the Old Bailey.[42]

Billing rapidly reprised his telegram stunt as a cheap form of electioneering. The cabinet was still deliberating on whether to accept all the recommendations of the Dalziel report (see above) when Billing telegrammed, saying:

> 'since announcing my intention to support Capt. Spencer at East Finsbury to force the hand of your Government to intern all enemy aliens in this country, the recommendations of the committee appointed by you have been brought to my notice. That there may be no doubt in the public mind as to our sincerity and good faith in this matter, I make you the following offer: If you are prepared to give an undertaking that the recommendations of the committee appointed by yourself shall be substantially carried out without delay, we are prepared to withdraw our candidate, as we offered to do and for the same reason, in the recent Clapham by-election.'

Lloyd George did not bother to reply.

Belsher received immediate support from the Seamen's League in a letter from Havelock Wilson who explained that Cotton, the Coalition candidate, had failed to respond satisfactorily to questions from the National Seamen's and Firemen's Union as to whether he supported their demands for an economic boycott of Germany. Wilson announced that he planned to address several meetings in support of Belsher, the independent, and, when doing so, confirmed that he was an out-and-out supporter of Lloyd George so long as the latter was out to win the war. At this stage in his career, Wilson was a potent figure, given strength by public appreciation of the part played in the war by British merchant seamen in the face of what were viewed as German crimes at sea. Cotton was not unsympathetic to the seamen's union's policies

---

42 *Northern Whig*, 11 July 1918.

but was unwilling to agree to their call for a boycott of German goods and trade specifically for six years after the end of the conflict.

Initial local interest was slight but grew as the three campaigns each organised substantial programmes of indoor and outdoor meetings. Cotton enjoyed several advantages including that he was well-known and well regarded as a long standing, and hard-working, local London County Council councillor; that he had the full support of the Unionists and that he faced a divided opposition. However, Belsher attracted significant external support, stemming from his strong support for a comprehensive economic boycott of Germany. In addition to Havelock Wilson, his meetings featured as many as seventy seamen who were working for his campaign. He had also secured the unofficial support of organised labour, if not of the Labour party. This included Ben Tillett, the highly-patriotic Dockers Union leader who had been elected as an Independent in the Salford North by-election the previous year (see chapter 11) who telegrammed: 'Good luck! May you win! We want conscientious patriots and courageous men in Parliament. Fight the good fight. Fight and win. The workers will help you. B Tillett. Dockers Union.' Belsher repaid the compliment by stating: 'I am in favour of the doctrine that no change in trades union rules and practice should be made without the full and free consent of the trades unions: and I desire to see that every man and woman worker receives a good day's pay for a good day's work.'[43] Also unsurprising was a favourable interview appearing in *The Globe* which, by this point, was being edited (albeit anonymously) by Leo Maxse, who was a declared supporter of Belsher.

Belsher additionally emphasised internment, saying that he fully endorsed the position supported at a mass meeting held in Trafalgar Square on the Saturday during the campaign (13 July). At this, a resolution had been passed unanimously:

> 'That this mass meeting assembled at Trafalgar Square regards the proposals made by the Home Secretary on Thursday in the House Commons as futile, and useless to deal with the alien enemy, and refuses to accept any compromise on the part of the authorities. It demands the immediate internment of all aliens

---

43 *The Globe*, 15 July 1918

of enemy blood, whether naturalised or unnaturalised, the removal of all such aliens from every Government Office and calls upon his Majesty's Government to take whatever steps necessary to put this resolution into effect.[34]

Further backing for Belsher came from the Patriotic Club (described as the oldest working men's Radical Club in London) which declared for him, the first time they had not backed the official Liberal candidate in any election.

In the face of the strong showing by the establishment wing of the patriotic movement, Billing and Spencer had been starved of attention and were making little impact – one press report noted: 'it is significant to observe how soon the sensation created by the absurd stories that were current through the use of the 'Black Book' have faded into oblivion.'[45] But this was to change, dramatically, on the eve of poll. All three campaigns held multiple meetings and thousands gathered to attend. Towards the end of Belsher's main meeting, Pemberton Billing and Spencer arrived with an estimated thousand or so supporters. The outcome was 'turbulent scenes'. According to the press,

> *'Some of the crowd made a determined attack upon Mr Belsher's motorcar, and though the police did their best, every bit of glass in the vehicle was smashed ... A large body of police eventually drove the crowd back, but it was with difficulty that they were able to clear a way for Mr. Havelock Wilson.'*[46]

Then, at another Belsher meeting, the report continued:

> *'A determined attempt was made to rush the hall. Stones and sticks were hurled at the building, and every window was shattered, the occupants having to barricade the place to prevent entry. The small force of police was overpowered, and reinforcements were sent for. Mr. Billing was addressing the unruly crowd from his motorcar outside the hall, and whether or not the crowd were unduly excited by his references to aliens and military shirkers, they set upon every person who was apparently of alien nationality or of military age. The police had to rescue a number of these persons, who were rather badly treated. As soon as police*

---

44 *Pall Mall Gazette*, 13 July 1918.
45 *Derby Daily Telegraph*, 16 July 1918.
46 *Birmingham Daily Post*, 16 July 1918.

reinforcements arrived Mr. Billing was requested to conclude his remarks. He did so after considerable argument, and the police then turned their attention to clearing the streets.[47]

Billing's version of history, as published in The Vigilante, was different. He claimed that sixty roughs, 'the very scum of the docks', had been brought in to harass Spencer's supporters and that it was they who had attacked several ex-servicemen. He also said that the 'bullies' were eventually chased to Moorgate station by a crowd of two or three thousand women (wives and widows of ex-servicemen).

Polling day started with a low turnout but there were reports of the constituency being worked by many seamen and firemen in support of Belsher. He issued a flyer reminding voters that he was supported by Havelock Wilson and Ben Tillett and distributed cards saying that he would win by 990 votes. The Billing campaign also was active early, to counteract the fact that the area was covered with posters either for Cotton or Belsher; soon, most of these had been fly-posted with 'Vote for Spencer' slogans. Cotton issued an appeal to Irish voters in the constituency to back him and re-iterated his cry that: 'This is no time for freak candidates and old Bailey antics'. Each of the candidates had numerous supporters in the field and much use was made of horse-drawn vehicles. Horse-drawn as restrictions remained in place on the use of petrol. Billing later reported that the Petrol Committee had allowed him 20 gallons for the election for two vehicles, Spencer's and his own. He reported that they had used only a single motorcar and 18 gallons of the petrol. There were also reports of much enthusiasm and 'hordes of ragamuffins' surrounding each of the six polling stations.

The general opinion was that Cotton would win due to his local links and popularity, a divided opposition, and the toughening of the Coalition's stance against aliens. Certainly, he had made sure to mark out his ground on the 'aliens' issue, reminding voters that as early as October 1914 he had seconded a successful motion at the London County Council calling for the internment of all aliens; in addition, he told electors that 'my mind is quite made up that I

---

47 Ibid.

shall never speak or associate with Germans again'.[48] Meanwhile, there was a view that Billing's reputation, and therefore influence, was in decline while, by comparison, Belsher was felt to have run a strong campaign. The eventual result, therefore, came as a surprise to the extent that Belsher polled fewer than 200 votes and was easily outdistanced by Spencer.

Dec. 1910			
Baker	Liberal	2,023	52%
Mason	Conservative	1,900	48%
Majority		123	
Electorate & Turnout		4,855	81%

16 Jul. 1918			
Cotton	Liberal	1,156	60%
Spencer	Vigilante	576	30%
Belsher	Independent	199	10%
Majority		580	
Electorate & Turnout		4,990	39%

The declaration was made to a crowd of two to three thousand. Cotton told them that the only issue had been support for the prosecution of the war while Spencer, bizarrely, said it was a positive that not a single naturalised German had voted for him. Some felt the result might indicate the slow return of 'sane' politics, given that Cotton had seen off two extremist campaigns. *The Times* saw the strong Coalition performance as a condemnation of the 'rowdyism' of the other campaigns. East Finsbury did not have a major impact on government policy, although in one of his first acts in the Commons, Cotton

---

48 *Daily Telegraph*, 16 July 1918.

voted against the government's actions on enemy aliens as he felt that they did not go far enough.

He received scant reward from the government or Lloyd George. In the December 1918 General Election, boundary changes meant his East Finsbury seat was subsumed into a new constituency of Finsbury. Cotton stood as a Liberal, but the Coalition coupon was given to Martin Archer-Shee, the Conservative MP for Finsbury Central with whom Billing had engaged in fisticuffs. In 1919, Cotton also stood down from his LCC seat but was then appointed as an alderman.

Belsher returned to political obscurity and did not stand for election again. Spencer parted company with Billing when the Vigilantes were wound up in 1919. In 1918, he had published an antisemitic tract, *Democracy or Shylocracy*, which was later republished by Beamish's organisation, The Britons. In 1922, Spencer was imprisoned for an antisemitic libel. There followed a career that veered between bankruptcy and marrying heiresses. He died in the Bahamas in 1957.

13.
WINDOWS ON THE HOME FRONT

Britain's first world war by-elections deliver fascinating insights into the changing hopes and concerns on the Home Front. Much is revealed through the issues on which they were fought and the nature of the candidates and their campaigning. The stories captured in these battles at the ballot reveal how attention shifted, and moods changed as the war progressed. Generally, the political truce held firm, and sight should not be lost that while 29 British[1] by-elections were contested, 85 were not; these were potential opportunities to indicate popular dissent that were spurned.

Frustrations begin to grow – too little war, not too much

The first significant British contested by-election, **Merthyr** (Nov. 1915), came a little after a year of fighting. The people of the world's largest Empire, one possessed of a dominant navy, were frustrated at the failure to make military progress. But Merthyr provided reassurance that even among 'militant' working-class communities, support for the struggle was strong. The labour movement demonstrated that its patriotism was a greater motivator than any allegiance to ideology or international class consciousness. The South Wales miners remained prepared to strike to protect their industrial rights and

---

[1] As noted in the Introduction, by-elections in Ireland have not been covered.

incomes, but they were not going to send to parliament someone with even a taint of lack of resolve regarding the war.

The next two by-elections, **Cleveland** (Dec. 1915) and **West Newington** (Jan. 1916), confirmed that those wishing to continue pre-war struggles or attitudes were now shouting in the wilderness. In these, Horatio Bottomley had some fun and the militant socialist, Joe Terrett, tried to depict restrictions on alcohol as a fundamental attack on British rights. The immediate pre-war years had seen high levels of industrial unrest and the threat by the London Trades Union Protest Committee to down tools to preserve their members' right to drink was an echo of those halcyon days. But the voters knew that more serious matters were afoot; a few backed the independents but those who did were more concerned about the attitude of 'wait and see' than with buying rounds.

It was the Zeppelins and the remarkable figure of Noel Pemberton-Billing that combined seriously to threaten the government forces such that a close-run contest in **Mile End** (Jan. 1916) was rapidly followed by defeat in **East Hertfordshire** (Mar. 1916). Voters now realised that the conflict was all-consuming. And the issue of the 'air war' provided a single cause which united multiple strands of concern. Perhaps above all, there was frustration at the inability to do anything much to prevent the killing of women and children in British cities. Where were Churchill's hornets when they were needed? Prevented from flying by Liberal sensitivities? The defensive response appeared weak, or incompetent. Some people were undoubtedly genuinely fearful of the threat to life and property. But there was greater anger at what was viewed as half-hearted commitment to the conflict. What these people wanted was harsh reprisal raids, raining harm on German citizens. Gott Strafe Deutschland. Pemberton-Billing was tapping a rich seam. A perceived-to-be hesitant Liberal-led Coalition was on the back foot and in Billing it faced an attractive and competent opponent. Here was someone who seemed to know what he was talking about (with a track record of successful derring-do), telling the voters that what they wanted could be delivered easily, if only sufficient 'ginger' were applied to the Liberals.

Against this, government forces couldn't settle on a consistent response. In Mile End they tried (as they were to do in several subsequent elections) to nullify opposition by co-opting its policies and criticisms. Thus, as regards the air war, Warwick Brookes seemed almost as much against the government for whom he was a candidate as was his opponent. Yet, in East Hertfordshire, the Coalition campaign backing Brodie Henderson distanced itself from an overwhelming focus on an air war which, as they rightly pointed out, in strategic terms represented only a small part of the struggle. But the call to display a stiff upper lip and to concentrate on feeding the army with men and the guns with munitions didn't offer a satisfactory response either to fear or retaliatory bloodlust. Nor could the Coalition decide how to play Billing, the man. Was he a well-informed hero who should be plying his trade in the Royal Naval Air Service rather than seeking a place in Parliament or was he a scaremongering charlatan who had left the forces under a cloud? It tried both, often at the same time. Eventually, it was not to be enough. The government was unfortunate to come up against a force of nature like Billing, at the time and place that it did, and it paid the price.

Discontent rumbles on but is held at bay

The experience of East Hertfordshire was a stark warning to the Coalition business managers. However, although other tricky contests were to come, they managed to hold the line, partly through more astute political 'tradecraft', such that East Hertfordshire was not rapidly followed by further defeats. The eventual fall of Herbert Asquith stemmed from high politics, not by-elections.

The next two contests, **Harborough** (Mar. 1916) and **Hyde** (Mar. 1916) came too soon after Billing's victory for him to play a part. Instead, the battleground terrain comprised of complications stemming from conscription and continued rumblings (largely driven by the 'trade') about restrictions on drink. The government had an easier ride on these issues than it had against 'the Airman'.

On conscription, Asquith paid the penalty for a badly phrased commitment, but he comes out of the controversy better than those who attempted to use against him the issue of the 'attested married men'. He had said that married men should not be called 'until the unmarried men were dealt with', but he clarified that 'dealt with' meant, 'I hope by voluntary effort, but if it be needed in the last resort by other means'. Once the first Military Service Bill had been introduced in January 1916, then the single men had indeed been 'dealt with'. The Prime Minister's pledge was intact.

Still, the attested married men did have legitimate reasons for anger. It was certainly true that a proportion of single men were not being 'dealt with', even with the passage of conscription; undoubtedly there were some 'hiding in government offices' and elsewhere. Also, concerns about the financial consequences of taking married men away from their families were genuine. At the point the government started to call them up it did not have adequate arrangements in place to enable them to 'keep their homes together'.

Although the attested married men protested loudly, they didn't have a coherent position that stood up to scrutiny; certainly not one which could unite sufficient opposition to defeat the government. The zeitgeist remained to fight the war harder, so any cry to delay sending men to the front was going to raise eyebrows. And the attested married men, specifically, were in danger of putting forward an illogical argument, namely that they expected, as the people who had come forward to promise to serve if called, that they should not be asked to do so until after those who had not volunteered. Asquith's mistake arguably was in not committing immediately to 'compulsion all round'. He should have realised that it was not viable to leave the married men who had not volunteered as the only ones not effectively conscripted.

The attested married men's by-election advocates could only really campaign for 'compulsion all round'. But that would not gather to their banner the single men or the unattested married men and, indeed, would represent something of a pyrrhic victory for themselves. It was not an attractive basis on which to campaign and consequently the august Thomas Gibson Bowles was seen off as was, with a little more difficulty, another enthusiastic Henry Houston-led campaign in Hyde.

But Billing was able to play his part in the next by-elections, in **Wimbledon** (Apr. 1916) and **Tewkesbury** (May 1916). The first of these saw a very close-run contest, where much more Machiavellian and committed Coalition campaigning proved just sufficient to defeat a highly credible opponent. Had the campaign been a few days longer, or the constituency a few square miles smaller, then another government defeat would certainly have been the outcome. The Coalition campaign in Wimbledon was devious; hiding a peerage until the very last minute, imposing the fastest-ever campaign in a county seat (and, what's more, in the division with the second largest electorate in the country); and getting its candidate's election address to the printer three days before the vacancy was made public. It was also massively resourced with an estimated 800 people involved in canvassing. But such tactics were needed as the government faced an almost perfect storm formed by an impressive opponent in Kennedy Jones (so impressive, he was to be returned unopposed, now as an official Coalition candidate, at another by-election later in the year), working in harness with 'the man of the moment' in Billing and enjoying full backing from the Northcliffe newspapers. Perhaps it was no surprise that the government escaped with a majority of less than 2,000 in a poll of over 16,000.

However, relief was at hand for Asquith in the shape of the vestiges of feudalism in the British countryside. It was his clear good luck that the next contest was in Tewkesbury, the bastion of the Hicks-Beach family. Even here, Lord Northcliffe was pressing hard for a result to 'ginger' the government, and the independent candidate, William Boosey, later revealed that Northcliffe personally had asked him to stand. But this was far too great a mountain to climb; a Hicks-Beach candidate in a seat where no Hicks-Beach had been defeated since the seventeenth century was invulnerable. Geography was also important. Unlike Mile End, East Hertfordshire and Wimbledon, the threat from the air was purely theoretical in rural Gloucestershire. Denied that issue, Boosey was still given some topical ammunition with the disastrous fall of Kut and the rebellion in Ireland. But it was never going to be enough. The lack of saliency of the air issue also meant that Billing was less effective as a campaigning force; he brought some excitement to the campaign but departed, according to the Liberal organisers, as a 'failed rocket'.

Thinking the unthinkable

Autumn 1916 saw the first attempt to use the publicity opportunities of a parliamentary by-election to suggest exploring whether a negotiated settlement to the war could be reached. This opening peace-by-negotiation campaign was a free-lance effort by a minor figure. There were a few, small organisations in the country, religious and political, willing to challenge the martial orthodoxy. None of them had yet deemed the time right to put such views to an electoral test. However, at **North Ayrshire** (Oct. 1916), an effort was made. A Baptist Minister from London, albeit one with Scottish connections, was not well-placed to make an impact in a brief election campaign north of the border. The candidate, Humphrey Chalmers, was on the periphery of peace movements but not a major figure; and he supported the economic policies of the left but was not a member of any of the socialist groups. Consequently, he ran an under-powered, individual campaign. By offering a portmanteau of policies, in addition to advocating exploring negotiations, he tried to draw together malcontents of all types. But his ideas about negotiations were either naïve or disingenuous; Germany would never agree to discussions on 'minimum terms' that included 'very full satisfaction of all the wrongs done to Belgium' and 'the restoration to France of Alsace and Lorraine' alongside 'the reconstruction of the damaged parts of France' and multiple other requirements. If there was any surprise in the outcome, it was probably that he attracted as much as 15 per cent of the vote.

The next peace-by-negotiation effort was of a very different nature and scale. The campaign in **Rossendale** (Feb. 1917) took place in changed circumstances. Most importantly, Asquith had now been jettisoned for David Lloyd George, making a move toward peace even less likely unless pressure could be applied. Yet, the raising of the prospect of 'peace without victor or vanquished' by President Woodrow Wilson and Lloyd George's action in finally spelling out war aims increased the saliency of questioning how and on what terms the war might end. At the same time, war weariness was growing, and the military news was disappointing. The candidate in Rossendale, Albert Taylor, was much better placed than Chalmers to raise the banner. He was a popular local trade union leader who had stood firm for his own rights as a conscientious objector. Being imprisoned on the initiative of his Liberal opponent's agent (who was also the local Recruiting Officer) undoubtedly helped his campaign which was, in any case, a far more professional one than anything Chalmers could sustain. Taylor received strong support from key figures linked to the UDC and his main campaign organiser was Charles Roden Buxton. The outcome was almost a quarter of the vote being cast for a candidate advocating negotiations.

Yet, if Rossendale cheered the advocates of a negotiated peace, the next two elections, just weeks later in **Stockton-on-Tees** (Mar. 1917) and then **South Aberdeen** (Apr. 1917) would bring them firmly down to earth. The mood had changed once more, and the 'peace' campaigns had flattered only to deceive. In Stockton, a well-regarded local Liberal and Quaker candidate, Edward Backhouse, also supported by the Union of Democratic Control and other campaigners and resources from outside, fell to a crushing defeat, polling only seven per cent. Excuses were made that the area had a strong armaments industry and that the local ILP was weak, but the 'peace' vote was derisory despite a well-resourced campaign. By now, expectation was growing that the United States would soon enter the war and perhaps the memories of the massive casualties of 1916 were fading while the 1917 campaign season was yet to begin. For whatever reason, it was a chastening experience. And South Aberdeen only confirmed the trend. Here, the peace campaigners had a celebrity candidate who had no problem in funding and running a strong campaign. A former Liberal, Frederick Pethick-Lawrence had married a suffragette campaigner and become a committed socialist. He was able to run a high-profile campaign but had walked into a complex political scenario. The local Liberals were divided and eventually selected an Asquith rather than a Lloyd George supporter as the 'official' candidate. A Lloyd George stalwart was dissuaded from splitting the vote but there was still a 'hyper-patriotic' third entrant who claimed to be a more appropriate representative of the Lloyd George government than the official Liberal nominee.

Pethick-Lawrence out-campaigned the other two candidates and he certainly did not try to sweeten the pill of his pro-negotiations standpoint as he called in speakers as provocative as Ramsay MacDonald and Charles Roden Buxton. His reward was a highly hostile welcome with meetings being besieged and broken up. The outcome was another shattering rejection for 'peace-by-negotiation' with Pethick-Lawrence securing only seven per cent and being outpolled more than four times even by the unofficial patriot. Again, the chastened campaigners cast around for explanations and excuses. It was likely that some who might have been tempted to vote for Pethick-Lawrence backed the Liberal, out of fear that he could be outflanked by the patriotic independent. But that was whistling in the wind. The reality was, now proven by multiple electoral contests, that however badly the war might be going, and however tough life was becoming on the home front, still the resolve of the British public to 'fight to the finish' was holding.

A mixture of emotions
The remaining notable by-elections of 1917 reflected a range of issues and attitudes but support for the war held in each of them. **Abercromby** (Jun. 1917) was born out of criticism of the government, but was in no way a call for less military effort. It reflected a full acceptance on the part of the electors of

the country's obligation to carry on the struggle. The complaint was simply that volunteers and conscripts needed to be treated properly in doing so. This was not a threat to withdraw backing for the war, but rather a demand for 'fair' treatment. The veterans' protest was not sustained for long because the government realised it had to respond; better support for the victims of war would ensure continued backing from the wider population.

Next was a purely local journey back into the realms of 'peace-by-negotiation' but again one that was rebuffed. Nothing would stop Edwin Scrymgeour from essaying his fourth campaign against Churchill in **Dundee** (July 1917) and he had most definitely added opposition to the war to his previous armoury of uncompromising support for prohibition. His experience was very different to that of Backhouse and Pethick-Lawrence. He achieved a respectable increase in his vote from six per cent in 1910 (in a two-member contest) to just less than a quarter this time. Also, he did not suffer any substantial assaults, either verbal or physical, to match those experienced elsewhere. Instead, like Taylor in Rossendale, a local champion was at least granted a hearing, even if a very clear majority still had no interest in the 'peace-by-negotiation' message.

In contrast, the next by-election saw an attack on the government from the opposite flank. Now an increasingly strident Pemberton-Billing returned, starting with his running a candidate in **East Islington** (Oct. 1917). His main policy was still that of the air war which was again high on the agenda of Londoners after a raid in July 1917 that had resulted in the deaths of 18 young children at the Upper North School in Poplar. Billing aggressively argued that the government was doing too little to wage the war. But he added to this a leavening of conspiracy theories, leading to his declared mission to 'purify politics'. This was an attack on alleged corruption among the leading politicians of the main parties. However, he was not to have this ground to himself as this by-election also saw the first electoral outing of Henry Page-Croft's National Party which offered a high-octane mix of tariff reform, anti-German extremism and a concentrated attack on corruption, particularly 'honours-mongering'. Allegations of corruption in high places were being used as an explanation, or excuse, for why Britain was failing to impose its superiority over Germany. Yet, despite an air-raid on London during the campaign, the Coalition held on although Pemberton-Billing's continued high profile meant that his candidate outpolled the new National Party by three to one.

The success of Ben Tillett at **North Salford** (Nov. 1917) just over a week later was another example of how popular calls were for more war rather than less. Tillett did not succeed so much because he was a dockers' union leader but because he was a recognised, dominant 'patriotic' figure. Offered the chance to back such a charismatic advocate of total war and reprisals, the electors were easily prised away from endorsing the dull establishment candidate offered by the Liberals.

1918 – cracks in the political truce and hysteria about enemy aliens

In the fevered times of 1918 and amid very real fears of defeat due to the German Spring offensive, calls for ever-harsher treatment of 'aliens' flourished. Yet, in the same period, elections were also being fought by renegade labour movement candidates who were finding the truce ever more irksome. True, the Labour Party had been brought into government, but this was felt by many activists to be only on sufferance. But if their internal 'patriotic' versus 'internationalist' split was to be healed, ready for the return of peacetime politics, then the party was going to need more freedom than being tied to the Liberals and Unionists currently allowed. Ironically, it was Labour's partners in government who acted as the catalyst for change. Initially, Lloyd George was supportive of the idea of Henderson attending the Stockholm international conference of socialists while the Labour leader himself was unsure. But then, in a significant volte-face, while Henderson became convinced of the idea his government colleagues went cold on it. The 'doormat incident' of August 1917 followed in which Henderson was excluded from a meeting of the War Cabinet while his colleagues discussed whether he should be allowed to go to Stockholm. This so offended Henderson that he resigned from Cabinet in a move which was to open the way for increasing reconciliation within the Labour Party and its growing preparedness for the end of the political truce. In many ways, Henderson achieved the best of all worlds. He left government and was able to devote his considerable skills to preparing Labour for peacetime politics while the Labour party still enjoyed the kudos of sitting at the top table.

The four by-elections after North Salford, namely Prestwich, Keighley, Wansbeck and Gravesend all featured candidates with links to the labour movement that, despite remaining loyal to the truce, Labour had been unable to control. In **Prestwich** (Jan. 1918), the local Labour party had been keen to stand. It was thwarted as its preferred candidate declined to do so because he did feel bound by the truce. But many local Labour forces took the indirect opportunity to oppose the Coalition that was provided by the locally strong Co-operative movement's decision to enter electoral politics for the first time. **Keighley** (Apr. 1918) was an even more blatant breach of the truce and marked a final sortie by the peace-by-negotiation forces. William Bland's candidature was officially as a representative of the ILP and a few Labour MPs, such as Snowden, took an active role in the election.

By this point, whether you believed the war was going badly or well, it was easy to adduce arguments in opposition to the quest for peace-by-negotiations. If you thought it was going badly, and the major German offensive had not yet been broken, then Brest-Litovsk, the harsh peace treaty imposed on the Russians, suggested hoping for mild terms from the Germans was a pipe dream. If you thought it was going well, the near-fatal submarine war of the previous year was being turned round, rationing was proving effective, and the Americans were, at last, arriving in numbers, why offer negotiations when total victory might be in sight? But, regardless of immediate circumstances, the ILP branch in Keighley was keen to build on its position. So, theirs was a campaign that embraced peace-by-negotiation, but in a wider context of arguing for socialist policies and working-class representation. The national 'peace-by-negotiation' stalwarts (such as Snowden – who started his political career in the town - Jowett and Ponsonby) came piling in to back a local candidate who had stood for the seat previously in a 1913 by-election. The election was difficult for hardline 'patriotic' voters since the 'official' candidate was an Asquithian Liberal who hinted at some sympathy with the pro-negotiators. It is unclear whether that helped the ILP candidate Bland (due to 'bitter enders' staying at home) or hindered him (due to some with sympathy for negotiations deciding the Liberal was an acceptable choice). Either way, the ILP took a third of the vote, a further example of a well-established local candidate (like Taylor and Scrymgeour) significantly out-performing those who had only their support for negotiations to rely on (such as Chalmers, Pethick-Lawrence and Backhouse).

Those campaigning for 'peace-by-negotiation' were principled men but they never won the electoral support of more than a small minority of a public more inclined to complain about too little war, rather than too much. Indeed, the surprising truth is that there was more (secret) questioning within the governing elite about whether 'the fight to the finish' was truly a viable policy than ever there was among the public.[2] Nevertheless, in public, Lloyd George's administration trumpeted its unwavering commitment and certainty in ultimate success; the public followed him, and the British home front never wavered.

Wansbeck (May 1918) then confirmed the ever-growing problem of trying to hold labour in the country, if not Labour in parliament, to the political truce. Here the movement faced an impossible choice, believing both that the seat should be in the gift of the miners and that, to abide by the truce, the Liberals should be given a free run. The Liberals chose not to help Labour (nor themselves in the long run) by selecting a miners' candidate of their own, favouring a ship broker instead. The Labour national executive urged commitment to the truce but the Miners Federation of Great Britain called on the local Labour Representation Committee to select and run a miner. They got their way and, to compound the resulting confusion, the chosen candidate, Ebenezer Edwards, was widely known as a pacifist (although he prevaricated somewhat on this during the campaign). The outcome was an extremely narrow win for the coalition, but also a growing realisation that Labour needed to cut its apron-strings to Lloyd George (and the Unionists) to prepare for success in the peacetime politics to follow. Beyond doubt, Edwards' strong performance reflected that he was a miner and was achieved despite his 'dubious' position on the war.

Less than two weeks later came polling day in **Gravesend** (June 1918). Yet again, despite official Labour adherence to the truce, another renegade claiming labour allegiance entered the lists. To be fair, this candidate, Harry Hinkley, was even more unofficial than most. He was the local chairman of

---

2 See the analysis in B Millman, Pessimism and British War Policy 1916 – 1918 (2001) which reveals serious doubts among much of the military and government regarding whether a final victory could be achieved.

the British Workers League and so standing on an ultra-patriotic platform. The League had agreed to abide by the truce, but Hinkley was having none of it.

Faced with unruly individuals from both wings, patriotic and peace-by-negotiation, the Labour top brass decided they could hold the line no longer. On the very day of polling in Gravesend, the formal decision to withdraw from the truce was taken. Henderson had already devoted the time since his resignation from government to the task of building up Labour as a realistic challenger in the General Election, whenever it came. Now, the party had the freedom, should it so choose, to run candidates at any future by-election as well. So, it is ironic that from then until the end of the war not only were there no official Labour candidates, but there were also no more irregulars either. But possibly that is not surprising. While the war continued, Labour remained at least as divided (Patriotic or Peace-by-Negotiation) as the Liberals (Lloyd George or Asquith) and there was little point risking internal dissension for the sake of single seats potentially only months before a nationwide election.

Consequently, the final two contested by-elections of the war were untroubled by unofficial (or official) Labour candidates, and, in a final flurry, Billing was given a platform to raise ever more extreme paranoia. Against the background of the genuinely frightening German offensive of Spring 1918, and with war-weariness at its height, public xenophobia was reaching an aggressive peak – one which Billing (and others) were only too willing to stimulate and exploit. **Clapham** (Jun. 1918) became vacant the day before Billing's remarkable acquittal at the Old Bailey where jurors were persuaded to find him not guilty of criminal libel for his claim, among other claims, that both Asquith and his wife, Margot, were on a list of 47,000 establishment figures being blackmailed by the Germans. Billing's candidate's only platform was a demand for ever stronger action against enemy aliens in the country, including that any allowed to retain their freedom rather than being interned or repatriated should be forced to wear a lapel badge indicating their nationality of origin. The election was held as public opinion about these aliens was reaching fever-pitch. Anxiety about the German offensive was compounded by concern over 'the enemy within' and demonstrations were held calling for ever more extreme action against such aliens. Billing's candidate claimed his special policy was to 'intern every German in the country, denaturalise every German and to deport the brute'. It was insufficient to win but, as in several other elections, the Coalition was forced to echo the Independent's call with their candidate summarising his own position as "Win the war, Intern all enemy aliens'. On the back of the hysteria, Billing came within 1,200 votes of another famous victory. More importantly, in response to the scare, Lloyd George again ratcheted up government policy by appointing a carefully selected committee designed to recommend harsher policies. The subsequent Dalziel report stimulated more aggressive action by government, leading to further people being interned or recommended for repatriation.

The final contested by-election of the war followed less than a month later in **East Finsbury** (July 1918). Once more there was a Billing candidate, but the militant challenge was split as another independent patriotic candidate also came forward. Both campaigned exclusively on the aliens' issue. The government had not yet formally accepted the recommendations of the Dalziel report and so the issue remained unresolved. The alternative patriotic candidate was heavily backed by Havelock Wilson's Seamen's Union and, like Billing, was campaigning for greater internment of aliens and the closure of all foreign-owned businesses. This last election of the war was concluded in a fevered atmosphere. Mass meetings were held demanding harsh sanctions against aliens and the two guerilla campaigns turned violently against each other on the eve of poll. The split 'intern them all' forces managed to poll 40 per cent between them as, once more, the Coalition held on in part by again stealing their opponents' political clothes.

But this marked the end of rebel candidacies at by-elections. There were to be a further nine vacancies before the Armistice, but none of them attracted a non-government candidate. Instead, there was a growing recognition that the German offensive had blown itself out and that, with American forces at the front now giving the Allies a clear numerical superiority, the hope of victory (if not necessarily in 1918) was increasing. Attention in the labour movement was switching to preparing for politics after the peace while, with war weariness largely replaced by confidence in victory, the other campaigning issues (such as aliens, air defence, etc.) were no longer as potent as before.

Even in the darkest hours, the Home Front held

What emerges from these by-elections is a home front population that was stoically supportive of the country in its struggle. Candidates who had a tinge (or more) of pacifism were generally roundly defeated; the only ones who attracted respectable vote shares were those who were also well-established local trades union or community campaigners. That sub-group allowed some conduit for the expression of annoyance at economic privations. But it is interesting that no candidates emerged who sought to fight exclusively on the economic issues facing the working class. That reflects three points. Firstly, economic groups were impacted differently by the switch to a wartime economy. Inflation certainly hit some very hard, but the increase in demand and workforce shortages also benefitted others through sizeable pay increases. Secondly, the war followed the industrially turbulent years of 1911-14. In those, the trades unions had demonstrated significant economic power and, patriotism or not, they were willing, in extremis, to continue to use that power during the conflict; the economic channel was more potent than the political one. Thirdly, the labour movement's parliamentary structure was very successfully co-opted by the other two parties; at last, Labour was invited to the top table and its parliamentary leaders did not want to jeopardise that achievement.

Thus, the British civilians of the First World War did not buckle in their support, due to economic privation or pacifist principle or even, as the going got tough and the years dragged on, from a loss of will, or an assessment that a negotiated peace would yield a better return than carrying on to a bitter end. In that last point they were more realistic than the idealists of the Union of Democratic Control; none of the outline suggestions for terms on which to speak to the Germans came anywhere near what might have been accepted by them as a basis for talks. And very few were they who were prepared to adopt the socialist concept of the solidarity of the international proletariat in place of the innate patriotism of the British working man. In that resilience they were, arguably, more iron-willed than their political and military rulers, some of whom lost confidence in the certainty of victory. When given their voice in by-elections, the public overwhelmingly supported candidates who wanted the government to go further and to fight harder.

What also emerges is that these by-elections mattered. The government cared about the outcomes. Indeed, they did so sufficiently that they were willing, where necessary, to indulge in procedural dirty tricks to fend off defeat. They were also willing, frequently, to co-opt their opponents' policies to nullify the attacks. They cared for several reasons. Politics were in abeyance. Parliament was quite often in recess and the scope it offered for opposition was greatly reduced by the large number of MPs (especially Unionists) who were away at the front. So, a contested by-election provided one of the few chances to gauge (or influence) domestic opinion. The universal cry of the government candidates that the results would be monitored in Berlin and amongst the allies, was true. Also, in a time of very considerable censorship (and self-censorship) a poor election result was something that could not be controlled and would be known about across the country (It is notable that local newspapers throughout the land carried reports from the by-elections, even from those held hundreds of miles away).

A glimpse of the political future?

How far were these by-elections a foretaste of the shape of politics to come? The 1918 general election was to continue the trend of strong support for 'patriotic' candidates and a shunning of those who had had any truck with pacifism or negotiation. That was the dominant pattern in the wartime by-elections. Yet, this tide was to turn quickly and the rise of the Labour party in the 1920s did not differentiate between candidates from different wings of the movement – in part, reflecting Labour's greater effectiveness in putting aside its wartime divisions than was achieved by the Liberals. In that respect, the 'predictive' power of the by-elections was short-lived.

But what did continue were the weaknesses in the Liberal party and the trends that emerged in the wartime by-elections became inexorable. Some key Liberals moved to Labour, often via the Union of Democratic Control. Some were encouraged out through opposition from Liberal constituency organisations to their hesitancy (or stronger) to back the conflict. Thus, a figure such as Arthur Ponsonby found himself campaigning for candidates against official Liberals; Edward Backhouse, an august Liberal (and Quaker) figure, stood against his own party. And the Liberals failed to recognise the trend of the time with the working class wanting to be offered 'one of their own' as the candidate in strongly working-class areas. The world was changing but the Liberal establishment was not changing with it – a problem that would grow with the increase in the working-class electorate brought about by the 1918 Representation of the People Act, combined with ever-greater Labour political organisation. Moreover, the internal divisions between the Asquith and Lloyd George wings severely impacted the party, evidenced by divisions regarding candidate selection in these elections even prior to the cataclysmic damage inflicted by the Coupon general election.

The contrast between Liberal and Labour is very clear. Labour, despite real ideological differences, managed to present itself in the 1918 election as a united force that was gathering strength. The Liberals had already lost important men during and because of the war and was now formally divided into warring camps. Some signs of the forthcoming 1945 Labour victory were there to be seen in the by-elections of the second world war; likewise, the sorry future fate of the Liberals can be discerned in the relevant electoral contests of 1915 to 1918.

The first world war by-elections are not a psephological goldmine; they are far too quirky and abnormal for that. But some clues are present as to how peacetime politics would develop. Even more, they offer a fascinating insight into the attitudes and morale of those on the home front during the conflict. A few citizens, out of principle or ideology, opposed the war, but they were always a small minority. Some took time to adapt to the privations and restrictions on 'traditional' liberties, but the great majority did not. As the war ebbed and flowed, some in the civilian ranks occasionally wavered, but never for long. A few, especially at times of real strain, fell prey to near hysteria. But the overwhelming majority remained not only supportive of the country's policy of fighting to the end, but also keen to see the commitment strengthened, not weakened. The country supported 'carrying on' but, far from being content with 'keeping calm', a clear majority wanted more war not less. In these by-elections, they elected Stanton, Pemberton-Billing, Churchill and Tillett and they rejected Winstone, Taylor, Backhouse and Pethick-Lawrence. The contrast with the German home front which, ironically, was far more damaged by the 'porous' blockade than Gibson Bowles realised, was considerable. Consequently, there was no 'stab in the back' for the British military, electorally or otherwise.

APPENDIX

Brief details are provided of the contested by-elections that are not covered in the substantive chapters; generally, these feature quixotic individuals or were fought on lesser policy issues.

Glasgow Central – 16 July 1915

In line with the party truce, the first twenty-one wartime by-elections in Great Britain were uncontested; Glasgow Central was the twenty-second and featured a late, surprise announcement of a second candidate. The vacancy arose due to Unionist MP, Thomas Scott Dickson, being appointed a judge. The local Liberals happily stood by the truce, and the Unionist Association unanimously selected John MacLeod, an accountant who was chairman of the local Recruiting Committee. That, it was assumed, was that. The writ was issued on 8 July and nominations were set for 13 July with polling, if necessary, to be three days later.

Then, entirely unexpectedly, a rival Unionist came forward. This was Gavin Ralston, who had fought West Fife unsuccessfully in 1900 and 1910. A native of Glasgow he was a barrister at the Inner Temple. He explained his decision by saying that he had no personal objection to MacLeod but alleged that the selection committee had deliberately held back all the names of applicants (including his) except for two with the result that the Association had been unable to make a fair selection.

Ralston's decision required a rethink by the Unionists who had not planned any meetings in the expectation of a walk-over. They rapidly arranged to campaign, as did Ralston. MacLeod began with a pleasant lunch at the Liberal Club and afterwards addressed a meeting in the smoking room. Both the Liberals and official Unionists regretted that the truce had been broken. Ralston's first public meeting was poorly attended and had no chairman; he apologised for not having had time to secure one. Both candidates pledged full support to the government in fighting the war and Ralston's 'campaign' was recognised as purely personal; he claimed that MacLeod was barred from being an MP as he held an office under the crown, but in saying that he was in error.

One brief scare for the official campaign was that the Irish Nationalists in the division, numbering around 2,000, threatened to support Ralston in protest at evictions in Belfast of soldiers' families; however, a telegram from Thomas O'Connor instructed them to remain neutral. Polling was muted, in part because the election fell on a local holiday, but MacLeod's campaign was bolstered by the Liberals who issued posters backing him. The result, a foregone conclusion, was a massive victory for the official candidate:

Dec. 1910			
Dickson	Conservative	6,888	54%
Murison	Liberal	5,907	46%
Majority		981	
Electorate & Turnout		14,809	86%

16 Jul. 1915			
MacLeod	Unionist	5,341	95%
Ralston	Independent Unionist	266	5%
Majority		5,075	
Electorate & Turnout		17,632	32%

A letter from MacLeod's daughter revealed what it had been like for her father. She noted his minor inconveniences: 'Imagine him getting up at 7.30am to make speeches at the dock gates. His sacred second cup of coffee had to go to the wall that day!' At the 1918 election he was elected at Glasgow Kelvingrove. Ralston was to die, suddenly, in 1924. The nature of the man is reflected in his obituary from *Motor Sport* magazine which recorded that he had been a keen member of the Royal Automobile Club in London's Pall Mall and notable for how he had cross-examined the officials at the recent AGM about the strict interpretation of the rules regarding the serving of refreshments late at night; the magazine summarised him as 'a great stickler for exact interpretations'.

Berwick – 16 August 1916

Berwick was the second by-election fought by the quixotic Dr Arthur Turnbul[1]. A doctor and surgeon who served in the Royal Army Medical Corps, he had already achieved notoriety when, on 29 March 1916, he dramatically entered the House of Commons by jumping from the Strangers gallery, in protest against poor protection for British troops from shrapnel. He subsequently wrote to *The Times* to apologise for his behaviour but noted that the government had now promised to increase the rate of supply of helmets.

Turnbull then established the National Union Covenant. He held meetings around the country, giving a 'patriotic address' entitled: 'The Allies' terms of peace to the Kaiser' and calling for a new and representative Parliament to be elected which would have the authority to pursue the war vigorously. Overall, Turnbull was arguing for a shortened war and putting clear peace terms to the Germans from the perspective that a new parliamentary mandate would allow Britain to fight the war harder and more efficiently. He anticipated that faced with the knowledge of British unity and determination, Germany would accept terms more rapidly. By mid-1916, he was cooperating with Horatio Bottomley and an advertisement for the National Union Covenant (calling on people to subscribe at a cost of one shilling) appeared in Bottomley's magazine, *John Bull*. The 'covenant', as well as reiterating Turnbull's call for a new parliament that could outline terms to the Germans, also called for

---

1 The first, in which he made negligible impact, was an Irish by-election in South Londonderry in May 1916.

an efficient government organisation, echoing Bottomley's campaigns for a government run on business principles.

Immediately after the *John Bull* advertisement, Turnbull stood as a 'national and non-political' candidate for the Berwick by-election. He was backed by Bottomley and Henry Houston was appointed his agent. During the campaign, Turnbull received a letter of support from Noel Pemberton-Billing. His election address called for a mandate regarding the war from every adult over the age of twenty-one through a new election; a clear statement of the terms of settlement upon which the British Government would be prepared to negotiate and the cessation of what he called ' faddist' legislation on the Drink question.

Despite Bottomley's assistance, Turnbull had little impact gaining only 621 votes (14 per cent). Francis Blake went on to hold the seat at the 1918 General Election but stood down in 1922.

Dec. 1910			
Grey	Liberal	4,612	61%
Hoare	Conservative	2,962	39%
Majority		1,686	
Electorate & Turnout		9,445	80%

16 Aug. 1916			
Blake	Liberal	3,794	86%
Turnbull	Independent	621	14%
Majority		3,173	
Electorate & Turnout		9,454	47%

Mansfield – 20 September 1916

Turnbull's final outing was at the Mansfield by-election and here he had more impact, although he was still unsuccessful. The by-election followed the death of the Liberal MP, Sir Arthur Markham who, although one of the most prominent mine owners in the country, was immensely popular with the Mansfield and Chesterfield miners. Markham had further increased his popularity by being robustly in favour of the strongest possible prosecution of the war. In that role, he had been a regular thorn in the side of the Coalition government, for which he sometimes fell victim to Asquith's reposts. On one occasion Markham asked if it was really necessary for the Coalition government to employ eight Whips given that 'the House of Commons will do exactly what the Prime Minister wants it to'. Asquith responded: 'My hon. Friend takes an unduly sanguine view. I fear his, for the moment, is a counsel of perfection.' In something of a surprise, however, the local Liberal association did not adopt a candidate likely to be particularly attractive to the miners, but rather chose a former Liberal Unionist, Sir Charles Seely. Turnbull's intervention was again unanticipated until he arrived in the constituency supported, as previously, by Houston. In his initial statements he stressed he would be emphasising the issue of high food prices, and the *Nottingham Evening Post* noted: 'Dr. Turnbull holds that the same pressure of public opinion which was necessary to obtain an adequate supply of munitions will be needed to effect a reduction in the price of food.'[2]

Bottomley arrived early in the campaign and stressed that a vote for Turnbull would be 'a message of encouragement to the men fighting in the trenches'. He was to be the dominant element of Turnbull's efforts, speaking nine times. Turnbull claimed that he was like Markham, in that he would not stand idly by if there were problems but would act to deal with them. Against this, Seely announced that he was standing 'as a supporter of the present government' and, specifically on the issue of high food prices, he argued that 'Government interference with prices invariably produced a result opposite to that aimed at'.[3]

Towards the end of the campaign, Seely drew attention to some of the positions Turnbull had adopted at Berwick. He attacked him for having said that 'as the war will entail the loss of a million more lives, and we shall not succeed in driving the Germans across the Rhine, the war should cease forthwith' and contrasted this with the Turnbull posters in Mansfield which

---

2 *Nottingham Evening Post*, 4 September 1916.
3 *Nottingham Evening Post*, 13 September 1916.

read 'Vote for Turnbull and no patched-up peace.'[4] The outcome was that Turnbull polled a surprising 4,456 votes (37 per cent) leaving Seely with a majority of just over 3,000.

Dec. 1910			
Markham	Liberal	11,383	73%
Cockerill	Conservative	4,200	27%
Majority		7,183	
Electorate & Turnout		19,752	74%

20 Sep. 1916			
Seely	Liberal	7,597	63%
Turnbull	Independent	4,456	37%
Majority		3,141	
Electorate & Turnout		24,749	49%

Press analysis expressed surprise at how well Turnbull had done with most interpreting his vote as a protest mainly against increasing food prices. Seely's own assessment was that

> 'our opponents polled every dissatisfied man from one end of the constituency to the other—every man who was dissatisfied with the Government for what it had done, dissatisfied for what it had left undone, every man dissatisfied with the Liberal and Conservative parties, and every man who had a grudge against the leaders of the Labour party.'[5]

The Evening Despatch identified: 'The reasons are that he made a great point of the high prices of food, and his cry was 'Cheap food for the people.' He also

---

4 Quoted from the *Berwick Advertiser*, 18 August 1916 in the *Nottinghamshire Evening Post*, 18 September 1916.
5 *Nottingham Evening Post*, 21 September 1916.

severely criticised the delay in giving adequate pensions to wounded men and allowances to soldiers' widows.'[6]

Seely was to stand at the 1918 General Election for Broxtowe but was heavily defeated by Labour. He did not stand for parliament again. Turnbull returned to a medical career in Scotland.

Winchester – 19 October 1916

The vacancy at Winchester arose in September 1916 following the death on active service of the sitting Unionist MP, Col. Guy V. Baring. He died at the battle of the Somme where he was a Lieutenant-Colonel in the Coldstream Guards.

The Coalition candidate chosen was Major Douglas Carnegie, son of the 9th Earl of Northesk, who lived locally and had connections to Winchester. According to the *Portsmouth Evening News*: 'Like his predecessor, Major Carnegie comes of an ancient family, members of which in their successive generations have served the State with distinction, the family arms bearing the word Trafalgar, commemorating the fact that the seventh Earl fought with Nelson at Trafalgar.'[7]

Politically, he was a supporter of the Tariff Reform League and, in August 1917, would join the short-lived National Party headed by Sir Henry Page Croft. Just a couple of days after Carnegie had been selected the unexpected announcement came that there would be a contest. His opponent would be Charles Woods who was described in the press as having travelled widely, especially in the Balkans and Turkey, and to be the author of several books on military and diplomatic subjects.

The *Liverpool Echo* summarised Woods' programme:

> *'He stated that he owed allegiance to no party; he is standing on grounds of public policy, and not for the purpose of agitation. He is prepared to support any Administration which subordinates political expediency to the great national interests and works wholeheartedly for the successful termination of the war. He*

---

6 *Evening Despatch*, 22 September 1916.
7 *Portsmouth Evening News*, 7 October 1916.

favours the British Empire for the British people, more stringent treatment of all enemy aliens, and the taking of the people into the confidence of the Government.'[8]

Woods' election address mentioned several additional policies. He called for a full (and, as far as possible, public) investigation into blunders made by the government, including the Dardanelles and Mesopotamia; opposition to the 'dumping' of enemy labour and goods in the country after the war; reform of naval and military pensions; opposition to 'unjustified secrecy, as being an insult to the intelligence of a self-governing people'; and opposition to leniency to enemy aliens and the official employment of persons with enemy blood and enemy connections.

Specifically, about drink restrictions, he stated: 'I am opposed to the present system of restricting the sale of drink, and I am in favour of any necessary restrictions being under the control of the local Licensing Authority, and not of a Board which has no connection with the district and which is not directly controlled by Parliament.'[9]

The election attracted little attention but was notable for Woods' curious approach to campaigning. According to the *Liverpool Daily Post*: 'Instead of the usual stump oratory he has entertained his constituency with a series of twelve lectures. Yesterday, he lectured on 'Constantinople as I saw it' and before that on 'The Dardanelles', with Sir Martin Conway, the celebrated Alpinist, in the chair.'[10]

The *Liverpool Daily Post* painted a humorous picture of how this approach might be developed:

> *'The elections of the future, if the lead of the Independent candidate is followed, offer possibilities of such entertainment that we can foresee general elections becoming popular pastimes. What an attraction would a lantern lecture by Mr. Asquith prove, upon, say, 'Things I could tell', with Mr. Bottomley in the chair: or still more popular we think would be Mr. Lloyd George on 'Peeps at the Paris Conference' with Mr. Trevelyan as chairman. Then there would certainly be a following, in a few constituencies, for Mr. Snowden on 'The Development of*

---

8 *Liverpool Echo*, 9 October 1916.
9 Copy available at University of Bristol Library, Special Collections
10 *Liverpool Daily Post*, 19 October 1916.

Conscience', illustrated by objectors in prison costume. Apart from war topics the subjects would be extensive. Mr Churchill might lecture on 'Unobtrusiveness', Mr. Balfour on 'The Art of Plain Speaking' and Sir Edward Carson on 'The Cult of Gentleness'.[11]

After a low-key campaign the result did not come as a surprise. *The Globe* said 'Polling opened at Winchester to-day very quietly, with scarcely any outward signs except that the supporters of Major Carnegie (the Coalition candidate) were wearing photographic buttons'[12] while the Dundee Courier added: 'The Winchester bye-election concluded in the same way as it began – in profound dullness. Working-men paid more attention to their late potato-digging. Consequently, the rival parties sent motors to the allotments to bring men to the poll'[13]

Dec. 1910			
Baring	Conservative	1,719	60%
Ricketts	Liberal	1,121	40%
Majority		598	
Electorate & Turnout		3,202	89%

19 Oct. 1916			
Carnegie	Conservative	1,218	72%
Woods	Independent	473	28%
Majority		745	
Electorate & Turnout		3,515	48%

Despite the eccentric nature of Woods' campaign, he managed to secure more than a quarter of the vote, revealing some discontent with the progress of the

---

11 Ibid.
12 *The Globe*, 19 October 1916.
13 *Dundee Courier*, 20 October 1916.

war and the performance of the government. However, one observer put this down to committed campaigning by the independent and complacency on the part of government supporters: 'The poll was a small one; a great many citizens contenting themselves with the belief that the Government champion was safe. Had the Ministerialists worked as indefatigably as the Independents, Major Carnegie would have had a great many more votes to the good.'[14]

Shortly after the election, Woods was again in the news. He had been a Lieutenant in the Grenadier Guards and had served in the Boer War. However, in 1907, in a very public case, he had appealed against a decision that he was not capable of operating as an officer. Woods claimed that the decision was unfair and stemmed from antipathy towards him among his fellow officers as he studied too hard. Despite a strong fight by Woods, the Army Court of Inquiry found that he: 'is inefficient as a regimental officer, and that his retention in the service is not in the interests of the Army'.[15] He resigned his commission under protest and his father wrote a letter of complaint to every MP.

This event became relevant when in June 1916 Woods was conscripted as a Private. He refused to join up and was charged under the Military Service Act. He argued that he should be exempt as he was a retired officer. The case caused great interest in the press. A magistrate decided that the charge had been proved but refused by reason of the nature of the case and the high attainments of the appellant to impose any penalty or even to convict. The case was eventually heard before the Lord Chief Justice who asked the Attorney-General

> 'if the authorities thought that in the circumstances Mr Woods ought to be forced under the Act to serve as a private when he had held a commission in the Guards. Mr Woods only gave up his commission because it was held that notwithstanding his talents, they were not those which really fitted him to be a regimental officer. It was hardly a case in which the authorities should proceed strictly according to law. Could not the matter be dealt with without the Court having to pronounce judgment upon it?'[16]

---

14 *Derby Daily Telegraph*, 20 October 1916.
15 *Gloucestershire Echo*, 10 December 1907
16 *Dundee Evening Telegraph*, 27 October 1917.

In the end the case was adjourned and never heard of again.

Carnegie was to stand down at the General Election and did not seek election again.

South Monmouthshire – 17 July 1917

The sitting MP, Ivor Herbert, was made a peer in June 1917, thereby occasioning the vacancy. There was speculation that his son might be chosen as the replacement Liberal candidate and an alternative suggestion that Herbert had been 'kicked upstairs' to provide a by-election in which Charles Masterman might find his way back into government. Masterman had been appointed as Chancellor of the Duchy of Lancaster early in 1914 but then proceeded to lose the resulting by-election in his Bethnal Green South West constituency and also failed in another attempt in the Ipswich by-election (the last contested election before the war). He was appointed instead as head of the War Propaganda Bureau (Wellington House).

The eventual choice was Sir Garrod Thomas who was preferred over Herbert's son. A contest was triggered by the decision of a local independent, Bertie Pardoe Thomas, to stand. He was a member of the Newport Town Council, an ex-President of the Newport Chamber of Commerce and a shipowner and shipbroker. He stood as an 'Independent Democrat' arguing that parliament should be composed of businessmen. He supported restricting the drink trade with *The Times* describing him as being 'an advocate for the abolition and suppression of the drink traffic and opposed to any state purchase'.

The contest involved several co-incidences; two candidates, both called Thomas, one of whom, Garrod, was a consulting physician for the Royal Gwent Hospital while the other, Bertie, was a director of the same institution. Garrod said that he considered Bertie a friend, but that did not stop him from attacking his opponent's manifesto as 'containing nothing but fault-finding and destructive criticism'.

Garrod Thomas held a few meetings while Pardoe Thomas did not and, since the latter was not well-known in the area, a decisive victory for the official candidate was anticipated and delivered:

	Dec. 1910		
Herbert	Liberal	8,597	56%
Forestier-Walker	Conservative	6,656	44%
Majority		1,941	
Electorate & Turnout		19,134	80%

	17 Jul. 1917		
Thomas	Liberal	6,769	90%
Thomas	Independent Democrat & Businessman	727	10%
Majority		6,042	
Electorate & Turnout		22,991	33%

The successful Garrod Thomas was not to stand again for Parliament, while Bertie Pardoe Thomas ran in the 1918 General Election for Newport, once more as an Independent Democrat, this time polling only 647 votes (2.6 per cent).

South Hereford (Ross) 4 May 1918
This by-election was notable as the first occasion the now ten-year-old National Farmers Union (NFU) backed a candidate. The vacancy arose following the death (in action) of the sitting Conservative (formerly Liberal Unionist) MP, Colonel Percy Clive.

The Unionists rapidly adopted Charles Pulley as their candidate. He was a prominent local landowner with 300 acres and a famous herd of Hereford cattle. His selection disappointed local Alderman Thomas Preece, a retired farmer and chairman of the Herefordshire County Council Agricultural committee. Consequently, Preece accepted a nomination to run on behalf of the Herefordshire NFU which had been angered by the Unionists choosing a candidate without prior discussion with them. Despite a very close result in December 1910, the Liberals agreed not to run and the local LRC did likewise, advising workers to abstain.

The novel policy of running a 'farmers' candidate' attracted interest elsewhere, such as Northumberland, where farmers were considering running a candidate at the general election in Berwick-upon-Tweed. The President of the NFU was supportive, saying that: 'By nominating a Farmers' Union candidate in South Hereford we have laid the foundation of a much larger campaign'.[17]

The NFU claimed that their candidate was leaving party politics aside; his main priority was security of tenure, followed by better wages, housing and social conditions for farm workers. The NFU recognised that electoral success would be impossible unless the entire farming community was united and its President claimed: 'Let it be understood we do not want class legislation, nor want farmers in Parliament merely to watch agricultural interests ... What we want is our representative to fight for justice for all the classes of the country.'[18]

The NFU, whose focus was on the interests of tenant farmers, was strong at the time of the election, claiming that in the past year membership had almost doubled from 30,000. However, the campaign proved too short for the NFU neophytes to make an impact, even though Preece had the support of a Liberal agent imported from the Cotswolds. Consequently, the official candidate recorded a comfortable victory.

Dec. 1910			
Clive	Liberal Unionist	4,748	51%
Webb	Liberal	4,627	49%
Majority		121	
Electorate & Turnout		10,946	86%

---

17 *Newcastle Journal*, 1 May 1918.
18 Ibid.

Appendix

The NFU went on to run six candidates in the 1918 General Election, but none was successful. They then changed tactics and sponsored some Conservative Party candidates, a number of whom were elected in the elections of the 1920s.

4 May 1918			
Pulley	Unionist	3,260	65%
Preece	NFU	1,784	35%
Majority		1,476	
Electorate & Turnout		11,412	44%

ACKNOWLEDGEMENTS

Both as political combatant and observer, I've always loved a good by-election. Some can change the political weather and even those that do not will produce quirks or amusing incidents that stick in the memory. So, I was surprised to discover how sadly neglected were the idiosyncratic elections of the first world war. That encouraged me to investigate them and to bring their fascinating stories to a wider audience.

In turning my inchoate research into this book, I have benefitted from invaluable assistance. Especially, I wish to thank Professor David Dutton, Emeritus Professor of History at Liverpool University, for so generously giving his time to review an early draft. David's knowledge of the politics of the period is immense. He guided me round historical minefields, recommended invaluable additional sources and, gently, pointed out grammatical idiosyncrasies. I also really appreciate Professor Sir John Curtice sacrificing part of his Christmas break (after a particularly busy election year!) to read the book and provide a generous foreword. This is my first sortie into the complex world of publishing and I could not have asked for a better or more simpatico guide than Martin Hickman and his team at Haythrop Books. They showed kindness, focus and commitment to turn the concept of *Battles at the Ballot* into this volume, which has benefitted greatly from their editing suggestions.

Acknowledgments

Lastly, I wish to acknowledge the inspirational teacher who inculcated in me an abiding fascination with political and social history. It is no easy task to encourage such a thing in a callow sixth former but Joseph Fyles, who taught me at Queen Elizabeth's Grammar School, Blackburn, bequeathed to me a life-long interest; for that I am deeply grateful. I hope readers enjoy the book as much as I relished researching it.

ABOUT THE AUTHOR

The retired owner of a market research company, **John Leston** is the author of published research reports for organisations such as the Department for Work and Pensions and the Financial Conduct Authority.

He holds a First-Class degree in Philosophy, Politics and Economics from Magdalen College, Oxford and studied at Nuffield College, Oxford. He has been a parliamentary candidate on two occasions and was leader of the Liberal group on Berkshire County Council.

More titles from Canbury Press

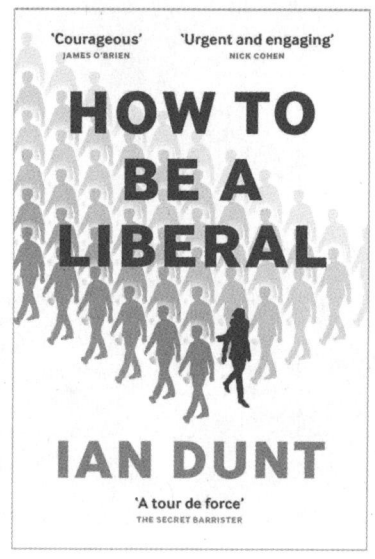

How to be a Liberal
The Story of Freedom and the Fight for its Survival
Ian Dunt
Hardback
ISBN: 9781912454419
Price: £10

'Required reading for anyone interested in politics and philosophy'
Prospect Magazine